Human Shadows
Bright as Glass

Human Shadows Bright as Glass

Drama as Speculation and Transformation

Howard Pearce

Lewisburg
Bucknell University Press
London: Associated University Presses

© 1997 by Associated University Presses, Inc.

All rights reserved. Authorization to photocopy items for internal or personal use, or the internal or personal use of specific clients, is granted by the copyright owner, provided that a base fee of $10.00, plus eight cents per page, per copy is paid directly to the Copyright Clearance Center, 222 Rosewood Drive, Danvers, Massachusetts 01923. [0-8387-5353-1/97 $10.00 + 8¢ pp, pc.]

Associated University Presses
440 Forsgate Drive
Cranbury, NJ 08512

Associated University Presses
16 Barter Street
London WC1A 2AH, England

Associated University Presses
P.O. Box 338, Port Credit
Mississauga, Ontario
Canada L5G 4L8

The paper used in this publication meets the requirements of the American National Standard for Permanence of Paper for Printed Library Materials Z39.48–1984.

Library of Congress Cataloging-in-Publication Data

Pearce, Howard, 1931–
    Human shadows bright as glass : drama as speculation and transformation / Howard Pearce.
      p.   cm.
    Includes bibliographical references and index.
    ISBN 0-8387-5353-1 (alk. paper)
    1. Theater—Philosophy. 2. Drama—History and criticism.
I. Title.
PN2039.P37 1997
792'.01—dc21   96-48858
                                                                 CIP

PRINTED IN THE UNITED STATES OF AMERICA

> Yet the absence of the imagination had
> Itself to be imagined. The great pond,
> The plain sense of it, without reflections . . .
>   . . . all this
> Had to be imagined as an inevitable knowledge,
> Required, as a necessity requires.
>   —Wallace Stevens, "The Plain Sense of Things"

> We resembled one another at the sight.
> The forgetful color of the autumn day
> Was full of these archaic forms . . .
> The total of human shadows bright as glass.
>   —Wallace Stevens, "Things of August"

Contents

Acknowledgments	9
1. Speculation: Seeing and Imagining	13
2. Mimesis: The Play	28
3. Ideas: Audience and Author	63
4. Ideas: Human Being and World	103
5. The Play: Presenting, Recollecting, Projecting	151
6. Call and Recall: The Play of Imagination	233
Notes	249
Works Cited	262
Index	267

Acknowledgments

I WISH TO EXPRESS APPRECIATION FOR BEING GRANTED RELEASE TIME to work on this book, for a sabbatical term from Florida Atlantic University and for two summer terms from the Charles Schmidt Endowment.

Grateful acknowledgment is made for permission to reprint previously published material:

The section of Chapter 2 on Harold Pinter's "The Black and White" is reprinted, revised, from my article in *Contemporary Literature,* vol. 33, no. 4 (Winter 1992), by permission of The University of Wisconsin Press.

Samuel Beckett's *All that Fall* (1957) is cited with permission of Grove Press, as is material from Harold Pinter's *Complete Works,* volumes *One, Two,* and *Four* (1990).

Quotations from *The Cherry Orchard* are cited from *Anton Chekhov's Plays: A Norton Critical Edition,* ed. Eugene K. Bristow. Copyright 1977 by W. W. Norton & Company, Inc. Reprinted by permission of W. W. Norton & Company, Inc.

Martin Heidegger's *Being and Time* (1962) is cited with permission of HarperCollins Publishers.

Citations from the poetry of Wallace Stevens are from *The Palm at the End of the Mind,* copyright 1971 by Holly Stevens, reprinted by permission of Alfred A. Knopf, Inc., and with permission from Faber and Faber Ltd for British Commonwealth publication.

Tennessee Williams's *Glass Menagerie,* copyright 1945 by Tennessee Williams and Edwina D. Williams, is reprinted by permission of New Directions Publishing Corp.

Human Shadows
Bright as Glass

1
Speculation: Seeing and Imagining

This Wooden O

Speculating on the nature of drama seems uncalled-for in a world that preserves and proliferates the genre and makes it, in one form or another, accessible to virtually everyone. The stage attracts audiences with musicals when they fail to fill seats for "serious" plays. Movie theaters appeal to a range of temperaments and tastes in offering films—adventure, mystery, bloody horror, inane comedy, melodrama—as diverse as their possible audiences. Those audiences, when they are not going to see plays or films, watch television at home, not only the various sitcoms, detective series, and soap operas but also the videotapes of films that they might have seen at the cinema. Indeed, the popularity and casual acceptance of this genre attest to its endurance as immediate, spontaneous, and desired experience for a world—at least for sundry audiences in that world—unneedful and often suspicious of retrospection and speculation about it. The drama's diversity and ever-transforming, recombining representations of a world, its kaleidoscope always proffering the new, seem to offer a spectrum of qualities of experience freeing it of the necessity for recollection and thought about it and therefore of the consciousness of its residuals, effectively covering up the need to question.

I know that this beginning with the question, presuming that it is to be taken seriously, seems to tolerate looseness of conception and to allow diversity to scatter into the indistinct. In this beginning I have failed, for instance, to distinguish the stage event from the film. Recognizing that it is legitimate and fruitful to make the distinction and to define each, stage play and film, by the opposition, I might express admiration for the economy of the film's representation that develops, in its own way and as distinct from the techniques of the stage, the elements that Aristotle assigns to the presentation as "spectacle." Yet the possibility of this antithesis seems grounded in the essential kinship of stage and film—the dramatic mode, the pure mimesis, that is distinguished by Plato and Aristotle from the monologic lyric and the mixed narrative modes; instead of considering the differences as boundaries of discrete categories I would prefer to engage in play between such contraries and in speculation about their correlation.

Not fortified by an expectation to answer such questions about drama with authority or finality, I would hope to find footings and explore qualities of the dramatic experience that seem to be essential to both stage and film, which have in common that presenting that is not the nature of fiction and lyric poetry. What might seem a too-self-conscious naïveté here, a calculated innocence, is an endeavor to move toward and remain receptive to essences that might appear and provide a means of seeing as clearly as possible and concealing as little as possible. My turning back to Aristotle's comments on drama, his distinguishing between tragedy and the epic, might well be a move back toward looking behind the complex question of mimesis. Essentially, what makes the dramatic art possible, as drama, what we think of and refer to as the "play," is its presentation as spectacle: according to Aristotle, "agents accomplish the imitation by acting the story out."[1] Our concerns for those troubling and inviting, difficult and gratifying questions of mimesis, character, and thought arise from the fact that "the imitation is of an action and is accomplished by certain agents." Drama, a performance art, whether on the stage or on film, engages the spectator in the immediate act of seeing the performance and in that presence invokes absence; in the flesh of the actor and the materiality of the scene the play calls up what is not simple presence to be seen and heard—calls forth character and world and a myriad of presumptions and anticipations about truth and illusion, about knowledge and being, about value and interpretation.

It is this complication of what seems to be our most immediate, unquestioning grasp in experiencing the play, it is the battery of assumptions behind assumptions, that calls for returning to consider again the most elemental matters. Thinking of the action "accomplished by certain agents" takes us, perhaps, to a beginning, a place to begin, a thought to begin with. Aristotle's need to explore ideas of action, character, thought and language, and spectacle and harmony derives from and builds on the essence that drama presents in presenting: relationships, connections. The single actor, as body and voice performing, is in direct relationship to another individual, an audience/spectator; and in being perceived she or he is one polarity and a necessity in the relationship between—as we are accustomed to think—subject and object, experiencer and the experienced. The supposed purity of action in this moment, as I abstract and talk about it, is of course contaminated, fulfilled, and troubled by, and achieves significance in, the vast possibilities of connections. The moment is derivative—laden with accumulated ideas and assumptions—and generative—inaugurating thought and rethinking—and the connections extend and multiply, are repeated and echoed, endlessly, out of the known and toward discovery.

Thinking from this first idea toward other connections, both those anchored in perception and those that primarily depend from and entail us in ideas, reveals the need to consider the activity of engagement itself. That character evoked by the actor, not Jean Simmons herself but Ophelia, is not material creature bound in the present event but a capable being who can even relive the events leading to her death. She is there for us as character unconfined by an actress playing her. She is there for others in the play, and they represent the relationships we have with them: they are subjectivities engaged with objects who are other subjectivities. As Jean Simmons is for us an actress playing Ophelia, Laurence Olivier is for her an actor playing Hamlet. As the other subjectivity provokes questions of his or her identity (now not Olivier but Hamlet for Ophelia)—whether what is seen is true, whether roles are assumed and identities created—Hamlet is for Ophelia a presence that invokes again, in the world of the play, that problematical (and, I want to say, ultimately mysterious) relationship we have with the character. Hamlet represents for Ophelia the presence that announces its detachment. And I in my world move in such relationships with others, experiencing and being experienced by others who discover, as I do, character through and in spite of the mask/portrait of appearance. The other can never be known entirely and purely.

In talking of the persons in the play, I have referred to the world of the play. It, too, is incarnate in the performance and eludes it. The performance, this staging, is in relationship to the world that has to be evoked as not resolved in and bound by this performance. It is tempting and all too easy to think of the world evoked as a historical world solid and factual in its time, as the Athens of Sophocles or the London of Marlowe. This single relationship might then become the motive in all questions about the play, as on the other hand thinking about psychological or moral effects turns us toward the play's relationship with our selves and our world. That world of the play is, however, like the character, a world of ideas, beliefs, assumptions, and associations that is generated out of the material presentation, and the difficulty in grasping what is already eluding us cannot be resolved by simple and single correlation of the play with historical worlds beyond, either the world from which it came or the one to which it plays. It is purposefully in relationship both to the world that produced it and to the audience's world, to the world interpreting it, relating the way character relates.

The world of actuality that comes to the theater to see a play is a world in time, a flow of presence, making meanings of mere facts—we experience character or world in what appears—by invoking purposes and designs that elude the facts and remain problematical, mysterious. This mystery of the world of the play I refer to is perhaps no more profound than the mystery of character, but it gives me pause even in my calling it "mystery." The characters in their relationships represent not only the relationship of one with another but also the relationships that constitute a world or worlds that are, as communities, implicated in other worlds—mine, their own diverse versions of reality, yours, and others'. These worlds, in some tenuous or problematical impingement, abutment, treat the other world as characters treat other characters; and those attitudes might range from certainty that the alien is known to an openness to discover what might not yet be familiar; the discovery might be *recognition*, an appearance of the familiar out of the strange, or a shock of cognition that might require revision of the already assumed (as when the illusory or unreal suddenly becomes real and the solid substantiality of the real is questioned). Achieving a mobility in negotiations among these worlds calls for allowing for possibilities and connections beyond the tangible present, requires participation in that constitution of worlds that takes us beyond the private and subjective.

In invoking the ideas of community and participation I have let the questions about the nature of drama become more diffuse and more pressing: considering what drama is might lead to speculation about whether perhaps we can pin it down by questioning where it occurs. Is it that event on stage? If it is not satisfactory for me to say that it is there, when I have argued that the characters and worlds of the play are evoked by the performance, then other questions might emerge. Aristotle talks about it being accessible even without the acting out by agents. Is it, if not bound by that moment, to be sought in the text? Or is it ultimately to be discovered as the world constituted as a conception of the playwright?

These questions will not disappear in what I have to say; but if we can think, now, of text as originative, and again, of the generative mind of the playwright, we are playing back and forth in the opposed directions I have broached as a metaphor of mobility. If we think of the playwright as determiner of the play, we are already plunged into the difficulties that surround us in the presumption that we know a subjectivity beyond the perceived, which to some extent always remains inaccessible. There are times when we must ask her or him,

"What do you mean?"; or reach back in time and ask, "What did you intend?" If we think of the written text as determiner, then the presumption is not of a subjectivity beyond but of an object of perception that yields pure and direct experience. We know, of course, and the language of the text reminds us, that it is not sufficient to think that seeing marks on a page is pure perception of words, syntax, thought, form, action, characters, and world. When we talk of "images" in the language of the play, we are using language metaphorically, and metaphorical language directs our attention beyond the presumed elemental correspondence between word and thing. We cannot escape the conditions of experiencing plays: that plays presented refer us to presumed sources (authors, texts, worlds); that they are constituted in the relationships of objects perceived by subjects perceiving (actor/stage and audience, text and reader); and that those embodiments of subject and object in relationship are essential for seeing in the first place.

Distinguishing connections as between subjects and objects is not, however, finally sufficient for thinking about the play. I have attempted to recognize and illuminate an essence, which is connection and relationship itself, in the corporeality of the play's presentation; that event seen and heard reveals beyond the seeing and hearing and establishes relationship between the play and the presentation, between character and actor. I have suggested that the individual spectator is of that essence, undeniably and indelibly there in the immediacy of experience, yet as utterly an establisher of relationship and participation beyond her/himself as is the tangible presentation of the play. In the relationship between audience and play, neither one nor the other is sufficient in itself to determine the event as incidence and significance. The audience is already involved in its world's installed understandings that make possible the experience of play as play: if in its world plays were unheard-of, what the audience sees would not be a play. The play is a play, not because the individual determines it to be so, but because he or she lets it be so, is entrusted by established conditions and agreements to be audience to a play. And whether approving or disapproving, liking or disliking, what has been experienced, the spectator as subject refers the play back to the audience's own world: in judging or speculating about this play in its relationship to other plays that have been experienced in the past or might yet be experienced; in, if it is bad or good enough to warrant thought, sharing those thoughts or feelings about it with the world. The more important talking about the play becomes, the more the individual spectator exhibits dependency on established conventions of understanding that make possible that conversation. The more capacitated by confidence in these understandings, the more that spectator feels responsible and empowered, by having entered the world of the play, to draw conclusions about it or at least to speculate on its connections with his or her world.

Essential to that relatedness of plays is their referentiality of plays themselves, as plays, to worlds, to the primary world of the play evoked by the performance or the text, to the possible secondary worlds within that world or beyond it—plays or narratives within plays as other possible versions of reality; impinging dimensions of heaven or hell or foreign cultures or the pastoral retreat that again offer other possibilities of truth and being; individual interpretations of character and event that, because they derive from and relate to others, are not detached and solipsistic but relational postulates. Being engaged in this referentiality involves us in correlations: between the palpable and ideas; among ideas. When I say "between" the material and the conceptual, the thing and the idea, the implication I intend is that I point to a relatively distinguishable and ostensibly lucid dialectic. It is not, however, a simple matter to check up on ourselves as we engage with the play by seeing and understanding. We might well presume to have seen what is not there; more provocative, disturbing, and entertaining is the possibility that what appears bears in itself its own illusoriness. When I say "among ideas," I mean to suggest that ideas have been so constructed and elaborated—into philosophies, theologies, politics, psychologies, aesthetics—that our understandings have been conditioned and formed, by the plethora, to reflect that excess and to entail us in more than seeing and understanding. If in experiencing the play we recapitulate and venture ideas of ourselves and our worlds, our ideas of plays and authors and audiences, we are immediately engaged in sensory experience, we grasp meaning and understanding through the play and interplay of ideas, and we perform the event of the play in an activity of the imagination.

Thinking about the imagination as an activity in the experience of the play, the seeing or the reading, gives notice that what I have said about seeing and understanding, their essentiality, is only a beginning. As the actual seeing and hearing of a performance are enabling but not sole requisite to experiencing the play, thinking the experience of the play needs to take account of imaginative engagement in the event. In this experience the imagination is operative and serviceable, as we in our time still conceive of imagination itself. Some of the Romantic uses of the Imagination no longer serve us, since for us it has been brought down to earth and lacks the metaphysical sanctions that gave it a privileged status (even above reason and understanding); but the distinguishing characteristics of the imagination—the presentation of images, the involvement of the sensory and the emotional with the conceptual, and the making/discovering of connections, relationships—identify it as somehow in play when we are engrossed in perceptions and recognitions in the event. It is the imagination that justifies our talking about "images" in the language of the play; an image such as the "bird" or "animal," as it occurs for instance in Aeschylus's *Agamemnon*, is the concrete thing evoked, not perceptually at hand.[2] It is neither a thing seen in the play nor an abstract idea in the mind of the spectator. That image in the *Agamemnon* bears powerful emotional force in our engagement with characters and events, in our seeing relationships and making connections between the watchman who identifies himself with the dog, the chorus's extended and complex metaphors of birds of prey, the more profoundly disturbing metaphors of birds, and their songs associated with Cassandra. The imagination's activity of freely extending connections, playing out toward other possible relationships, might circle (like the bird) from the appearance of song > attached to the idea of birds > associated with Cassandra > around and back to the idea of its own song about which the chorus sings. The imagination is free as it finds and makes connections to play back toward the other images of the animal and the ideas of human beings like the watchman-as-dog.

This activity is never, however, pure making or discovery, as if personal and autonomous. It is not a totally free imagination, powerful and sequestered, any more than perception is without connection to its world of possibilities. Culturally bequeathed ideas and language (that word "bird") engage as possibilities of relationship with images and ideas in the play, and the audience is pivotal. As a bearer of the past in the immediate action, the audience reflects the way the play bears its past into the present. The audience can be thought to be imitative, rather than a subjectivity free to make whatever total design it wills, in that it reduplicates the making of the world of the play (I do not mean the making of the text of the play by a solitary playwright) and the making of community out of the past. The past is borne into the present in the memory and in the capacity of the present to resound. That resonance plays among perceptions and ideas and language derived from the past and plays with their possible relevance in the moment. The evocation and putting into play of images, characters, actions, language, and ideas is instigated by the play, which in its form as well as in its language, character, and action is allusive. Allusion is enacted, plays out toward the absent, in metaphoric language and in the indirections and obliqueness of the play as well as in what we ordinarily think of as allusion, the speculative verbal reference to or mention of figures and events of the past or the absent.

This bringing of the past into the moment is a retention, a recall, for the purpose of enriching, filling out, and seeking greater significance in the moment. In the *Agamemnon*, again, an allusion to Heracles or to Philomela opens up possibilities for seeing in terms of, in relationships, not only in the world or worlds and characters of the play but also in the world of the audience; and the imagination is invited to play back and forth in time, toward the past and toward the future. Even the imagination, in our time, of a world degenerated, of loss and deterioration, of the absence of past forms and assurances, continues to allude to what is felt no longer to be. The imagination might be so caught up in its own illusion that the world as detritus seems to be seen purely and not imagined; the imagination might be so enamored of the generated idea that what is thought to be seen does not seem to be, as it is, dependent and inseparable from the acts of alluding and imagining.

This Little World . . . This Earth of Majesty

Searching in language to find a word to characterize our time, our "detritus" for instance, rather than Richard Second's "majesty," invokes the past and a certain kind of change in that what is, is thought to be the result of a natural wearing away. Detritus is, in the restricted sense of the word, the result of disintegration; it is the inert remains, the settlings, of what has been worn down by nature's forces; and, once invoked, it in turn invokes a way of seeing characteristics of our time that was not a possible way of grasping the world in times past. The play reflecting this world might represent the consequence of that kind of change, natural forces like erosion operative in time: the resultant character, language, and form that are incapacitated and cannot even bear the responsibility of sustained and coherent thought. In our thinking about a history of drama, the ideas of disintegration and detritus might imply tracing a historical process from the distant past to our present or our recent past, from the tragic and epic to the naturalistic, to the dilapidations of dada, to the bare or littered, wordless or cacophonic absurd. The play might then become, in this metaphorical conceiving, like detritus: the minimal remains that seem, because of their metaphorical value *only* seem, to bear no meaning at all and to announce meaninglessness.

The imagination playing upon that sense of loss might, on the other hand, find other language—for instance the word "relic"—that tempers the brutal truth of the imagined detritus. Relics are gathered remains that are endowed with or themselves bestow significance, being lifted up and thereby having become venerable; and the essential idea of relics carries with it the primordial idea of detritus, the idea that they are not experienced as separable from their origins, the past and change. If the remains of the past are not imagined as absolutely dead, mere lifeless matter as utmost fact, they might provoke allusion to the past that points to the life, even the affective power, remaining in the play. The play's capacity to make connections, even in denials, with more than the momentary scene suggests that it not only retains and conveys some power from that abandoned past—or the past's abdications—but also presumes efficacy in the anticipation that it will find and involve audiences. The past might be felt as necessary for and provocative of this playing, I suggest, in the way my finding and proposing a word like "relic" is more overtly allusive than using the word "detritus"; and that finding becomes an action entertaining ideas and implications in the opposed terms.

Since the word "relic" in our time is often used even more pejoratively than "detritus," implying the dead remains of specifically human desires and accomplishments, the allusion refers us to a past when relics could be genuine and efficacious. Chaucer's Pardoner is possible in his world not only because, as Siegfried Wenzel has argued, "in Chaucer's time the association of pardoners with fake relics was not as uncommon or even unparalleled as is currently believed,"[3] but also because genuine relics could be thought to exist and were cherished. Wenzel cites texts, reaching back into the thirteenth century, that reveal both an acceptance of the genuine powers of relics and a condemnation of the "false pardoners" of the time whose relics are "nothing but the bones from a farm animal . . . stinking and dried up and worthy of every abomination" (39). Chaucer's Pardoner seems to capture, already in his time, both that sense of the true worth and power of relics derived from the past and the contemporary disparagement of them, his own. If relics have according to him "magic powers" to "heal sick animals, protect against jealousy, multiply grain, and so on" (37), those powers are affirmed as potential in the Pardoner's subversion of them. Our disaffection, our greater comfort (or lesser embarrassment) with images of detritus than with saints' bones and fragments of the cross, cannot quite nullify our appreciation of the idea of the past empowered still in the present. And if we are more at home thinking about the play as minimally representing a fragmented, chaotic, or meaningless world, we still, bearing these thoughts, feel its residual power and let ourselves be involved and carried beyond those ideas of detrition.

Imagining the play as relic has been here, then, an activity of thought beginning with detritus in a "dwindled sphere"[4] and moving toward the relic that is cherished and that says more about the recollection and significance of plays in our time than does the idea of detritus. That activity is admittedly a play of the imagination, an activity of discovering connections and making sense out of the sensory. Speculating on the play as detritus or as relic reveals through the metaphors that what appears to be one might be another, but if seen as one or the other, or as something else, it nevertheless appears to be something.[5] In the identification of the thing that appears, it is brought into a scheme of meaningfulness, and herein lies another primordial theme, the possibility that it might not be what it is seen to be. Recovering the metaphor of the relic affects the perception of the play and qualifies the felt relationship with it. What appears to be strange, incoherent, and meaningless; what strikes us as simply an image of our "dwindled sphere"; is after all a product of the imagination as well as perception and—like Wallace Stevens's "plain sense of it, without reflections, leaves, / Mud, water like dirty glass"—invokes metaphor in the very "absence of the imagination" that has "itself to be imagined."[6] The play engages us in appearances that seen, understood, and imagined yield not a certainty and finality of understanding but a venture toward further understanding. The possibilities of disclosure in characters and worlds represent the inherent mystery, the not yet known, and the essential desire for recognition in experience. As worlds play toward and against each other, interpreters of those worlds, anticipating reinterpretation or surprised by the alien coming home to us, the familiar becoming strange, themselves depict that necessary and potentially remunerative interdependence of worlds.

This brief exercise in considering the drama as imaginative play grounded in the constitution of our world is intended to be little more than a posing of questions I have found stimulating and essential to speculation—themes of seeing and understanding and the imagination; of relationships and interconnectedness, involvement and interdependence; of characters and worlds and discovery; of temporality and loss, perpetuation and memory; and implicitly of other aesthetic questions, for instance the old concern that abides in our world, whether imaginative literature is inconsequential and merely amusing or is serious, whether drama fulfills its calling by providing an abundance and diversity of soporific entertainment or calls an audience toward significance. Considering the degrees of uncertainty, speculation, and tentativeness—the enablement of playfulness—I advocate, I do not hope to provide final and decisive answers or solutions.[7] I am committed to the idea of play in talking about plays, and if I of necessity as well as desire treat philosophical themes I do not hope to argue toward epistemological or ontological certainty. Although the nonseriousness of play contaminates the sincerity of the presumed professional charge in writing a book, the ostensible absence of imagination in analysis would call out "to be imagined." I hope, however, that this confession will not obviate the possibility that the absence of philosophical rigor here is no mere negation of serious thought about serious questions. The imagination is in play as integral and necessary to what might become a professional—historical, analytical, philosophical, or other disciplinary—enterprise, which in refining, rounding off, completing a serious argument can cover up and in effect deny the essential play of the imagination.[8]

The representation, Aristotle's *mimesis,* is clearly about strife, conflict—the stuff of drama—both in the represented conflicts that attend and occupy characters and in the warring ideas and worlds that are the conditions of such conflicts and the means of engaging an audience. The play is thus, in both its representations and in its being a representation for an audience, confrontational. It is a challenge to make and discover connections. It is, additionally, in setting up the possibility of those connections, an affirmation of relationship and connection. It is unitive in its acts of bringing together—in seeing, in imagining, in mimesis, in the inescapable being of one with another in community, in the past borne into the present toward the future. If the play provokes understanding of strife and contraries—war, animosity, odium—in the consolation of probabilities or necessities, it represents in its events and characters and in its relationship to an audience the possibility of reconciliation and love, of the participation and interdependence of the one with the other. Aristotle's proviso that for the strongest emotional involvement of the audience in events evoking pity and fear the action should be between characters with "strong ties of affection"—rather than enemies or those with "no relationship, whatsoever, to each other" (Golden, *Aristotle's Poetics,* 24)—is a concern not only for the play's representation of love in strife, strife in love, but also for the emotion and idea of love in the audience's engagement with characters in events. This idea might in our time seem as improbable as are knowledge and conversation in a dwindled world represented by a dwindled play. But, it seems, in the "plain sense of ... water" generating the metaphor of "dirty glass," in the image of ourselves as the poor, bare, forked animal Lear complains about, universal strife or chaos has not been and perhaps cannot be purely realized so long as we go on imagining, talking about, and seeing and feeling the relical powers of plays.

The play accomplished as nexus of presentation, recollection, and projection becomes, then, not a fixed and changeless identity but a possibility and a beginning, a metaphor of being. Its power to touch, to make connection, to form an attachment, is manifest essence. In that essentiality it represents an affirmation of the need and desire to experience another presence, to reconfirm the endurance of the past in thought and memory, to anticipate the value of that dramatic experience in what might become of it: astonishment as well as recognition, a necessary letting go as well as understanding. The play's touching us, involving and reminding us, and letting us go on to play beyond it cannot reassure with finality and certainty. In establishing an event responsive to the need to discover, to see and understand and imagine, it can only offer a structure of relationship that, like new love or adventure, is anticipative, is a beginning.

Conceiving of our time as a world that can think of the play in these ways is not to deny that we have thought and might still think of plays as detritus representing detritus. But the possibilities in approaching the idea of play as I have suggested germinate from other than dismaying possibilities of thought about our world in our time. In talking about an activity that plays back and forth between seeing and imagining, I have echoed ideas and language appealing to and loosely recapitulating a major inclination in twentieth-century thought. The attempt to establish a way of seeing, to clear the vision and to reformulate relationships between subjects and objects, was a needed step in the thought of Edmund Husserl, who sought reconciliation in the agon of Western philosophy's realist and idealist combatants. Husserl proposed a humble stance in going back to the things themselves, looking again and trying to see more clearly, approaching that experience deprived of the blinding certainty that "things" were, on the one hand, really "out there" in the world or, on the other, merely in the mind of the experiencer. The metaphor of seeing persisted in Husserl's addressing the question of experience to the idea of the individual experiencing; and it brought to light a hope inherent in the possibility of our being in touch with another.

Martin Heidegger's attempt to fulfill and accommodate Husserl's undertaking took account of the essential complicity of the individual perceiver in the world already lighted and darkened by the human activity of making a world, lighted in the constructions that have made the earth habitable and darkened by the covering up that this habilitation incurs. Heidegger adapted Husserl's metaphor of the individual, in time, intently focusing on, moving around, and coming back to the object of perception—the motion for Heidegger becoming movement in a circle of wider sweep, the subject becoming more embroiled in the conditions of a world that make possible seeing anything as something at all. The appearances that present themselves are a giving that calls for readiness and anticipation, for the receptiveness that is open to astonishment. The human being is a participant and contributor in the making of the world, involved in and provided by its constructions and concealments beforehand. The give and take of moving from Husserl's clarification of seeing toward Heidegger's world bestowing appearances is the motion I have proposed as an activity of engagement with the play.

The play's power to involve an audience in the events of its world, to be a presence that appears and leads into engagement, is considered by Hans-Georg Gadamer to be a transformation that brings the audience into a structure, a relationship of being with the event of the play. In his ideas about drama as play, game, and festival, Gadamer has pursued with Heidegger a way to affirm the communal nature of being human without sacrificing Husserl's concern for clarity and directness of experience. The presentation of the play is for Gadamer a transformation, and it is affective. The audience in becoming one with the play is like the player in the game who is so intently absorbed in the play that the play takes over and the player is played. From Husserl to Gadamer there is both this movement toward opening up the arena of experience and a continuance of the idea that experience is grounded on earth. That grounding in immediate experience affirms the possibility that drama, rather than being restricted to the demonstration of powerlessness and detritus, expresses—in the participatory act of audience and play, in the event—the hope, the possibility, of relical power remaining in the drama.

If my thinking defects from the rigorous thought of these philosophers, it strikes out as a necessity of the imagination. If the outcome of play is not predetermined and if the appearances that appear and the objects of experience can yield clearer perception, the uncertainty of what is given by the activity must remain open and affirm possibility. It cannot reassure beforehand that failure and detritus, inconsequentiality and deception, are not also possible in the event. Plays and worlds, characters and playwrights, ideas of virtue and truth, purposes and desires, if they might truly astonish, must have as well the capacity to disappoint in as many ways as they can happily astonish. Approaching the play as if it might have that relical power does not preclude the possibility of pardoners.

Hence it must be with trepidation that I here approach a play or plays out of desire and—I think this word apropos—love. These plays I talk about have called for speculation, which is not a settling and proving of ideas but merely a reflecting and reflecting on. Other plays, "great" and minor, could abundantly attest to an aesthetic phenomenon and a continuing need for the aesthetic in our time. What has preceded and what follows should come together to make a case for giving closer attention to and caring about this special kind of relationship. This coming into relationship, perhaps promiscuously, with first one play and then another, involves trying to see them in the relationships that appear, whether as if historical influence and allusion or as speculation and metaphorical relation; and it involves speculation on the relationship itself, the way I think I—and we—experience, see, give to, feel and think about, let be, extrapolate from, judge, and therefore establish quasi-ethical relationships with plays. These exercises aim to reflect, then, the purposes and strategies of drama itself: to be somewhat and not too seriously instructive, to by mere example reaffirm the need for and love of the play, to capture that childlike spirit of insatiable anticipation and readiness to be delighted by surprise, to receive and accept the limits of seeing as the withdrawal itself that appears and beguiles.

What I hope for by talking about the experiences of plays as excursions into unique encounters and fulfillments is that my speculations represent not a betrayal of the truths *of* the plays for the sake of the desire to discover truth *for* the play, that my conversation about plays should retain in the presentation that idea of tribute to the plays' power to touch. If my thoughts seem discrete and eccentric in their responses to the plays' demands for ideas—which emanate from the plays as their stimulating, provoking, playing with ideas—they not only seize their own life and stand alone as speculation but also strive for connections, for the possibilities in repetition, for some representation of coherence and design. The plays' presentations, recollections, and projections stimulate and reflect the audience's desires for participation, for translation and transmission of experience. My negotiations between the eccentric and the common, between diversity and correlation, did not and could not rise beyond temporality to establish a changeless abstracted truth. There should appear here no presumption to full knowledge and analytical closure but only a desire for energized thought and imagination in consonance with the plays, only a hope yet to see and feel more.

Such truth as might appear should have emerged as possibility from the plays themselves and in the imaginative apprehension of their possible essences. I have attempted to represent a movement from the relative clarity of perception toward the freedom of imaginative play, yet I have discovered emerging, as I had not recognized beforehand, the compelling nature of ideas—of the artist, of male and female, of angels, of habitations and worlds, and of journeys to and fro—that seemed to assert themselves and to determine movement and form beyond my intentions, to reveal beyond my anticipation. It seems that in having been carried along, or away, by the relical powers of the plays, I have come to feel more strongly that, in the plays' building of worlds, they represent not only seeing and speculation, connection and transmission, but also the tentativeness of life as drama, the mystery of character and world, the wonder of touch and confederacy. These prefatory comments stand, then, vibrating between what has come before and what will ensue, as if they were integral in a process moving inexorably along temporal lines; they are not deceiving, however, since in the performance they reveal that this is in reality not foreword but afterword.

2
Mimesis: The Play

THE IDEAS OF "SPECULATION AND TRANSFORMATION" IN MY TITLE evidently raise questions about the audience of a play. I have proposed that the audience caught up in the experience of a play is engaged in a speculation that carries on into thinking back about the play. If, in addition, the play retains any of that relical power assumed for plays in the past, the audience is in some way and to some degree touched, affected by the experience. Our world seems to assume, at any rate, when it expresses concern about pornography and proper role models and the responsibility of imaginative literature to amend history's false truths, that a play can cause or contribute to speculation and that it does not leave an audience unchanged. My invoking ideas of speculation and transformation as thought about the audience is intended, however, to suggest in addition that the audience is in radical mimetic relationship to the world events of the play. An audience engaged in thought, speculation, the receptivity to and generation of a play of ideas, reflects characters so involved; and that activity might be considered, in recalling Aristotle's concerns about climactic events in the play, to have something to do with characters' Recognitions of things, other people, and themselves. The dramatic Reversal the protagonist and often others experience is repeated in an audience if its thought and passion are sufficiently bestowed on those "human shadows bright as glass" to become theirs and to receive theirs.[1]

Among the persistent difficulties in talking about drama—and poetry, and life as drama—is the problem of knowing the relationships between such entities as the shadows on the stage and the audience: the represented, the representation, and the perceiver. One way to talk about such relationships might begin with the language of Aristotle, raising the question of mimesis. It is all too easy to restrict the idea of mimesis to one objective and present reality, the stage, in its imitation or representation of another, perhaps absent, reality. If taken to be absent and therefore not immanent, that reality is the world outside the play, ordinarily thought to be some world passed away or, for the audience, the one we live in. Discussions of the play that direct attention to how truthfully it represents the real world of our moment can be dualistic and reductive, assuming on the one hand an unquestioned factuality of the real world and on the other the play's mere reflection, right or wrong, true or false, of the real. The critical and popular reception of the films *JFK* and *Schindler's List* is a striking instance of the assumption that the drama either reflects the real world accurately (as Aristotle suggests, properly shows how a horse runs) or lies. The unreal must attach itself to the real and thereby gain its own validity through correspondence. It writes the word that refers genuinely to the thing. The world against which the play is measured is already known as objectively real, though absent, and the play there before the audience must conform to the audience's conception of its referent.

In his more exacting concept of mimesis, Hans-Georg Gadamer argues against that duality of play and referent. The play's truth is immanent, as it is for Aristotle in his seeing the play's revelation of general pattern rather than historical particulars or literal accuracy. The playwright creates an action that is both an instance of purposive design and a shape being formed and revealed in the action. Gadamer argues that the play generates a representation of the meaning that belongs to it and appears in it, a meaning that need not correspond superficially to the truth of some remote dimension in whose reality it might not participate.[2] The locus of concern is shifted from the question of how and whether the play reflects an external reality to the involvement of the play and the audience. Here again, conceiving a duality, audience and performance, as in opposition, as subject and object rather than as opposed objectivities, is from a "natural standpoint"[3] only reasonable. The audience, knowing itself as it knows its world, is already constituted and comfortably assured that self and world are real, that they know each other relatively well and get along together in negotiating daily affairs. It knows, just as comfortably, that the play is a fiction that can be taken seriously only if it conforms to the audience's already settled convictions about its world.

This separation of self from the experienced representation, as the real opposed to the unreal, situates a chasm between them and maintains a defense against the one being implicated in the other. It would seem that there is some indeterminate implication, however, in that the distinction between self and actions or characters in the play ensues from the experience rather than being essential in it. In the performance of, for instance, a cognition-oriented genre, the mystery or detective play, the audience is engaged along with the characters in sifting evidence, identifying and holding on to clues, making guesses.

Too involved to think of self as not in the action, the audience—unless a separation occurs through other kinds of activities such as making "aesthetic" judgments or drawing conclusions about the author's purpose—is a genuine participant. Gadamer extrapolates his theory about dramatic involvement from the way players in games give themselves to the game. The willing subject is merged into the game, receiving an assigned role and the determination of kinds of actions that the player performs in being one with the game. It might even be said that the game plays the players. "All playing is a being-played. . . . The game masters the players. . . . The real subject of the game . . . is not the player but instead the game itself. What holds the player in its spell, draws him into play, and keeps him there is the game itself" (*Truth and Method*, 106). This statement reverses our conventional way of thinking ourselves as little islands of independent will, judgment, and governance; it is a way of revising the presumption that the self is an identity of thought and being apart from its experiences of and concomitance in its world.

Gadamer cannot be held entirely responsible for the idea that the game plays the player if the game Gadamer plays plays him. His metaphorical as well as literal conception of the game would include, as fellow players among others, Edmund Husserl and Martin Heidegger, who share the responsibility by establishing their own contextuality and by engaging with historical problems of ontology and epistemology. Husserl had tried to fill the gulf between subject and object by identifying it as the arena in which experience occurs. His concept of intentionality maintains the activity of experiencing as a possible moment of truth. What is genuine is the fact that we experience "intentional objects" that are there for us in the experience; and we are not, in the act of experiencing, abstracted as thinking beings apart from thinking the objects of thought. These objects might be perceived, remembered, dreamed, or imagined; we are engaged as if at a play, letting the images appear as they are rather than bearing against them a prejudgment that they are either of the mind or of the world. For Husserl, in our answering the call to the things themselves, which are those intentional objects not yet abstracted and placed "out there," the question of whether they are subjectively or objectively determinant is, in the direct experience, put in abeyance. They are significant, not because they can be differentiated as actual out there or merely imagined, but because they can yield knowledge of essential being (to which he refers with the Greek "terminologically unspent *Eidos*" [*Ideas*, 42]).

Husserl's way of beginning is, in this attunement of subject and object, comparable to the way we say we lose ourselves in a play when we yield to it. The self, bringing preconceptions about the play's truthfulness in representing a world and about other philosophical, sociological, psychological, and aesthetic convictions, yields those assumptions when fully engaged in the play of the experience. The engagement is not an abstraction from the experience but a spontaneous reduction of the majestic accomplished self to the mystery of involvement. Here, in naming this event a mystery, I would hope to be understood as letting go of attempts to understand and definitively explain it in philosophical, psychological, or aesthetic terms. For the sake of this discussion, Husserl's depiction of the experiencing event, mistrusted by many for the way it maintains the "logocentrism" of Western philosophy,[4] need not be accepted as absolute truth but only adopted as an idea issuing, like his Eidos, from the immediacy of experience. My naming it a mystery is a standing back from certainty while reserving a privilege to entertain ideas about it. The experience of the play remains, for me, a strangeness that I might try to explain, as do others when we talk about plays; but trying to convince a skeptic that I "identify with" a character or an action is no explanation but a restatement of the mystery.

I do, however, perform actions in experiencing drama that are not my autonomous self, thinking and feeling in isolation from the objects encountered, and I observe others apparently engaged in similar acts— or testifying that they do. If I suffer the embarrassment of crying with or for a character, that embarrassment does not negate the thing itself, which is my indistinct yet compelling attachment to the character and an emotional consolidation. Perhaps more disconcerting is the reaction I have to events designed to produce terror, horror, or unadulterated fright. If I were not in some way a participant in the action, I would not manifest signs of these emotions, such as tensing of the body, pulling away from the action before me, and feeling goose pimples or hair standing on end. Retreating from this activity, I wonder how I could be so affected by a mere unreality, especially when my critical judgment tells me I am watching a grade B horror film. Critical interpretations of the pleasure derived from such emotions might direct the question from psychological foundations, as for instance in Joseph Addison's explanation that we sense our difference and congratulate ourselves on not being the victim whose sufferings we see.[5] Aristotle had addressed the problem of emotional interchange in the experience of drama, linking the emotions of pity and fear (perhaps among other emotions). In that pity can entail that sense of the pitiable object's otherness, Addison's attributing to the audience self-protective operations of the psyche would seem to be a distinction Aristotle does not make; but surely fear does not hold me apart. It tells me that I am in danger, not that someone else is, and it confirms the fact that the threat from the dimension of unreality impinges against my safe world. It is not unfortunate that Aristotle did not try to explain causation psychologically in observing the play's breeding fear in the audience.

His account of the drama recognizes other shadowy recesses that, like fear, can be felt, known, and even described but cannot be traced in a regression to ultimate source. Is the catharsis he postulates as ensuing from the arousal of pity and fear to be thought of as a cleansing and elimination of harmful emotions or as an amelioration and balancing of emotions, thus in either translation instilling psychological health? If it is a response in the audience of *Oedipus Rex*, is it not as well an outcome for Oedipus himself? If something happens there, in Oedipus and in the play, and here, in the audience, the something Aristotle calls catharsis is open to interpretation, as is his explanation of hamartia. But Aristotle seems to lead us astray, or to allow us to become confused, when his commentary seems directed toward either the real world or the drama but might refer to the other, or both; when it seems to apply to character in drama or to the audience but might refer to the other, or both. Is there not a mysterious duplication in the audience's mimesis of the play's texture? Thinking in terms of Husserl's intentional relationship of subject and object, which is established in order to approach a description of essences discoverable there, I have proposed that what goes on in the event is not only a representation of relationship but also a manifestation of the limits of knowledge concerning it. The representation of relationships in the play, relationships that reveal the essential need for love in the love-destroying animosity and strife, in the assertion of individual power and domination, is mimetic of those relationships that enfold the audience. Discerning that the mimetic relationship of audience and play is essential—not that the one represents the other but that they are mutually implicated—does not produce closure but opens up the question to further questions. To say that in *Oedipus Rex* the qualities of equanimity and composure at the play's end do not belong to Oedipus alone, nor are they only a psychological condition in individual members of the audience, is to anticipate further questions about the audience.

Aristotle does not construct a persuasive case for the play's values being achieved communally, but the argument of his *Poetics,* seen as a defense of drama, seems designed toward that conclusion. The value of the drama to the republic, Plato had argued, is in its good effects for the state. To the extent that Aristotle's treatise can be considered a response to Plato, the inquiry might turn from the individual hero, Oedipus the king become an outcast, and his relationship to the individual observer, who is free to withdraw into her or his private Husserlean speculation and thus play the part of the outcast. This turning is anticipated in the acknowledgment that our concerns are not private and unique, however inherently we think ourselves as solitary and autonomous beings. The dignity Oedipus gains is not entirely a private accomplishment in spite of the gods' or other human beings' influence, though it can be read that way, but a mediation of self and world; and he bestows his reconciliation on the community in leaving Creon in command and his children in Creon's trust. Oedipus's sense of individual choice and personal responsibility and his drive to think things out to clear resolution set him apart from others, and the audience is one with Oedipus in the assumption of discrete privilege. If Oedipus is brought to a recognition, not just of clues that lead to discovery of the reality that lies outside himself but also of himself, the audience shares in the opportunity for recognition of the other, Oedipus, and of self through the other. If not only Oedipus and the single observer but also Oedipus's world and the world of the audience can be thought to undergo a catharsis, this transformation or modification of being retains the attribute of mystery and eludes the certainty of analysis; it is not an assurance of mastery and finality (the Oedipus at Colonus has become a possibility) but an anticipation wrought in change. It calls for a representation of mediation or reconciliation that thinks beyond the isolated paradigm Husserl installed in his epistemology.

Taking Oedipus as an example, I have appealed to Husserl's ideas as a way of beginning with the disclosure of relationships between the experiencing being and the world of experience. Husserl uncovers a foundation for rethinking the structure of relationship presumed to be established and clear, the objective observer standing apart from the objects of experience. My suggesting a turn toward the question of community is a move back toward implications in Aristotle's idea of mimesis that are recoverable in the idea of involvement Gadamer characterizes as the player's absorption into the game; and of course the way the individual is involved with the other initiates ontological, epistemological, and ethical considerations. The way of being human in the world entails, in Heideggerean deportment, a resignation of the autonomous self to being in the world; the redundancy of this statement is meant to underline *being in the world*. As a redirection of Husserl's insight, Heidegger's stress on being in the world turns the attention from the subject to the conditions of being, performing a reversal that Heidegger talks about as a turning, a *Kehre*.[6]

In Heidegger's thinking and in Gadamer's, this turn of thought is essential to revelation of what is as yet mysterious, what is not yet known or what has been covered up in installed structures of thought and language. Heidegger's searching of language—especially in his later work the exploration of metaphor—becomes, as search and exploration, a metaphorical journey in the circle of interpretation. Movement in the circle is not a journey toward an end, from point A to point B, and therefore a closure; it is an interminable quest that requires the possibility of turning away from a presumed and perhaps presupposed end in order to let what might seem to be behind and already known appear anew. This enigmatic way of expressing a thought might be a sign of a fresh discovery having been made or it might be a way of provoking, of making possible, fresh discovery. Heidegger's talk about *Dasein,* or *Da-sein,* is intended to "make an entity—the inquirer—transparent in his own Being" (*Being and Time,* H 7). As Dasein the human being is not an entity unto itself but manifests its "there-ness" as reversible expressions, there-being or being-there; and the word "Dasein" is devised to blur the distinction between the essential Being of beings in common and the individual's experiencing being. In this turn of thought the regnant individual is dispossessed of a kingdom and brought down to enforced affiliation, to recognition of the condition of existence, which is participation in the "throwness" or fallenness of all beings. The condition of throwness, *Geworfenheit,* "into its 'there'" (H 135) is not, however, a fall from grace, a deprivation, but the natural and inescapable ecosystem of human beings in their world: "indeed, [Dasein's being] is thrown in such a way that, as Being-in-the-world, it *is* the 'there'" (my emphasis).

The necessary reorientation of my thinking, the turn I must make, to think that I am the "there," or that I am of it, seems a formidable task when I read Heidegger. If there seems to be something mysterious and irresolvable in this task of thinking, I recall that I have already claimed to entertain such thinking about my experience of the play. To conceive of my identifying with another human being, fictional or real, to the point of being emotionally moved as if I were that other or to the point of better understanding myself through understanding the other is to announce to myself that I am not merely myself: I am also "the there." If I have been caught up in a game of interplay of idea and affect between my real dimension and the fictional, I am, as Gadamer says, played by the game. Following Husserl and Heidegger, Gadamer has persisted in exposing the meretriciousness of that gulf between self and other that keeps us safe and our intellectual possessions secure. To read him in the context of influences, from Plato and Aristotle through Husserl and Heidegger, is the more easily to accede to his denial of autonomy to the players in the game of drama.

Gadamer argues that the play is an event encompassing the audience, "comprising players and spectators" (*Truth and Method*, 109). The drama is, like the game, a "total mediation" in that it transcends the individual subjectivities taking part in it: "Neither the being that the creating artist is for himself—call it his biography—nor that of whoever is performing the work, nor that of the spectator watching the play, has any legitimacy of its own in the face of the being of the artwork itself" (128). Yet a discomfort remains in the proposition that the individual "being" of the playwright, call him Anton Chekhov, has no "legitimacy of its own in the face of the being of" his play entitled *The Seagull*. How can we be concerned with the play without making connections to the writer and his or her other plays, thinking of the plays as personal creations? As I proceed, this question will reappear as a consideration of the idea of the artist, which can be developed as a consideration of the idea of Husserl's *Eidos*. The artist and the audience are, along with all other beings human or not and all natural and cosmic phenomena and worldly creations like architecture, gardens, and plays, ideas in the circle of Dasein's interpreting: if the idea of artist is fixed, closed, final, then the way we read Chekhov is governed by that finality and we might need to turn around and go the other way to think again about what the idea of the artist has meant. The audience, too, is not simply a fact but a call for thought about what the idea of the audience has meant. Regarding for another moment the apparent depreciation of the spectator's legitimacy as discrete being will lead back to implications in the way Gadamer has subsumed the several identities into the being of the play.

Concerning the relationship between audience and dramatic representation, Gadamer has negotiated one of those turns in the hermeneutic circle as a bold move based in Heidegger's conception of Dasein. If the idea of Dasein gives pause to the individual, who hesitates before the possibility that the self's being *is* the there, then a difficulty emerges in the attempt to accept an epistemological as well as an ontological shift. Somehow the individual being is asked to yield autonomy, to stand open to the bestowal of knowledge as truths appear in appearances. For Gadamer the truth of the drama is "in the pure appearance (Erscheinung)" of what is being played (110). In the play's mimesis, "what is represented is there . . . [and] it has come into the There more authentically (eigentlicher ins Da gekommen ist)" (114). "Pure appearance" gives itself from the dimension of the play, the "there" that incorporates Dasein; and the play attains a reality and a truth that call into question the solid, enduring, detached identity of the spectator. The audience is free to assume a way of being with the play that puts the self in play in the event, giving both the emotional and conceptual constituents of self to the event. Yet the freedom of the individual caught up in the performance is contained in the realizing activity. In this turning of thought, Gadamer attributes a heightened seriousness to the play; and even though we by habit utilize this turn of thought and therefore are not unfamiliar with it, we do not as a rule take the play seriously. When we return to our ordinary business in a real world that seems to reward our assertiveness with enduring success, the tentative and momentary involvement in a play becomes like vapor, an unreality with little relationship to or effect on our real world. Yet there has been for that moment a play of inversion, the unreal attaining substance by taking us into itself.

We—in our daily affairs and in our entertainments—appreciate the play of ontological inversions, the real becoming unreal and the unreal real, the true false and the fictional true, in the pleasurable activity of playing with the question of reality; and our play with the metaphors structured on this distinction is underlain with the serious need to understand self and other and the conditions of their being. For instance, the individual's identity is presumed to be a reality and to maintain a continuity, but it becomes an unreality when it makes a sudden shift and is recognized to be a mask. "He is only playing a role": the real identity does not appear except as a reality constituted out of the recognized unreality. Yet there seems to appear a true identity veritably residing in his act of assuming the role that is not the truth. He is not other than the mask but the one who appropriates it. This is serious, the problem we pose in presuming the logical disjunction of the reality and the sham, and if we play with it we only the more enact the essentiality of our need for freedom to play between the two, to negotiate transformations and revelations concerning the real and the unreal. "His life is a parody of a soap opera": this way of seeing a real life as one of the most doubly false kinds of mimesis is hyperbolic, and it is a conversion of the actuality into a composition understood as bearing the taint of untruth. As an imaginative activity, it enfolds the truth in fictionalizing and is an admission that the more or less playful conversion is not to be taken as entirely serious, that it is a "light and winged" thing like Socrates' poet.

As our serious observations about important matters can be realized in lightening what is vexing about them, our lightest entertainments often yield pleasure because they are intuitively grasped as transpositions or inversions of dimensions that are vital to our subsistence in the world. When we apprehend a truth in what appears to be the light and playful, a sense of the truth emerging from the false, the serious from the nonserious, our pleasure becomes recursive, a turning back to the structure of relationship itself for grasping and playing with the transformation. I am thinking of the lightest and seemingly the most trivial sort of literature we regularly comprehend in a glance and with little attention, the daily or Sunday comics. Gary Larson's comic sensibility in *The Far Side* is characteristically manifest as a sense of discrepancy. The cartoon captioned "When potato salad goes bad" plays with two meanings of the expression "goes bad," depicting a bowl of potato salad in the refrigerator holding a gun on other inhabitants of that little world.[7] "Going bad" is not the same for food in the refrigerator as it is for human beings in the social dimension, and Larson plays on that difference. This verbal play between two worlds becomes more complex when the words are charged with associations and allusion, as in "The elephant man meets the buffalo gal" (97). The "Far Side" calendar of 10 July 1990—and identifying a cartoon this way points up its transitory nature—depicts two figures, a large man wearing a railroad engineer's cap and a miniature hobo carrying over his shoulder the hobo's symbol, the bandanna on a stick. The "engineer" looms above the hobo and a toy train, which has the designation "Ace Toys" on one of the cars; the hobo, who is walking away from an open boxcar, is evidently a part of that toy world. The engineer points into the distance and says to the hobo, "And stay off." Even though we should, with a certain delight, glance back at the calendar throughout the day, we probably would not spend time thinking about the essentialness of the structure that is the basis of the humor.

The engineer's relationship to his world of toys is not one of reality set definitively over against the play world, a superior and larger world with a lesser world inside it. There is a "real" hobo leaving the train, and the man in charge orders him away. Does the humor not lie in the confusion of complacencies? The hobo is matter-of-fact: he is merely leaving. The man of authority is imperious, angry, indignant, frustrated—at least we seem to see those qualities in his stance, his facial expression, his words. His thoughts might well be, "It's my train, I'm in charge here, who do you think you are? Get out of my world!" I find his attitude comic because of the way it exposes the discrepancy between assumptions about ordinary reality in the man's indignation against the play world's getting out of hand. His seeming obliviousness to the discrepancy heightens my reaction. He is, after all, an adult playing a child's game and taking it seriously. He seems undisturbed by the disruption of a reality, the hobo, appearing from his make-believe world as if belonging in his real world. Although much more might be said about the humor in this little dramatic situation, my point is that there is in our basic understanding an essential structure of play opposed to reality that is both of serious concern and also humorously exploited in Larson's imagining what happens when one invades the other.

Giving thought to such a slight instance is to range toward the thoroughly entertaining features of drama and the pleasures to be had in experiencing it. At the same time, the profound seriousness of the question of how we can take the nonserious seriously will continue to call for thinking about the presumed significance of drama. Beginning with the idea of mimesis and the persistent doubleness inherent in any thought about imitating or representing will inevitably invoke Aristotle, whether directly or historically through the manifold interpretations and reinterpretations of the idea of mimesis and the defenses of poetry that lead us into our own time. Aristotle's twofold assumption that we "find pleasure in imitations" and that we learn our "first lessons through imitation" (Golden, 7) remains as a challenge to both detractors and apologists alike. Having turned to Gadamer for a contemporary justification of drama as not merely significant but vital, I have tried to locate the inquiry at the points of juncture—I continue to think of it as mysterious—where two worlds meet, the subjective and the objective, the dramatic representation and the audience. This juncture as dramatic performance, thought of as both spatial and temporal, as a place of meeting and as transitional interval, is an event in a place where change occurs, is a place where the event of change occurs. Such junctures constitute the rhythm of experiencing life as in an arena, of human being being what it has become and becoming what it has not yet been.

The pure experience of the play is a transitional interval in which the action that takes place is the bonding of the spectator to and in the unfolding event. Although the conceptualization of this event analyzes the primary components as a duality of experiencer and experienced, subject and object, representation and audience, Heidegger or Gadamer's arguments for Dasein's mode of relatedness or the play's being a "transformation into structure"[8] render a challenge to the abstraction; an altered awareness of this relatedness would effect a recognition of the one's, the audience's, yielding or giving of self to the other, the play—that is, being taken in by and taken into the other. This understanding of drama provides an insight into its persistence and the endurance of its defenders, and illuminates as well its popular and casual appeal. Without reflecting on any value to be gained beyond the moment, potential audiences buy tickets to the theater or the cinema in search of entertainment. They flick the remote control of the television set to see whether, if a mystery or adventure or evening soap opera engages them, they might settle down to lose themselves for an interval. The essence of dramatic experience is this indeterminate articulation, indeterminate in that it is a juncture of entities in possibility. Unconstrained possibility in the meeting of the actual and the imaginative would allow for the emergence of profound truths, significant morals, reflections of life, intuitions about the self, bland entertainments, or trivial pursuits.

This hypothetical unreflective audience is not invulnerable, however, to thoughtful and impassioned attachment when even the slightest entertainment stimulates an excess of response. My tarrying over a cartoon in the daily newspaper is remarkable for its excess. Intensely emotional involvement in the pretenses and illusions displayed on the stage is clearly, given the unreasonableness and impracticality of it, excessive. To have shed actual tears at the death of Heathcliff's Cathy can be an embarrassment when we turn to face the real world. It is the nature of drama, and perhaps imaginative literature in general, to raise the mundane to the level of histrionics, to transform detritus into relics and thereby bestow significance on the contingent matter of life. Considered to be a mimetic activity, this bestowal of significance is the venture of "reading" meanings, the extension into and beyond the elemental perception so that it is more than a kaleidoscopic flow; it is ordinary perception duplicated in the theatrical event; and it occurs in the images presented from the author, stage director, and players as well as in the audience, whose mimesis is lavish participation. That residual power of transformation into structure might play across the range of possible affects, from amusement and titillation and fright to intellectual and emotional growth, to extension of the private self toward involvement with another and community.

The player's giving of self over to the game has come to be seen in the twentieth century as, for instance in Clifford Geertz's interpretation of the Balinese cockfight, a "deeper play" than could be understood in terms of Bentham's utilitarian economics.[9] The possibilities of excess are unconstrained in the activity of the imagination. An audience's surrender to the free range of possibilities that might be encountered in the representation is a readiness to be surprised, an anticipation that in the immersion of the self in the illusion an unexpected coherence will appear, that a continuity will be established not only as in the representation but also in the audience's sharing in it. The illusion so encountered in the protean workings of the theater catches the audience up in the game of illusion, which makes the theater itself an embodiment of the theme of abutment—the touching and blending of separate identities in a mysterious no man's land (I say no man's land because it is not to be conquered and possessed by either realist or idealist forces; to name it "no woman's land" might stimulate an even freer play of imagination) where self and other, world and world, join in a revelation of the theme of the actual's relatedness to illusion.

Herein is made possible the playful turning that entertains the question of reality assigned to us whenever we extend ourselves beyond the bland assumption that the momentary actual is in its fullness a sufficient reality. In his study of the metaphor of the theater and the dream in Renaissance drama, Jackson I. Cope cites Marsilio Ficino's account of an instance of this kind of thinking that occurred on a "philosophic holiday."[10] According to Ficino, while on an excursion in the hills below Fiesole he and Pico della Mirandola were imagining an ideal villa when, as "'we were giving ourselves up to this imaginary architecture, suddenly it stood before our eyes.'" Cope observes, concerning these philosophers' toying with ideas about the imagination and actuality, that "Life, like the perfect villa, suddenly appears before us in the light of that strange yet quotidian mystery which 'happens every day to dreamers.' But is it man's dream, or is he himself, with this world, but the shadow of a deific dream?" The stimulus to extend and dwell in this play of imagining reality has informed with renewed vigor the drama and the *theatrum mundi* metaphor of our time, as Cope shows in "sampling" the ideas of José Ortega y Gasset, Antonin Artaud, and Northrop Frye ("Prologue," 1–13) concerning the illusion of reality.

The stage in its actuality comprises that doubleness that Ficino and Pico apprehended in their imaginary villa's suddenly appearing as real. An actual presence before the audience's eyes, the play generates an imaginative reality that is taken to be merely of the ideal dimension. By a progression of thought, however, that imaginary and unreal world attains its authenticity, becoming true in its reference back to the real world or, if metaphysically justified, to the superior world beyond for which this world is a *theatrum mundi*. If back to an ordinary world that carries the onus of being an inferior reality, then the play either refers in a problematical way to the world that is a ground of illusion or indeed incarnates a superior truth that is the truth of reality. Whether referring to one dimension or the other, the play constitutes its world as referential and at the same time determining its own mode of being.

This peering into the face of paradox and watching definition slide away behind the veil of illusion does not resolve—and can do no more than broach—the predicament of the spectator. My discussion has so far uncovered and failed to distinguish two themes. On the one side is the quasi-philosophical question of the seriousness of drama as manifest in the ontological and epistemological relationship between audience and play, a relationship established in mimesis. On the other is the apparently less serious concern that the play instigates and answers to a playfulness in engaging the audience. Opening up for the audience and gratifying its impulse to approach and explore the unfamiliar, the play casts it into irresolution in the territory where illusion and reality are not always answerable to the analytical impulse. The idea of the *theatrum mundi* is pleasurable when it arises in the primacy of mimesis. It can be the point of departure for gathering the armies of theory and donning the armor of interpretive method in the march back toward resolution and certainty. The audience giving itself to the play, however, as yet enthralled in the felt eventfulness, performs the play of histrionic and exorbitant becoming one with another, like the actor playing another or like Aristotle's "well-endowed poet," who can "easily change character."[11]

The eventfulness of this immediate participation is recognizably thematic as I step back to notice that, in being a mimesis, the play is inevitably about mimesis, presents representation. It is, embodies, the idea of the Play. The play's representation is not primordially a representation of a reality beyond itself, if it is taken in Gadamer's terms to present, in its own appearance and in the way it appears, what is essential to itself; what is most essential to itself is its irreducible mimetic nature. The mimesis that Aristotle identified as essential to human nature is, as Aristotle insists, an action; and the play's action, its taking the audience into an eventful structure, is that mimesis. In the world of the play itself the eventfulness of union through imitating is made thematic more clearly—increasing the pleasure—when representations of mimesis occur in the mimesis. If in the evocation of mimetic action what the play is, foremost, is a representing actuality; and if, in its being what it is, it presents representation, its own being; then in the doubling of mimesis that can occur in the play, the play can be a mimesis of a mimesis. The presentations of representation in the play—the doublings of identity; the plays, games, dreams, and stories within the play; the masks; the roles, costumes, and disguises; the mirrorings, allusions, photographs, and pageants—intensify and increase, become an excess, of the idea of moving into another not yet known dimension and into the accompanying play of illusion that lures us further beyond the ordinary assumptions by which we bear and bear up reality. In its essence mimesis is a doubling, the one repeating the other, not as a mere copying or unprofitable duplication of the other but as a being in itself in mimetic activity.

To the extent that the audience engages in mimetic action, living through and reflecting the represented events, it performs much as if it were in that other dimension, the world of the play. The repetitions of mimesis in the play are then representative—duplicative—of the relationship of audience with play, as the audience's repetitions of mimesis are representative of the mimetic relationships within the play. The audience's pleasurable recognition of the principle of mimesis in the play, in the doublings of worlds and events and characters and the play itself, is a confirmation that the audience itself is an imitating and imitated being. There is a heightened appeal, an excess, in the drama that within its world, the world of *Hamlet* for instance, entertains the idea that somehow the truth of its world articulates with the truth of the play Hamlet wants played. The serious claim that the duplications of mimesis in the play are duplications reflecting and involving the audience's mimesis should to some extent illuminate their appeal, and though not to deny this seriousness I reiterate the Aristotelean point that the earliest lessons learned in performing or in seeing mimesis are pleasurable. In a world of detritus that pleasurable activity might seem slight, and perhaps in itself a yielding not to a transformative power of substantial worth but to the inconsequential illusion that at best entertains, at less than best might contribute to delusions, might sate the imagination or encourage its irresponsible self-delight.

Popular drama—in the theater, in film, on television—no less than serious dramatic literature, exploits the appeal of devices of the *theatrum mundi*. When Lena Horne sings the title song in the 1943 film *Stormy Weather,* the stage audience is watching a performance on a stage that pretends to be a real room, with a window, but clearly reveals its theatricality: the stage has levels and stairs designed for pyrotechnical dance numbers. The window, however, opens on a far more "realistic" street scene, in which the rain intensifies the mood of the torch song and dampens the spirits of the crowd on the street. The camera moving into that scene—a stage within a stage—tracks a kindred spirit who separates herself from the crowd and who, feeling the malaise of inner or outer stormy weather, affords departure to yet another dimension expressing and modulating the despondent mood, a dance fantasy, which takes place on another stage. From that world the camera brings the real audience back to the street scene, then back through the window into the room, and then back to the audience watching that performance. The stage audience seems to take part in the performance in much the same way that the film audience participates. Having a good time, both audiences would, if the show is effective, reflect the mood while being taken in and carried along from one level to another. Either, thus engaged, might reflect on itself being transported from one dimension to another, but that reflection should not, if the audience is genuinely absorbed in the action, vitiate the adulterated mood of sweet melancholy, sadness mingled with pleasure.

This pleasure of being taken into the scheme of revelations that might be true or false, and that invigorate the interest in the idea of the illusion, is manifest in more recent films that challenge orthodox assumptions about sexual identity. The successful Broadway play *La cage aux folles* explores the theme of disguised identity in its songs and plot and achieves theatrical éclat in the volatile and gay disguises and unmasking in the world of the play and in the play's reiterations of those disclosures for the audience. In a stage performance in the play, a twofold representation—for the audience of the nightclub that gives the play its name and for the audience of the play—the elegantly attired female chorus line, costumed in gowns and headpieces, ends the number with costumes whisked away revealing that the group is mixed, male and female. The star of the club is known to be a female impersonator, a man playing a woman, who in real life plays the feminine role in her relationship with another man, and her convincing theme song is "I am what I am."

Similarly, the film *Victor/Victoria* reveals in its title the double identity of its heroine/hero, who is as she describes herself a "woman playing a man playing a woman." In both these plays, disguise and the creation of illusion are enforced in a world that constrains roles and identities to the familiar, to preconceptions of what it means to be female or male. People are allowed to be what they are so long as they are what they are expected to be. To be beyond the pale is to exist in some dimension ill-defined and ambiguous, some *theatrum* that lacks the substantiality of the encompassing and encaging dimension. Breaking through the illusion of complacency, the assumption that everything real and respectable in reality conforms to prescribed definition, the eccentric challenges the orthodox and coerces new perceptions of the authentic that arises in and through the illusion. It is not in the theater, however, that those prevailing attitudes hold jurisdiction; the audiences in both plays transcend their worlds' expectations in being open to the entertainments that engage them in revelations through the veil of illusion. Evidently audiences, if only ostensibly for the sake of being entertained, are willing to let themselves be carried along into suppositions and speculations that lead beyond their ordinary perceptions and presumptions. They submit with delight, and they applaud.

In these glances at instances of the widespread appeal of the *theatrum mundi* metaphor, I continue to think of the audience both as an imagined, dramatized performer in the play and as an authentic—individual and communal—subject having a real identity apart from the play. To turn decisively toward thinking the audience as an idea generated by the play might be productive of literary analysis, an explication of the audience as thematic in the drama, a demonstration of the ways and to what effects it appears. It becomes a being in a world that can be read as speculation on reality, as an imaginative or fictional construct that is experienced by aesthetic means. To turn decisively toward the subjectivity of the real audience would be a move toward a different kind of certainty. The demonstration might result in, for instance, a psychoanalytical or a reader-response understanding of an actual, a theoretical, or an implied audience, or some other abstracted concept of the experiencing subject.[12] If I resist finding resolution in a clear and circumscribed site for interpretation, the risk is taken in the awareness that such moves toward certainty do not through abstraction achieve final, unassailable knowledge but themselves become counters in the larger game of interpretation. To think that I must logically choose one end or the other—to have arrived before I begin at the conclusive purpose of showing on the one hand what the objectivity, the play, performs or on the other what the subjectivity, the audience, experiences—is in the first place to have performed that analytical separation of the audience and the play. What I have said about popular entertainments has been intended to obscure the real and determining distinction between the audience in the film watching a performance and the audience watching that audience watching. What I hope to have gained is a sense of audience and play in harmonious relationship constituting that event Gadamer thinks of as a transformation into structure.

What I seem to have provoked is the problematical dramatization of myself as an audience who is both a separate identity and a being caught up in, at one with, the idea of the audience in the play. The play is not merely, in this confusion of identities, that thing out there to which I respond, but an event in which I perform; and I am in the event neither pure autonomous subject nor abject receptor lost in and effaced by the illusion. If I seem to go in one direction and then the other, or in both directions at once, in talking about the audience—and, as I proceed, other agents in the play—then what seems of value in these negotiations is what might be discovered or experienced along the way. Watching or reading, and recalling and speculating about, plays remains in the felt attachment like that process of reading imaginative literature Coleridge talks about in *Biographia Literaria*. It is not the goal, the resolution, that is to be cherished but the process itself: "The reader should be carried forward, not merely or chiefly by the mechanical impulse of curiosity, or by a restless desire to arrive at the final solution; but by the pleasurable activity of mind excited by the attractions of the journey itself. Like the motion of a serpent, which the Egyptians made the emblem of intellectual power; or like the path of sound through the air; at every step he pauses and half recedes, and from the retrogressive movement collects the force which again carries him onward."[13]

Although in Coleridge's characterization the reader is a private subject that becomes metaphorically disembodied, "like the path of sound through the air," the thrust of his argument is toward psychological or epistemological explanation. Implicit, however, is the power of the poem to instigate the "pleasurable activity of mind excited by the attractions of the journey itself." Coleridge has already, in Chapter 12 of the *Biographia,* entertained the question of knowledge under the guidance of Schelling. In experience itself, realist and idealist abstractions are not formulated and distinguishing: "During the act of knowledge itself, the objective and subjective are so instantly united, that we cannot determine to which of the two the priority belongs. There is here no first, and no second; both are coinstantaneous and one" (1:174). Coleridge's concentration on the experiencing subject, like Husserl's, invites the opening of the question toward the play of relationship posited by Heidegger and Gadamer. To take this direction seems implicitly to require assumption of a deferential mode of acting, to call for a devalued authority in the subject, to allow for the possibility that the subject, the audience experiencing the play, is subsumed among the ideas and images that appear in the play.

The audience as critic/theorist plays, then, the role of abstracted audience, no longer experiencing but reflecting on and speculating about the play, about relationships, about discovery. In looking back, this audience recalls, imagines, complicates the essential engagement of a moment in the desire to retain and to share, to talk about and pay tribute to the moment cherished. The desire in "the retrogressive movement" that "collects the force which again carries" forward is a desire that takes us beyond the personal, an anticipation that tribute to the play helps to preserve it as a relic for the future. This activity is mimetic in that its speculations are a reaching out from the past experience of a play toward an audience which, if taken in, reduplicates the mimesis and receives the power of the play to reach out from the past, to call and to reveal, to bestow its gifts. This one audience's speculations might become a mediation, merely a means— like the staging of a play—to make contact, to serviceably stand in for the play, to be mnemonic. Thus, the following essay on a slight sketch by Harold Pinter, "The Black and White," might serve as a retrogressive movement and a recall for an audience who already retains the play in memory and as an enticement to discover and share what might not yet have been known. The performance of speculations about the play, in the desire to interest, becomes excessive as recapitulation of the desire to see clearly and to indulge the impulse of the imagination to range freely. The reader's desire is mimetic of the desires of the characters in the play, and the reader like the characters desires familiarity and adventure in the projection and anticipation of world views and constituted dimensions of reality.

Mimesis and Vision: Pinter's "The Black and White"

Unlike Shakespeare's Lear on the heath, the modern "unaccommodated" human being might be observed anywhere, doing almost anything, frequently encumbered by triviality rather than facing nature's sublime power. The women in Harold Pinter's sketch "The Black and White" are too engaged in the moment to voice Lear or Job's questions. Intent on their satisfactions of the moment, they engage in an activity that appears trivial, inconsequential, ephemeral. Meeting near dawn at a milk bar that closes for only an "hour and half" for a "scrubround,"[14] they eat their soup; they talk about it, the bread, the place, the bus routes; and they talk about three other more imaginative things: the man who has, according to the Second Old Woman, made a pass at her; the problem of the First Old Woman's talking to strangers (which she denies); and the danger of adventure that can result from talking to strangers, the Second Old Woman's having been taken in by the "coppers." The momentary pleasure ends as the milk bar is about to close, the Second Woman intending to go "up to the Garden" and the First Woman, for the "hour and half," not "down" to the Garden but "up to Waterloo Bridge" (242–43). They are occupied during this minimal action, however, in interpreting their world, with questions and answers; and they might serve as a paradigm for one sort of interpreter, one who presumes to play the role of literary critic. Although their world is not comfortably structured or institutionally secure (the milk bar's closing frees them to the city), they generate their own consolations in their moment, in their place, and in their own movements. Although their field of vision is limited, they take satisfaction in the fact that they can see "what goes on. . . . It's better than going down to that place on the embankment" (242). As observers, they are indeed "unaccommodated."

"The Black and White" is so slight a "sketch" that it resists interpretation. Paradoxically, its minimal presentation of character and action, promising so little in the way of meaning, leaves an audience reluctant to accept it as it appears, and it thus improbably provokes interpretation. The resolution that is desired of interpretation is, indeed, the difficulty with works of art that appear as ephemera, emerging from shadow and receding before our will to interpret is sated. Yet when we advert to the idea of interpretation, we have already raised a structure of our relationship with the play. We are, as audience, *about* interpretation, inevitably, whether or not we contemplate this activity. Taking notice of ourselves as interpretively engaged, we might observe our likeness in the women. They too are *about* interpretation. The Second Old Woman presumes to understand unspoken motives in the man who has asked the time: "I told him all right. Go on, I said, why don't you get back into your scraghole, I said, clear off out of it before I call a copper" (241). She advises the First Old Woman to "stop talking to strangers, old piece of boot like you, you mind who you talk to." This concern for the unknown, for strangers, is romanticized as an attractive danger. The Second Woman's story about being taken "away in the wagon once" because she talked to strangers is an instructive, though brief, story for her audience, the First Woman, who predictably according to dramatic/aesthetic expectations identifies with her friend. When the Second Woman explains that the police "didn't keep me, but that was only because they took a fancy to me," the First Woman asks, "Do you think they'd take a fancy to me?" (242).

The story is for the First Woman what the play might be for its audience—a perhaps inconsequential, problematical chance to experience an entertainment and to entertain ideas about it, to enlarge ourselves through our relationship to it. The strange and alluring events, fictional or real, whether interpreted truly or fancifully distorted, carry with them not only risk but also the opportunity to connect. That imagined connection is for the women, understandably, sexual: with the Second Old Woman's man who asks the time, the other's (perhaps) talking to two strangers, and the "coppers" who "took a fancy" to the first (242). But this connecting can be thematized, can become speculative, as surely as can be the idea of interpretation. The idea of the women's—and our—relating to, going out to, others, to objects of our interest, is not merely a psychological fact to be proven either true or false; it is an idea involving understanding and relationship, and as idea about connecting it goes beyond the question of truth in representation. An understanding of the women is a having of ideas about them, and the way we connect with them is more than, though not uninvolved with, our perception or interpretation of them as characters. Our perceptions and understandings of them are as mere reiteration of the familiar, however, of what is already ours, unless we have "taken a fancy" to them and in this affection have freed ourselves to the play of imagination that seeks adventure and connections. We feel and entertain the idea that we are connecting; they are connecting; and we like to think some genuine connection takes place. I am thinking not merely of our "identifying" with characters in drama, that problematical activity Aristotle leaves unresolved in his assumption that we experience pity and fear, but also of the connecting Henry James makes crucial in *The Golden Bowl* and E. M. Forster makes mysterious in *A Passage to India;* of the essential and primordial connections between subject and object in Husserl's phenomenology.[15]

The one woman becomes an audience for the other in the brief story. We, Aristoteleans still, "identify" with the women, and in this problematical transcendence we assume a freedom to interpret them, to pursue a vision of what they are and mean. We might let the identification end with observing their apparent status in life, their vulnerability, their limited perspective. One result, a distancing pity, is an appealing safety maneuver, keeping us, if not coldly analytical in Brechtian *verfremdungseffekt,* at least apart, as other, as the pitier who feels the difference between ourselves and these women. If they mimetically stand for conditions in their world, we tend to read the play as social reflection, and our concerns about them as women, about their economic status in the state, become thematically paramount. Mimesis understood this way leads to interpretations that look at a unilinear representation, the women as standing for an underprivileged class—economic or gender perhaps—the play as bespeaking a world of ephemera and inconsequentiality. We might then judge the "truth" of the play by sociological, psychological, or historical yardsticks; and, less overtly perhaps, by the naturalist metaphor of our world's detrition.

We might, however, admire a certain strength and daring in the women's adventures. We might read the play with Aristotle's wonder—at the women's stamina and endurance, their bold expatiation, their curiosity, and their Odyssean impulse to see more. Thus read, they are ourselves hoping to understand and, when we have to let go of understanding, trying like them merely to see more. Relinquishing the visionary impulse, we might settle for the pleasure and immediacy of whatever this experience brings. Seeing involves us in not only questions of visual acuity and attention, seeing what is there, but also in recognition and remembering, and it inevitably serves the ulterior purposes of transcending the immediate—interpreting toward a *Weltanschauung* that is generative, ever toward the future. Heidegger relates seeing to what he names curiosity (*Neugier* [*Being and Time,* H 170]), a condition like idle talk (*Gerede* H 169), which is essential to our everyday being in the world, the falling. These "everyday modes of Being" (H 173) in the world tend to uproot, and are complementary.

Idle talk closes off, blocks discovery; for curiosity "nothing is closed off," it is "everywhere and nowhere." Heidegger's concern is that from this ordinary desire to see we move toward the wholeness of being, to Care, and by understanding the existential condition that includes curiosity "we have obtained the phenomenal ground for a 'comprehensive' Interpretation of Dasein's Being as care" (H 180). The apparent lightness of seeing, then, is a necessary ground of our hope to see more through imaginative discovery.

In the play's action, in the structure of events, the women's concerns suffer this reduction of imagining and conjecturing to the pleasures deriving from sight; their speculation, their toying with designs and desires, becomes reduced to the simple mastery of travel and observation. They let go of speculation for the immediate pleasures of seeing. The First Woman's territory ranges from Marble Arch to Fleet Street; she has "been down to Liverpool Street" but does not "fancy going down there, down Fulham way. . . . I've never fancied that direction much" (241). Her preferring to "see what goes on from this top table" rather than "going down to that place on the embankment" initiates a brief discussion about traveling and seeing—they will go, the Second Woman "up to the Garden," the First "up to Waterloo Bridge" (242)—and the play ends on a quizzical note, provocatively heightened by the women's recurrent and questionable mapping in terms of the up-down metaphor.[16] Going up to Waterloo Bridge, the First Woman will "just about see" a last all-night bus "come up over the river" (243). Her final question—"It don't look like an all-night bus in daylight, do it?"—ends the play with a question that mediates between elemental seeing and teleological comprehension. The dawn and the bus constitute perception that bears in itself the question of illusion, transformation. What seems to be can seem to become something else—the bus, the women, the play, the audience.

The women's mapping and mastery of landscape, their sense of knowledge and capability, their certainties and determinations, are the satisfactions we take in this strange territory of the play while we rely on the consolation of Aristotelean mimesis thought of as representation grounded in probability. Mimesis is not merely the dramatic design that represents for us the principle of design we anticipate, the underlying regularity and predictability of things. As affect, it is the reassurance we feel about the rightness of there being constancy and probability, in events and things. We reiterate the mimesis as satisfaction, a sense of resolution and comfort.[17] We have a map to a world retraced each time we experience the patterns we have generated out of previous experiences with drama. But that final question from the First Woman leaves us open to the unresolved that provokes the imagination, to the question of seeing that teases us beyond probabilities and resolutions, teases toward further understanding and imaginative design while abandoning us to irresolution. Indeed, the all-night bus, like this play and this woman, is of such elemental facticity and definability that, seen in a new light, undergoing some visual transformation, it provokes interpretation and at the same time leaves us to wonder.

My playing off mastery against mystery is aimed to establish two major thematic issues with the women in this little play, issues reflected by or in the audience. The women's movements, their plotless plotting of itineraries, instantiate an idea of mobility that is not without orientation and not without reliance on the familiar. They rely on the familiar and predictable patterns of buses, the known landmarks that provide boundaries as well as a base for their operations. Like them, the audience experiences a play as discovery, as new experience, but it relies on its expectations of established patterns and forms. The stage, the curtain, the communal group as audience, the actors presenting an action should, we ask, give us a sense of familiar designs: rising action, climax, falling action; believable and understandable characters; Aristotelean unity and probability of action; the mimetic assurance that this particular design gives us an instance of design itself. Those are our landmarks, and they make us comfortable. With this "sketch" or Pinter's plays in general we have learned not to be disappointed that some of these expectations are minimally gratified; we are becoming, perhaps, increasingly versatile and open to discovery; we might, we like to think, learn to live with fewer mimetic certainties as we open ourselves to and are opened by the play of imaginative perceptions. In this extension toward possibilities we are not, of course, satisfied and fulfilled in seeing a represented world reflecting the mere detritus of our world.

Thematic, too, is the women's playing with the mystery, their propensity to exceed such limits as we demand in the closure of mimetic probability. It seems to me not unwarranted to relate the women's playful impulse to what Aristotle identifies as an end—if not perhaps the ulterior end—of tragedy. Aristotle, arguing that the effects of tragedy are heightened by the audience's perceiving them as based in "cause and effect," as "having an air of design," observes that grounding events in probability or necessity produces something more than the assurance that things happen by plan or understandable design. Probability establishes a cognitive base but, given that base, "The tragic wonder will then be greater than if they [the events] happened of themselves or by accident."[18] Wonder seems to be a motive that lies beyond whatever assurance we receive from seeing that events in the dramatized world are meaningful, that they make sense. Again, although the irrational is the source of the wonderful, "It is necessary in tragedy to create the marvelous" (Golden, 44). While the women in Pinter's play seem to find solace in the predictability of their daily rounds (apparently ritualized in these pre-dawn meetings), their motives incline toward the unknown and, what might be observed about Aristotle's wonder, the ineffable, the undefinable, the je ne sais quoi. Their imaginations play upon a man's motives in asking the time and upon the embellished consequences of talking to strangers. The strangeness of that dawning world is imaged in the way an all-night bus is transformed by the light. Deferring the interpreting impulse, the inclination to leap, for instance, to understanding a relationship between night and day in that image of the bus (and thus to explain the play's title), to pin down with our understanding, we might be satisfied that we are opened up to the mystery, to the possibility of transformation, to the beauty of wonder of which the women are capable. If they become for us something more than pitiable, fragile signs of human existence in a diminished world, they enlarge our humanity and reflect our capacity for desiring more than mere existence, our invocation of the urge to see more. This imaginative impulse is tenuous and can be disappointed. Like the women, we are extending ourselves toward the unknown, toward the as yet undiscovered—and we are not unfamiliar with Odysseus. In thus entertaining engagement we take risks, and we know the expediency of letting go.

If Odysseus was a sort of voyeur, so are the women, and so is their audience. Our understanding of Odysseus derives from his consistency of character, his desire to see and to experience, even to the extent of enduring hardship and danger in order to hear the song of the Sirens—in short, his power to make us see our possible selves in him. If the women do not confirm the rich thematic associations of Odysseus's character and adventures, his fertile imagination and self-revelation in his own narratives, we can nevertheless observe provocative similarities, recognizing that in the differences we can consider ideas about opposed world views. Does the Second Woman serve as a Circean advisor to the first? Do the women suggest, in a sort of Joycean commentary, that the qualities we associate with Odysseus and recognize shadowed in them—endurance, imagination, curiosity, the urge to experience, to see—are still there in this dwindled world? Do such questions instigate the improbable affirmation that there is something wonderful about the women?

Allusions to other literary works like the *Odyssey*, oblique or inchoate as they may be, imply another version of a world against which this one is played off. Pinter's plays seem often to be self-referential, about the play itself, involving theoretical and aesthetic concerns, as in *No Man's Land*.[19] Although minimalist in their impact, they might be an incitement to thought, to speculation, to playing with an idea, to reflecting on the theoretical; as Wallace Stevens says of Reginald Marsh's "Wooden Horses," the painting is "not without imagination and . . . far from being without aesthetic theory" ("The Noble Rider and the Sound of Words," *Necessary Angel*, 12). They can thus be experienced as reflexive, as generative of ideas about the theater as a representation of a world, as a version of reality, thus invoking the *theatrum mundi* metaphor and encouraging the audience's proclivity toward assuming the role of critic who is a voyeur and an imaginer. The First Old Woman seems to look out on the world as if it were a stage, engaging the Second Old Woman as co-conspiratorial audience. Gazing out the window, she congratulates them on their prospect:

> *First:* You can see what goes on from this top table. . . .
> *Second:* Yes, there's not too much noise.
> *First:* There's always a bit of noise.
> *Second:* Yes, there's always a bit of life. (242)

The audience, appreciative viewer of a world seen through such a frame, is free to define and characterize itself in the act of observing the world. The women's pleasure in experiencing includes the power to transform "noise" into "life"; the audience has the privilege of reflecting and sublimating the earth's cacophony toward the meaningful, toward Heidegger's "world" that bears in itself the possibility that ends are beginnings, that with the women we anticipate the pleasure of discovery as we go on toward new experiences.

"The Black and White" echoes questions of knowledge and "seeing" more overt in some of Pinter's other works—for instance, in his dramatization of John Fowles's novel *The French Lieutenant's Woman*, which explores the doubleness of nineteenth- and twentieth-century perspectives, the doublings of the *theatrum mundi* and the mirror metaphors. The direct and primary problem in translating the novel to film was how to represent that doubleness of vision in Fowles's narration. Pinter's solution, of course, was to exploit the metaphor of the theater/dream, to play off one reality against the other, to present to the audience a fiction of actors filming a fiction. The doubling of consciousness represents from the first moment those questions of seeing and knowledge, the audience's perception of Sarah's image in the mirror becoming transformed by the discovery that what is seen is Anna, the twentieth-century actress playing the nineteenth-century Sarah. Less a satisfaction of the mimetic contract than this film, *The*

Dumb Waiter, like "The Black and White," exposes us from the beginning to the discomforts of the mysterious, in that the unknown is not grounded in the assurances of probability. Like the women, Gus and Ben in *The Dumb Waiter* live in fastidious circumstantiality while musing about the absent, the forces beyond their ken. We, like these characters, are led to seek comfortable knowledge, certainty, and a sense of control in the Aristotelean probabilities of presence; yet we accompany the characters in speculating on what is absent, with Aristotelean wonder. The great mystery that emerges in the action concerns the identity and motives of the absent boss, the director of this drama, the playwright who plotted it, the figure whose attributes an interpreting audience might identify with those of God. The mystery of this designer and controller is more ominous and immediately significant than that of the absent designing agents in "The Black and White," but in both plays the imaginations of the characters contribute to whatever objective threat there is. In the end, the audience of *The Dumb Waiter* is left grasping for and trying to embrace the insubstantial shade of those absent figures of authority; assuming the freedom to generate an imaginative construct of freedom and power, identity and being, motive and design; presuming to know the transcendent objectivities. As whenever we are engaged in other kinds of interpretation, we interpret the imaginative work of art with our imagination in play. We are engaged, not in a methodical process from perception through understanding to imaginative constructs of meaning and relationship, but in a play of redundancy, imagining and interpreting and seeing, all in complicity. One of the pleasures of remembering the work of art as aesthetic experience and anticipating a renewed experience of it is that we can always see more. The Women in "The Black and White" demonstrate this movement from presuming to see the scheme of things to just seeing and anticipating the pleasure of seeing more.

In both *The Dumb Waiter* and "The Black and White" characters engage in both kinds of seeing. The visionary impulse, the drive toward full transcendent knowledge, even when it requires imaginative constitution of meanings, is a perhaps unrealizable goal yet a need that is not to be forfeited merely because it involves risk and inconclusiveness. It entails the irrational, which Aristotle considered inappropriate to the design of probable events. The irrational is the source, however, of the wonder that he says is essential to the ends of that action. Writing about Albrecht Altdorfer's "The Virgin amidst Angels," E. H. Gombrich observes that "infinitude acquires a special pathos and beauty through its religious associations, but in principle, as Nietzsche knew, all claims to copy nature must lead to the demand of representing the infinite."[20] In observing this imperative in art, the desire to go beyond, to see more, I find Gombrich's exploration of mimesis and illusion more than instructive. While "the demand of representing the infinite" embedded in "all claims to copy nature" challenges us to see more accurately and truly, it leaves us open to the transcendence of wonder that is uncontainable and the sense of wonder that is authentic. When the critic relocates the infinite in the mimetic, assurances come, the certainty of knowing and interpreting is ratified in the closure of meaning. When the wonder is authentic, the critic cedes his or her saltatory authority and becomes ambulatory.[21] The end of mimesis is, in Gombrich's view of art, seeing and the possibility of seeing more: "The true miracle of the language of art is not that it enables the artist to create the illusion of reality. It is that under the hands of a great master the image becomes translucent. In teaching us to see the visible world afresh, he gives us the illusion of looking into the invisible realms of the mind—if only we know, as Philostratus says, how to use our eyes" (389).

Clear sight, seeing fully and accurately what is, is an immediate goal of the audience or critic. The critic, abstracted into a theoretical premise, typically loses in the abstraction that play of mimetic (imitative, reflective) engagement with characters like the two women in "The Black and White." Yet seeing clearly is the presumed objective, and "objectivity," of traditional historical or biographical criticism, producing that certain knowledge that comes of discovering a reality believed to be Shakespeare's or Pinter's mind, its purposes and meanings[22]; and it was the central value to be gained from the New Criticism in its encounter with the poem, that definition of our visual acumen. The New Critical impulse, however, while allowing for the aesthetic motive in seeing, disguised its mimetic aim in severing the work of art from its world and its author. Isolating and securing the poem against the problematics of mimesis as ordinarily understood— events in the work representing events in the world—the New Criticism established the fiction that the critic was simply and directly, given the necessary capability, seeing and understanding what the poem was, is, and will remain. The goal was to discern the principle, the design, and to know it fully, an ambition manifest in the assurance and certainty of the critic displaying *the* understanding of the work— often the secret understanding revealed as an entirety.

In spite of the multiplicity and diversity of our prevailing criticisms, this quest for certainty is evident in much of the theory designated reader-response, subjectivist, psychoanalytical, Marxist, and feminist. Each is an earnest attempt to realize the visionary impulse in a reading of reality, to resolve theoretical problems by fixing on a one-to-one relationship between subjects and objects. The presumption of a full vision of the work's relation to the world is a yielding to the illusion that the work simply tells—or fails to tell—the truth about some thing it represents. The fixed motive, however, the explanation of the world and the work of art as a relationship between A and B, purposefully restricts the relationship to something manageable, something that can be grasped and abstracted from the flux of experience, thereby voiding the very mobility and openness to discovery implicit in Odyssean journeys. To state these relationships reductively, of course, as a negotiation between A and B, between object and subject, the object might be the literary work or the world with the subject being the reader or the author. In simplest readings, a subjectivist or psychoanalytical theory can refer meaning to the reader's generating patterns of understanding, thus identifying the ontological site, the determiner.[23] Another psychoanalytical reading might use the work as a bridge to apprehend meaning in the author's mind. Pinter's psyche might then stand revealed, like the New Critic's body of the poem, as a phenomenon perceived clearly, atemporally.[24] A refinement of this operation can be seen in the Geneva version of phenomenological thinking, in which the author's mind is not an entity beyond the work but a revelation in the canon. Literary works yield motifs and patterns that can be attributed to an author beyond them, and it is easily assumed that such knowledge is more than a version of reality or merely a preferred fiction. Husserl's intentionality is, in the very act of invoking it, tamed and made serviceable to the grasping of objects. In engaging with the work of art, an imaginative intentionality reflects the problematical nature of what presents itself as neither necessarily fictional nor certifiably true.

Reader-response theory, developing from Roman Ingarden's phenomenological thought, postulates the work of art as a "concretization," an activity determined neither by the text nor the reader, but realized in the event.[25] This premise allows for a certain openness, for the impossibility of finishing—the word "finalizing" seems allowable here—in that for Ingarden there will always be "spots of indeterminacy" that a reader will try to fill, to determine. Ingarden's philosophical bent is, nevertheless, toward that closure that defines precisely what that ontological and epistemological relationship is between the reader and the work of art, as evidenced in his pursuit of earnestness in *The Cognition of the Literary Work of Art*. The assumption is that there is a single relationship that, by our paring away the manifold of context, can be seen as a mimetic activity. Ingarden's motive is generated like Husserl's from the need for philosophical certainty; but as a beginning it stands ready to amend old assumptions, to forgo them if necessary, to face things as they are even if they are recalcitrant. As with the other critical positions that have benefited from phenomenological insights, reader-response theory expresses an earnestness based in the mimetic illusion that sense can be made and order can be discerned if we take the problem seriously. We take comfort in probability and in the power that comes of assurance in the face of uncertainties. This partiality to mimetic assumptions, this belief that seriousness is dead serious, that "genuine" knowledge settles matters, gives us a certainty felt as power. Schiller characterizes this impulse as the *Formtrieb*, which "wants to determine for itself."[26] The formal and the material impulses "are equally earnest in their demands" (78). Schiller's activating principle, the unfinished process that is ever seeking balance without demanding the satisfaction of static realization, is the play impulse. It becomes a liberating quest, the allowing of wonder in the rage for closure, for final order, that never is to be found in some still form free from motion.

I have been moving from the play to theoretical questions, apparently, with the seriousness of both the form and the sense drives, yet my talk about the women and the play is about identities already imaginatively constituted. Looking more closely at the action and the two women would not be a corrective to the freedom of the imaginative play, a closure, producing all-resolving certainty, but a fresh start, a new look. If I confess that what has been said about the women, "they," generalizes them as a representation of and in their world, and if I then distinguish them as individuals, I shall hope to see them more precisely, nevertheless, just because I see them according to traditional expectations of dramatic structure and characterization.

Their being identified from the beginning as "small" (First Old Woman) and "tall" (Second Old Woman) (240) invites a distinction, and the action bears it out. Like Ben and Gus, indeed like Laurel and Hardy, they represent opposed principles of character. The play begins with two questions that reveal their propensities:

Second: You see that one come up and speak to me at the counter?
First: You got the bread, then? (240)

The First Woman is matter-of-fact, pragmatic, interested in what she sees before her (including the "view from this top table"), rather simple, and perhaps naive; the Second Woman instigates intrigue, reading (we have not seen what she saw, her evidence for this reading) ulterior motives in a man's asking the time, warning against talking to strangers (241), and relating her wonderful adventure of escape from the coppers because of her feminine appeal (242). They represent a difference between seeing, or perception, and imagination; and, difference notwithstanding, they are capable of sharing an experience, talking about it, appreciating it. They like this place where converting "noise" to "life" is a transformation affirming that, in spite of their opposition and the dramatic conflict, they are capable of harmonizing and producing in the audience a sense of the rightness of their becoming one in their pleasure, in their sharing an adventure before going their separate ways.

The willingness to allow, to see afresh and to see beyond, without the demand for closure, to become more than what Gombrich calls the "Egyptian," might be seen as a willingness to entertain ideas in play rather than to insist on resolving their ontological value. In his "Retrospect" to *Art and Illusion* Gombrich observes that "The 'Egyptian' in us ultimately stands for the active mind, for that 'effort after meaning' which cannot be defeated without our world's collapsing into total ambiguity" (395); but defeating the Egyptian is no more possible than would be living in "total ambiguity." When the fear of defeating the Egyptian causes disregard of the translucency of art, we reduce the manifold of connections to the purity of a simple relationship and retrain our visionary instinct on the visual and immediate.

If, on the other hand, the pleasure of seeing more demands more than direct sensory reception of objects before us, we are engaged with ideas in seeing what appears before us. According to Heidegger, the blank stare manifests a depreciation of ordinary perception:

> When we have to do with anything, the mere seeing of the Things which are closest to us bears in itself the structure of interpretation, and in so primordial a manner that just to grasp something *free,* as it were, *of the "as",* requires a certain readjustment. When we merely stare at something, our just-having-it-before-us lies before us *as a failure to understand it any more.* This grasping which is free of the "as", is a privation of the kind of seeing in which one *merely* understands. (*Being and Time,* H 149)

The mere seeing in staring "mindlessly" at something is not our way of approach in ordinary experience, and with the work of art we inevitably see the object "as." The First Woman's observation that their soup is "tomato soup" (240) entails meaningful seeing, even though it seems a stubborn retreat to the facts while the Second Woman is trying to tell her story of the man who asked the time. With the literary work, however, the structure of meaning is not posited as an event in the real world. It is the "as" performing in presentation, the seen speaking oblique meaning, and we play with it. This impulse to play with emerging concepts I have referred to as "thematizing." Thematizing is the entertaining of ideas that do not have to be fixed in order to hold value, do not have to be—really—propositions that are true or false; it might be merely speculative. Since such conceptualizing is in itself neither true nor false, assuming this view saves us from the need to determine the validity, the truth or falsity, of someone else's mimetic premise. The world, a *Weltanschauung*, is not the only referent of mimesis, nor is the audience, nor the author. Any referent can appear, and all referents, including the idea of the work of art itself, are inevitably and potentially what the work can be discovered to be "about." The discoverable, and consequently as-yet-undiscovered, the Idea of the Author for instance, can be instantiated in a figure in the play, in an allusion, in the *theatrum mundi* metaphor, in the biographical playwright or in the director—"real" or imagined. But as ideas they are ungoverned and remain ideas *of;* they are seen *as*.

Mimesis can be located, then, as a process of relations between the work and the world, between the artist and the work, between the work and the audience, between or among whatever dimensions might appear. Certainly Aristotle promotes our thinking about mimesis not simply as work reflecting world, but as an audience reflecting the character's experience, realized in the audience as pity and fear, and catharsis. In Aristotle's finding our earliest learning to be based in imitation, it is worth considering that we receive pleasure from learning not only in recognizing an act of imitation but also by engaging in mimetic activity. But conceived as a single dimension, this understanding of mimesis is not sufficiently removed from Plato's metaphor of the artist as mirror-wielder. Plato's objection to the artist as mirroring agent is a shield against plurality, uncertainty, invisible power, indeed, against an Ion's sense of wonder about the unseen. So long as mimesis remains restrictive, remains the consolation of recognition and knowing that empowers closure, our operations in the world are assured and reassuring.

Gadamer's hermeneutic challenges us to approach the strange not with anxiety about possible misinterpretation but with confidence: "Only the support of familiar and common understanding makes possible the venture into the alien, the lifting up of something out of the alien, and thus the broadening and enrichment of our own experience of the world."[27] Allowing for wonder through such discovery characterizes the mimetic imperative as not the end desired but the necessary means of beginning. Probability or necessity becomes the map by which we gain our bearings; the critical imagination can serve as our Circe, giving us particular clues and warnings as we venture into the unknown, yet not revealing all.

It would seem that a deconstructive critic would free us from our self-generated restraints, our reliance on the received word. When Jacques Derrida negates the mimetic relationship between the work and the world, there being no outside text[28]; when the word refers not to an objective "signified" but to what it intends; when Heidegger's X-ing a word while using it becomes a play with words like "differ-defer," it would seem that we have been set free into the wonderful. But Derrida's deconstructions, though erasures, fix in the play of language such dualities as absence and presence, re-logocentrizing through the play of paradox; they are driven by mimetic certainties. The critic in seeming to read beneath the text is nevertheless in a comfortable one-way relationship to it, is empowered to read what has been covered in the author's words. Thus privileged, the deconstructive author's voice becomes an imposing presence, a voice with a fixed cadence and a tone of finality. But the risk is absent; there is nothing irrational, in Aristotle's sense; there is no surprise, except as the critic becomes empowered as the sole artist, and the only text is his. There is no room for wonder. The ambulatory critic might prefer to go back to Aristotle, to his withholding of full understanding about wonder, or to Schiller, who insists that the form- and sense-drives are always, in time, seeking and failing to achieve atemporal balance; the play-drive keeps both in play, in time—even the theoretical formulation of them, which is realized only in the activity of art and never completed.

Stanley Fish's idea of a community of readers is an admission that the critic is yielding power, but an appeal to what might turn out to be Plato's promiscuous crowd is dangerous. My characterizing us as an audience shares with Fish's "notion of interpretive communities" ("Interpreting the *Variorum*," 148) a vulnerability to oppositional strong criticism, and I admit that, not having discovered scientific resolution to many questions about psychology, I do not know exactly how that audience reiterates "pity" and "fear" and "catharsis," nor that those terms adequately represent our mimetic activity.[29] I do not know to what extent our differences—sexual as well as other culturally marked differences—make shared experience improbable. I do think I know, however, that in primordial direct experience we act as if union of self and other is possible and general. We feel for and make sense of the other in spite of difference; our mimetic activity as an audience opens us to possible shared experiences and as a speculator/critic presumes that others can become our audience and repeat that connecting of experiences.

In the direct experience, ideas of identity and relationship are available as means of recognizing, of seeing *as,* and they amount to thematizing the audience, along with the playwright, the play, the world, the critic. All are units of possibility that are in their indefiniteness—their not being absolute, finished, and complete—vulnerable to interpretation and open to pluralizing. The member of the audience and the author, for instance, whom we usually think of as discrete historical beings who if we understand them will yield certain knowledge, are inevitably inaccessible except as a seen presence and/or in our ideas of them. Granting our uncertainty about them, even when we talk of them as objectively real, allows them a certain privacy and the freedom to be otherwise and to change. The consequently mobile author or audience might disappear or might appear, even in the text.[30] The idea of such a figure remains only an idea, perhaps merely a notion. My notion of Pinter, the playwright who crafted "The Black and White," is seemingly reinforced with some little knowledge of the man himself and a little more sure knowledge from having read or seen other plays of his, yet it is a notion deriving from and colored by ideas of the artist as craftsman, as capable intellect interpreting and presenting a world, as . . . whatever other available concepts of the artist might pertain.

The incompleteness of this view disappoints our instinct for probability and necessity, fails to settle matters in the recognition of the design; but that disappointment is a certain freedom in itself. The condition of freedom looks to the future, as Fish's community of readers and Heidegger's Dasein are anticipatory. This community, the audience, is in action. It is not merely drawing on and recognizing structures from the past, but creating a dialogue that is generative, speaking in a voice ready to be astonished. It is ready to hear something more, as if the play were proleptic. Its rhetoric is toward the future, unsettled, unsure of consequences, as Classical rhetoric did not presume to satisfy all requirements of logic but simply to use it for the sake of convincing probabilities. Stevens talks about the imagination in terms of inclinations toward the past or the future: "We cannot look at the past or the future except by means of the imagination but again the imagination of backward glances is one thing and the imagination of looks ahead something else. . . . [M]emory involves a reproductive power, and looks ahead involve a creative power: the power of our expectations" ("Imagination as Value," *Necessary Angel*, 144). If we are not constrained merely to follow our familiar rounds based in memory, to be reassured by what seems set and predetermined, to find satisfaction in *recognition*, we might be able to "see what goes on from this top table. . . . It don't look like an all-night bus in daylight, do it?"

This way of seeing is cognition, incorporating the necessary capability to know and to acknowledge the legitimacy, even the determinative nature, of the objectivities. What we want is clear sight, the engagement with the imaginative objectivity in an act of psychological *epoché*.[31] But cognition need not be constrained to the realm of indubitable truth. To have an idea of something, or ideas about it, as in the literary experience we inevitably and from the outset sense or create character beyond personality, is to engage with ideas about, not necessarily and finally to know. Imaginative constitution of such ideas is not merely false only because it is not final. "The Black and White" is a text, as I read or remember it, and it warrants my faithfulness. Yet my engagement with it is not intended merely to derive a certainty of its truth, its author's intention, its fidelity to one dimension of a *Weltanschauung*, its meaning. E. H. Gombrich's Egyptian, in his "effort after meaning," in his desire to establish and maintain the static atemporal forms of Egyptian art that Socrates so admired, assumes a power to determine and know beyond change and discovery. The premise that such knowing is attainable is the very denial that makes it so difficult to surrender to the appearance of the wonderful. To be sure of something strengthens our resolve, and we might in that strength build a fortress against the fear of being vulnerable to wonder. I would hope to attain some understanding of this play's value as a map; but, more important, it should liberate me to discover the unknown, it should open me up to the mystery, to the wonderful.

I would be gratified in appreciating the women as mimetic, as seriocomic representatives of social conditions. If I am sensitive to human vulnerability and isolation, to the way individuals are disfranchised and exploited, I can objectify the women as instances of precarious and unfulfilled existence in a dangerous and alien world. My imagination will connect with that of the Second Woman in sensing and reaffirming the world as a dangerous place. But that activity of separating into classes, affirming cultural difference, is yet a presumption that I have already made connection in transcending the ego. Recognizing myself reflected in the women, I might notice that their mood is not negativism and complaint about how the world treats them, the theme I have brought to bear, but a mood of enjoying the little pleasures of the moment—including stories about high adventure, allurement, and escape. If my desire is to transcend what I recognize at times to be a bleak condition in a menacing world, in a world of detritus, I can take pleasure, like the women, in little things like seeing what goes on from "this top table" or imagining that someone might "take a fancy" to me, little things that can transform conflict into mutual experience. Seeing the improbable in the women is a matter of recognizing and feeling satisfaction in their satisfaction that turns an inconsequential meeting into something dramatic. If I come to wonder at their power of endurance, their curiosity, their ability to wonder, their freedom and mobility, I am lifted with them into the power of wonder and freedom. Their potentiality extends even to invoking the idea of Odysseus the wanderer, the experiencer, the endurer, the imagination-blessed storyteller.

Such truth as appears, then, is the truth of metaphor, the connotative rather than the denotative, the play of ideas that might lead to larger vision. We rely on the denotative force of language as on the probabilities in the dramatic representation, and that reliance proves a ground for the interpretation that can extend to metaphoric connections and the freedom of wonder. The world of probabilities, Schiller's "contingency" and "necessity" (77), involved in exploring mimetic relationships leads to questions about the truth of the representation and, with language, the right or wrong of correspondences. Wonder and metaphor undermine the right/wrong, fact/fiction antitheses and open us to thought, to exploration. Dissuaded from immediate conclusiveness, we come to represent freedom in the uncertainty, in the possibilities of playful interpretation. As with metaphor, the apprehension of wonder opens us to thought and thought to us.

Especially in works like "The Black and White" the possibility of seeing is so limited, the "dwindled sphere" so confined, certainty so elusive, that we the audience might remain uncomfortably in an overpowering sense of desolation, deprivation, the pall of reality; but we are capable of connecting, of completely touching and being touched by another "in the stale grandeur of annihilation."[32] We balk at the idea of the visionary when the work seems to give so little. Yet the vision that goes beyond mere eyesight, albeit falling short of epiphany, provokes an awareness of mobility, liberation, freedom, being. A correct reading that might come of criticisms grounded in mimetic distinction between audience and representation, the representation and the represented, would keep our sights on matters of probability. Still, we would want the freedom and vision that can appear in the deceptive, even duplicitous, presences of a diminished world. Such an engagement reflects the larger Aristotelean design, the ranging from ontological resolutions, mimetic necessities, outward into a sensibility to wonder, a glimpse of the wonderful; like the women in "The Black and White," this sort of audience knows old patterns and familiar territory but does not find full and satisfactory resolution in them without the play of imagination. This peripatetic audience meets the women in the interstices, unites with them in the pleasures of seeing and imagining, and goes its own way—up/down to the Garden or down/up to Waterloo Bridge.

3
Ideas: Audience and Author

TO SAY THAT IDEAS AND IMAGES APPEAR IN THE PLAY, AT FACE VALUE an unremarkable observation, asks still unresolved questions about ideas and images, about appearances and seeing and imagining, about subjectivity and autonomy and the perilous depreciation of the subject's authority. A critic's speculations as an excursion back toward the play, "The Black and White" for instance, move toward ideas among the play's appearances, but not without those ideas as made possible by thinking already in the audience's world. Those ideas the critic "has" are derivative, coming from the play on one side and the audience's historical world on the other, and her or his pleasure in discovering them and inviting another audience to enjoy thinking about them serves purposes beyond the personal and beyond the moment. If in the experience of the play the audience has been taken into, has become *of,* that transformation into structure, then isolating ideas from the fullness of experience moves among them as in a mimesis. The play is mimetic, representing possibilities in its world and, for the audience, that audience's possibilities in imitating and in recognizing its proper imitating in its world. The play as idea presents itself as an idea of representation and a presentation of idea-generated worlds; and its implication for the audience is the audience's ideas of a world and its world as ideas. The idea of those ideas as in a play of illusion—and speculation on them as in complicity with the play of imagination—assign to the audience an unresolved role, one of engagement in the play of illusion and imagination.

Assuming a deferential manner toward images and ideas, perhaps in itself appearing as a calculated pose of humility, might be from a different perspective a necessary qualification for living in a world *in extremis*. If our philosophers have led us downward to the absurd or to the minimalist prospect of the human landscape, our poets and playwrights too have shown us to exist in an ecology of detritus— shattered icons, displaced authority, the ruins of time. Robert Frost saw the poet's bird, the nightingale, transmogrified into an oven bird, who sings "Loud, a mid-summer and a mid-wood bird."[1] This degraded bird says of his world that "the highway dust is over all," and "The question that he frames in all but words / Is what to make of a diminished thing." The question is precisely what to make of a diminished thing, as Wallace Stevens imagined those "finally human, / Natives of a dwindled sphere," in the posture of "finding / What will suffice" ("Of Modern Poetry," *Palm,* 174–75). The ideas of the poet's bird of inspiration becoming an oven bird and the "finally human" living in a "dwindled sphere" are merely ideas expressed in images, neither universally true nor inevitable. They are images generated out of a felt dilapidation in the contemporaneous.

They are an illusion neither true nor false, merely the interpretive grasp, within the theater of the world, of what that world seems to be and how it sees itself. If it is, in "the plain sense of it, without reflections, leaves, / Mud, water like dirty glass, expressing silence / Of a sort," then the felt incoherence and the observed detritus are a coherence of the imagination. The stage and the *theatrum mundi* remind us that illusion is not the exception to a solid base of reality but the condition itself and the possibility of reality. Stage illusions, the very illusoriness of the drama itself, as we meet the eerie insubstantiality and it touches us, sometimes more profoundly than we could anticipate, tell us that the illusion is that of which we make our reality. Illusion is not, in this locale, a foredetermined other-than-actual, easily identified and dispensed with as the not real and the not me; it is the play, *ludus,* between those polarities. It is like the drama; what appears in the play and in life can be abstracted into a dialectic of actuality and unreality, a dialectic of opposed ideas. As a transformation into structure, however, it is not essentially an abstract state, is not to be accounted for quite truly in the ideas of reality opposed to and corrective of illusion nor in the visual field of the metaphors of dreaming opposed to waking, real world opposed to stage. The visualized dualities are, in being experienced in the event and being temporal action, a rhythm of stillness and flow, opening and closure, anticipation and discovery. They engage us as an appearing that carries in itself the admonition to look attentively, to turn and look back at its fulfillment in time, to look beyond its moment at its fulfillments in potentiality.

The activity is ever anticipative, in that what provides assurance and certainty through discovery might yet turn again, the established, recognized edifice proving to have been an illusion. Abjuring the certified truth that has become false, the play might move forward in the realm of the uncertain, where all is, on first appearance, merely appearance; and the nullified truth may again become true. In the moments of appearing the illusory appears, but not beforehand distinguished *as* illusion opposed to reality; and the actual appears *as if* actual, by the charmed presumption that the evident is evidential. The appearance presents itself in the mediating atmosphere in which readiness to make something of the appearance is a requirement of the imagination.

Since appearances, as perception, are nothing more or less than an appearing, it seems lamentable that we should be directed by the thinking of our interpreters such as Husserl and Heidegger down toward the transitory and ephemeral in our search for connections and better understanding. *Ubi sunt* the verities of the past? And what significance to be counted worth obtaining can be found in the always changing, unreliable, mere appearances? Yet the imperative to fix upon certainty, to set the illusory aside and embrace the real, holds us in its grip; there is reconfirmed in our time, in our sense of having progressed, the impulse to cancel old truths, to render them obsolete, in the act of installing present truths as if they were inviolable, absolute, and as if they in their originality were uncontaminated by the inherited. In this imperative to make truth in our world as if for the first time, the ideas of where we have been, and where we are as a manifestation of that potential, are depreciated in the erasure that maintains a certain, fixed boundary between the truth (of the present) and the untruth (of the past), between the achieved actuality and its unfolding as a moment of the past.

On the other hand, the stage and its representations of the opening up to new dimensions of reality show, in the appearances of its illusions, the event of discovery calling for readiness, anticipation, yielding to the unknown that might become known. The dramatists' imaginings of a world of detritus only answer their world's presumption of progress and show that the very act of depreciating the past is not merely a denial of its abiding relical power but, in the confirmation that proud assurances can be illusory, a representation of the need to connect. Heidegger's immersion of the autonomous self in the play of *alethia*, the unforgetting, and the *lichtung*, the lighting and lightening (*Basic Writings*, 384), entails letting the appearance appear as it is, and in this sufferance the old verities, as well as those perhaps not yet thought of, remain operative in the play of possibility; the current verities are vulnerable to that play of the trusted image or idea's removing its mask, a revelation that does not render the mask irrevocable. In our being brought down into such involvement, in the diminishment of the human image and the crumbling of the eternal, metaphysical edifice of a world, the discomfort and anxiety might dictate retreat to a secure new knowledge or lamentation that all solace and assurance are gone with the departed images (which amounts to a new knowledge). For both Husserl and Heidegger, however, the necessity of beginning anew is opportunity rather than affliction. Being dispossessed of the nostalgic assurance in the idea of the garden (or being abandoned by the eidolon) is movement not into a final, inescapable prison of god-deprived nature but toward the dark somethingness in which we light our own way, or allow the lighting by our readiness, and anticipate finding "what will suffice."

Stevens, in the play of language I have quoted, opens us to the possibility and the responsibility of what it means to be "finally human" in a "dwindled sphere." Lamenting that we are the finally human, worn down to mere skeletons of the heroic, broken into comic shards of the tragic like Samuel Beckett's Gogo and Didi, is to presume that the comic grotesque image is fixed, intractable, the end; that it cannot "go on." To observe an aperture in meaning, to declare that we are finally, at last human, is to recognize in the turn being made, and in what is made, that there is potential in the image. The possible transformation belies the isolated, static image of "autumnal space," whose poverty is not stasis but becomes "a few words spoken." In a Heideggerean shift, the individual being does not reassume performable autonomy but attains complicacy in the way the unaccommodated space becomes a look and words. Through this renewing activity, connection with another might be, in and at least for the moment, complete. Cosmic certainties are reduced to the tenuousness of a moment, a touch. To be finally human is to be an end and, at last, a beginning. In the idea of negotiations between the alpha and the omega, between one possible meaning and another, the need is not to choose between them but to yield to the possibilities in both meanings; both meanings appearing as a play of ideas, their appearance does not carry the imperative of choice. It bears, on the contrary, an invitation to look again and more closely, to let the ideas appear free of the prejudice that if one is true, a truth that is predetermined by the form of thought and must be ascertainable, then the other must be false; and we are engaged in the play of appearances on the stage of the *theatrum mundi*.

Gadamer's "transformation into structure," accomplished in the event of the play, is that subsumption of author, players, and audience in the structure of relationship, and it involves furthermore an appearing of idea in the action. The temporality of this action is evident in Gadamer's thinking of it as a transformation that involves the audience and takes it in. The event is not, then, the play's plot as a mimesis, though that conventional mimesis is involved; it is the action that is "total mediation" and through which the play achieves "ideality, so that it can be intended and understood as play" (*Truth and Method*,

110). The play's achieving ideality is the emergence of ideas in the event, not only ideas discernible in what we conventionally think of as the representation, in the way the gray and bare world of Beckett's *Endgame* recalls a romantic past in the moment's delirious activity, but also in the transformation that achieves the "ideality" presented in the play's being "intended and understood as play." The event's being understood as play comprises in it the idea of play as transformation into structure. This sense of the play is not achieved in what Gadamer eschews as "aesthetic differentiation" (117), since an audience engaged in "aesthetic" appreciation of the performance—whether for instance the actors and the staging are satisfactory representations, whether the actor playing Hamlet is interpreting the character well, whether the author's ideas about life and truth are realized in the performance—detaches itself from the play and isolates components for the sake of making aesthetic judgments. In this sense of aesthetic appreciation, the spectator takes a stance apart from the play as private subjectivity, refusing in effect to yield to the transformation into structure.

As the ideality of the play appears in the "total mediation," then the transformation into structure is an appearing of ideas, the foremost being the idea that enfolds, in the transforming, the discrete participants in the event and in the idea of play. Among those participants, the ideas of audience and author, their relationship as they reach to each other across the play and the ways they are thought to enter into the event, do not achieve a precedence but remain merely players engaged and endowed by idea. The idea of the audience, as I have talked of its being structurally involved in mimesis, is like the idea of the author endowed by possible established, diverse, sometimes contradictory ideas defining it. As in the represented events the ideas of identity and disguise occur—in, for instance, Vindice's disguises and performances for audiences in *The Revenger's Tragedy*—they are about transformation and discovery. The play is a representation of ideas of identity, transformation, and discovery in which the audience participates as being *in* the transformative event and as being *of* the achieved ideality. As idea of the audience, the audience is not merely a real subjectivity apart from the play, but neither is it pure abstraction. It is of the play of appearances seen as something in their ideality, which is merely the play of ideas in appearances. Its being in play means that it is integral to the "concept of play" wherein "the difference between belief and pretense is dissolved" (*Truth and Method*, 104). If on the one hand the audience seems to be depreciated to mere ideation and its genuine selfhood lost in the play of ideas, then on the other it has become freed of the constraint of being merely an isolated identity unrelieved by the disruption and reconstitution of the self in transformation, by the possibility of being "completely" touched, by the anticipation that comes with the idea of being finally, at last human.[2]

The ideas of audience and author in this play of appearances might come to light, as pure ideas, in Husserl's manner of approaching the immediate. Husserl's stripping down the encrustations by which the known and serviceable determine the apprehension of what is met in experience is a matter of ridding the experience of obstructions to clear sight. Disavowing any pretense to play the sophist or the skeptic (*Ideas,* 100), he would merely be prepared to see things as they present themselves, and his taking them as intentional objects is of fresh serviceability in placing the questions of whether they are real or illusory, whether in the subject or out there in the world, in suspension. Husserl is careful to distinguish between random supposition, free flights of fancy, and the unconsidered enforcement of structures such as subjective/objective and real/unreal. He distinguishes as well between casually making an assumption, "taking for granted" (99), and the "living conviction" from which we need to be "disconnected." This disconnecting, "abstention," or "bracketing" would deter making a "judgment which is compatible with the unshaken and unshakable because self-evidencing conviction of Truth" (98–99). Apparently this divesting oneself of the certainty of and reliance on old verities, this depriving the judgment of the "unshaken and unshakable . . . self-evidencing conviction of Truth," should give pause to the one seriously engaged in the pursuit of truth. If Truth has been depreciated along with the seeker of truth in a world of detritus, then the seeker is left to stand before things themselves, the intentional objects apart from which the subject is not pure, abstract, objectless thought—nor are the intentional objects pure, subjectless entities.

In this complicity, the human expectation is that things will make sense. What might be dismissed as detritus cannot be dismissed, because it is seen as remnant of something; it makes sense in being what it is. Husserl's rigorous approach to the things (sachen) is the fresh beginning of the finally human who, having ceded the unshakable conviction of Truth, must rediscover essences, essential truths, in what is given. Essence or idea, Eidos, is no longer bestowed from a dimension of Truth beyond the temporal nor available through the "living convictions" that have been disconnected; if "pure essence" is to appear in "essential intuition" (49), "*all* thoughts *partially mystical in nature* and clinging chiefly to the concepts Eidos (Idea) and Essence remain *rigorously excluded*" (50). Eidos, freed from the mystification of convictions that "cling," emerges from direct experience. The idea of the audience would not, it seems, deprive any particular audience of its actuality and self-sufficiency, but any particular audience would be an instance of the idea, if that idea is of the essence of audience. The idea of audience, its essentiality as audience, if understood in the light of its being in and of the transformation into structure, is not to be found in its capacity for making "aesthetic" judgments over there outside the play but in its being taken into the fabric of the play, its being in play. The audience's direct experience of the play is that fusion that occurs in the experience and makes the audience a participant. Its becoming one with the play involves it in the structure of relationships of discovery and becoming.

The activity of discovering Eidos is essential, be it taken seriously as life activity or imaginatively as play. Husserl sees us engaged in that activity, whether genuinely discovering essences or governed by "living convictions," and the contemplation of intentional objects might be of the actual, present "facts," or objects of memory or imagination: "thought concerning pure essence—the unmixed thought, not that which connects essence and facts together—needs for its *grounding* and support an insight into the essences of things" (51). Since ideas of the audience, or other ideas such as the "author" or the "finally human," "*do not make the slightest assertion concerning facts*" or their existence beyond the experience, they might seem to remain up in the air and therefore, as mere ideas, unprofitable. Admittedly, if the conditions for discovery are those of change, loss, and metamorphosis, then discovery is conditional. Instead of expecting to attain and settle comfortably in timeless truth, the adventurer lacking the support of changeless convictions trusts to the possibility of discovery itself. Since that discovery is enabled by giving in to the possible revelations in appearances, allowing essential ideas to appear—without attempting to pin them down to what the audience or the author is already thought to be or not to be, as discrete psychological entity— is an acceptance of both actual and imaginative experiences for their potential illumination.

Approached in this ambulatory spirit of inquiry, the world becomes like the stage, in that what seems to have been found as an essential and serviceable knowledge is capable of a transformation compelling reorientation. John Keats identifies this amiable accommodation as "*Negative Capability,* that is when man is capable of being in uncertainties, Mysteries, doubts, without any irritable reaching after fact & reason—Coleridge [on the other hand] would let go by a fine isolated verisimilitude caught from the Penetralium of mystery, from being incapable of remaining content with half-knowledge."[3] Keats's "fine isolated verisimilitude caught from the Penetralium of mystery" might, mutatis mutandis, seem an anticipation of Husserl's Eidos or essence, appearing not through an "irritable reaching after fact and reason" but in the capability "of being in uncertainties, Mysteries, doubts." The profound mysteries of human being in a world are not resolved in the stage's reflection and elucidation of those mysteries; rather, in its freeing the audience from the "real-life" necessity of resolution it momentarily suspends the responsibility to separate fact from fiction, reality and self from illusion. In giving the audience an illusion of itself as Eidos, the play neither falsifies it nor deprecates its actuality but engages it in the play of possible ideas.

This play of ideas that incorporates the idea of the audience among other ideas becomes a substantial world as idea of reality, and it achieves "ideality" as a transformation into structure. The "living convictions" that are brought to bear on this idea of a world make demands of it that it cannot meet, since it does "not make the slightest assertion concerning facts." Yet the questions persist: whether people really "act that way"; whether the play's images of male and female accurately meet the contemporary definition of role, sexuality, and status; whether the playwright intended this interpretation, who she or he is, how his or her theories of art and political beliefs are revealed; whether reality is indeed and in fact "dwindled"; whether the play tells the truth that human beings are to be explained most essentially in terms of Freudian psychology, Marxist doctrine, or the animal metaphor of naturalist convictions. If these demands for relevance are not to be repudiated—and as genuine concerns and ideas about reality they should not, could not be—they can be disarmed or disconnected, in the play's capacity for holding all participants in its suspension and in the magical transformations that can occur. The play achieves the wonderful, and it is wonderful to experience that depreciation of burning questions in the appreciation of the play's ideality, to be in play and—subverting the value in Plato's expression—to be beside oneself. It has become commonplace to modify Coleridge's statement, concerning his and Wordsworth's convergence from opposed beginnings in their collaboration, that the poem produces a "willing suspension of disbelief for the moment" in that it can be thought of as producing a spontaneous suspension of belief.

When we forget to ask questions about the author—Shakespeare, Harold Pinter, Sophocles, Luigi Pirandello—while the play has us, the idea of the author nevertheless remains operative in the action. The idea of an author being somewhat less specific than the idea of the playwright, it is sometimes more serviceable to refer to the author—or even the artist—in pursuing the idea as idea. To think of the author Pirandello as the idea of the playwright in *Six Characters in Search of an Author* is meaningful, of course, since there is a playwright named Pirandello in the play, though not on stage. Since a playwright is traditionally thought of as in essence a creator of a dramatic text, an author as a creator of these or other verbal texts, and an artist as a creator of art in a broader sense, the ideas of playwright, author, and artist have functioned metaphorically to identify the creator of representations and worlds; the God of Testament is playwright, author, or artist of this *theatrum mundi*. Since the play represents a world made by such a maker, since the idea of the play as imaginative creation entails the idea of its creator, the play's transformation into structure cannot effect the disappearance of all thought of this agent.

In Gadamer's rigorous hermeneutic the overcoming of assumptions about isolated subjectivity is paramount, as is evident in his insistence on the enfolding of the audience within the transformation into structure. This motive leads him to efface the individuals—actor, author, and audience—who are implicated in the cognitive value of the play, in what is there presented for recognition. Even though authors are recognizable as real agents in the world, the play in gaining the autonomy of performance seems to dispense with them in Gadamer's locating the event in community and his seeing attributes of the play connected to those of festival (*Truth and Method*, 122–24). I tried to make the point earlier that the play's proposal to the community is that the dramatic presentation of a world, as an idea of a world, puts into play the idea of its being a mimesis, neither pure illusion nor pure correspondence to fact. I have tried to suggest by extension that if a representation is, as Gadamer insists, to and for an audience, then the audience enfolded in the event is of that mimesis and attains the status of idea in it. I think the idea of the maker remains operative in the event, primordially in that the mimesis is never taken to be a natural phenomenon but a creation. To yield not to the play as play but to the illusion, as if the represented world were an actual one, would be to forgo the actuality for the illusion, to mistake the imagined characters for real beings and perhaps proceed beyond feeling with them to trying to understand their psyches as if they were actual, as if Hamlet were governed by our world's Freudian understanding.[4] From the intuition of the author in the work the appreciative audience qua biographer or psychologist might seek the real author beyond the work. Beyond the work, indeed, there lies the world of fact in which audiences and authors play their parts, along with philosophers and firemen. In the performance, however, the idea of the artist remains no more than an idea and no less an idea than is the idea of the audience; it is inextricable from the play as mimesis.

The last century, like the Renaissance, has seen a heightened and overt dramatization of the role of the artist in the work, not only as a creator and designer of the world of the work but also as participant in that world. Like the audience, the author is both of the mimesis and in the mimetic world. Pirandello plays with the idea of that playwright who wrote the drama "The Game of Parts" (Il giuoco delle parti), which is being staged as *Six Characters in Search of an Author* begins[5]; the humorous play by Pirandello is interpreted symbolically and pretentiously by the director, and the actors' laughing at him is a depreciation of the historical playwright, making him an absent minor character in the action. His absence is not tragic or even of consequence, because he has left the book that constitutes his identity and names him in the play. In the play, the absent author who has abandoned the script of the six characters' lives generates, by his abrogation, the essential problem in the play, the search for identity and realization, without the book, through performance of actions. The audience's role in the play is, like the author's, distributed in the tragic comic action, in fragmented and diverse instances of audiences. The actors, as professional interpreters of identity, find themselves playing the role of audience to the characters who, deprecated as mere ideas, represent to the audience the struggle for identity at any cost. The audience and the author appear in the drama of incompletion in a play designated, in the original version, a "comedy in the making." In the idea of incompletion, both the author and the audience perform a mimesis of the events in the play, in that they are ascertainable identities and at the same time elusive nonentities, fragmentary and suggestive appearances. The actual author and audience are not accessible to analysis and definition that would resolve them into the structure, although the ideas of author and audience are operative both in being transformed into the structure that is mimesis and in being repeated in diverse images in that mimesis.

If the idea of the artist is available, it is not an idea certifiable only by established, unequivocal role and function. Although even Plato's concepts of the artist as inspired, as having no proper craft, and as requiring restraint endure as ways to think of the artist, it is in the play of potential ideas of artists appearing in the worlds they create that the artist appears. Subsumed in the play of ideas, author and audience become essential constituents in the play's transformation into structure. The inaccessibility of the private subjectivity, audience or author, is not absolute but qualified and interrupted by revelation in the contention between derived assumptions and the appearances that might reconfirm, revise, or challenge those assumptions. The convictions by which we read the artist have been troubled by the derogation of value from exalted images, but if the image of the author depreciates, fragments, along with the detritus of the images of a world and human beings in it, most essential to emergent images is their not being fully disclosed and fixed. The author has neither eroded beyond recognition nor disappeared, but arises inescapably as protean artist. The image might retain the moral imperatives that warranted the vocation of the Victorian poet, might disparage that bestowed responsibility, might speak against conventional morality and stand for immorality or a new morality. The author might promote or allow the mystification that attributes the poet's power to spiritual sources—god, the muse, the collective unconscious—and thus become a shaman, an Orpheus, or a priest.

Yielding to the authority of the democratic appraisal, the artist might survive by promoting an image of the work as entertainment, thereby minimizing or negating the responsibility to communicate universal truth or uphold the values of society. As the artist's authorization becomes progressively destabilized in a world of change and uncertainty, the idea of artist as craftsman might be transmuted into the manifestation of skill directed, not toward the true representation of a world, but toward the doubtful intimacy of artist and audience. The pure entertainer only amuses, distracts, titillates an audience. A commonplace attitude toward the contemporary artist who presumes to do other than, or more than, pleasing expresses not mistrust but repudiation of the charlatan who, like Socrates' poet, has no skill except in deceiving the public with pretenses and ruses: anybody could make a few swift lines suggesting a nude as easily as Picasso did; anybody could wrap pink plastic around islands; anybody could foist on the public a play lacking proper characterization and action, significance, and therefore worth. Furthermore, in collaborative efforts the single artificer might escape into the safety of the committee; even in the novel translated into film, where is the responsible agent to be found? Who and where is the artist?

The scenario of alienation and distrust poses an undecipherable and crafty artist against an audience, who might in turn be a crafty exposer of the artist's sham, a pretender to aesthetic taste and therefore dupe, or, among other possibilities, a willing accomplice. The idea of the author unsanctioned by traditional definition of role reveals, however, not simply alienation but the question of identity shared by audience, characters in the represented world, and author. If the author assumes the mask of author, it is, because it is the assumption of a role, a variable mask or many masks, elusive or contradictory, deceptive or revelatory; and audience and author are collaborators in evolving a relationship of understandings: understandings of the work of art that relates them in its mimesis and understandings of the structure of relationships that envelops them. Although misunderstandings might abound, the understanding that both author and audience might appear in the play is a sign that both are in play in a structure of relationship, "total mediation." As the dramatic representation does not exist apart from the audience, neither does it gain an autonomy apart from its creator, who appears at least in the very idea that the work is a work.

The idea of the drama game that absorbs participants is known to be, and is experienced in the playing as, a game of identity and recognition. Suspicion and alienation are not the only possible deportment in the relationship of author and audience when the author appears as deceiving or elusive, as crafty or irresponsible. The enticement to identify with or sympathize with the characters created by that author is the attraction that makes the confidence game. Confiding in and establishing intimacy in circumstances that assure no sure safe transit or profitable outcome puts participants in the game at risk, as in any game. The idea of the play as a confidence game, entailing risk in the commitment to approach and touch, to give oneself, requires of all players the willingness to collaborate. As Mike, the mentor and confidence man in David Mamet's *House of Games,* says, "it's called a *'confidence'* game. Why? Because you give me your confidence? No. Because I give you *mine.*"[6] Mike's reassignment of confidence from the "mark" to the artist who is perpetrator of the con game emphasizes the fact that the game is not only a matter of creating and playing among illusions but also an assumption of roles and reversals in the sharing of identities, in coming together in confidence. Maggie plays the role of audience, first taken in and watching Mike's cronies perform and then insisting that she participate in the game. In the climactic discovery, which results in her transformation into artist, she stands in the shadows watching the con men, as if backstage, discussing their play, their roles, their skill as performers; and she recognizes Mike as the director of that play within the play.

Mamet's idea of the confidence man as artist has antecedents, notably in Herman Melville's novel of that title; and Melville's theoretical statements about himself and Nathaniel Hawthorne as artists pursue the question of confidence and the elusive image of the artist. On discovering the works of Hawthorne, as Melville recorded his effusive appreciation in "Hawthorne and His Mosses," he fictionalized his own identity as "a Virginian Spending July in Vermont."[7] The masking might well be considered in the light of Melville's personal ambivalence toward his audience, but the essay is an exercise in constructing an image of the two writers and their relationship as author and a reader who is in turn author. Asserting the premise that "the names of all fine authors are fictitious ones" (*Works*, 13: 123), Melville identifies an essence of Hawthorne's mind, his "blackness," but allows other readers a different reading: "Nor need you fix upon that blackness in him, if it suit you not" (131). He is "content to leave Hawthorne to himself" (137), since Melville or any reader will in forming a bond of confidence in the "fine author" imagine "to himself some ideal image of the man and his mind" (138–39). The "love and admiration" grow as Melville returns to the stories, discovering more of that ideal image of Hawthorne as represented in his characters, in spite of the fact that the writer is indeed a confidence man, giving and receiving confidence through creating illusions. Melville, taking readers into and giving them his confidence, warns them that they might be "trifled with, disappointed, or deceived by the triviality of many" of Hawthorne's titles (139), because that writer "takes great delight in hoodwinking the world,—at least, with respect to himself."

The ultimately unknowable private Hawthorne, protecting his identity as Melville finds the idea of himself in the idea of Hawthorne, establishes authority and gains confidence through the reader's willingness to allow him his game of revelation and concealment, to give him confidence. The uncertain aim of Hawthorne in the trivialized titles—"whatever motive, playful or profound" (140)—reveals the author as creator of illusions who in gaining the reader's confidence commissions the reader to engage in the discovery of essence. If he can "deceive—egregiously deceive—the superficial skimmer of pages" and even "dolefully dupe no less an eagle-eyed reader than myself," he empowers the sympathetic reader to see through the image, to discover in the "'gentle' harmless man ... [in] his sweetness" the "sublimity" apprehending "blackness" that "seems lost" in the mask (141). The devices for taking a reader or audience into this confidence game, variable and limitless as they might be, most essentially require the establishment of identity, the familiarity by which the mark sees the other as self, as "like me"; and the strategy is to take the audience beyond the familiar, to test limits, to engage in excess. As Melville pursues the image of the author in the created character, that exorbitance tests the bland assumption that the character speaks for the actual author, as Hamlet is quoted as if speaking for Shakespeare, and becomes a challenge to discover the essential idea of the author in the role. If the "Master Genius" appears in the "guise 'of a young man of poor attire,'" the character represents "a parity of ideas ... between a man like Hawthorne and a man like me" (142). Whether the confidence game intends that the mark be lamentably duped and bilked or led toward the discovery of such Romantic truth as Melville finds in

Hawthorne, that revelation is to be found only in the playing out of the confidence game.

Melville's image of Hawthorne seems to capture an essence, not only of Melville's concept of the individual writer Hawthorne but also of the idea of the author, the author who in creating the work reveals a conceived world and characters along with the idea of the creator, for an audience that is to be taken beyond the limits of the familiar. Evidently that idea of the author is interdependent with the idea of the audience who desires to go beyond, who anticipates, who moves in a readiness to be astonished. In his own works Hawthorne seems to bear out Melville's image of the elusive revelations of the author, not only in Melville's seeing the "triviality of many of the titles." Melville's "eagle-eyed reader" becomes in one of Hawthorne's character sketches a "disagreeable figure" of real life who is a "remarkable character."[8] The writer meets the character, "altogether a filthy and disgusting object" who still bears "signs of having been a handsome man in his idea" (90–91). This figure, "in his idea," retains the idea of a "handsome" past in the "disgusting" detritus of the present. Thus meeting in an atmosphere of alienation and resentment from others, author and character are drawn together in mutual recognition. In the author's revelation of his recognizing affinity with the lawyer-become-soap-maker, he is led to see in the man a dignity and self-respect that makes them one in spirit. The character of Hawthorne's memory, or imagination, in turn sees their likeness in the idea of interpreting the other, in their being united as Melville's "eagle-eyed reader," the bond of confidence being confirmed in the soap-maker's identification with the author: "'My study is man ... but there is something of the hawk-eye ... about you too'" (92). The author reveals in the character the discrimination and circumspection that he hopes to reveal in himself for the reader and to have realized in the reader; and the revelation is made possible in the abilities to present images that might be deceiving and to read those images by an excess of confidence, by opening self toward appearances in order to find the truth of self and other.

Hawthorne's image of the author as keen observer and mediator does not disavow the qualities of deception and unreliability that Melville saw in him. The idea of artist as craftsman grown crafty, Plato's mirror-wielder become sleight-of-hand-man, confiding guide transformed into confidence man, appears in shadowy figures throughout Hawthorne's tales. In the unsafe world of romance, benevolent figures like the kind gentleman in "My Kinsman, Major Molineux," may have dark designs, and in "The Minister's Black Veil" the spiritual guide to the mystery behind the illusory appearance might in assuming the veil become himself an image of horror. In the prefatory note to "Rappaccini's Daughter" Hawthorne deprecates his authorial image by feigning the role of pontifical critic of the story's author, "M. de l'Aubépine" (the hawthorn; 10:91), judging that his tales "may amuse a leisure hour as well as those of a brighter man" (92). This "playful or profound" artist reveals and conceals the idea of the artist in the characters he creates and in the image of himself, claiming in the extended establishment of an identity in the introduction to *The Scarlet Letter,* "The Custom-House," that he is "disinclined to talk overmuch of myself and my affairs" (1:3). Taking the reader into his confidence, warning that this autobiographical excursion is not simple confession but a preservation of "the inmost Me behind its veil" (4), he declares a purpose to gain the reader's confidence and to give the reader his. The "Custom-House sketch has a certain propriety, of a kind always recognized in literature, as explaining how a large portion of the following pages came into my possession, and as offering proofs of the authenticity of a narrative therein contained." The propriety "always recognized in literature" is that propriety Aristotle advanced as the playwright's responsibility to make his events and characters believable: "tragedians still keep to real names, the reason being that what is possible is credible: what has not happened we do not at once feel sure to be possible: but what has happened is manifestly possible: otherwise it would not have happened."[9]

If the facts of the story of Hester Prynne are grounded in history, they can be trusted to have happened, and if the "large portion" of the narrative is Mr. Surveyor Jonathan Pue's facts presented by the author in his depreciated and minimally significant "true position as editor," then embedding fiction in fact and depreciating the role of the maker of fictions provides the credibility that gains the reader's confidence. The romance under the canopy of historical truth is the place "where the Actual and the Imaginary may meet" (*Letter,* 36), and "details, so completely seen, are so spiritualized by the unusual light, that they seem to lose their actual substance, and become things of intellect" (35). The actual Jonathan Pue meets the thing of the intellect, the idea of the author; the actual Nathaniel Hawthorne meets the thing of the intellect, his imagined character Pue. In an imagined scene, Mr. Surveyor Pue, as "predecessor" (34), calls for the author's "filial duty" (33) and exhorts him to give Pue's memory "the credit which will be rightfully its due" (34). Hawthorne's joke, as in the play on his name in "Rappaccini's Daughter," lies in the regression of identities. The stern provider of historical data to the author of the fiction is after all an author of his own historical "facts," having "*made up* his narrative" (32; my emphasis) from "oral testimony" derived from the memories of "aged persons" who remembered—and plausibly imagined—Hester Prynne. As collaborative artists, Pue and Hawthorne become one in reaching out toward others and toward further confidence in collaboration.

It is not only in this self-conscious playfulness and self-dramatization, and other stratagems such as the Shandean toying with text, that the idea of the author appears. Even in twentieth-century images of the author abjuring authorship, as in the chance fragments produced by the anti-artist of dada, the idea of the creator of the work of art appears concomitant to the structure of relationships. In drama, the naturalistic program of Emile Zola recast the author in the image of scientific observer uncontaminated by the idea of play involving an audience, and the resultant isolation seemed a secure defense against ideas of the artist as craftsman or confidence man, shaman or inspired madman. The drama of realism, assuming the craftsmanship of the playwright, effaced the author in another way sanctioned by tradition, eliminating the language that gives particularity to the creator, the tone of voice and play of ideas that go beyond necessary, minimal stage directions. The play was presented as if it were primarily a mimesis, not of the structure of relationships, but of the actual world it represented, and both it and its author encouraged their being measured by their conformity to actuality. The author, presumably a mind sincerely dedicated to revealing in the mimesis the world's true condition, particularly such social ills as the political corruption Henrik Ibsen makes thematic in *An Enemy of the People* or the oppressed woman as represented by his Nora Helmer, Hedda Gabler, and Helene Alving. Yet this idea of the playwright is determined by the working conviction that he distills reality in the finely crafted structure of events and in the characters' truth and that he retreats behind the shadow of the structure to let it stand alone.

In the twentieth century the plays of George Bernard Shaw, for instance, reveal, in the philosophical-journalistic-novelistic excesses of the playwright, an emerging of authorial presence from the ostensible effacement of naturalism or realism. Stage directions become essays extending beyond the practical requirements of production, even beyond the probability of capturing information, insights, and speculations in the stage representation. Eugene O'Neill, whose *Long Day's Journey into Night* encourages the impulse to autobiographical or psychoanalytical comprehension, nevertheless transcends the presumption that the author is entirely accessible to realist, naturalist, or neonaturalist presuppositions. Compared to the terseness of the voice giving stage directions in the plays of Ibsen and Chekhov, O'Neill's interpreting author—providing, to be sure, intuitions enabling the interpretation of character—moves out of the shadow. Mary Tyrone is introduced as having an identity not limited to immediate impression and as affecting author, audience, and others in her world in particular ways: "What strikes one immediately is her extreme nervousness. Her hands are never still. They were once beautiful hands . . . [but] now they have an ugly crippled look. One avoids looking at them . . . conscious she is sensitive about their appearance and humiliated by her inability to control the nervousness which draws attention to them."[10] In the indefinite pronoun "one" (Is that "one" conscious and humiliated or is she sensitive and humiliated?), this author stands together with all potential audiences interpreting and perhaps even sharing the feeling of humiliation with the character. In introducing the setting, the playwright identifies the contents of two bookcases by titles and authors, as if merely observing facts, but the apparent scientific objectivity is excessive enumeration, since an audience would not be likely to see the words on the books and recognize the writers collected in the "small bookcase at rear" as a group that Tyrone in act 4 names: "Atheists, fools, and madmen . . . Whoremongers and degenerates" (135). Tyrone's idea of the artist being disappointed by the "modern," he names other degenerate writers—Baudelaire, Whitman, Poe—designated in the stage directions in act 1 by "etc." (11). This author who yields authority to an audience encouraged to fill the "etc." performs an act similar to that primary stratagem of Hawthorne's author, laying a groundwork of realism and fact in order to give the audience an illusion of probability and thus to gain free access to the imaginative, the poetic, the romantic. In so doing, he withholds from the audience ideas he intends in the revelation of facts, joining with the audience as collaborator.

The audience is, then, both reflecting and interpreting the author. Grounding *Long Day's Journey into Night* in realism and naturalism, a *weltanschauung* readily apprehended in his plays, O'Neill can "deceive—egregiously deceive—the superficial skimmer of pages" and an audience gratified to see reflected back to itself its own firmest convictions that it is blind, driven by natural forces: economic determinism, sexual needs, psychological conditioning. Deceived as well is the alienated audience that abhors the message it finds to be gloomy pessimism, preferring like Tyrone a romantic view it does not find in this author's works. Perhaps there is a degree of concealment, as well, in the romantic reading of the play that ascertains the end of the journey and consequently the idea of the play as an affirmation against that pessimism, as heroic or tragic. If the play can be said to be about both naturalistic conditions and idealist illusions, it is then about the improbable possibility of the second appearing from the first; and the play is not so much about idea abstracted from the event as about the process of revelation and discovery of self in the recognition of other, audience as well as character, author as well as audience. The play's title seems to refer to the mimesis of the play as a downward descent into darkness, impenetrable and conclusive; but that journey into unalleviated darkness is not the only journey made by author and audience. The descent and diminishment into a world of pettiness, estrangement, shattered dreams, and impotence leads to reunion and understanding, the improbable touching the characters realize in act 4, and it is a fragile and tenuous connection. The audience experiences the characters' representations of the alienation and animosity that belie love, experiencing the play's rhythms of disclosing self to another in an attempt at honest revelation and the ensuing withholding of self in deceptions and lies, the withdrawal that repudiates the possibility of union. The audience shares in this movement toward realization of its own capacity for touching another in the transformation of strife into sympathy, understanding, and love. The liberation of the family's love from confinement in resentment, suspicion, anger, and despair is a release into hope and the illusion of possibility. And the author participates not primarily "autobiographically," but as agent and idea presenting significance in the events.

In the world of the play images of the artist appear not only in the family as actors who have made for themselves a *theatrum mundi* but also in the idea of the artist as poet; and that poet raises questions for himself about the role and function, the powers and identity, of the artist. The illusion or dream that the poet Edmund finds walking in the fog is not the realization of a dimension where transformation energizes by obscuring the easy distinction between actuality and illusion, but an irreconcilability of the two, which might well be thought of in the antagonism of naturalist and romantic assumptions; in the fog "Everything looked and sounded unreal. Nothing was what it is. That's what I wanted—to be alone with myself in another world where truth is untrue and life can hide from itself" (131). Edmund's hope in this illusion is the romantic realization of self in the escape from the trammels of communal demands and the social concerns of the realist artist. His eloquent account of transcendent moments of "ecstatic freedom" (153) echoes the voice of the romantic but, lacking the romantic commitment to the reconciliation of opposites, he falls from those moments back into the natural world where he "would have been much more successful as a sea gull or a fish. As it is, I will always be a stranger who never feels at home." This image of the artist, too casually read as a real avatar of the actual Eugene O'Neill, remains an idea of the possible artist played against the other creators of contradictory truths in the play. Notably his father, whose unbridled pragmatic accommodations to actuality enslaved him in "easy repetition" of a role that, although "a great romantic part," was "the big money-maker" (150), represents the artist as performer for the audience's entertainment and betrayer of his own idea. He exalts and isolates the "great" poets of ideas and illusions like Shakespeare, who inspired him, thereby isolating and depreciating himself. The author who appears as maker of the play, fully represented neither by an image of the artist in the play nor in the isolable ego of the actual playwright, shares with other ideas of the author the propensity to discover commonality with the created characters and with the imagined audience. The actual playwright Eugene O'Neill never reconciled the imperative to be realist artist.

Creating a drama of discovery, of the need for recognition of self in others, he represents and pursues an action that should in a world of probability or necessity lead only downward to obscurity, divestment, and despair. The improbable touch occurs, nevertheless, in the dwindled sphere. The dedication to Carlotta, the playwright becoming like his character Edmund a poet, is an affirmation that the journey can transcend brutal deterioration, that light can appear out of darkness. If the author's voice seems excessively confessional and private in the words "These twelve years, Beloved One, have been a / Journey into Light—into love" (7), it remains the voice that establishes an identity in the play and attracts the audience to itself as well as to the fictional characters, or the fictionalized real memories, in the representation. What is revealed in the dedication is not restricted to the literal twelve years with Carlotta that have been for Gene a journey into light; if that journey has "enabled me to / face my dead at last and write this play," the journey back into darkness has illuminated and transformed the playwright, who now can write the play "with deep pity and understanding and forgiveness for / all the four haunted Tyrones." Reading the dedication as a poem, as it appears, would emphasize its place in the tradition of dedications, tributes, or prefaces that are integral, playfully or seriously, deceptively or forthrightly, to the play. If Carlotta is an identifiable audience and the play is "a tribute to your love and tenderness," she "will understand" how a "play / of old sorrow, written in tears and blood," is not "a sadly / inappropriate gift . . . for a day / celebrating happiness." Denying the "old sorrow," like the denials that unite the Tyrones in a common effort to maintain counterfeit lives and retreat into their fog of illusion, their drugged dream or their fiction of facing reality, would be a refusal to accept the minimized possibility of being human and consequently a refusal of the potential lighting of the darkness. The dramatized author accomplishes that unlikely transformation of darkness into light in finding or creating, in Carlotta and in the play's audience, an audience who can understand and play a part in the tribute. Any actual, historical audience, like Carlotta (who remains, since apparently receiving the tribute in that moment of first presentation, an idea in the play of presentation and anticipation), becomes transformed into the structure of ideas as participant assigned a role.

The audience's playing that part is, as with the author and the characters (real or imagined, present or absent), if a full participation, a "total mediation," not merely an intellectual engagement and understanding but a matter of sensing, feeling, and imagining roles and identities, relationships and involvements with others. Author and audience are accomplices in the play's revelations, losing and finding themselves in others, disappearing and reappearing in the structure of relationships: of ideas, of worlds, of characters, of worlds within and beyond worlds. Engagement in a play like Pinter's *The Dumb Waiter* implicates an audience in the gestalt of feeling and speculating on relationships between characters and worlds. The audience as character plays a part extending toward, touching others; feeling for and identifying with them; reaching for understandings; and imagining the lives and worlds of Pinter's characters. In this play, as with the idea of the play itself, the audience is not utterly absorbed beyond the play, as play, into the represented world, the room of *The Dumb Waiter*, at a loss for or abandoned by the idea of the author making worlds. As the immediate world is in its apparent detrition full and complex, as if calling for unstinting absorption, it takes into the structure of relationships both audience and author and reaches imaginatively toward, alludes to, other worlds.

Power and Permission: Pinter's *The Dumb Waiter* and the Brome *Sacrifice of Isaac*

> Pinter: "someone called Pinter..."
> Abraham: "Fader of heuyen, that formyd all thyng"

The idea of the artist might play between, on the one hand, the biography or actual being of a writer like Harold Pinter and, on the other, the representations of the creator that are his plays, which become a canon collected in several volumes named *Complete Works*. Although the question of the playwright's identity seems to be resolvable from the facts of life and work, the ideas of the author—his or her capabilities, powers, qualities of mind, purposes, social or metaphysical functions, relationships with other artists and audiences—are brought into the pursuit of this artist. Similarly, the life of the play calls attention to its unique being and its interrelationships with and allusions to life beyond itself. As maker of worlds, Pinter creates in, for instance, *The Dumb Waiter,* a world both incarnate, manifest in the text or performance, and derived from ideas of worlds to some extent shared by writer and anticipated audiences. As the author of this and other texts, he creates and reveals a personality that, like the play, seems to embody all that is itself while projecting that self toward a world beyond, toward a past and a future.

Pinter asserts, "I'm not a theorist" (*Works: One,* 9). His comments following this statement, however, suggest that rather than eschewing all things theoretical he resents being understood categorically and would not expect to be thought innocent of theory. If he is "not an authoritative or reliable commentator on the dramatic scene, the social scene, any scene," then he is not an *authority*—poetic, dramatic, sociological, political, philosophical—on abstract theories and principles. The image he presents of his authority *as author* is nevertheless clear. He describes himself as a writer reflecting the perpetual concern of artists about their assumed role and image as artist. John Keats, for instance, presents himself as very much the kind of artist Pinter claims to be.

Keats's "poetical Character," as opposed to Wordsworth's "egotistical sublime" (a complex of traits including perhaps what Pinter thinks of as the "theorist"), places the character itself in question. Rather than being philosophically placed and intellectually resolved, the poetical character Keats represents "is not itself—it has no self—it is every thing and nothing" (To Richard Woodhouse, *Letters,* 387). His enjoyment, "gusto," embracing of "foul or fair," and changeableness all present a manner of self-satisfaction, and this character, who "shocks the virtuous philosop[h]er, delights the camelion Poet." The declaration of character deficiency produces a vivid image of a strong character and a congruity of thought in spite of his seeming to be whimsically antiphilosophical. If he is a self-delighting chameleon, "not one word I ever utter can be taken for granted as an opinion growing out of my identical nature—how can it, when I have no nature?" This image of the poet frees him of the responsibility to be an "authority" on aesthetic, philosophical, theological, and social affairs. Therefore, while he maintains a "solitary indifference . . . for applause" (388), he avows a commitment to write that, seemingly stable and assured, can be transformed in a chameleon-change: "Even now

I am perhaps not speaking from myself; but from some character in whose soul I now live."

Pinter's characterization of himself echoes this disavowal of responsibility and seriousness while displaying the playwright and thinker's intensity of commitment. Since any "categorical statement . . . will never stay where it is and be finite . . . no statement I make . . . should be interpreted as final and definitive. One or two of them may sound final and definitive, they may even be *almost* final and definitive, but I won't regard them as such tomorrow, and I wouldn't like you to do so today" (*Works: One*, 9). The writer claims for himself the same freedom his audience has, and an audience corresponding in temperament to this writer would grant his freedom not to be fixed.[11] The overbearing artist grants no such freedom to his audience and thus expects, as applause, a full understanding of "his worthiness, his usefulness, his altruism," which "can be seen in full view. . . . What is presented, so much of the time, as a body of active and positive thought is in fact a body lost in a prison of empty definition and cliché" (13). The poet of the "egotistical sublime," although he is according to Keats "a thing per se and stands alone" (*Letters*, 387), creates for himself a prison of solitude; paradoxically, he makes himself dependent on an audience to reflect and thus to affirm his positive image. Like Keats, Pinter might feel indifference to the applause of a fickle audience, especially when in Dusseldorf he takes "thirty-four curtain-calls, all to boos" (*Works: One*, 10), and he knows that "Praise and insult refer to someone called Pinter" (*Works: Four*, x). The egotistical poet's prison is solitude because the audience he needs to reflect him is merely applauding or booing the false image of his name. If the chameleon artist grows haughty in disavowing responsibility—"to audiences, critics, producers, directors, actors or to my fellow men in general"—his color changes in a reflection that takes his audience into confidence: "I warned you about definitive statements but it looks as though I've just made one" (*Works: One*, 10). The warning serves as ironic reminder "to let you see that no dependence is to be placed on what I said" (Keats, *Letters*, 387). The effect of this intimacy is to allow distance; it is an agreement to meet for mutual satisfaction and to let be, to grant to another the freedom to be.

In exploiting the traditional question of the poet's character, Pinter and Keats engage us in a play of sincere insincerity. Both ask understanding from the audience, and that understanding would entail, if we play by their rules, allowing the writer not to appear as full presence. The poet or playwright would not have us presume that he is to be "seen in full view." He would assert his right to retreat, like his characters to "wilfully elude," to "withdraw into the shadows"

(*Works: Four,* xi). The presumption to "know" the writer is our desire and our hazard. How can we talk authoritatively about Pinter's works if we do not know him? But in becoming the authority we readily presume to capture his fixed identity, his biographical reality, his stable, unchanging authority. We reflect, as a result, the egotistical sublime that we project onto him. At the risk of seeming quixotic, I would take him as seriously as he takes himself and assume the privilege of taking myself just as seriously. Pinter and I become no more "finite" than the mere idea of author and audience. As Pinter uses the word, his pronouncements will not become fixed and "finite," because "there are at least twenty-four possible aspects of any single statement," and interpreters will interpret as they will (9). I take Pinter's words "finite," "final," and "definitive" to be a stressing of the closure, the limited identity, of the poet who lives in the "prison of empty definition." If Pinter is recognized as loath to say anything that is "final and definitive," potential transformations are instigated on both sides—from the author and from the audience.

We can, however, be consoled by the possibilities inherent in transformation and uncertainty. Relegating both the words of the writer and the words of the critic to the realm of ideas, specifically—for the moment—to ideas about author and audience, we find release from mere seriousness, from the determination of the "finite," and we consequently engage in the play of the possible, which involves us reciprocally with such ideas—and more. We come to represent a quality of thought Heidegger traces back to Plato and Aristotle. Observing that Plato finds *astonishment* (*Erstaunen*) to be the beginning, the "point of departure" for the philosopher, Heidegger considers that beginning, the *archê*: "It names that from which something proceeds. But this 'from where' is not left behind in the process of going out, but the beginning rather becomes that which the verb *archein* expresses, that which governs."[12] For Aristotle, too, astonishment is the beginning and the "determining path of philosophizing." Heidegger feels a need to retrieve this understanding, which philosophy has forgotten in its quest for certainty: "Astonishment is *archê*—it pervades every step of philosophy" (83). If for Aristotle, as interpreted by Heidegger, astonishment is the beginning of philosophy and determines its direction, it remains a motive force toward which philosophical method and reasoned thought serve a purpose. Similarly, Aristotle's relationship between probability and wonder is a negotiation toward astonishment from the ground of probability or necessity, structure, design, revelation of purpose, and the assurances of logos.

The capacity for astonishment is, in my appreciation, the beginning and the aspiration in our relationships with poetry and drama. Our primordial connection with the work of art is based, not in the ostensible need for resolution and the desire for completion that we transfer from the business of life, but in the anticipation and discovery of something not in our power. Heidegger characterizes our relationship with Being as such an ambivalent encounter: "We step back, as it were, from being, from the fact that it is as it is and not otherwise. And astonishment is not used up in this retreating from the Being of being, but, as this retreating and self-restraining, it is at the same time forcibly drawn to and, as it were, held fast by that from which it retreats. Thus, astonishment is disposition in which and for which the Being of being unfolds" (85). I think it not presumptuous to invoke this relationship in suggesting a reciprocal play between audience and drama, audience and author. Heidegger, in his attempt to reestablish philosophy's concern for Being, grants poetry the task of revelation: "Art, as the setting-into-work of truth, is poetry. . . . The essence of art is poetry. The essence of poetry, in turn, is the founding of truth. . . . Art lets truth originate" ("The Origin of the Work of Art," *Basic Writings,* 186). We allow the work and its creator to be "as it is and not otherwise," and in giving this permission we gain a freedom to be as we are and not otherwise. Pinter's relationship with his characters reflects this play of power and permission: "The relationship between author and characters should be a highly respectful one, both ways. And if it's possible to talk of gaining a kind of freedom from writing, it doesn't come by leading one's characters into fixed and calculated postures, but by allowing them to carry their own can, by giving them a legitimate elbowroom" (*Works: One,* 14). Ultimately Pinter must listen to his characters, and he must suffer pain through them (*Works: Four,* xi).

Pinter's objection to "theory" is to a priori judgments about dramatic form and character and about Life. "But," he fears, "we have a marked tendency to stress, so glibly, our empty preferences. The preference for 'Life' with a capital L, which is held up to be very different to life with a small l, I mean the life we in fact live" (*Works: One,* 12–13). The "fact" is, in Heidegger's terms, "as it is and not otherwise." Consequently, what Pinter brings to "bear upon a production, these are not intellectual concepts but facts forged through experience" (*Works: Four,* xiii). Husserl's *zu den sachen selbst* ("to the things [or facts] themselves") is a call to the "things," but things no longer presumed to be objective existences in the isolation of objects "out there."[13] "Facts" are immediate and real, and they entail the complicity of a subject. Intelligence and theoretical insight are, then, unfolded for Pinter in the encounter with the immediate: "I am referring to an intelligence brought to bear on practical and relevant matters, on matters which are active and alive and specific, an intelligence working with others to find the legitimate and therefore compulsory *facts* and make them concrete for us on the stage" (Pinter, *Works: Four*, x; my emphasis).

In talking about one of Pinter's plays I entertain the idea that the "facts" of the play and its characters are the origin of power and the means of astonishment. What we see in Ben and Gus in *The Dumb Waiter* is a revelation in "practical and relevant" terms of the "active and alive and specific," of "compulsory facts." The facts themselves raise the question of power—the power, or lack of power, represented by the characters; the power of the artist to represent power and seeming powerlessness; his control and his restraint in allowing the unknown to remain unknown. An audience might in turn reflect the characters' disquiet in, like them, seizing upon the facts, attempting to interpret them, and hoping for resolution and understanding. The world of Ben and Gus, however, does not yield certainty, and it seems to reflect the uncertainties of ours. I am thinking of their world and ours as two dimensions opposed and referential, as essentially mimetic. Even this felt structure of a duality is, of course, reductive, since our world is not a single, homogeneous reality and their world is created not only as the playwright's version of a world but also as the characters' interpretations of their reality. Ben and Gus's worlds and ours are mimetic in the easiest understanding of Aristotelean mimesis: we take theirs to represent or to reflect ours. This relationship is mimetic, too, in the extended sense of our engaging in mimetic acts, our reflecting and in some sense repeating the conditions we encounter. We feel their malaise and reflect their need to understand.

This sense of the world to be discovered as a world not yet definitive seems to me essentially imaginative and metaphorical. It is founded in an apprehension of the duality expressed as reality versus fiction, truth versus falsehood, world versus stage, and waking versus dream. The capacity for astonishment is there in the work's power to astonish and in the audience's readiness, from the beginning, to be opened up to other worlds. The opening up of another world, both the overt metaphor of the play-within-the-play, for instance, and the pervasive ambivalence felt in exposure to that "other" world of the stage, is a matter of discovery, of adventuring into a strange world. The *theatrum mundi* metaphor sharpens that sense of challenge in its questioning the assurance and satisfaction of our dwelling in reality. Another version of reality appears, and the simple opposition of stage/reality is, in Husserl's terms, "bracketed."[14]

The playwright need not invoke the metaphor directly, as Pinter does in *The French Lieutenant's Woman,* to reveal that he plays upon the idea. Writing about his characters and their language, Pinter assumes not only that they reflect our condition but also that a reality, their world, exists beyond the presence of action and language: "So often, below the word spoken, is the thing known and unspoken. My characters tell me so much and no more, with reference to their experience, their aspirations, their motives, their history" (*Works: One,* 13). Sensing a vital and genuine dimension that extends beyond what can be grasped directly, a dimension not of discovered fact but of potentiality for understanding and appreciation, "the thing known and unspoken," the artist constitutes the present as a sign of incompletion. Auguste Rodin declares that unseen domain to be real: "My nudes are done, which is to say that the bodies beneath the draperies are done.... You see, it is the part one doesn't see—the most important part—which is finished."[15] The audience is invited to venture with the playwright into that other dimension: "Between my lack of biographical data about them and the ambiguity of what they say lies a territory which is not only worthy of exploration but which it is compulsory to explore" (*Works: One,* 13). Pinter's metaphor of a territory to be explored sets up a relationship between the characters we see and hear speak and an "under" or hidden world, a world analogous to the stage world inside a stage world. He furthermore refers us back to our own world, including us as a reflection of that relationship between the revealed and the unrevealed. "You and I, the characters which grow on a page, most of the time we're inexpressive, giving little away, unreliable, elusive, evasive, obstructive, unwilling. But it's out of these attributes that a language arises. A language, I repeat, where under what is said, another thing is being said" (13–14).

Like the metaphor, the text or performance is a language "where under what is said, another thing is being said." It might practice evasion and be unreliable, but it is nevertheless a text. We approach it seeking clarity, feeling it out for a sense of probability, and it reassures our understanding. Even as we explore a strange new territory, the explication serves to ground us. Biblical exegesis has confirmed, historically, not only the text's validity in and of itself but also its mission to elucidate the rightness and dependability of the world beyond, a world that we have presumed to substantiate through our understanding of the text, a world to which the text refers. Pinter expects us to appreciate and accept our role in granting permission to the text's being "as it is and not otherwise"; but he expects as well, and respects, our imaginative or interpretive need, our desire to venture toward greater understanding, our readiness to be astonished.

My recalling texts—Pinter's inductive speculations, Heidegger's talk about astonishment and origins—appears as a sort of fundamentalist reading; but my interpretations aim merely to invoke those texts as themselves referring. The doubleness of the text lies in its requiring clear reading or "seeing" on the one hand and, on the other, in the imaginative play prompted by the fact that it refers, like the speech of Pinter's characters, to a world beyond. It plays toward—it *al*ludes—as *il*lusion plays against. To play, *ludere,* is to be liberated from the matter-of-fact, and allusion refers, in that freedom of play, from the restricted understanding of the matter-of-fact toward another as-yet-uncertain, sometimes astonishing dimension. Alluding to something calls into question the *qualities* of truth and reality of the present experienced object. If in a play a character alludes to Hamlet or King Lear or Ecclesiastes, then the allusion asks the question, "What is the connection?" It sets up a metaphorical relation whereby the audience needs to know, to be involved as understander and interpreter of what the allusion means in the context. The theater/dream metaphor thus refers to a world not already definite and confined in the temporal and spatial bonds of the moment, in the probable or necessary. The range of such play is unconfined, and may be toward the pious or the parodic, even the "ludicrous," as in *The Dumb Waiter.*

The Bible is a text that refers back in time, to origins and sanctions, invoking the powers that endure and bringing them forward to us as relical. Like the *in medias res* convention and the flashback in imaginative literature, which reach into the past for making connections and for instigating interpretation, for revelation and for discovery, the biblical text retains a past, for the present and future. The past worlds thus evoked and discovered fill a need in the realization of the present: for instance, when myth appears in Strindberg's *A Dream Play.* In invoking other worlds, whether we sense them to be a source inherited from the past or the appearing of another contemporary dimension such as the dream or the drama within or beyond our drama, the text maintains its precise literalness and leads beyond itself; it is definite while at the same time enticing us toward thought. It might be felt as a duplicitous presence, certain in its demonstration yet, as Keats complains to his Grecian urn, teasing "us out of thought / As doth eternity."[16] The danger felt in the hypnotic charm of a timeless object, the idea of timelessness contradicted by our inescapable consciousness of our temporality, evokes a troubled and urgent sense of that temporality. The poet's awareness extends from the world of the urn's hidden and unknowable past into the future, and Keats bestows upon the urn a new and anticipatory text concerning the limits of thought, the admonition to accept the limitation of truth to a present, to an apprehensible beauty.

The Brome *Sacrifice of Isaac,* a text we take to represent a world view not only distant in time but also in many ways antithetical to ours, can be considered a relevant past to *The Dumb Waiter,* and Pinter's play can be thought about as if alluding to the earlier drama.[17] Allusion puts a relationship into play and sets up a structure of textual duality, the "present" text referring or instigating reference to another text that manifests its own "presence" as well as representing a world. Through this correlation the worlds of the two plays, in this case the "medieval" and the "modern," generate reflection, a repetition that in Heidegger's terms is "a *reciprocative rejoinder.*" For Heidegger, the rejoinder is made "*in a moment of vision; and as such* it is at the same time a *disavowal* of that which in the 'today', is working itself out as the 'past.'. . . Repetition does not abandon itself to that which is past, nor does it aim at progress. In the moment of vision authentic existence is indifferent to both these alternatives" (*Being and Time,* H 386). Observing such connectedness with the past is not, then, to remind us of its power of determination, of our mere naturalistic inheritance, nor to free us from it, to escape to the future by means of progress. Repetition is relical; it is productive of vision, understanding, characterizing relationship.

There are in the medieval understanding two primary dimensions of reality, the assumption of reality as two worlds, the God-secured eternality of that world as opposed to this one, which is a *theatrum mundi.* In the twentieth century, a different version of reality assumes only one dimension and becomes monistic. With allusion to that medieval view, we have two versions—what we might think of as "modern," "absurdist," or "existential" as opposed to medieval Christian. When one refers to the other, then where does the truth lie? Pinter's play is not proposing the modern as the truth disavowing or negating the untruth of the past, obliterating the past and affirming the path of progress, but rather setting up a reciprocality, allowing a going around, entertaining the question of reality; it is not the resolution of the dichotomy in favor of one's truth over the other's fiction. The allusion to the past world expresses the ambivalence of the theater/dream metaphor: when an unreal dimension appears and asserts its reality, the real context in which it has appeared is no longer simply the real.

In characterizing our world as we see it represented in Pinter's play we are not forgetful of the past, readily observing his characters' lack of awareness, their failure to be grounded in the sense of a vital, relical past. In discerning their lack of both knowledge and power, we are engaged in ideas about the range and degree of the ability to know and to act, ideas evident in *The Sacrifice of Isaac.* Ben and Gus seem to parody patterns in the earlier play; to allude, without consciousness of that past, to its characters and world; to concern themselves promiscuously with inconsequential objects that are reflective of its consequential objects; to seek reassurance in texts that perhaps speak to and for them as parodic of the way texts speak in *The Sacrifice of Isaac*.

In both plays events are instigated by an absent determiner of actions, a figure of power and authority. In both, the action moves, with distractions, toward the obligated characters' fulfillment of purpose through obedience, toward an execution or a sacrifice—at any rate a killing. In *The Sacrifice of Isaac*, God sends an Angel to deliver His command to Abraham: "Owre Lord comandyth the for to take / Ysaac, thy yowng sone that thow lovyst best, / And with hys blod sacryfyce that thow make."[18] Abraham's immediate reaction to the message is compliance, and although he expresses his anguish as doubt—"I may not fynd yt in my harte to smygth . . . / . . . hym to kyll" (ll. 300–4)—his commitment is firm: "I wyll no lenger let for the" (l. 313). Delays are calculated to produce a heightened sympathy and perhaps even a gentle, compassionate humor, as when Isaac's questions grow importunate. With the climactic revelation by the Angel, heaven and earth are reconciled and God reveals Himself, voicing His purpose and His promise to Abraham; Isaac's relief is expressed in the free play of humor; and the Doctor conveys assurances to the audience about the meaning of the drama. Abraham's hesitation stems not from uncertainty about God's benevolence nor from distrust of His will, but from his own bonds to his son, from his humanity. Over and over he attributes his anguish to his "hart," the seat of love for "chyld" and "wyffe" (l. 84) and the ground of allegiance to God: "With all my hart to the I call" (l. 2). Abraham's knowledge of his origins and God's promise of his place in history elevate and ceremonialize his act, and he can be proud: "Loo! Ysaac, my son, how thynke ye / Be thys warke that we haue wrogth?" (Ll. 403–4). The play is resolved by incorporating the Doctor's demonstration: Abraham's action is a prototype for the audience, and they are challenged to imitate Abraham's example. God has affirmed this purpose to the Angel: "All men schall take exampyll be hym / My commawmentes how they schall kepe" (ll. 45–46).

Observing the confidence of that world—in God, in self, in community, in history—only stands to show the deficiency of confidence in the world of Ben and Gus. Although these characters understand and comply with strict rules of obedience, they do not even know the identity of their Boss. He could be named Wilson, but Wilson might be merely another agent, their messenger. Whether he is the master or not, he might be upstairs sending down orders or he might not be here yet. Their instructions have been clear since early morning, but they are rudimentary—merely to once again perform the act when the time comes, without understanding motives and consequences. Read as a parody of Abraham, Ben demonstrates Abraham's unfaltering obedience without his certainty of an all-embracing goodness. Messages are as inconsequential and bewildering as are the actions of Ben and Gus in their time-squandering diversions. Events are not a play of conflict between resolution to act and avoidance: they lack direction; they scatter. Gus's escalating anxiety isolates him yet further from Ben, who is simply resolute. Read as a parody of Isaac, Gus's idle curiosity in the beginning develops into ineffective importunities, his questions arising from a deep anxiety bred of insecurity rather than a voicing of the child's questions of a trusted father. Ben and Gus's obsessive need to know, to be in control, is dissipated on incidentals such as the newspaper, the china, the ball games; it comes into focus only in the pointless—according to Gus—preparatory litany. Their ritualizing knows no purpose and engenders no consequence, since it is preparation for repetition of an action that is, they think, sure and invariable, an action that is rote and unsustained by previous enactments and unsustaining of meaningful consequences; their assumptions are in sharp contrast to the memorializing impulse of Abraham or, in an earlier world, of Orestes in Aeschylus's *Choephoroe*. Instead of resolution the play ends in intensified readiness, with Gus substituting for the nameless victim—a grotesque inversion of the substitution in *The Sacrifice of Isaac*. Isaac is saved by the substitute "scheppe"; Gus becomes the substitute. In the Aristotelean sense, the play has no end—no mimetic resolution, no catharsis. In contrast to the medieval play, its events attain no iconic status. It presents no paradigmatic action or actor to be venerated; it does not delineate history as perpetual reenactment to be imitated; it denies to its repetitions (in the represented action) the power of relic.

The structure of the world of *The Dumb Waiter*, and objects in it, both echo the earlier play and deny efficacy in its configuration. Whereas in *The Sacrifice of Isaac* space, like time, is regulated and clear, direction is an element of the confusion in *The Dumb Waiter*, and known space is constraining rather than liberating. The world of the earlier play is designed as a theater of events played beneath the heavens above—the heavens that would be retained in a later theater and become represented as the planetary, therefore astrological, design painted on the "heavens" of the stage. Characters playing out their lives below enact events in the presence and under the scrutiny of the author above. This metaphor belonged, of course, to the play's world and carried a weight of belief, confirming the significance of actions and the responsibility of actors to perform well. On the world as stage, the relationship between the two worlds, the superior and the inferior, is represented in the setting. The Angel is to "schow" Abraham "the wey on-to the hylle / Wer that hys sacryffyce schall be" (ll. 41–42). A free ascent "In-to the Lond of V[i]sion" (l. 63), "On-to yon mownte" (l. 123), for the purpose of an offering is a gesture of trust and accord. It is a movement in God's direction, a movement exposing Abraham's actions before His eyes, a performance for Him.

In the performance of Ben and Gus there is, rather than gestures in the sight of a "Fader of heuyn, that formyd all thyng" (l. 47), negotiation with an inscrutable force and suspicion—of the power above or "out there" and of each other. The closed circuit of the dumb waiter from "up there" to "down here" produces in the beginning only written communication from above and, from below, frustrated attempts to be heard and frantic efforts to comply with orders. The import of commands progresses from the dinner orders in writing to, with the discovery of the speaking tube, messages heard only by Ben, finally the instructions Ben apparently hears and repeats: "He has arrived and will be coming in straight away. The normal method to be employed. Understood" (*Works: One*, 164). Although these exchanges are with whoever is up above, his identity is uncertain. If it is Wilson, he is outside as well, since he is thought to be the one who slips matches under the door; and his power is felt to be ubiquitous, his epiphany uncertain. Ben and Gus, constrained in a basement room without windows, are directionless, their journey having been made in the early morning dark. Ben, passing the time in listless waiting, is irritated by Gus's movements, his wandering in and out, his search for cigarettes, his talk. Their uncertainty about where they are and where they were on a previous assignment becomes ominous; and when Gus appears from the door leading to the outside, after having exited through the door leading into the kitchen and lavatory, spatial orientation is confused and movements are inexplicable. Instead of performing meaningful actions and moving with purpose in a direction, they wait for orders, and their movements lead nowhere, toward nothing. In a fragmented world, where there is no hope of moving toward an elevation, no desire to move nearer to a caring source, they perform the same action over and over, without end and without understanding.

Like their digressive actions, the stage properties that capture their attention and become their business of the moment are accidentals: the china, the "deficient ballcock" (133), the bedclothes that "pong" (136), the "photo here of the first eleven" (133), the newspaper, cigarettes, tea. One of their trivial concerns, fire, devalues and proliferates that image of *The Sacrifice of Isaac*. Abraham and Isaac, duty bound, set out prepared: "Both fyer and wood we haue redy" (l. 139), only Isaac being troubled by the fact that "queke best haue we non on this hyll" (l. 140). The "fagot" and the "fyer" are necessary components of an act that is to prove Abraham's worthiness. Ben and Gus have come without matches, seemingly a negligible omission when as the play begins Gus discovers a "flattened matchbox" and a "flattened cigarette packet" in his shoes (129); but when the twelve matches arrive in a sealed envelope, "they'll come in handy" (140). The conflict that ensues concerns whether they will be used to "light the kettle" or the "gas" (141). Fire has become nothing more than a trivial utility like the gas, a means of heating water for their tea. The mystery of its provider is forgotten for the moment, although as Gus's questioning grows frantic he extends the question "Why did he send us matches if he knew there was no gas?" (161) to the question of the provider's identity: "Who sent us these matches? . . . Who is upstairs?" The power to provide fire has nothing to do with the mission of Ben and Gus, except that finally, when the voice from above has rejected the offerings—"The Eccles cake was stale. . . . The milk was sour. . . . The biscuits were mouldy" (156)—and demands "a cup of tea" (157), "There's no gas" for boiling water. Ultimately they lack the fire required to satisfy the demands of the invisible orderer, who seems like them to represent the principle of distraction. Not only is there a dysfunction in their "fagot" and "fyer"—first no matches, then no gas—there is no genuine need for them. The men's "scharpe sword" (l. 292) is the revolver that each of them carries, and using these weapons entails no fire for ritual sacrifice. Objects exist as disconnected phenomena of the moment, useful perhaps to some limited end but as isolated as the characters, who have limited knowledge, minimal relatedness, finite purpose.

If Pinter's characters are not to be understood as originating in "abstract idea or theory" nor interpreted as "allegorical representations" (*Works: One,* 10–11), their limitations as represented characters and as an idea of human being realize a dissociation from their present context and from the past. Consciousness of a serviceable past might include Ben and Gus's remembering Abraham or Agamemnon's roles in ritual sacrifice, but their references to the past extend no further than their recollections of football games and previous assignments, and the sites of both work and games are problematical. Their disorientation does not, however, negate the past and the possibility of seeing the men against some meaningful structures rather than against nothingness. Their relationships to each other and to whoever gives them orders allude to the relationships between Abraham and Isaac and

God. If God is a "Fader . . . omnipotent . . . that formyd all thyng" (ll. 1, 47), his power as author of "all thyng" created an ordered world and his vision maintains watchful care over his creation. Abraham is not only a child of God but also a force and influence on future generations. God's "assay" of Abraham's love is for the purpose of establishing his place in history and his usefulness as a model, and his reward is "blysse withowt yend . . . wersoeuer ye wend" (ll. 399, 402). God's promise will follow Abraham and his seed in their dispersal.

The power over Ben and Gus is itself dispersed and comes from no certain direction. Although messages descend, matches appear from outside and "he" is felt as an uncertain and threatening power, an absent force that can appear out of the dark ("He might not come. He might just send a message" [144]). His messages come not with the voice of an angel but as ominous, inexplicable demands—notes ordering food, a voice through a speaking tube, and the silent form of twelve red matches. His capricious manifestations reduce ultimately to games of menace. Gus is indignant that, having "been through our tests," having "proved ourselves" (162), having performed by understood and agreed-upon rules of the game, they are now being subjected to some sort of arbitrary and inexplicable games: "What's he playing all these games for?" A godlike force in felt power and apparently superior knowledge, this absent figure has freedom to be anywhere and nowhere, to parody the reassuring image of God as circle whose center and circumference are everywhere and nowhere.

If Abraham reflects that authority of God in his relationship with Isaac, Ben reflects Abraham in his relationship with Gus. Ben, the "senior partner" (142), is like Abraham in assuming the superior role, playing father to Gus. Not only does he demand and lead the preparatory litany toward the end of the play, he begins the play by reading lessons to Gus from the newspaper: "It's down here in black and white" (130). He presumes to know the answers to questions about plumbing, explaining that the tank has "a deficient ballcock, that's all" (133). In giving Gus lessons on how to live life, he observes that Gus has no interests; and he holds himself up as an example of one who has interests—"woodwork . . . model boats"—that occupy his time and leave him free, "ready . . . when a call comes" (134). Unlike Abraham, however, he does not fulfill the role of mentor with love as a motive, rather competition. His challenges to Gus's thoughts, designed to maintain distance and superiority, repudiate Gus's information, the facts, as well as his ability to think logically. When Gus concludes that the Villa must have been playing the game he remembers "here, in Birmingham," Ben counters, "They were playing away" (138). When Gus wants to see the Spurs, they too are playing away, and when Gus concludes that they might then be playing the Villa here, Ben responds that "The Villa are playing away"—equating past and future events to arrive at his final illogical dismissal of Gus's interest, "They're all playing away" (139). His wielding power over Gus includes intimidation about the uses of words, the argument over whether they light the "kettle" or the "gas" ending with Ben's vehement ill logic: "Nobody says light the gas! What does the gas light?" (142). He is finally vindicated by the voice from above: "You know what he said? Light the kettle! Not put on the kettle! Not light the gas! But light the kettle!" (156)—the expression having been used in the first place by Gus. Ben's diversionary tactics in response to Gus's increasingly insistent questions are reduced finally to the demand, "Shut up!" (161), and to physical assault. Abraham, deeply troubled by Isaac's full participation in the sacrifice, responds to the boy's question about the "scharpe sword" (l. 148) with an aside to "Fader of heuyn"; but he does, in spite of his grief, tell Isaac the truth: "Ysaac, Ysaac, I must kyll the!" (l. 167). Whereas Abraham's dual roles, benevolent stewardship of Isaac and faithful dependency to God, establish him as type to be emulated, Ben's creation of himself as a model for Gus merely exemplifies how his meaningless time might be filled unproductively.

If as opposed to Abraham's God the god of Ben and Gus remains hidden and elusive, other vital figures are absent from *The Dumb Waiter* as well. The idea of the female remains for Ben and Gus an enigmatic sign of discrepancy, an attractive mystery that kindles a brief dissertation on Woman. The "girl" they killed on an earlier assignment "was a mess.... They don't seem to hold together like men, women. A looser texture, like. Didn't she spread, eh?" (146–47). The implied inferiority of the female, her "looser texture," sets her apart and below the realm of men, but an earlier implication, in their discussion of the "child of eight [who] killed a cat" (131), is that the female has a special difference, and their solution to that mystery exonerates her. When Ben reveals that this child "was a girl" (132) and then, checking the newspaper, reports that "her brother, aged eleven, viewed the incident," they interpret the evidence, which is "bloody ridiculous," to conclude that the brother committed the crime: Gus offers, "I bet he did it," and Ben agrees, "I think you're right." The brother's crime of killing a cat is compounded by a despicable act against the girl—"A kid of eleven killing a cat and blaming it on his little sister of eight! It's enough to—" evidently, as Ben earlier and later completes the statement, "make you want to puke" (130, 163). Ben and Gus glance, negligently, into the alien world of the female and interpret her as, if perhaps inferior, nevertheless appealing—soft, vulnerable, victimized by the male. She can, however, be a source, an influence, and a defense. When Ben attacks Gus's use of the expression "put on the kettle" (141), Gus defends himself, first in that "they" say it and then in an appeal to his mother:

Gus: I bet my mother used to say it.
Ben: Your mother? When did you last see your mother?
Gus: I don't know, about—(142)

Ben, with his authority as "senior partner," wields the power of fallacy in dismissing Gus's mother as an authority, perhaps implying in addition that Gus lacks filial care, that he is remiss in not having seen her, not having remained close to his mother. If she is somehow abandoned by her son and therefore vulnerable like other women, she remains nevertheless a mother to whom the child turns in this moment of need.

Isaac's mother is, like Gus's, a missing and needed source of comfort: "I wold to God my moder were her on this hyll! / Sche woold knele for me on both hyr kneys / To save my lyffe" (ll. 175–77). As intercessor, she represents the qualities of sympathy and care, motherly devotion and faithfulness, that are to be recapitulated in Christ's mother; and Isaac, feeling those qualities in their absence, reciprocates with care for her feelings, asking Abraham to "Tell ye my moder no dell; / Yffe sche wost yt, sche wold wepe full sore" (ll. 256–57). The mother's human feelings would, in Isaac's understanding, render her incapable of carrying out the father's duty, and these attributes are the point of the Doctor's interpretation of the play.

His demonstration of the play's message becomes a challenge to the audience, specifically the "sores" who should emulate Abraham, a question whether they would obey the command to slay a child or would "groche or stryve therageyn" (l. 446). His supposition is that some "iij or iiij or moo" would so strive, as would "thys women, that wepe so sorowfully / Whan that hyr chyldryn dey them froo, / As nater woll and kynd" (ll. 449–51). His turning to the women as a class argues that women by nature are more vulnerable to mere human feelings than are men; they are "soft." The very qualities that make Abraham human and cause his anguish are exaggerated in women, an exaggeration that sets them apart as inferior. But these are the attributes that make them fully human, eliciting Isaac's genuine sympathy for his mother and his world's sympathy for the mother of Christ— and their expectation that she will intercede. The women should understand themselves by identifying with both Eve and Mary, who would, according to Irenaeus, "by a virgin's obedience undo and put away the disobedience of a virgin."[19] Such deference to a paradoxical superiority or at least specialness in women seems to be inchoate in Ben and Gus. Their limited purposes and the restricted structures of their actions, however, preclude full awareness and inhibit their reciprocality with others, male or female. They maintain inherited assumptions, living convictions, that amount to prejudice rather than consciousness.

The Doctor's interpretation for and engagement with the audience is an enlargement of relationships unrealizable in the silence extending beyond the final moment of Pinter's play. Here there is no resolution, no reassuring confederate who assumes the authoritative role of wise counselor or who displays the benevolent concern for others, including the audience, of this conventional figure, the Doctor. His apparent function is to provide a supplemental text to that of the play. His set speech to the audience composes, however, a play-within-the-play design, the play of the Doctor enclosing the play of Abraham and Isaac. His play is as if factual, as if an intimate pastoral homily with text. Yet he is a character played by an actor, and as protagonist in his play he performs an action in direct engagement with an audience. Commenting on a text drawn from biblical text, he can point to the meaningfulness of that action with a show of assurance that his audience is capable of playing its part well. He brings a message to the audience as the Angel does to Abraham, and his message assumes the assurance of a true source and presumes an action on their part—that they can "feytheffully serve hym qwyll ye be qvart" (l. 462). He speaks with authority, invokes the power of the play of Abraham and Isaac to illustrate in its mimesis the ideas of responsibility and obedience; and he grants to the audience their power and capability. Individual communicants are reminded that they are endowed with the power to obey or to disobey, and they are capable of receiving the import of the actions they have witnessed, capable of seeing clearly and of understanding. Their response should be a "reciprocative rejoinder," not an abandoning of their repetition to the past nor an aiming at progress but an "authentic existence" in their own lives.

E. H. Gombrich interprets a painting depicting this play's action, this ritual moment of sacrifice, "on the walls of the synagogue of Dura-Europos," as a "timeless re-enactment" rather than "as an imaginative account of a past event.... It owes its very strength to this direct contact with the beholder" (144–45). The Doctor in the Brome *Sacrifice of Isaac* accordingly speaks with a voice comprehending the timeless world of God, the past world of Abraham and Isaac, and the present world of his audience. The audience's reciprocality engages them in all three dimensions and with other people in their own. This consoling frame of reference would allow benevolent laughter, a good humor in the Doctor's treatment of his audience, the audience's acceptance of duress being qualified by the motive of the Doctor in conveying God's intention; and the assurance is that the purpose of God, the author of all things, is to "Bryng vs all to heuyn blysse!" (l. 465).

The disconnected and discordant voices of *The Dumb Waiter* speak inauthentically with exorbitant authority yet echo that abdication of benevolent godlike authority by the playwright: "his worthiness, his usefulness, his altruism." Ben wields language as a means of maintaining position and power, and the authority of words elsewhere in the play appears in silent voices, texts. Although matter-of-fact news stories provide a basis for perverse interpretation, the voice of the newspaper is cool and uninvolved; it reports facts, information, and things, and it is unencumbered by the responsibility to see beyond immediate circumstances. The magnified response of Ben and Gus is disbelief and indignation, not so much concerning the facts of the story about the "man of eighty-seven" killed by a "lorry," the veracity of the text, the news account, but their inability to imagine why the events should have occurred. Ben's proof of the truth of the account is convincing evidence: "It's down here in black and white" (130); they believe in the authority of the press's written word. The factuality they find reconfirming their trust in a present text is an assurance that does not extend beyond the text itself. It leaves them puzzled and frustrated in their inability to understand and control events and beings that remain always beyond their grasp. Their sense of alienation seems to project toward the enigma of human actions and motivations: Ben exclaims, "A man of eighty-seven crawling under a lorry!" The written orders for meals are equally matter-of-fact in tone and equally productive of consternation, beginning with a request for "steak and chips" (147) and ending in a series of bizarre requests for "Ormitha Macarounada" (153), "Char Siu and Beansprouts" (154), and finally "Scampi" (162). Not knowing who originated the demand, they are without the power of influence or even explanation, and when Ben speaks to the commander on the other end of the speaking tube he is deferential and obedient to an anonymous authority. These agents of that power must perform finite, disconnected actions that do not engage them in reciprocality, in sharing love and responsibility, freedom and allegiance, understanding and interchange. Their trust is in the finite literalness of a text, its facts that do not extend toward full understanding and that allow a free, unregulated, even bizarre play of imagination.

Neither do they reflect the freedom and mutuality of the author, whose negotiations with his audience and characters are, albeit decentralized, humanly permissive for self and others. There is in this world no god who is center and circumference, but rather beyond one's gaze a centerless expanse of darkness or void in which one must find a way. If the author is elusive, will withdraw from sight, will change colors, his characters are permitted to conceal themselves from others, including the audience. The audience might in turn feel the characters' disquiet, their "thrownness," in that this condition involves them, in Heidegger's terms, in the mimesis of "idle talk . . . in a mode of groundless floating," along with "curiosity [which] discloses everything and anything, yet in such a way that Being-in is everywhere and nowhere," and "ambiguity [which] hides nothing from Dasein's understanding, but only in order that Being-in-the-world should be suppressed in this uprooted 'everywhere and nowhere'" (*Being and Time,* H 177). The idle talk, curiosity, and ambiguity Heidegger characterizes as essential traits of this ordinary being are not only essential to the represented characters Ben and Gus but also signs of their connectedness to their author and audience.

If the audience are made uneasy, however, in the experience of an apparently pointless ambiguity that seems to have no source, of the "groundless floating" of "idle talk" and irrelevant chatter, of the indiscriminate and random disclosures of curiosity, they are nonetheless granted the permission that the author gives to his characters. The audience might recognize themselves in a restricted perception of Ben and Gus, their practicing avoidance through aggression, their compulsion to hide through confrontation, their imperative to dominate grounded in a sense of helplessness; but such recognition could entail allowing freedom and letting be, since the audience is not free to presume full knowledge of others. They exist in a little world that is not enveloped securely in a comprehensive, meaningful design. Texts refer ambiguously, as if only a matter of curiosity and idle talk; and lacking the authority and clarity of the Doctor who brings things round in *The Sacrifice of Isaac* they allow an eccentric freedom. Yet such permission, the audience's engagement and performance lacking the consolation of all-resolving knowledge and power, lacking the requirement of total, final, comprehensive understanding and control, is not merely a loosing to the eccentric or grotesque imagination.

It is in the relationship of characters and audience a relical power remaining in the play, a power to discover the self in confrontation with the bizarre and strange. In the unavailability of full understanding the audience might come to realize self and world by letting go of "definitive" knowledge and standing open to astonishment. Accepting the limitation of thrownness, being human on earth, the audience would dwell in a constituted reality as do Pinter's characters, who allow only so much of themselves to be revealed, as do Rodin's unfinished nudes; and they would embody the ideas of power and freedom, freedom not to meet the demands of finality, final purposes, ultimate meaning, all-encompassing explicability.

As in the audience's relationship with such characters, their freedom not to be known definitively echoes the author's. The playwright is, like audience and characters, in the process of being made as well as being maker. Rodin's *The Hand of God* reveals the expressive and sharply defined hand of God in the act of creation, itself emerging from the uncreated, the unrealized—a flux of stone. His creation, the human, mirrors this disclosure in appearing out of the unformed, in being only partially revealed. Artist and God and creation are not to be considered entirely accessible, the artist Rodin's creation representing God the creator synecdochically, His hand only, as God's creation retains potentiality in not being "final and definitive." The author's power is in retaining his own potentiality while letting possible worlds appear incompletely, and the encompassing silence allows reference beyond the immediate while demanding attention and care. Pinter's imperative for the author implies that like him the audience needs to give heed to others, to their words, to the text. The playwright does "a double thing. . . . You arrange *and* you listen. . . . And sometimes a balance is found, where image can freely engender image and where at the same time you are able to keep your sights on the place where the characters are silent and in hiding" (*Works: One,* 14). This "double thing" involves the reciprocality of agents neither overpowered nor omnipotent, neither determined nor determinant; and the structure of their relationship is grounded in Husserl's "perfect freedom" of cession.

Through a sense of meaning in structure, an apprehension of the relatedness of author, characters, and audience, the audience can entertain the ideas of affinity and care, stand open to the astonishment of understanding, and might confirm the power of imaginative involvement and the freedom in being and letting be. If puzzled, if thrown for a loss by the fact of the play's being—"that it is as it is and not otherwise"—the audience nevertheless have the capability to "step back . . . from being." In "this retreating and self-restraining" they permit the play to be "as it is." If "at the same time" they are "forcibly drawn to and . . . held fast" by the play, the result need not be felt merely as the dismay of powerlessness but as "astonishment," which is both the origin and the prevailing impetus of a venture into the inexhaustible experience. Pinter's "territory . . . worthy of exploration" extends into the alien unknown, where astonishment might be the illumination borne toward or released in the darkly concealed. Consequently Pinter's audience might recognize themselves as opposed to the Doctor's audience, who felt their freedom to act in a structure of assured aims and ends; yet for the audience of *The Dumb Waiter* that identification of a difference is heightened by awareness of the past. The old conformability of God, author, others, text, and audience is not destroyed but diffused. Ideas of those entities remain as felt dimensions—audience and text and author, author and characters and audience, text and allusion. In the concomitant ideas of freedom and power and knowledge, other ideas—of oppression and vulnerability and nescience—might be felt as generative rather than definitive. In yielding to the text the audience are empowered to let go of the elusive characters, to discover in the enigmatic image of the author more than the mobility of his disappearing act, more than isolation and chameleon change; they are left free to be astonished by the enduring power of the play, by the possibility of genuine touching and understanding beyond the presence of the disfranchised yet still puissant ideals—God, Author, and Abraham.

4
Ideas: Human Being and World

EXPERIENCING A WORLD AS ILLUSION, A STAGE WORLD OR THE known as actual when it changes before our eyes or is discovered to have been not what we thought it was, is in the presentation of the illusion a suspension of elemental and unquestioned trust in its matter-of-factness. As it becomes a question calling for interpretation or revaluation, it represents a loss of comfortable trust in the unquestioned. Acknowledging that recognition might come clearer when the certainties of knowledge are handicapped—that riveted concepts of a world and others in it, including ideas of artist and audience, amount to a denial of what they might appear to be if allowed to come momentarily into the clearing—seems to be a cession of authority and privilege and a vulnerability to contingency or chance. If, however, the unaccommodated idea can appear in the image, if Eidos is still accessible when ruling ideas have been dethroned and take their place among provisional ideas, then the dwindling of idea and the human image that entertains it in a diminished world becomes the postulancy of a beginning, a rediscovery out of impoverishment.

The idea of Idea itself might seem to be impaired, as when the persona in T. S. Eliot's "Preludes" searches for words to express the images of the world that appear in perception or imagination. In a world of "grimy scraps / Of withered leaves" and "dingy shades," and "other masquerades,"[1] this poetic consciousness longs for an idea expressible only as attenuated image of suffering god; but the haphazard demoralizing images of a world express, to be sure, the way "morning comes to consciousness" (13), revealing a consciousness not only attuned to them but also desiring something more than a meaningless or demeaning flux of images. As opposed to the synecdochically complacent "short square fingers stuffing pipes" (14) and the "eyes / Assured of certain certainties," the poet has the romantic urge, from the vantage of debasement, to see more, to imagine, and to apprehend transcendent reality. "Moved by *fancies* that are curled / Around these images, and cling" (15), the debased images being stirred and activated by "fancies," the activated consciousness is moved as well toward "The *notion* of some infinitely gentle / Infinitely suffering thing" (my emphases). The Romantic idea of the Imagination is reduced to "fancies"; the idea of Eidos is reduced to "notion." Although in and of this world, this consciousness can nevertheless project that notion of unconstrained gentleness and suffering from the actual to the infinite, from time's "masquerades" in the *theatrum mundi* to the cosmic circle, where "worlds revolve like ancient women." As "Preludes," banal images of human beings and the world are appearances in an activity that is in its temporal expression a matter of atonal prae-ludus and an anticipation of some cosmic or transcending harmony.

The projected images of human beings and a world cloud the sight only so long as they retain the unconsidered privilege of determining thought and preserving old certainties. To know with unassailable conviction that the earth is round and no longer flat is to remain secure in an unshakable position, felt as unshakable in spite of the earth's tremors because the earth's position and shape are known to be, begging the question, unquestionable. To know that the sphere is an element in cosmic design, or lack thereof, is equally unshakable, given the certainty that is felt to be indisputable. Here there might be, however, and is, disagreement. Knowing human beings as men and women, children and the elderly, heroes and cowards, despots and victims, angels and devils, and the myriad other images that might be human can be no less conclusive when we have made up our minds. We know the difference between youth and age, and we see it in the exemplars of the types. The young are (pace Jaques) energetic, brash, thoughtless of others, and ignorant; the old are slow, cautious, considerate, and wise. Having a mind made up is to know, for instance, that self-interest governs all actions and that survival is a matter of doing unto others before they do unto you. A disruption of such conviction, tantamount to Husserl's bracketing, might be thrust upon the believer when this conviction is challenged and troubled by a contradictory image of kindness, mercy, or love.

The moment of disruption imagined here, the moment between the eidolon and the eikastic—in which the opportunity to see otherwise allows retrenchment or adaptation; rebuttal, denial, or growth; blindness or perception—is that opportunity of the stage to take its advantage in unguarded moments. The play's revelation of potential recognitions and change represents this dare to look more closely and see what has not been seen. It is an opening up of a world and beings in an atmosphere of freedom, putting in abeyance the necessity to make determinations and come to resolutions that might alter or reconfirm real and personal identity, that might shake the foundations of a secure actual world or brace those foundations. The immediate experience is a fabrication, seductive because it need not be taken seriously, but it is also a presentation, an embodiment, of the ideas by which worlds and beings, real or imaginary, are read. If the ideas of the author and the audience seem imposing in considering the idea of the play, the characters and worlds in the play are no less generated by ideas of reality and responsive to apprehension of them as ideas. Since the characters in the play *represent, as idea,* rather than being actual, their primordial idea is the presentation of uncovering, the unfolding of character, in the context of pretense, of role-assumption, of the disengagement of the actual.

Recognition of and identification with characters does not, however, ensure a yielding of self that gives to the other a precedence of influence; the character discovered might be taken to the self, adopted, and adapted to the certainties that have been constructed as definition of the self and world, of the self's honorable engagements in its real world, where values are constructed in the structures of actuality. Although not real, not acquaintances or public figures, not known by "living conviction" to be historically or supernaturally real, characters in the imagined world allow, in their indefiniteness, that mysterious confusion in which the doubling of identities might become the excess of conviction rather than the excess of imaginative play. To admit to moments of unconsidered, impulsive conflation of self with other, character with actor, is to recognize the humorous strangeness of, for instance, meeting the actor who plays a doctor and asking him to diagnose symptoms, or, less humorously, to identify an actor with a role to the extent that they are thought of as one in nature, values, quality of mind. It is to recognize that audiences can fall so in love with a character that they assume the charming mannerisms or habits of the character, and they become, in perhaps dress, gestures, and even self-image, one. Ben Jonson was perceptive in the troubling observation that "we so insist in imitating others as we cannot, when it is necessary, return to ourselves."[2] Taking the unreal to ourselves and transforming it into the real, or endowing the real with a tincture of that unreality, is in essence an exorbitant factualizing of the imaginative. It is to translate the imaginative so that it becomes *unreflectively as if* real. If these instances seem outré, the more typical naturalization of character occurs when audiences measure and judge a character by those unshakable convictions that are ready at hand and necessary to everyday performance in the world. If an audience believes that individuals are responsible for their own lives, should face reality, and should take practical means to resolve problems, it might retain that belief as an imperative for everyone, including Blanche Dubois in

Tennessee Williams's *Streetcar Named Desire* and Lyubov Andreyevna in Anton Chekhov's *The Cherry Orchard*. Neither character can meet that demand, but both achieve an intensity in seeing things their way and attracting audiences to themselves, enticing audiences to yield to them and their ways of being.

When moving into understanding and sympathy with a character that seems an alien spirit, an audience activates the capacity to put into abeyance those predispositions and habits of opinion that govern practical encounters with others. This impracticality is inordinate respect for the other under circumstances that seem, because of their being mere pretense and play, to have no serviceable consequences. The audience is engaged in an excess of imaginative play, which is in itself a transformation—momentary, unpremeditated, disencumbered—and this opening of self toward the other is an opportunity to discover, in the deprivation of attitude and governing beliefs, character being revealed in the process. The revelation is a notion of, for instance, Blanche Dubois's ideas of people, individuals and types; and the audience not only receives, in the idea of Blanche, her being through and for others like Mitch, Stella, and Stanley but also sees those others and her world through her eyes. As an interpreted character, she represents in the world of the play the human conduct that is interpretation of others through on the one hand prejudice, alienation, and essential guiding assumptions or, on the other, adaptation to their ways of seeing. In the play's conflict characters might accommodate their ideas by which they interpret others, becoming circumspect, or they might impose their paradigms as irrevocable. The mimesis can be thought of as double, or mutually reflective, in that the character's possible ways of seeing reflect the audience's, and the audience's way of seeing the character repeats, in the experience, those possibilities.

Blanche and Stanley represent for the audience ideas in conflict, and they construe one another in terms of opposed world views. As Stanley says, "The Kowalskis and the DuBois have different notions."[3] Blanche, who shares with the playwright the poet's inclination to create through illusions an idealized, spiritualized image of human nature, represents for Stanley the idea of falseness, in deed and in persona. She echoes Aristotle and subsequent theorists in her desire to transform actuality through "magic": "I misrepresent things.... I don't tell truth, I tell what *ought* to be truth" (117).[4] Even in recounting for Stella the detrition of their world of the past, Belle Reve, she translates the actions of "improvident grandfathers and father and uncles and brothers" into "epic fornications" (43). The Dubois are epic in proportion; the Kowalskis beastly. Her thinking appeals to heroic, literary, and mythic images from the past, Stanley's to the naturalistic. She was born under the astrological sign of the Virgin (77), plays to Mitch "*la Dame aux Camellias*" (88), and in scene 11 wears a jacket that is "the blue of the robe in the old Madonna pictures" (135); she characterizes the young man who comes to collect for the newspaper as "a young Prince out of the Arabian Nights" and "My Rosenkavalier" (84); and for Mitch she plays a coy game of looking for the Pleiades among the stars, "going home from their little bridge party" (86). She delivers for Stella a dissertation on Stanley and his tribe: he is "sub-human . . . apelike . . . survivor of the stone age" (72), against which the Dubois are seen as capable of appreciating art and poetry and having survived their epic past with "tenderer feelings," evidently a belief that there remains in a debased world, albeit tenuously and not without risk, the possibility of touching one another. Stanley's stratagems for exposing her deceptions and her morbid sexuality are grounded in those naturalistic instincts she attributes to him. Although ideologically opposed and locked in conflict against the general idea of what the other stands for as well as against the other's immediate threat, both characters manifest attributes of the other. Stanley's revelations expose the naturalistic underside of Blanche that she would conceal, and he reveals in the end that he is capable of "tenderer feelings," murmuring to Stella, "Now, now, love. Now, love" (142).

Instead of these agonists' coming to recognition of themselves through discoveries about the other, it is the other characters in the play, most importantly Mitch and Stella, who, making judgments about Blanche, come to know and appreciate the fuller humanity of both Stanley and Blanche. Mitch and Stella, lacking the unrelenting conceptions of Blanche and Stanley, are caught in the agony of the conflict of ideas, and their lives are transitional; allegiant to Stanley and his world, both are at the end of the play "sobbing" for Blanche (141–42). In that Blanche and Stanley are passionately intertwined in a struggle to preserve their worlds and maintain their identities, they represent for the audience the idea of what it is like to be essentially determined by the inflexibility of the self, the prejudice, that comes up against an alien, misunderstood otherness and repudiates it. Stella and Mitch, lacking the imaginative or practical ability to transform or mediate those contradictions, represent the complaisance that involves them with others in ideas that are neither fixed faith nor determinative convictions. Unlike an audience, which might in extending itself toward Blanche and Stanley lose its certitude in the presumed inconsequentiality of its involvement and be momentarily redeemed from assertion of judgment by the play's suspension of belief, they are profoundly caught up in the conflict of values. Their anguish appears to be debilitating, but since unresolved it leaves them caught up as well in the anticipation of change and amelioration, the hope that is essential in their capacity for giving themselves to others and taking others to themselves.

The idea of touching another's life significantly is there for characters in the play and through them for the audience, and it is an available idea because the characters reflect, from the past, that possible conception of human attributes. Blanche's celebrated parting words—"I have always depended on the kindness of strangers" (142)—echo from the past this idea of enlarging oneself in the extension toward others. In the opening scene, confused about the inferior locality to which her journey has led, she has indeed arrived, as Eunice tells her, at "Elysian Fields" (15). The descent into a lower world, which can be felt in our time as O'Neill's long day's journey into night, can be conceived as well in terms of generative mythical pattern or classical locus. In book 6 of Vergil's *Aeneid,* for instance, Aeneas's descent into the terrifying underworld takes him through horrors down at last to the Elysian Fields, where a world of peace and beauty is inhabited by the virtuous dead. Here dwell heroes and "devout poets . . . who spent their lives in artistic invention or who by reason of their merit caused men to remember them"[5]—those who performed for and gave to others, and are remembered by them; and here dwells Anchises, who performs for Aeneas that "kindness" Blanche seeks. Although Blanche has been subjected to Stanley's terrorization, she has encountered in others, in Stella and Mitch, the possibilities of kindness and sympathy that affirm the possibility of reaching out toward others in a debased world. Her being recipient of that kindness from Stella and Mitch does not, however, free her from her own strength, which in the agon with Stanley is destroyed.

In gathering meaning to itself by echoing diverse human images from the past, the play might represent the particular image of the artist creating worlds, apparent realities, by manipulating illusion. The profusion of human images that might appear in the play—noble entities drawn from the past; improbable and faint echoes of the types of nobility; fragments of the virtues that heroes, demi-gods, and saints have stood for—entail ideas of authority and power, vulnerability and victimization, male and female, servant and master, parent and child, privilege, status. The concepts instantiated in images in a play like *Streetcar Named Desire* constitute a framework by which the people of that *theatrum* understand relationships and conflicts. In revealing themselves, their ideas, and their prototypes for an audience, they might well extend the limits of their reality by doubling the illusion of the play's reality, by—like an artist—performing and creating illusions. Whereas Stanley and Blanche's opposed conceptions of the world produce a kind of doubling for the audience, a character like Blanche plays the artist in creating an illusion within the play for both the audience and other characters in the play. Stanley's residing essentially in the flesh, his comfort with the elemental card game as opposed to Blanche's games of seduction, is a position from which he instinctively attacks pretensions and illusions, and her playing for others can be interpreted as lies, delusions, deceptions, insanity. When she creates fictions, concerning "Mr. Shep Huntleigh of Dallas" (128) for example, he accuses her of "lies and conceit and tricks" and orders her to "take a look at yourself in that worn-out Mardi Gras outfit, rented for fifty cents from some rag-picker" (127). Performing, masking, telling stories, and presenting plays within the play, creating little dramas and assigning roles, are repetitions in the play *for* characters in that world, who are cast in the role of audience. That audience, encountered by an unreality that might be true in essence, might repudiate it or yield to its suasive power, let itself be caught up in the structure of revelation, recognize itself in the strange unreality, suffer transformation and growth, and risk unsettling revelations of identity, even devastation. The play's audience, in that structure of revelation, is mimetic both in the knowledge of relationship to characters and in reflecting the idea of its own world; in play, the audience offers itself, performs as if for its audience, neither as pure actuality nor as mere unreality.

The idea of purposeful play in the creation of character and action, both in play making and in making illusions within plays, inevitably exploits those potential semblances by which the particular being is identified. The creation of illusions within the play reflects the play's illusion in that, in both dimensions, purposes can range from mere entertainment for self and others to the heuristic, to willful deception, to self-aggrandizement, or to other motives such as self-defense. Characters drawn as eidos in Plato's republic, in nineteenth-century realism, or in Marxist programmatic literature should represent for the audience clear and persuasive instances of values to be understood for their applicability to the real world. Characters ostensibly there only for a moment's entertainment are, while not of such serious function, no less indebted to ideas of character. Either sort embodies purposes, and when characters visibly engage in shiftings of identity, transformations, or creation of illusions, disguises, and plots, they intensify those moments of disruption that disorient and therefore demand heightened attention and interest. If those disruptions magnetically attract or fascinate their audience, their excess draws the audience into closer commitment to the play of illusion, creates closer attachments; and it increases the risk of involvement and perhaps a sense of vulnerability to those machinations.

In Pirandello's *Henry IV,* the audience is like the audiences in the play in being taken aback, bewildered, perplexed. The games of revelation and duplicity are played by and within the play. Ostensible purposes give way to ulterior designs, genuine identity becomes a mask, the actuality of the stage world becomes a stage created for the sake of illusion. The baroque action is an intricate scheme of tricks and revelations, disguises and disclosures, con men and marks, schemers and fools, and in this perplexity the purposes are to explore the questions of validating identity, of confirming a locus of reality in the flux of appearances. The questioning moves not toward a certainty of validating hopes but into the illusion that destabilizes without assurance. The characters in the play represent, for the audience, itself on the one hand standing fixed within its framing world of certainties and on the other mobile in its impulse to participate in play, its desire for movement, its need to let be free the imaginative possibilities that can develop as the one-dimensional solid reality accedes to its complicity in a play of illusion.

The purposes and expectations of the characters who come to the "Solitary Villa in Italy in Our Own Time"[6] are rooted in firm convictions about themselves and others. They are certain that the protagonist, who is named only as the character he portrays, Henry IV, is a madman. Their good intentions have been instigated by Henry's sister, Charles di Nolli's mother, "dead for more than a month" (153), who with the "firm conviction that her adored brother was just about to be cured" extracted a promise from Charles that he would "never neglect" Henry, "would have doctors see him." Accordingly Charles—with doctor Genoni, Charles's fiancée Frida, her mother Donna Matilda, and Matilda's lover Baron Belcredi—plans to practice on Henry a "violent trick" (177) that will shock the madman back to sanity. Charles declares that "we have come for a very serious purpose which you all know is important for me" (152). Doctor Genoni's calling the enterprise a trick in no way disputes that utter seriousness of benevolent intentions to cure Henry. The Doctor's professional understanding of human nature qualifies him as the traditionally approved idea of the doctor, helping others through knowing them better than they know themselves. If the Doctor seems to live comfortably in an assigned role of earnestness, Belcredi seems fixed in an antithetical role. Frida's perception of him, that "He acts the fool by profession" (151), is not denied in his ready wit, his ironic insights, his playfulness with what others take seriously. Being told that Henry calls the Pope a pagan, Belcredi says, "The Pope a pagan? Not bad that!" (162). In the last act he maintains an ironic, perhaps sarcastic, distance from Henry's intensity. He responds to Henry's profound repudiating of the counselors who have betrayed him—his placing them, along with the valets, among the others who have laughed at him—with unsympathetic wryness: "Well, imagine that . . . That's not bad . . ." (205). Doctor Genoni's unwavering dedication to their purpose, governed by his preparedness to understand only through the eyes of psychiatry, is no more the constraint of role than is Belcredi's intellectualizing the game. Genoni earns for his earnestness only the reward of failure, his interest and involvement being ostensibly merely professional; Belcredi, involved in the events of the past as well as present, taking lightly his close associations with others, maintains his role of the fool to his death.

Matilda's reasons for participating in the action, her motives and desires, are less clearly ascertainable than those of Belcredi and Genoni, whose identities are anchored in role. She is not defined and contained by her roles as woman and lover, by the guilt of her participation in the disastrous fall that left Henry insane, by her potentiality for playing the curious audience, by her apparent eagerness to assume a role. When Charles declares that Belcredi need not be there and the Doctor seems to question the need for Matilda's participation, she declares, "I mean to see him too, naturally. I want to see him again" (162). To Frida's plea that Matilda come away with her, she responds "(*imperiously*): Let me do as I wish! I came here for this purpose! (*To Landolph.*) I shall be 'Adelaide,' the mother" (162–63). Her declaration of fidelity to serious purpose seems implicitly clear, but her formal tone announcing the role she will play hints at an excess of pleasure in playing a part in the drama, as Frida seems enchanted to find herself playing a role in costume. Matilda's unhesitant choice of a role for the ruinous pageant was an identification of herself, by name, with the "Marchioness Matilda of Tuscany" (155). Her taking the role of Henry IV's "implacable enemy," a relationship she claims to have recognized only later when Henry took his role because "he wanted to be near me in the pageant as Henry IV" (156), confirmed for Belcredi his perception that she could not "stand" Henry; but she insists that she "didn't dislike him." In her explaining her attitude as characteristic of women in general, who can only laugh at men who show them "a pair of eyes glaring at us with a contained intense promise of eternal devotion," her apparent trivialization of a lover's seriousness seems to be a stratagem for self-protection, if not the instinct to play by her assumed identity; her impatience with "all that is pondered, or tedious" (157), did not, however, protect her from the recognition that her "own laugh mingled with those of all the others—the other fools—who made fun of him."

Matilda's perhaps imponderable self-contradictions are received in the spirit of analysis by others who are convinced that they see her truly. Belcredi reads her playing her part in the trick as "simply enormous ... an abnegation" (182), true to the type, any woman; but when she declares, "I owe it to him," Belcredi depreciates the abnegation as "just enough to prevent you losing caste in other people's eyes—and just enough to offend me." She is, as he sees her, like all women in protecting her status and image and in practicing wiles to stir the jealousy of a lover. Henry sees her as one in a class with the others, male and female, in taking part in a "counter-joke for me" (201), although she denies the charge "(*impetuously*): No, no! What do you say? It was done for you! I did it for your sake!" Matilda's identity is not resolved in any interpretation of her, and she remains a mysterious possibility between truth and deception, character and guise. Belcredi's final depiction of her suggests that rather than being fixed in one of those assigned roles she is seeking identity through role and relationship with others. She is, Belcredi says to Henry, "all fascinated by your words, by this *conscious* madness of yours"; and to her, "you could even remain here to live it out, Marchioness" (206). Her apparent readiness to assume a role is an attraction to the other, actual or imagined, to possible images of self and a lover; perhaps it is an expression of the lingering need in a debased world for authentic touch.

The fascination for Henry's words and his conscious madness that Belcredi sees in Matilda seems to be a fascination for the alien, the attractive illusion, perhaps both to the attractive lover and also to the idea of finding self in the other, of reconciliation and reunion. In her assuming the identity of her counterpart, the Marchioness Matilda of Tuscany, she discovers a relationship with an enemy, Henry IV; but that antipathy in the imagined historical dimension conceals, as the modern Matilda's contempt for an importunate lover conceals, the possibility of reconciliation and benevolence. Although at the end of act 1 Henry extracts a promise from Matilda, playing his wife's mother Adelaide, to intercede for him, to "beg His Holiness for pardon" (172), Matilda in act 2, with Landolph's assistance, cites history as saying "that the Pope gave way to the supplications of the Marchioness Matilda and the Abbot of Cluny" (184). The modern Matilda's desire to free Henry from his madness echoes Matilda of Tuscany's acting to free Henry IV from the Pope's excommunication. It seems that Matilda's saying in act 1 that she had not given her choice of a role for the pageant "any importance" (155) has concealed the truth she tells in act 3. This revised account reveals that she knew Matilda of Tuscany interceded for Henry IV, and "that I intended to take advantage of this fact—at the time of the pageant—to show him my feelings were not so hostile to him as he supposed" (184). If in the debilitated and cynical real world genuine and tender feelings, compassion or love, must be concealed in a mask of aloofness, contempt, or ascendancy, then the roles assumed in a condition of thrownness might well be a taking of cover. Indignation toward the world, Henry's hiding himself in a mask of insanity, and the protection the role affords, seem to be the essential condition in which an alienated life can be lived in a depraved world. The roles of counselor, doctor, or lover seem to be contaminated by self-interest and sophistry. The ambiguity or duplicity of Matilda leaves open the possibility, however, that the authentic, the sincere, and the capacity for love are merely covered up by pretension and the artifice of alienation, are not impossible.

In this atmosphere of disaffection, the assumption of roles might improbably release the uncommon potentiality for being genuinely involved with another. Henry's estrangement does not erase his sister's wish and Charles's attempt to carry it out, nor does it repudiate the possible motives Matilda finds and cultivates in her playing Matilda of Tuscany, in appealing to the past for an image of the intercessor. Henry's eloquent appeal to the counselors at the end of act 2 is an argument for the beauty of the dream of the past, but it is not a solipsistic dream. If they would play their roles for themselves, not for him as audience, they could realize themselves not as in isolation but as a community: "the men of the twentieth century are torturing themselves in ceaseless anxiety to know how their fates and fortunes will work out! Whereas you are already in history *with me*" (195; my emphasis). The darkness of his world, increasingly terrifying, does not afford the full illumination by which Plato's prisoner, released from the cave and ascending into the sunlight, would find the truth. The moon, the poet's inspiration, with "her" light transforms and creates an altered reality: "see what a magnificent night scene we have here: the emperor surrounded by his faithful counsellors" (194).

Although momentarily fascinated by the beauty of his dream, Henry's counselors betray him; but their demonstration of infidelity does not deny the possibility of devotion in a faithless world or in an ideal or illusory one generated by the artist. Old John, coming "every night to play the monk" (196), provides an opportunity for the counselors' crass pleasure in their having "*the chance for another joke.*" Henry's rebuking Ordulph for wanting "to play a joke on a poor old man who does it for love of me" evokes Landolph's admonition to Ordulph that "It has to be as if it were true." The "as if" true is what the artist makes when his moon transforms the actual. John's playing, for Henry, the role of the monk who records the history that Henry dictates represents a bond of love and commitment that has not been broken by Henry's revelation of his sanity. In the role of the "humble monk who is devoted to me" there is achieved, by John and Henry in collaboration, an illusion of truth that transcends the ordinary. The improbable emerges from the world's illusions and deceptions "as if true," and "only so, truth is not a jest."

Consigned to a world in which pretense might be a plea to let the genuine reveal itself, in which pretending "as if" might let truth appear in the jest, the audience/interpreter is constrained and at risk in making sense of things. In the world of the past, for Henry, Matilda, and Belcredi the youthful sense of freedom to trifle with icons of their past, scarcely known or known only as important and serviceable to their own privilege to play with life, becomes in the present events a deadly serious game played into the darkness. Their failure—Belcredi's death, Matilda's release back into the world of time, Henry's terrified recognition that he is bound to his attendants in this place "together ... for ever!" (208)—is not the failure of the epic or tragic hero who, out of tune, is brought back into harmony with the world. This world is in itself discordant. The acutely painful difficulty in establishing a world and gaining a sense of place is comically expressed in the opening scene as Berthold tries to discover where and when he is. Having studied for his role the world of Henry IV of France, he learns, now in costume and on the job, that he is in the world of Henry IV of Germany. Not recognizing his costume as of the eleventh century rather than the sixteenth, his having prepared for the role by studying history is to no avail. The place itself, although "furnished and decorated so as to look exactly like the throne room of Henry IV in the royal residence at Goslar" (139), is unstable; sometimes being "at the castle in the Hartz ... or at Wurms" (140), it "jumps about with us, now here, now there," temporally and spatially mobile.

In such a world of easy substitutions, in which the tentativeness of both person and place affords little sense of belonging, of being at home, of being together with others, the possibility of founding relationship is enfeebled. Henry's seizing Frida is a desperate gesture only, she being a substitute for Matilda in the costume of the Marchioness of Tuscany. As a gesture of love, its obliquity bespeaks the untrustworthiness of love. As a gesture of defiance, Henry's enticing Belcredi to front him is a futile and fatal indirection. Futile gestures of love or combat, under the embarrassment of disbelief in love and heroism, altruism, courage, and fidelity, remain in a world of detritus signs of belief, echoes of the illusory world of the past. Belcredi's alienation speaks for the sardonic comedy that makes everyone an observer, disengaged and disbelieving while holding on to the shreds of values that would make human actions meaningful. To capture that illusion of continuity, making a little world and fixing it out of time, imitating the real as it should be in a Platonic world of idea, Henry embraces the illusion that he and his faithful counselors are locked away from time and change and betrayal, performed in a secure construct of art that transforms or transcends the actual.

Building and maintaining an identity in a fluctuating world seems a serious and consequential responsibility, as would be, concomitantly, caring for the identity and well being of others from whom identities are derived or with whom identities reflect. The fascination with the play of illusion and interplay of illusions contaminates the purity of seriousness but does not deny it. The characters' excesses, their fascination with the possibilities of discovery and transformation that might appear in the strange apparition of an unreal dimension, are not merely the pursuit of trivial entertainment or the expression of idle curiosity. Their need for alliance with others demands the risk, the chance that meeting the other in the faint hope for reunion might only confirm the horror of estrangement and impotence. Knowing that the trick and shock they intend for Henry is a risk, they chance it for the sake of reunion in reality and sanity. The shock for Henry in confronting a painting of the Marchioness transformed into the living woman, and then the living Marchioness doubled in another, would, Genoni believes, shatter his world of illusion. The helpers are less aware of implications in their complicity or prepared for the consequences of their own engagement with the artifice of illusion. The astonishment, the disorientation and requisite adjustment to what appears unexpectedly and in spite of presumed knowledge and calculated preparations, bestows on them the role of an audience. They can be swept into the illusion and lose themselves; they can continue to force a conversion of the illusion into the actual; they can repudiate the illusion and return to the security of their supposedly indisputable reality; they can yield to the interdependence of the actual and the imaginative, the play or devised show as a trick, that represents the as-yet unresolved condition of experience.

Ideas of identity play from the past toward the future, in characters' needs to be expressions of ideas of what it is to be a human being, to find themselves according to possible, available models and to make themselves for their own lives, for what is to ensue. The idea of the woman who is intercessor, debased by Belcredi and deprecated by contemporary voices calling for acceptance of the changes that disable the chimera, remains among the dynamic icons by which roles are defined and assumed. A specifically feminist iconoclasm would confront the ensconced Virgin Mary in an attempt to negate the idealized image of woman. So long as the idea or the negation of it retains an unconsidered power, however, a felt need and compelling expectation, it persists as one of the possible regulatory referents of sincere actions and conceptions. Put into play in the speculation of the imaginative performance, it attains the luminosity that is allowed the mere appearances that seem to be inconsequential, merely the play of images and ideas. Brought into play, it is in effect brought down among the diverse images that are all in the abeyance of conjecture. To observe represented characters presuming the validity of the idea or repudiating it, adoring or mocking it, speculating about it, discovering through it, is to perform with them in the play of their represented activity.

Devotion to gods and their agents—angels, intercessors, priests, avatars, congruous representations of the unitary idea of godliness—preserves the duality of a deteriorated, fallible world dependent upon a superiority or flawlessness in another dimension that can direct, govern, or redeem the fallen world. The real world beyond, different in kind from this *theatrum mundi,* makes or unmakes people and affairs in this puppet play. In the searches within this world's fallenness for the traces of lasting truth, the duplicity of a spiritual confidence man is made possible by the conviction that the eternal can and will appear in or through mortal agents. If, on the other hand, the angel is brought down to reside or appear in dasein, in the sundry possibilities of the idea of angel as it might appear in human beings, the idea suffers a reduction that makes it "finally," at last, human. Wallace Stevens's angel, like Paul Klee's, is thus brought down. Klee's angel of earth, perhaps freed from earth by wings but still hovering near it, finally descends to walk on it. Transmuted, in one instance, into the "Hero with Wing," the figure retains the angel's wing in an incongruous pastiche of reference to gods, heroes, and the human: he stands with one wooden leg planted in earth; helmeted, he displays one arm as machinelike; the other is a mutated wing, clearly unserviceable as a means of flight back to heaven.[7]

Stevens's "necessary angel of earth" neither brings messages from another world nor inspires the hope to attain it. Yet it incorporates the ideas of an angel's bearing messages and inspiring: "in my sight, you see the earth again, / Cleared of its stiff and stubborn, man-locked set" ("Angel Surrounded by Paysans," *Palm,* 354). The angel's message concerns seeing things as they are, without the "stubborn, man-locked set" of convictions that impose the unreal on the actual. In the dramatic quest of "Notes Toward a Supreme Fiction" for a "first idea"—not first as archetypal, original, or atemporal, but first as primary, most essential, most earth-endowed—Stevens's poet imagines Canon Aspirin's angelic ascent to the view of earth *sub specie aeternitatis* and his obscene descent, like the descent of Milton's Satan to earth, "to the children's bed" (*Palm,* 229). Canon Aspirin "imposes orders," but for the poet "to discover an order" is "Not to impose, not to have reasoned at all, / Out of nothing to have come on major weather, / It is possible, possible, possible. It must / Be possible" (230). Thinking his way toward "the real," the poet thinks "The fiction of an absolute" and abruptly tells the "Angel" to "Be silent in your luminous cloud and hear / The luminous melody of proper sound." If the poet can imagine "the angel in his cloud," he can also imagine the angel descending, not like Canon Aspirin's pouncing angel, but forgetting "the gold centre," growing "warm in the motionless motion of his flight" (231) and perhaps feeling an "expressible bliss" indistinguishable from the poet's. Turning to the "too weedy wren," the poet tells it to "whistle aloud" and declares, "I can / Do all that angels can." This human voice of earthly maker neither denies the efficacy of the angelic nor betrays the human in a deference to superior knowledge and power from another world. In the incorporation of the idea of the angel into the human, the imagined is vitalized as incarnate in the "ignorant man" (207), and this man, ignorant because attempting to put in abeyance the "stubborn, man-locked set" of idealized images and determining convictions, receives the endowed images to make of them what he can. Thus brought together, human being and angel transcend the separatism of rank and privilege and accomplish a "possible, possible, possible" marriage of the actual and the ideal.

Ideas of the human incorporate inherited images with the images that are enabled through transmutation, iconoclasm, or the creation of new models. They presumably cannot, in the circumstances of time and change, attain finality, making the claim of the ideal. In an ever-changing adaptation and accommodation to the actual as it is being realized, they entail the anticipation that along with other change the idea of what it means to be human will change. As the theater represents the juncture of the familiar and the strange, in the representation itself for an audience and in the moments of encounter and discovery when the characters in their world meet the alien, it too realizes that marriage of the actual and the ideal. A world brought down to earth is a world that bears in that descent the images that have constituted it.

Images of possible worlds, self-defining dimensions, are not preserved in a coherence of stability and changelessness but in the possibilities of worlds impinging, meeting in love and separating in strife, relating to one another. Heaven above, the enclosed garden of Eden, a Ptolemaic cosmos with earth fixed at the center, aspiring cathedrals, throne rooms composing a center of power and influence, home and hearth: orienting images announce the security of place and connectedness. Familiar reminders that the world is an architectural habitation for human beings, a place designed and constructed as a play is construct, these structures confirm the centripetal force that realizes cohesiveness and order in the idea of enclosure. The seeming permanence of the constructed place, like the timelessness of the work of art, endows it with an idea of changelessness amidst change and destruction. Whether structures of a motionless other world opposed to the fluctuant earth or havens fabricated within that undiscovered and open territory, that interminable extensiveness of the unknown, that darkness or nothingness beyond what is already grasped and contained, they are consolations and safeguards against external dangers and threats, the satanic intruder from the darkness beyond or the enemy beyond the moat. They obviate the risk of adventure for the dweller within the covenant, providing in the familiar the consolations of certainty and predictability; and they provide for the adventurer a retreat from encounters and risks met beyond the secure place. In the enclosed garden or home's idea as a first place, it invites the return to origins, the uneventful condition before strife. The idea of an enduring place, like the perfected ideas of perfect beings, becomes a felt certainty that redeems, a reliable refuge from the uncertainties of change, discovery, and transformation.

The established sites of preservation constitute, however, the structures of a world, as Heidegger conceives it, generated out of and inseparable from earth. The Greek temple, "standing there, opens up a world and at the same time sets this world back again on earth, which itself only thus emerges as native ground" (*Basic Writings*, 169). The work of architecture does not stand over against the raging storm outside, as in opposition, but gives meaning to the storm, "makes the storm itself manifest in its violence." The temple is built from the earth and "gathers around itself the unity of those paths and relations in which birth and death, disaster and blessing, victory and disgrace, endurance and decline acquire the shape of destiny for human being" (168). The architectural structure, representing the human endeavor to make a human habitation and to be safe at home in it, is on the one hand a struggle against the earth and on the other a collaboration with it. "World and earth are essentially different from one another and yet are never separated. The world grounds itself on the earth, and earth juts through world" (172). Since the work of art manifests its being as a product of human endeavor, it is neither timeless reality nor merely thoughtless occurrence. In it, furthermore, "createdness is expressly created into the created being, so that it stands out from it, from the being thus brought forth, in an expressly particular way" (182). The theatrical event's createdness is not the createdness of artifacts or equipment, in which the createdness "disappears in usefulness"; in the literary work "this thrust, this 'that it is' of createdness, emerges into view most purely." Essential to its revelation is the idea of itself being a structure like other configurations of world grounded on the earth and generated, made possible, by the idea of making something of something. The ideas of stability, endurance, and origins carry with them the ideas of strife and danger, against which in being opposed to that destructiveness they seem to establish security and endurance.

The theater, representation of a world, essentially reiterates the construction of enduring edifices from the raw actuality of earth and the anxieties earth provokes—its threats of storms, dwindling and disgrace, disaster and obliteration—as well as its encouragement to record achievements, build temples and statues, and pay tribute. The play represents in its essence the making of order, coherence, and endurance as if it were lifting itself into timelessness. In its illusions, the stage contemplates the structures the world has made and dramatizes the strife that does not sever the bonds of earth and world but confirms their interdependence. Revealing in its own structure, its edifice, the human artifice by which worlds are created, it represents the confected nature of entitled place and its inevitable complicity with earth. If the imposing edifice of the stage itself can be toppled, fragmented, or transformed, its comforting representations too can be challenged. In *Role Playing and Identity*, Bruce Wilshire begins his exploration of the theatrical metaphor with an instance of experimental theater's removal of the solid screen between the drama and reality (ix–xiv).[8] The stage in a "semi-darkened warehouse in New York near the docks" achieves its meaningfulness because the objects appearing on it are not clearly theatrical, thus reassuring the audience that this is not actuality but a play; nor are they unequivocally real objects untransformed by the idea of theatricality. Although "actual things in plain view—not things dressed up or illuminated so as to appear to be what they are not," they effect a change in the audience, in which it adopts "a way of freely interpreting the world" (xii). The theater is a presentation of established ideas of a world and human beings in it, in a speculative event. In bringing ideas down to that juncture of earth and world, in presenting ideas of a world's architecture as in play, including the idea of the theater itself, the play achieves a luminosity that is "as if true," like the history John, playing a monk, records for Henry IV.

As opposed to the purity sought by a stage that confronts an audience anticipating its pretense with things actual and what they are, the stage might catch that audience up in the idea of its illusion. It might be contaminative rather than corrective. Pretending to be, for instance, a home or a church, it might express the idea that it treats its audience as if the audience were of the illusion—that is, not purely an actuality there beyond the stage's activity but entailed in the idea that questions how and what truths will emerge from illusion. In the drama of nineteenth-century realism, the stage represented the discipline and restraint of verisimilitude in drawing a curtain away from one wall of the home that practiced a similar discipline and restraint. The ideas of control and order in the represented world are reflected in the crafted dramaturgy of the play. The minimal view of that private world, like the opening in a camera lens that declares its glimpse to be from a fixed perspective and a certain distance, pays respect to the privacy; but this prudent look becomes less than circumspect in that the audience, cast in the role of objective observer, is in effect peeping through an opening that for the characters is a wall protecting them from prying eyes. The conventions of this drama conceal, in the fourth wall, awareness of intrusion; but the play repeats the idea of intrusiveness in the way the audience reflects the prurience of outsiders who enter into the action, bringing with them their alien vision. The audience is, then, a representation of the intruders in the play and bears in itself the question of ethical involvement as they do.

In Ibsen's *Ghosts,* the home is a citadel against the world, carefully fabricated and maintained by Mrs. Alving. Perhaps no more egregiously intrusive than Pastor Manders is the carpenter Engstrand, who maintains a mask of piety in order to gain advantage, keeping a watchful eye on others and circumstances to see what he can make of them for himself. Manders, bringing his strict code of values and conduct into the home and imposing it against the "Fine fruit" of Mrs. Alving's reading, "these disgusting, insidious freethinking books!"[9] attempts to recall her to his sense of decency, abandoned by her when, she says, she began examining his philosophy, "seam by seam." Helene Alving is a woman convinced of the legitimacy of these new ideas of freedom from the strictures of old ideas. Yet when—after a year of marriage she fled to "seek refuge" (226) with Manders—he sent her "'home to your lawful husband,'" she determined to transform the home she saw as corrupted and debased by her husband's profligacy, "the appetites he indulged" (225), into an image of those traditional values. Marital fidelity, rectitude, sobriety, and her devotion to the duties of wife and mother shaped a facsimile of the ideal home, even though, to protect Oswald from the actual influence of his father, it was necessary to keep him, her only child, in school away from home. Manders's charge that she has been "instinctively ... drawn to all that's undisciplined and lawless" (227) belies her commitment to the Apollonian image, and she later confesses that she is too much a "coward" (236) to shatter icons, specifically the "beautiful image" of his father she fostered in her "son's imagination" (237). Instead, she has devoted her life to maintaining and enhancing the image she knows to be false and the ideals in which she no longer believes. She has attempted to preserve her home against the depredations of licentiousness on the one hand and on the other the stultifying doctrine that binds her to the past.

In identifying with Mrs. Alving, feeling with her the oppressiveness of Manders and Oswald's ideas, the audience might feel with her the indignant virtue, the sense of rectitude, she feels against others' imperatives. It might bring to the experience, from and representing its world, its own vision as if clear and pure and its own rectitude as if authoritative. Manders's authority resides in the church, and the antithetical values that Oswald brings home with him are represented in the images of Paris and Rome. As the nearby town is for Mrs. Alving a world maintaining the past's fundamental beliefs against her ideas, a world with a watchful eye like Engstrand's—who has a curiosity that helps Manders to take care of his own image—the world of Paris is for Oswald a life of "beautiful freedom" (224); there artists maintain homes in what Manders names "illicit relations! ... plain, irresponsible free love!" (223). For Manders, Oswald should have grown up in a real home, which he defines as, in contrast to the artists' homes in Paris, "a family home, where a man lives with his wife and his children." Manders's conception of the decadent Parisian world, in which he sees freedom as licentiousness and vulnerability to such consequences as social disease, is for Oswald the idea of a world of honesty as well as freedom. The purity of that world is threatened by the respectable aliens from Manders's world, who being tourists ostensibly come to see but who act on the world, exposing the free and honest citizens to corrupting ideas of "things and places we never dreamed existed" (224). The ideas of freedom and honesty played against ideas of social order, continuity, and life lived by inherited moral roles and codes are the ideas in strife in Mrs. Alving's home. Her determination to maintain the past in the facade, for the world and others, including her son Oswald, conflicts with her desire for a private honesty and freedom that she would establish for herself and pass on as an inheritance to her son. Having endured and suffered the depravity her husband brought "here in our own house" (229), when he brought into the home what he had before kept "secret away from this house," when "the infection came right within our own four walls," she intensified her efforts to live by duplicity, by the contradiction in her public image and her private values.

Her intense sincerity blinds her to a third essential quality of the free and honest home that has broken with the imperatives of the past. In the bitterness of her struggle, she fails to see that her secret announcement of freedom from Manders's god raises the question of purpose. If the world is not Manders's reality, "a vale of tears" where "work is a curse and a punishment, and . . . life is a miserable thing that we're best off to be out of as soon as possible" (257), the alternative to that belief is an acceptance of life for its satisfactions. Mrs. Alving's life has not been lived according to the satisfactions to be had in a genuine epicureanism, having been governed instead by the unconsidered assumption, the concealed pious premise, that seeking pleasure on earth is sinful self-interest and amounts to licentiousness and debauchery. Although desiring happiness and "often" thinking that "law and order" are "the root of all our miseries on earth" (236), she lives still by the austere eidolon of a god who watches, as the town watches, for breaches among His children. Oswald returns home with a fear, engendered by her mask of piety and the illusion of tradition she has maintained, that in the strictures of this home there is no awareness of "the joy of life" (256): "You don't know much about that here at home. I never feel it here." The world created from and responsible to earth, unaccommodated by promises of reality and happiness in another dimension, should be, according to Oswald, "Light and sun and holiday scenes—and faces radiant with human content" (257).

Mrs. Alving's complicity in the creation of illusions while desiring truth leads not to embracing a new reality, constructing a new place, the old illusion departed, but to consternation. Believing in and devoted to discovered ideas, she cannot realize new truth in her home, which still lingers in the shadow of the church. Instead of achieving a liberated acceptance of others, a freedom for self through letting others be for themselves in an atmosphere of creative play, where an artist like Oswald is free, and "everything" in his painting "is involved with this joy of life," her ardent earnestness releases none of that joy. Her anticipation of future happiness does not countenance a Dionysian upsurge of communal vitality but holds to the archaic premise, contradicting her belief in the liberation from old ideas, that one Apollonian order must be substituted by another. In act 1 she tells Manders that "After tomorrow, it will really seem as if the dead had never lived in this house. There'll be no one else here but my son and me" (232), a son and a mother who wears the mask of tradition and masculine authority. Enclosing him with her in a house (in which she will not allow him to smoke [221]), she will have escaped from "this long, horrible farce" (232). Aware that she has played the role of writer and director of the play of deception that preserved for Oswald the false idea of his father, her repudiation of the past as an illusion leads to the terrible reality of the past in the present. She has discovered at the end of act 1 that Captain Alving still lives in Oswald, and the revelation that Oswald carries his father's taint, speakable only in French as the *vermoulu* (250), confirms the power of ghosts (*gengangere*, perhaps better translated as "phantoms").[10]

The phantoms that stalk embody the persistent determinative power of eidolons, revealing their sway in minds for whom they are unquestionably true and, as well, their strange endurance against the wills of minds who would deny them and pronounce them fictions. Mrs. Alving's discovery of the mysterious interweaving of truth and fiction transforms the "long, horrible farce" she has played for the world into the private tragedy, the terrifying reality, that leaves her alone with Oswald in the home devoid of joy. The world she has constructed as a *theatrum mundi* has become, she discovers, the prison to which she has condemned herself. Rather than being manifest only as a conflict between the home and the intrusions from the world beyond, the antithetical ideas of control and freedom, of honesty and deception, hold sway within her, in her inability to play the monstrous mother by using the morphine to kill her own child and her inability to achieve the happiness of a mother in full possession of and giving total care to that child. Her recognition that Alving was not the antithesis of paternal virtue she had seen him to be, that when they married he "*was* like a child" full of "the joy of life" unfulfilled in his world (266), she experiences a withering of certainty about her own role in his becoming what she saw and a growing doubt about her own image devoted to the idea of mother. An audience contemplating this corrosion of identity in Mrs. Alving might well feel for her while failing, with her, to see that it bears and maintains its own deceptions against the interlopers and self-congratulators who keep an eye on her and who, as voyeurs, in their own ways represent the audience.

In the world beyond Mrs. Alving's private sorrow, the "horrible farce" continues to be played on a stage where the false ideas of Manders collaborate with the crass dishonesty of Engstrand in preserving and promoting the world's delusions. The "home" will be a parody of Mrs. Alving's ideas of home, as Manders and Engstrand parody her tragic sense of life in their farce. The two intruders, who have used their seeing into the home to promote their own ends, work toward self-aggrandizement in the guise of piety. The illusion of truth Manders sustains is under the control of the unconditional deception of Engstrand, who in practicing blackmail to obtain control of the property where the orphanage burned invokes the idea of the immaculate messenger from eternity, referring to himself as "your guardian angel" (264). Engstrand has in act 2 equated the two "refuges," the orphanage and his home for sailors. His is dedicated to protecting the virtue of "orphans of the sea," the "sailor . . . wandering ashore," from that world's "temptations . . . so manifold" (245), he playing the role of father: "in this house of mine he could live like under a father's protection." The idea of home is parodied in the way Mrs. Alving's false tribute to the image of her dead husband, the orphanage, becomes Engstrand's "house for wayfaring seamen—that's going to be known as 'Captain Alving's Home'" (264). Mrs. Alving had precisely divided the family inheritance, her part to be entirely her son's and Alving's to be the edifice named the "Captain Alving Memorial Orphan's Home" (215). The true depravity of Alving would be transformed into an image of pure virtue, the selfless, identity-denying charity of an orphanage. Through Engstrand's power to deceive and manipulate Manders, Alving's name will be given to the shady edifice that will provide for the "wayfaring seamen" more than a haven; it will offer, with Regina's assistance, "a little life in the evenings" (207).

Deeply implicated in the "horrible farce" of life, Mrs. Alving has had no power over it. Her construction of a false home as world, in the idea of the orphanage but more profoundly in the lifelong construct of her own home, has not protected her from the voyeurs and meddlers who sought advantage. Her now disavowing her part in the project, giving to Manders "all the papers" and "power of attorney" (262–63) to dispose of the property as he chooses, frees her only to the encounter with a terrifying reality within the home rather than the serenity of a home safeguarding freedom, honesty, and happiness. The horrible light cast by the burning orphanage, revelation of the disastrous potential of earth, has been an exhibiting of the darkness out of which phantoms walk, perhaps to be read as both an inner and outer darkness, and the mocking sunrise brings, not the "lovely day . . . bright sunlight" (275), but the terror of darkness in the sanctum sanctorum of the home.

The home remains an idea of refuge for the voyager, for the young man returning, preserved as memories and expectations. As the home constitutes the proximal source of values and formation of identities, return to it renews its concentration and reinforcement of the ideas of self and origins. Oswald's return does not anticipate a changed or changing mother, and the home retains for him the ideas of constraint as well as protection. If his fascination with his father's pipe evokes discrepant memories, recalling the image of a father's cruelty from which the mother still shields him, the conserved static image of mother is fixed in his mind, and he is vulnerable to her need to transform him back into her "own . . . dearest boy," to indulge him as when he was "a little child." He had hoped that Regina could perform the act that an indulgent mother cannot perform, giving him the lethal dose of morphine, which he can demand of his mother only in desperation. Unlike Orestes and Clytemnestra in the central play of Aeschylus's *Oresteia,* the *Choephoroe,* Oswald, returning near death to the refuge of home, and Mrs. Alving, preserving that refuge, rely on the potent idea of the home to bring him back and keep them together.

The ideas of home in *Ghosts* echo ideas in the earlier play; the son returning not to die but to achieve resolution knows what home should be. Although Mrs. Alving bears certain resemblances to Clytemnestra, she adheres to the stable image of herself as absolute mother even as she contradicts it in her desire for transformation of herself and her world; Clytemnestra has already yielded, in the *Agamemnon,* to the desires and satisfactions that profane the idea of mother and desecrate the home. She has in the *Agamemnon,* however, justified the killing of Agamemnon by portraying herself as preserving values of their world, as devoted mother of the daughter Agamemnon has slain. Desperately trying to create for Orestes the soiled image of his father and to retrieve Orestes's memories of himself as her child, Clytemnestra would save herself from the horror of her dreams, the serpent she gave birth to and suckled. Her plea for pity is to the son who should withhold his vengeance: "Stop! Stop! My son. Pay due respect, my child, / to this breast of mine, at which you sucked as a baby" (ll. 896–97). For Orestes, the journey home is to the place depicted by the chorus as "desolate hearth . . . ruined palace . . . / Now sunless, detested by all of mankind" (ll. 49–51). The heroic image of his father, the despicable image of his mother, the degraded sister—roles played in the setting of a corrupted home—these constitute in the personal dimension the complex of grounds that justify Orestes's desire for vengeance; and the drama is played on a grand stage of which they are all aware.

As opposed to the exterior animosity felt in Mrs. Alving's world, that grand stage defines and gives significance to the personal actions, the individual accomplishments, that are performed before the present world as for an audience, for audiences of the future in the sweep of history, and under the watchful eyes of the gods. On the personal level, Orestes is destined to take his place in history among the heroes of his house, and in the social dimension he is destined to complete his suffering in the *Eumenides,* effecting the transition to a new dispensation. His self-justifications include the personal, "Grief for my father" and the "oppressive ... want of wealth"; the social and historical, "that my fellow Argives, the world's most famous, / ... may not be subject to a pair of women"; and the metaphysical, "Apollo's orders" (ll. 300–304). The enslavement, corruption, and darkness of the house are the darkness of human wickedness, the depredation that has brought down "Royalty once viewed with respect ... the majesty of rulers" (l. 55): as human aberration, they might be corrected and transformed, whether by vengeance or justice. The darkness beyond is the darkness of mystery and hidden purposes, never to be seen into except in the illumination it produces, through the god of light, Apollo's oracle; through the revelations of dreams, messengers, signs. If the gods and the dead appear out of that darkness to plead, threaten, guide, or command, they reveal their understanding and will that are in relationship to and affecting the events of the present; but they also reveal, in their mysterious appearances and in the withholding of full knowledge, an encompassing reality that transcends human understanding and vision.

The human understanding that knows the limits of vision might devise images of another world, Olympus or Hades or Elysian Fields, but it knows the dangers and incompleteness of approaching those images and recognizes in the mortal dimension the necessary readiness to receive and interpret the import of signs. As in the world there is deception, alienation, and misunderstanding, what comes in moments of revelation from beyond is not simple and absolute truth but carries in its revelation the warning that it might be false, incomplete, ambiguous, dangerous. Hermes, a presiding spirit in the action, is messenger from the other world and intermediary, and he is shrewd and cunning. Electra asks him to proclaim, from "below the earth ... / to the nether gods ... / that they should listen now and heed my prayers" (ll. 124–26). The oracle has, in Orestes's account, threatened Orestes with nightmare torments, the horrors of "things from the earth ... / creatures that climb on the flesh with savage jaws, / gray leprosies ... / visitations of Furies ... / bright-eyed things in the darkness" (ll. 278–85), if he "should not pursue my father's murderers" (l. 273). If Apollo has declared that Orestes "should be wholly free of criminal guilt / if I did this" (ll. 1031–32), he has not prepared Orestes for the assault of the Furies. By imperfect human reasoning, if not doing the deed will bring the punishment of the furies, doing the deed should not result in that same punishment.

Building the edifice of history, in home and palace, in sites of conflict and dangerous journeys back and forth, is the making of meaning out of the past and the unknown that stretches beyond. In both dimensions, the supernatural and the human—which are setting for the drama of contemporary events as they articulate in history both past and future—the possibilities of truth and goodness, of light and understanding, of unity and continuity are expressions, through actions, against equally possible falsehood, darkness, and destruction. Meaningful action must be taken with risk, in the uncertainty of conditions and consequences, and action with risk is both interpretive and creative. Orestes's journey home is the anticipation of reunion and transformation, reunion of the humiliated outcast with others who will participate in the event and transformation of the disgraced world and, through the re-empowerment of union, those who are debilitated in it. The revelation of design and purpose through making connections, achieving a meeting of minds, reflects the uncertainty and tenuousness of connections between the human and supernatural worlds. Not knowing the potential of the other world nor that of others in this world, the depths of malice and destructiveness possible in human beings, is a repetition of not knowing the potential for destruction and disaster that might come from the earth, with its storms and fires.

The deeds to be performed in the drama of Orestes's return, the killing of Clytemnestra and Aegisthus, repeat that idea of destructiveness; but Orestes's capacity to act requires elaboration as well, making those deeds creative, transforming gross killing into ritual purgation, and performing them through invention. The creation of a regenerate world begins in images as signs and the showing of evidence, the appearance of things. The signs of Orestes that appear for Electra, the lock of hair he left on Agamemnon's tomb and his footprints, spontaneously stimulate a sense of mystery in her and in the Chorus, fear. She searches their mere appearance for meaning, seeing in the lock "news. Listen and share it with me" (l. 166). Uncertain of significance, divided in her inclinations to find reason for hope and augmentation of despair, she cannot choose whether to "fling it away" as her mother's hair or to accept it as reverence to her father's grave, to "share my mourning, / an ornament to this grave, an honor to our father" (ll. 197–200). Nor is the appearance of Orestes sufficient proof, nor his language identifying the person standing before her as Orestes. Her fear to hope and her mistrust of hope's evidence impede the process of discovery, and she considers the possibility that this person might be trying to trick or trap her,[11] revealing not the truth in what appears but undecipherable hidden purpose. Only with another showing of a sign is Electra convinced that this person is Orestes, this sign being more than resemblances in hair and footprints that would link her to Orestes, more than words can prove. The object is unique, a garment she wove and embroidered for Orestes, the thing itself rather than something like another.[12] The images that appear to Electra, apparently her chance discovery disassociated from overt purpose to reveal something to her, prompt her search for meaning; the image presented to her as proof of identity resolves the question. In the designs of the gods and human beings alike, it is necessary to persuade by giving evidence and proofs, both physical and verbal.

Orestes's displaying the bodies of Clytemnestra and Aegisthus to the representatives of the community is a spectacle showing his destruction of the desecrators of the house and the land. He is demonstrating, in his reformative actions, the making of world in conformity with the creative purposes of the transcendent dimension; reflecting those purposes, he is transforming and making purposeful earth's strife and destruction realized in Clytemnestra and Aegisthus. Opening the palace doors is a disclosure, a lighting of the interior of the home made dark by defilement. Orestes's illuminating act is mimetic, reflecting the illuminations generated from the other world,[13] and it is intended as unitive, an attempt at full disclosure, for an audience, of both the change he has effected and himself as agent of that change. His deed and his representation of it, however, are no more perfectly clear and indubitably true, needless of proof, than are the deeds and words of the gods.

Orestes must make of the community an audience for his demonstration, and this action reveals the idea connecting that stage audience with the play's audience, Athenian or modern. The interior of the royal palace becomes a stage for the tableau, and the audience of Argos, represented by the chorus of slaves, is prepared and eager to discover its own fate in the portrayal. As the edifice, the palace has stood for the coherence and continuity of the people, a centripetal force of the world's beneficent and sheltering architecture, and its degradation has contaminated the world and afflicted the welfare of the populace. The actual Athenian audience of Aeschylus would find itself in relationship to a historical past, not only literally in its connection to the lineage of Argos[14] but also in the thematic identification of shared values and powers represented in the event and displayed through the open palace doors. It would stand ready, with the people of Argos, to interpret the events, to see its history displayed in the ideas of home and palace, of kinship and shared fate, of strife and love, of degradation and exaltation. Orestes's exaggerated performance is calculated to persuade and move his immediate audience and to reach across to audiences of his future in a demonstration that individual action can be meaningful and efficacious in connecting and sustaining worlds.

The public and cosmic importance of his actions for a world, their historical range and significance, and his consciousness of their being played out toward the future, evoke in that world itself the idea of a *theatrum mundi* more directly and emphatically than does the closed and private world of *Ghosts,* in which to be seen is easily to be embarrassed. Mrs. Alving's sense of the odious comedy of life, her bitter feeling that her efforts to eradicate ghosts from the past have failed, does not look toward a future beyond the failed illusion that she could achieve happiness in isolation with her son. The play ends in the stasis of consternation and the dissolution of meaning, and the fourth wall protects her from any consciousness that what has happened to her makes a difference to the world beyond her little stage. To the extent that her efforts have been toward making of a world, would-be audiences are constituted with the taint of Manders and Engstrand's motives. Her private world wants the fourth wall, and the world outside goes on playing its game of fixed beliefs in collaboration with deceptions, Manders's eidolons locked in the malevolent embrace of Engstrand's deluding manipulations.

Orestes's performance for an audience is with the full consciousness that his actions are significant and of consequence, and his relationship to the world affected requires that he make that significance known to them. His world is aware that it is of the fabric of history, which is made not merely by conquest and bloodshed, building kingdoms and consecrating marriages, suffering disgrace and disaster, but by preserving and transforming events, keeping them in the memory, translating them into stories, oral and written records for the future. The Chorus has a ready store of knowledge about how "Earth breeds many horrors, / fearful and strange . . . / monsters, foes to humans . . . / lightning . . . / anger of stormwinds" (ll. 585–92); and it can tell stories challenging "everyone not flighty in mind" (l. 603) to recognize Clytemnestra in the idea of woman's dark passions and her capacity for evil deeds: in the stories of Althaea; of Scylla, in "legends of old" (l. 613); of the women of Lemnos. Told for rhetorical effect, as preparation for the action about to take place, these examples end with the challenge to an audience: "Am I not right in my choice of legends?" (l. 638). Events grounded in strife and danger, being memorialized and transformed into idea, confirm the significance of the past and give access to it; and likewise commemorating the present lifts it up into the design. Orestes's asking Agamemnon "What can I say, what can I do," to send "light and joy to compensate your darkness?" (ll. 316–19) expresses the desire to illuminate his own actions; and his assurance that "this mourning to honor the Atreid stock . . . / is likewise meant as an act of love and gratitude" (ll. 320–22) both confirms the efficacy of formal mourning and discloses that he wants his actions to become memorialized.

His presentation of the bodies of Clytemnestra and Aegisthus is an appeal to his audience to see the images, both the dead and himself the living; to understand and testify to the rightness of his acts; and to preserve them in memory for the future. He begins his apologia with an appeal to those present, "you that hear these evils, see this too— / the contrivance for tying up my unhappy father" (ll. 980–81); and ends it with a plea to the future: "I bid the Argives witness for me in the future / to Menelaus, how these ill deeds were wrought" (ll. 1040–41). The demonstration is directed toward the gods as well, a supernatural audience witnessing the events: in showing the robe to the audience, Orestes is aware of the god's watchfulness: "Spread it right out . . . / for the Father to see— / not my own father, but the sun, who beholds all things" (ll. 983–85). The visible sign, the bloodstained robe of Agamemnon, is elaborated with words to capture the imagination: it is a "net," a "bath curtain for a corpse," a "trap," a "crafty device" (ll. 998–1003). The robe, like the clothing he has shown to Electra, is the thing itself, is commanding evidence; but the identifying language as an act of preservation attempts to strengthen and assure the clothing's identification with the wearer and the wearer's connection to the viewer.

In presenting himself, Orestes similarly shows his anguished condition and gives voice to it: "I proclaim this to my friends; / I declare that I killed my mother with full justice" (ll. 1026–27). The image of himself is displayed in terms of ennobling purpose and his action as the transcendence of the moment. The enhanced drama of his defense again calls for the proof of vestment, and in attiring himself in the emblems of the suppliant he presents an image to be retained by the spectators. Going out, once more an outcast from home and community who must return to the oracle of Apollo, he is "a wanderer, exiled from this land / in life and death, leaving reports like these" (ll. 1042–43), leaving not only his words but also the words that will be generated as recollection of him. In contrast to the ending of *Ghosts*, where the stark brightness of the sun outside cannot penetrate the cave-like darkness of the home, the Chorus connects the opening of the home's darkness to horrible events of the past, relating them as the storm that has "blown on the house of our kings" (l. 1066): "Thyestes' piteous woes" (l. 1068); the death of Agamemnon. Anticipating not only the events of the *Eumenides* but also the meaningfulness of this play's action for the future, the Chorus bestows on those of the future the role of interpreter and appraiser. Thinking beyond the moment, it considers the uncertainty of meaning, whether Orestes is to be remembered as "a Savior . . . / or am I to call him a Doom?" (ll. 1073–74); and the irresolution establishes this action in the fabric of

4: IDEAS: HUMAN BEING AND WORLD 131

history, which must be held together and continually made as the drama of the future unfolds.

The uncertainty of ultimate meaning—the indeterminacy of human potential for benevolence and malevolence, the unpredictability of earth's operations, and the impenetrableness of the darkness out of which the supernatural appears—is manifest in the requisite circumspection dramatized in this play. There is hope for connection and conformability to the world beyond, a trust that engaging even in illusions as well as conflict the individual plays a meaningful and consequential role. The characters are aware that essential to life played as of dramatic consequence is the ground of illusion, both the illusoriness of appearances, which may or may not be what they seem and require clear perception, and the falsehood that is intended to deceive. Unsure of the gods and of others, their need is to demonstrate or to have revealed to them the essential truth that might rise out of the unreal or the fictional. Orestes's nurse, Cilissa, is advised by the chorus to accept herself as involved in falsehood in order to effect the ends of truth, to tell Aegisthus to come, as she was bid by Clytemnestra, but not to tell him that Clytemnestra asked that he come armed and with servants. She will thus become the messenger who justifies the aphoristic "a hidden plan depends for success on the messenger" (l. 773; [other translations heighten the epigrammatic quality in that the messenger straightens "crooked" language]). Orestes, too, makes a truth of fiction when he assumes for Clytemnestra the false identity of a messenger with news that Orestes is dead. The dissimulation, the concealment of his true identity, is an untruth that reveals the incipient truth, the Orestes who has not yet been realized, not yet become the suppliant who will then become the Orestes of legend. Aware that actions can dissipate into the surrounding oblivion, the indistinguishable and immemorial flow, the capable, potential hero affirms through the power of imaginative creation the significance of events in time and the possibility of securing, through bold extravagance, through invention, a place in them.

Ideas of a superior world—superior perhaps both in the sense of being above and beyond and of being secure, stable, safe, and lasting—involve the inferior world in its imperatives of purposefulness and endurance. If Mrs. Alving's world becomes a dark token of these ideals, assaulted by the gaze of intruders and deprived of a rightness beyond them, it nevertheless, as idea, remains accessible to the imagination and a motive in building a world. The stimulated imagination composes not only images of human beings exemplifying freedom, power, and heroism and images of ideal places represented in palaces, temples, and homes but also images of humiliation and destruction, horror and death. The "panicky rumors" Aegisthus attributes to the women, the imaginings that "leap in the air, to die away in nothing" (ll. 845–46), are like the dream imaginings of Clytemnestra and the terrifying images evoked by the oracle for Orestes and transmitted by him to others. The destroying images can incapacitate, can annihilate, and they affirm the inextricability of human beings from thrownness, from being on earth and in the world. They can activate as well the impetus to transform and transcend through the building of ideas and truths in architectural images and powerful images of accomplished human beings—saints, heroes, kings, madonnas, mothers, fathers, mentors, angels, muses.

Images of the world as detritus or delusion, as deteriorated in time, the "waste of lilies" imagined "as an inevitable knowledge," are no less generated and embellished by the intensifying, the histrionic activity of the imagination than are the congratulatory images of *bildung*. The feverish imagining that breaks forth in Aeschylus's characters intensifies their determination to make significance on a stage of time; the threatening images of bleak negation become oppressively dour in Mrs. Alving's awakening to the drama that shuts her in silence; the madness of Henry IV calls for the presentation of images whose shocks drive him further into his dark theater where sanity has proven madness. An audience apprehends those images as assertions of truths in the plays' worlds: truths of peril and destruction that dismay and debilitate; truths of construction that are retained from the past as truth against meaninglessness and destruction; and the audience receives those truths as if its own and bestows its own in finding itself reflected there. Between the truths of destitution and of enduring eidolons, the truths of building ambulate, ever generative and transformational. For the audience, the author of a world like that of Robert Altman's *Come Back to the Five and Dime Jimmy Dean, Jimmy Dean* remains among the ideas of beings and worlds—including the god of heaven and maker of this world—that come into play in the meeting and reflection of worlds. The film play reminds its world that the work of art is not timeless although, like those persistent reiterations, those enduring ideas of human beings and those of secure places that seem to resist time, it bears in its representation and in its relationship to the audience the ideas and illusions of secure endurance.

Reflection and Reunion: Altman's *Come Back to the Five and Dime Jimmy Dean, Jimmy Dean*

The stage is no *speculum* if the mirror is understood to reflect an image—an object—and to be an object for the audience—a subject.[15]

The mirror metaphor is objectionable, however, only if it retains the Platonic demarcation. Plato's mirror, the metaphorical trick of the artist's trade, gives him the power of false creation, the freedom to generate illusory fragments of the world. The mirror-wielder's versatility in manipulating the mirror, in reflecting "all there is in the heavens . . . yourself and the other animals and furniture and plants," qualifies the "marvel" as a maker of "appearances" (*Republic*, 10:395). Effecting mimesis is limited by the capabilities of the mirror. Its perspective is finite, reflecting only what it can catch, what it can "see," and its image might be interpreted as doubly removed from reality because the three dimensions of material existents are reduced to two; perspectival power of this lone mirror is inferior to the twin human mirrors that perceive depth, roundness, and distance. Deceptive as well, it involves a viewer in reversals of right and left, so that, for instance, using scissors before a mirror can be awkward. Because it is constrained by time and place, the gadget is furthermore limited. It can reflect only what is presented to it, what is visible from its position; and it can reflect only what is present here at this time. Even these limitations have a certain interest, however, when we consider that, given the artist's capability of movement, the mirror is ambulatory, its reflecting activity inexhaustible; and the fixing of the photograph and the "moving picture," both restricted in function like Plato's reflector, captures an image at a moment in time and preserves it into the future.[16]

This photographic power of retention implies a temporality not inherent in Plato's mirror: the ability to bring an image from the past forward into the present. For Gadamer the verbal text is like this mirror, in that "Language itself . . . has something speculative about it" (*Truth and Method*, 469), and "The word 'speculative' here refers to the mirror relation" (465). The relationship between the mirror and the reflection is structure and reciprocality, and this structure includes the observer, who becomes "speculative" as opposed to dogmatic (466). Gadamer argues that, engaged in this relationship, the speculative person is able to "reflect" on, to contemplate: "a thought is speculative if the relationship it asserts is not conceived as a quality unambiguously assigned to a subject, a property to a given thing, but must be thought of as a mirroring, in which the reflection is nothing but the pure appearance of what is reflected." This interpreter is receptive not merely to the surface reflection but to the revelation—the appearance—of structure, relationship, ideas, including the interpreter her/himself. Gadamer's interpretation of reflective relationships argues for both the legitimacy of "pure appearance" and the unpremeditated discovery possible in "speculation."

I have displayed Gadamer's thoughts about the mirror, at least in part, because they address structures essential to his discussion of how the play as theater relates to play as game and how the past comes into play. Although Gadamer discounts the spectator's "reflections" that are purely "aesthetic," his interpretation of the mirror suggests that the stage, too, engages a viewer who becomes "speculative" and therefore integral in the reflective structures. When the game becomes the play, the transformation into structure includes the audience. The audience apprehends, through the presentation, the play's "total mediation" (120) and becomes speculative, mirroring what appear as "the work's own possibilities of being" (118). In the play's transformation into structure, a represented past event retains that reflective structure in that an audience is essential in experiencing a world in the mirror that, like the photograph, presents a past and draws the audience into relationship with it and its world.

The photograph and the play present an image that in the very presentation raises the question of their devices, their tricks of representation like the "trick" of the photograph in Pirandello's *Henry IV*—the perhaps inconsequential, ephemeral, illusory, insubstantial images that are merely two-dimensional, even reversed. One of the problematic references to a world is to the reliability of the event of representation itself, its manifestation of the play's truth; as a work of art it displays the manners, codes, and techniques of drama, the assumptions of genre. The work of art is speculative in its existence as art rather than as science, history, or theology. Is *this* play merely one of those trivial entertainments like the shell game, in which the pleasure lies in our inability to win the prize of understanding? Does it elicit the ephemeral wonder of Plato's "marvel"? Or is it as drama revelatory of continuity and value? If we are to become spectators to a world, that world is not in the first place true and not necessarily verifiable. It is speculative, and we enter it in a mode of discovery. It might be experienced as a *theatrum mundi,* opening us up to the devices that instigate an adventure into the unknown. One such device, the play within the play, might prompt speculation on how Gadamer's ideas of the mirror and the play are pertinent to encountering worlds within worlds; and the premises of his theory might establish a point of departure for entering the worlds of such plays as Robert Altman's *Come Back to the Five and Dime Jimmy Dean, Jimmy Dean.*

I am not insensitive to the possible confusion in my using the word "play" to refer to a film, a stage play, and the activity we call playing, mere playfulness. I have begun in an unprofessional confusion of film and legitimate drama, with an intention to move toward recapturing the sense of wonder in experiencing the art Plato discounts as produced by those pantomimic gentlemen. A film is to be considered, if we cede the professional critic's aesthetic analysis of technique, an opportunity for participation like that event of the theater. I think Gadamer's moving in thought from play activity to drama as spectacle and ritual carries along—into the serious—the idea of play as entertainment and amusement. The popularity of films with all sorts of audiences keeps the idea of play open to the possibilities of speculation and transformation in the self-presenting of that world and the interdependence of authors, audiences, and worlds.

In talking about Altman's film play I do not mean to detract from the stage play written by Ed Graczyk, without whom this film could not exist. I assume him to be an author mirrored in the author I call Altman, both being particular manifestations of the idea of the author, whether thought of as standing beyond the range of the camera in the film or writing the text of the play. Since I am concerned with the film as a "text" being "read," my ideas generate from and incorporate images and ideas particular to the film as well as images and ideas attributable to the author Graczyk.[17] This sense of collaboration might lead to a consideration of both similarities and differences between Altman's film and Graczyk's play. For instance, a felt difference for me involves structure. The film's continuous action evokes a sense of structural division when Edna Louise enters in her party dress to a deserted scene, producing a poignant moment of stillness and emptiness of the "stage." In the play she enters after the second act has begun, evoking immediate responses from others.[18]

Altman's film engages the audience in a past event, a celebration taking place in 1975, and that celebration recalls events of twenty years earlier. The world of 1955 is revealed by means of the stage-within-the-stage device, a mirror that represents past events contained within a film that presents an action to the audience. Evoking the past, although superficially a matter of the fan club's reunion, transforms the puerile rite of hero worship into spiritual confrontation. Haunted by ghostly presences, the participants are challenged to see more, to experience recognition, and to undergo transformation.

The camera is not simply Plato's mirror, not a mere mechanical recorder of a primary dimension (the world of the reunion) and an inner dimension (the past world that appears in the mirror); nor is that mirror a mere reflector revealing literal presences of its world of the past. To characterize the "camera" is to recall the mobility of Plato's artist, whose ability to reflect is identified with his device. So considered, the camera not only synecdochically incarnates the artist but also represents what it makes visible; we are not given the camera but the image: the drama on film is the text we read. Both the film and the mirror yield the appearance of a world, but ideas of their powers are more adequately represented by Gadamer's mirror than by the surface of Plato's reflector. They are implicated in their appearances. The camera moves within the five and dime, tracking, panning, cutting; revealing more than the actions and appearances of characters in this setting. It reveals the mirror's world, which is a reversed image of the five and dime the audience sees. It reveals, too, in the present, what is not there for all the characters. While Mona is puzzling over Joanne's identity, Joanne stands looking out the door and the image of Joe appears superimposed on Joanne's, Joe already having appeared to Mona in the mirror. Facing us, he raises his left hand to his cheek, and when Joanne turns back to us she has duplicated the gesture with her right hand. Joe, of the mirror world but not in it, and Joanne, of this other dimension, are each an identity, a self; and both are reflections of one another. If the mirror gives that image of Joe to Mona, it is not simply an artifice for revealing that other world to the audience. It not only elicits the other dimension but also presents an image to a character in the present action. Such facility, on the parts of both the camera and the mirror, is engaging, and the observer experiences "the real mystery of a reflection" in "the intangibility of the image" (*Truth and Method*, 466). When such representation engages memory and the past has a seeming presence, the audience is commissioned to see beyond the moment's representation, to realize its role as an interpreter capable, in an activity of the imagination, of seeing more than the present.

As Mona warrants her idealization of James Dean by allusion to Christ, the audience is empowered to see the image of Mona reflected against other remarkable images from the past and to draw relationships between her world and the worlds of those others. Mona's creation of her role plays toward identification with the Mother of God; she was, she says, "chosen to bring the son of James Dean into the world." Her self-glorification is not unseen by the others—Joanne calls her the "Virgin Mona"—but like the audience they are aware of her fragility in that compulsive withdrawal into illusion. Like Laura in Tennessee Williams's *The Glass Menagerie*, she cannot face the unameliorated reality of her world: the nature of her son Jimmy Dean, the mere humanity of the son's father, the unglamorous and desiccated stage of her life, her all but invisible walk-on in *Giant*. As Laura creates and retreats into her little world of glass, Mona erects a shrine to her god and adorns it with relics reclaimed on holy pilgrimages. For both Laura and Mona, it is better to play the artist and construct a world of illusion than to contend with intractable people and events in a disappointing and changeable world. In their fragilities the debilitated Mona and Laura reflect the idea of the vulnerable female, the innocent Eve, the madonna who must be elevated and shielded.

Attuned to such ideas and images that persist from its past, an audience can relate such an idealized image to Petrarch's Laura but also to the frail Hedvig in Ibsen's *The Wild Duck*. Hedvig, like Williams's Laura, is physically weak—Laura is crippled and Hedvig is going blind—and Mona's asthma is associated with her "premonition of death, like James Dean has." Hedvig's world of illusion is created and sustained by the family, who themselves, according to Gregers Werle, live in a world of illusion. Her crippled duck (like its benefactress debilitated) and its attic are the refuge to which vulnerable characters retreat; like Laura and Mona, Hedvig escapes into a world of illusion from a world of illusions. For all of them, the world of actuality is stained not only by harsh reality but also by the illusions of others. Gina and Hjalmar in *The Wild Duck* indulge in what Gregers deplores as self-delusion; Amanda in *The Glass Menagerie* imposes her fancies on her children; Juanita and Sissy counter Mona's illusive versions of reality with their own.[19] The real world has held up to Mona, and her fellow dreamers, its cherished counterworld that is both a reproach and a mirror. It is not only a true reflection of the impulse to construct a privileged estate but also a commentary on the fragility of the dream world. The power of allusion lies, for the characters as well as for the playwright and the audience, in its evocation of ostensibly puissant validating images. For Mona they are incorporated uncritically into the materials of her fabrication; for the audience they announce their appeal and call for interpretation.

The past, which is invoked by the characters and the play itself, is for the audience a reservoir of meaning, an access to understanding continuity and significance. As Mona recalls figures from the past who serve as commentary on her assumption of role, who establish a reciprocality of significance, the play generates ideas about identity, about sex—male and female identities—about doubling and duality (and concomitantly the pejoration of doubling, duplicity). Those ideas too raise questions about origin and foundation. The fact that there are no men at the reunion is essential to the action. The only male in the fan club being Joe, the reunion is a celebration by women, and the absent male is, like the female figures alluded to, an icon to be interpreted. In Sissy's eyes, Lester T. was an ideal lover and husband, sexually potent and responsive to her allure, her "boobs." She preserves her idea of his devotion to her by a fiction, and Joanne, exposing a contradictory image of him, reveals that he has abandoned Sissy, that he is not working in Arabia but in Kansas City. Juanita's Sidney, too, was protected, Juanita having "tried to hide him from God" by concealing his true nature in pious attire. He was, however, in Joanne's reconstruction, merely human, a drunk. Joanne has already told Juanita that when she used to find him drunk he was "hiding from you, Juanita, and God." Mona has safeguarded Jimmy Dean from the world by keeping him a child, an innocent, and Sissy assumes Joanne's function in exposing Mona's "lie." According to her, Mona has not taken the boy to "one goddam doctor," and the comic books he reads are girlie magazines, provided by Sissy; he is not only a man but one who satisfies Sissy's idea of manhood.

The men are not finally salvageable from mortality except by falsification, by the construction of an idealized image. James Dean, the god of the disciples, is the perfected image, and Stella Mae's pornographic picture of him is for Mona a sacrilege. Since Joe's love for Mona was merely human, his question whether she could "ever love me like you love him" failed to displace James Dean, to whom Mona was "promised." Mona's shrine to James Dean, with his photograph centrally displayed, and Juanita's picture of Jesus Christ are competing images of godhood, as Juanita's gospel music competes with Sissy's earthy country ballads. God vies with god; mere mortal strives against god and with human being. It is understandable that Joe's competition with James Dean for Mona's affection has ended in Joe's defeat. The idea of the human as reflecting, imitating, or incarnating god derives from old embedded images of god the powerful, the savior, the good. The idea is preserved both in fragmented appearances of attributes in individual males and in abstracted remembrances of perfection, and Mona's idealization and memory have overpowered Joe's mere human goodness.

If ancient concepts of god the omnipotent are implicit in the women's idealizations, the idea of god the omniscient is similarly understood; for instance, in Juanita's having tried to hide Sidney from God—as she finally admits along with her admission that Joanne's interpretation of Sidney is true. Mona's god, too, is watching, a point made in the irreverent song of the disciples, "The eyes of James Dean are upon us," and in Mona's continuing to gather relics for her shrine. God's faculty of perception is distributed as well, among the women who reflect his attributes, in the idea of seeing, not only in their deficiency of vision, their lack of insight about themselves, but also in their need to know all, their endeavors to see—even when what they see is an illusion. Their studying the picture of themselves in order to discover Joanne's identity is a comic representation of the hunger for knowledge, and Mona's slow, haunted perusal of Joanne expresses the gravity of that need. Mona's elegiac refrain, "deceiving to the eye," is a pathetic and incipient recognition on her part of the weakness of her sight and the illusoriness of her visions. When Joanne appears and seems to see with preternatural clarity, asking whether Mona is "the mother of his son," she reveals that she has read the faded signs announcing the child and elicits Mona's observation that she "must have unusual eyesight."

Joanne's mysterious appearance and the others' sustained efforts to discover her identity install the game of discovery in the play, the game that expresses the fundamental need for transcendental knowledge: of others, self, world, and reality. The play is a drama of discovery and, like the characters, the audience is engaged in the play of seeing and understanding. The need to know can be satisfied casually in the apprehension of the image or the dramatic representation, in the receptivity of the viewer to what the mirror represents; and indeed there is a need to see clearly what is thus given, to read the text. But the audience's engagement is in the game the characters play, not only in their scrutinizing the picture of the group (of 1955) hoping for recognition but also in the play of imagination, in their becoming reflective, negotiating toward the revelation of meaning and the establishment of understanding.

The dialectic of discovery involves the interpreters in a relationship with an image that not only represents the meaning and value to be discovered but also defers to the structure of relationship thus established. The photographs of James Dean are such an image, Stella Mae's picture of him contradicting Mona's and therefore accenting the complicity of assumptions—what Gadamer calls "prejudice"—in interpretation.[20] Essential images thus connecting the interpreter with the world interpreted are the photograph of the group, the world of the past represented in the mirror, and the moving picture, the "outer" world of the "stage" the audience is studying. Those images are not necessarily genuine and simply "true," however, a circumstance any interpreter instinctively understands. Images are always potentially illusory, grounded in the condition Husserl recognizes as a need for seeing clearly—by going back to the things themselves and by bracketing assumptions, putting them out of play. The Cartesian idealist's certainties Husserl had to contend with began in the distrust of eikastic knowledge, for instance the unreliability of Plato's objects that are distorted when seen in water (*Republic*, 10:402). E. H. Gombrich's mirror is deceiving: we know (or if we do not know we can experiment and learn) that if we trace our image on a mirror "clouded by steam" and step back it will be half-size; yet we continue to see our image in that mirror as life-size (*Art and Illusion*, 6). Consequently, seeing genuinely entails the possibility of seeing accurately that is only possible in the play of illusions.

We know, however, that human artifacts and works of art are created and that we might be doubly vulnerable to illusion in our engagement with the play, as in experiencing trompe l'oeil painting. Mona is aware of the power of illusion in art, recognizing that the facade of Reata, the now-crumbled stage set, was "deceiving to the eye." Her desire for the dream, however, rationalizes the illusoriness as "the way they do things in the movies." In the past action, when she used the expression "deceiving to the eye" concerning the set, she declared that "it is real." Understanding the illusoriness of the world created and represented in the stage set, Mona has been nevertheless driven to exalt and detemporalize it. She insisted that she, Sissy, and Joe could escape their barren world to buy Reata and live there in their glass menagerie or attic forest. Although her constrained recognition does not result in the reversal Sissy experiences, she can in the end declare that, along with other illusions, the god she worshiped was/is, like art, an illusion. When she appears in the mirror at the end of the film, the illusion that has faded is the god she thought was perfection incarnate, and now she declares James Dean himself to have been "deceiving to the eye."

Perhaps even more important and more problematical in experiencing such created images is the knowledge we have of an agent or agents who produced the images—the artist. No uncomplicated *speculum,* this mirror carries in its appearance, as constituent of its truth, the maker of the image. If the photograph of the group seems to be a simple mirror, it is complicated in the reflection of it in the two worlds, and those reflections seem to be produced by a Platonic artist in that reflections produce reversed images. Although it is not requisite that we accept Plato's implications about the artist, it remains possible that such a maker is a charlatan, a deceiver, a trifler producing that unreliable image. The idea of the artist potentially incorporates, however, those attributes that the characters seem to reflect, even if fragmentarily, and that we recognize as godlike. Omniscience and omnipotence in god might be just that: absolute power and vision/knowledge. Ordinary human beings might project those powers onto an idealized human being while mirroring the traces of those attributes in their games of seeing and controlling. The author/director/artist is similarly a projection, whether idealized as omnipotent and omniscient in governing his little world; conceptualized as perhaps a supreme craftsman; or, among other possibilities, suspected to be a manipulator of images to no avail, maneuvering us in the shell game we should not hope to win. If the audience is to claim the right to reflect those attributes and to play the game of knowledge and self-determination, which has not yet been determined to be a shell game, the effort to interpret will necessitate both imaginative openness to the not-yet-discovered and seeing with clear vision.

As I have tried to suggest, mirroring—in photograph, mirror, or film—engages the audience speculatively with the idea of the mirror: the idea is there in the film's moving from the literal world of the characters' present into the mirror, which represents their past world. The camera has the power to move into that world of the past and thus to suspend the mirror's identity as reflecting agent. Images from the past world can appear in the present, as when Joe appears superimposed on Joanne. The problematical appearance in this superimposition raises the question: why, in this clearly significant doubling, does Joe raise his left hand to his bloody face while Joanne, as she turns around, raises her right? Surely, if this phenomenon were accidental, without meaning, images inverting the right and the left would not recur and seem to announce their significance as mirror reversals. There will always remain the possibility, of course, that there is no significance, that such inversions are merely accidental consequences in filming a scene, and that there is evoked no idea of an author as craftsman or authority controlling these images. Another image that in itself might be unremarkable, however, seems to point up that inversion and to support considering its significance. The photograph of the fan club in their new red jackets, brought out to aid in identifying Joanne, shows Joe and Sissy on the right. When the group appears in the mirror, with the Mona of the present facing us in front of the mirror, studying the photograph and remembering the past, the image is reversed, with Joe and Sissy on the left. It seems unlikely that a director would strive for naturalistic representation in this doubling, aiming merely to give the audience a verisimilitudinous image of what happens when images are reflected. Besides, precise calculations on the part of the audience would be necessary for this interpretation, the reversal being explainable by taking into account not only the photograph and the mirror, for the audience, but also the mirror as reflector of the group in the past. Rather than pursue this possible explanation, I suggest that the reversal seems to represent the idea of the mirror, its reversals, and the specific reversal of the right and the left, which would lead us back to the doubled image of Joe/Joanne and forward to the end of the play, where we see Mona, Sissy, and Joanne in the mirror—in that order from our left to our right.

Joanne returns to the five and dime on this day of the reunion, appearing mysteriously and instigating those protracted efforts to discover her identity. In pursuing this activity with the characters, the audience might well be led to consider the doubling and Joanne's transformation as central to interpretation. Joanne, in control of the situation and enjoying the power that comes of having secret knowledge, toys with the others, even after she has been identified as Joe. Sissy having asked Joe to take off his wig, Juanita refers to Joanne as "he," and Joanne responds, "Unlike all of you, I have undergone a change." The doubling of identity and the idea of transformation recall received interpretations of human nature, notably Carl Gustav Jung's psychology. Repeating patterns embedded in a collective unconscious, individuals manifest the schismatic personality that fortifies the female or the male component, the anima or the animus. Consequent to this divorce, the individual is needful of a reunion, a meeting with the suppressed element of self. To the extent that this other is repudiated, it might appear as does the Jungian shadow, who like a ghost can frighten, can produce a spontaneous rejection.

Joanne induces this reaction in Juanita, who is the most obdurate of the group, and even though Juanita experiences recognition concerning Sidney and to some extent herself she refuses to acknowledge Joanne as Joe, rejecting Joanne's hand (echoing Mona's rejection of Joe), and pointedly calling her "Miss." While the denial of the shadow leaves Juanita still in need of transformation, Sissy's calling Joanne Joe—"you son of a bitch, can I buy you a drink?"—is merely one sign not only of her having recognized herself as well as Lester T. but also of her having accepted the full identity, including the sexuality, of Joe/Joanne. Joanne might consequently, in a Jungian interpretation, represent the integrated persona, the reunion of male and female. If recognized as a shadow, she would arouse the memories of the other characters, not only the happy recollections of their youth and hopefulness but also the dark events that involved brutality and betrayal, events that lie deeper than the ostensible reason for the reunion, the lamentable and merely accidental death of James Dean.

These darker events, coupled with Joanne's appearing as a stranger in this world, might allude to other possible and perhaps more illuminating referents. Sissy, Mona, and Juanita have maintained, however tenuously, a semblance of order in the daily compromises they make in order to abide as a group, and the drama is about not only the spiritual conditions of the individual and the community but also the interrelatedness of the one and the group. The fan club engages in a communal return to the past, but the image of the past that appears, even before the appearance of Joanne, comes and troubles rather than satisfies their nostalgia. Joanne's intrusion is not only mysterious— inciting interpretation by the others—but also disruptive, causing resistance in them, as is the coming of Dionysus in Euripides's *The Bacchae*. The fact that the action concerns a group of women celebrating a god and at the same time being challenged to undergo a transformation strongly suggests an allusion to Dionysian rites (and perhaps to the origins of tragedy). Their opportunity for liberation, finally, the uncovering of the truth, is effected through the wine of Bacchus (in actuality beer and hard liquor), through Dionysian intoxication. If the obvious allusions to Christ as a counterpart of the idealized movie star and to the Virgin Mary as Mona's warrant for her illusions illuminate the play's ironic meaning in the discrepancies, the meaning in the Dionysian rite reveals a substantial and serious need for the dread interloper who approaches from the past.

As Friedrich Nietzsche characterizes the present need, it is founded in the "terrible witches' brew concocted of lust and cruelty [that] has lost all power under the new conditions."[21] The past is indeed not a matter of neutralized events from which we are liberated but rather advances into the present in the "Dionysiac reveler," who "seems still to hark back (as the medicinal drug harks back to the deadly poison) to the days" before pain and anguish were submerged in the Apollonian dream of majesty. "For now," in the Dionysian rite, "in every exuberant joy there is heard an undertone of terror, or else a wistful lament over an irrecoverable loss." These Maenads in the film have forgotten themselves and anticipate the celebration as a happy reunion for the sake of "the wistful lament over an irrecoverable loss." What they discover in the intrusion of the past is the "undertone of terror," the cruelty and brutality they have disavowed.

In the past Joe's sexual duality had released the alien, the iconoclastic, the dangerous in a world controlled by representatives of the Apollonian, whose maintenance of values presumed the exclusion or the suppression of the Dionysian. Sidney not only hid his own undernature from the world but also constructed an idealized image of himself. His festivities were disguised as pious meetings, he being an upright official in the church, and he was mayor at the time the baby Jimmy Dean was on display to the "swarms" who came to see the child. "Apollo's majestic rejection of all license," his "proud, imposing image" (*Birth of Tragedy,* 26), militated against Joe's being one of the McGuire sisters, and when Joe was brutalized, with the "whole town" in attendance, Sidney was there.

Since Joanne's appearance is mysterious, her motives clouded, her reason for attending the reunion is surely not satisfactorily explained in her claim that she has "as much right to return to this reunion as anybody"; she might have a complex of motives, ranging from curiosity or self-justification to vengeance or the desire to revive feelings for Mona, perhaps to wake Mona from her dream. She seems to embody the ambiguous motives, both the benevolent and the destructive, of Euripides' Bacchus, as for instance when she attempts to terminate the story of Lester T., warning Sissy that she might regret hearing more. As Joanne's actions reveal, her function, like that of Dionysus, is to affect the world of Apollonian illusion by shattering the dream, which is the others' "cadaverous and ghostly" sanity (*Birth of Tragedy*, 23). If the apparent sanity of waking reality is an illusion and the principle of reality appears from another dimension, an "outside" world, then the world is indeed a stage or a dream. Joanne comes as an emissary of a larger landscape and as a voice from the past that, mirroring the past, reveals its impact on and continued investment in the present.

Nietzsche not only establishes such a relationship in the mission of Dionysus to the Apollonian world but also envisions that world itself as "aesthetic product," as theater, poem, architectural work. The historical world thus conceived would situate itself within a larger dimension and project a metaphysical status to the world beyond. Apprehension of or conformance to that reality beyond would redeem the artist from the subjective. "To the extent that the subject is an artist he is already delivered from individual will and has become a medium through which the True Subject celebrates His redemption in illusion" (41). The world is a stage, an illusion, a mirror, a dream; and it is created by the supreme artist.[22] Considering Nietzsche's depiction of this creator, the idea of god again appears, echoing Plato's idea of god the artist of the ideal bed. The idea of god remains, then, not only in traditional theological constructs or in individuals idealized in conformance with venerable models—that is, ideas of god's omniscience, omnipotence, creativity, and goodness instantiated in characters in the world of the play—but also in the idea of the artist of the play we experience.

The structure of relationship between this play and its artist mirrors the structure of our *theatrum mundi* and the world beyond, and the artist of the microcosm relates likewise to the creator of the world. For Nietzsche, "Only as the genius in the act of creation merges with the primal architect of the cosmos can he truly know something of the eternal essence of art. . . . He is at once subject and object, poet, actor, and audience" (42). If both Nietzsche and Gadamer argue for a suspension of the discrete subjectivity of the individual, the observable and dramatic difference in their designs is that whereas Nietzsche adopts the established model of a male god as the architect of the world, Gadamer emphasizes the multiple and temporal reflective activities of mirroring, displacing the powerful image of the artist. Nietzsche's extrapolation, however, anticipates Gadamer's freeing the activity from the image of a cosmic Subject. Whether ontological or metaphorical, Nietzsche's representation of god as artist, as creator of what we think is the real world, would recommend understanding all individuals and actions as actors and performances, including the figures of author and audience. Nietzsche's artist not only "merges with the primal architect of the cosmos" but also *becomes* "subject and object, poet, actor, and audience" in a manifold of reduplications. The multiple reflections for Gadamer are essentially temporal. The structures of relationship among characters, actors, audiences, playwrights, and worlds exist in the event of the play, and it both mirrors what appears as a truth and, like the game, does not privilege any of the participants. The author functions in this manifold as does the audience, and the idea of god that appears through the artist remains merely an idea of potentiality, uncertain and unresolved among other possible views of the artist, including that of the Platonic magician. The creator of a world is assumed to have power and vision; to design and determine as well as to observe it. But the truth represented in the created world might reflect on the failure or inadequacy of God and His instantiations. As the women in this play long for and seek the absent male, their hero or god, the only male who remains with them at first appears to be disguised as a woman and then is recognized as transformed, as having become woman. The Artist Himself might withdraw, refuse self-disclosure, appear transformed—as trickster, deceiver, challenger, destroyer of values; might in effect manifest the Dionysian not only in the world of the work but also in the image of the artist her/himself.

Such an artist might appear innocuous, at first touching lightly and negligently the objects and people in the five and dime, as does Joanne, with an apparent disinterest that betrays more than idle curiosity. The light touch of the camera's opening moves becomes, like Joanne's, interested and caring. Joanne does reflect characteristics of the artist in that she knows and sees more of the action being played than do the others, and in that she directs actions. She promulgates stories that call up the past and reflect on the present action—for the direct benefit of Juanita, Sissy, and Mona in that their versions of reality are challenged—and she serves as playwright or director in correcting the stories they tell. If her initial deception leads to painful disclosures, they are not intended to produce alienation and disillusion but restoration, reunion. Expressing sympathy for Mona, whose fictions about her son and about her having been "chosen to bring the son of James Dean into the world" have been shattered, Joanne embraces her and says, "I chose you, Mona. I loved you." Although Sissy is finally the only one capable of accepting herself and Joanne, Joanne has offered everyone an opportunity to see and to change—everyone except Edna

Louise, the simple and uncontaminated type of the virgin mother, to whom Joanne lovingly says, "You glow."

Incomplete though it is, the reunion—of self with the self, the other, and the community—echoes Nietzsche's "intense throng of Dionysiac revelers" (23) in the drunkenness that liberates, in the cruel laughter that greets the revelations of secret fantasies. The limited success of Joanne's ministrations implies that, beyond the allusion to the Dionysian motive, the artist of this play sees the *theatrum mundi* as darker and more problematical than that potentially regenerate world of Nietzsche. Nietzsche's "bond between man and man" appears fragile here, the capacity for waking from the dream being limited. After the others have gone away, Mona's refusal to become "reconciled," to become "actually at one" with Joanne and Sissy could hardly be considered a sign of "universal harmony" or of "nature itself" entering "to celebrate the reconciliation with her prodigal son, man." An artist of the darker vision, this creator has not eluded the sounds of mockery and cruelty echoing from the past. Yet the outcome of the action is an affirmation of the need for laughter, not only the derisiveness of iconoclastic and curative laughter but also the genial laughter of forgiveness in reunion and celebration.

Joanne's story about Lester T., a painful revelation that he did not adore Sissy, is punctuated with laughter and ends with Lester T.'s crying because Joanne was laughing; Joanne's telling of it ends in laughter and Sissy's question, "This is not fun is it?" It is after the harsh laughter has died out and the gentle laughter prevails that Mona is brought near to reconciliation and falters. We can hear, however, echoes of the beneficial laughter Nietzsche invokes in his "Critical Backward Glance": in learning "the art of terrestrial comfort" the student of Nietzsche will, "with a peal of laughter, send all metaphysical palliatives packing" (15). This play in its tentative realization of laughter demonstrates that "terrestrial comfort" is indeed terrestrial, temporal, momentary resolution. Since the past is not abolished, laughter sends "all metaphysical palliatives packing," including Nietzsche's "True Subject," the author and god of all. Since the sojourning author of the present, restricted to a moment in time, lives under no divine aegis, the image of the artist is realized as that of a lesser god. This artist, like Joanne, tells a story that is not assured to be universally redemptive.

The tricks of the camera and the mirror are appropriate for the artist who like Joanne makes an unassuming beginning, the artist who is appropriately unassuming in a world that is disintegrating as his camera records it. The duplications and inversions achieved by these reflectors raise questions that grow progressively more serious and culminate in the problem of an ending. If reunion is desirable for his recalcitrant characters, the merely human artist, without willing access to a genuine beatific vision, must rely on his devices—the camera, the mirror. What happens in the final scene with Sissy, Mona, and Joanne reveals the lesser—the less assured and less powerful—artist at work, the type Aristotle identifies as one who, unable to resolve his plot, resorts to the deus ex machina. The conflict has ended with Sissy and Joanne alone in the five and dime, Mona having retreated into the rear of the store. She has tried to join in the laughter but has been unable to. As Joanne and Sissy stand before the mirror, Mona appears in it—not behind them and the camera, reflected in the mirror, but "inside" the mirror. Joanne, seeing Mona, points toward her in the mirror and tells Sissy to look at her. Mona declares, "Deceiving to the eye, that's what he was"; and Sissy, apparently untroubled by Mona's ghostly manifestation, the discrepancy in the mirror's mysterious power, suggests that they play the McGuire sisters. While Sissy, still in the present, goes to the juke box, Joanne appears in the mirror with Mona, who is wearing the red fan club jacket thrown over her shoulders. When Joanne goes to fetch Sissy into the mirror, the camera follows them in. While they are singing "Sincerely," the camera pulls out of the mirror and there is no mirror: the illusion of a present world has decayed and become past.

The strange trick of the camera and the disappearing act of the mirror resolve the action in irresolution, and the trio fade before the audience's eyes, like ghosts of a present action that has moved into the past. When the camera pulls back and the credits begin to appear, it moves into the devastated rear of the five and dime, moves about haunting the ghost of a world, moves toward the sunlight, and finally backs into the rear. Its tracking of characters that come in out of the sunlight has become a stalking of the haunted place, as the protagonist in Henry James's "The Jolly Corner" creates metaphysical disquiet by an inversion, by becoming the stalker of the ghost, by changing places with him. In the play's appearances, the mirror and the camera have displayed the freedom of the imagination to range, to produce and retain images, to control and arrange; and in this return to the past for reunion Aristotelian probability has been further suspended. The machines of the god, the artist god synecdochically in the machine, are the camera and the mirror, and they take the present action into the past only to affirm its necessary entailment in the past of the audience.

In this mysterious improbability of reunion in the deceiving mirror the audience is once again reminded of the mirror's inversion of right and left—in fact imitates the inversion, in that Sissy's right is the audience's left. Sissy, standing in the middle, places Mona on her "ever-popular right hand side" and Joanne on her left. Sissy has assumed the role of the artist in directing this performance, in placing, assigning, arranging. In her contrivance the audience might well discount, again, the possible motive of verisimilitude, the superficial placement of each according to her identity as one of the McGuire sisters. The "ever-popular right hand side" is the side of rectitude, orthodoxy, adherence to established order, the appropriate placement of the unregenerate dreamer. Even though Mona, like Juanita, has been brought to incomplete recognition and acceptance, her Apollonian dream persists, as evidenced in her withdrawal and reappearance in the mirror, in the safety of her attic or glass menagerie. Joanne and Sissy's approach to her, a startling eventuality, is possible only as a return into the world of the past, where Mona reigned as eternal virgin mother. Joanne, the instigator of discovery and transformation, is appropriately placed on Sissy's left, since she is the sinister, the disruptive, the mysterious Dionysian stranger. This earth-bound trinity represents the confluence of the Apollonian and the Dionysian, the perishable merger of contrary principles that centers the transformed dreamer, the would-be star of the Ice Capades whose earthiness made her vulnerable to the destroyer of dreams.

This tenuous union, the forced happy ending that announces the improbability and at the same time the necessity of laughter, the improbability of salvation except as the artist devises it, is reflected in the capacity of the camera to enter the mirror and suspend its separate identity. This complicity has been established in the superimposed images of Joe and Joanne, their right and left hands bespeaking identity, and in the inversions of the group in the mirror and film representations. Before its own frantic and solitary searching (bereft of others to reflect but not an audience) in the decaying world of the five and dime, the camera takes its audience on a final journey into that past world and returns, fulfilling the cyclical design. Placing the celebrants in that fragile construct, it withdraws like Mona into the world of the five and dime, and its retreat is back into an illusory world that has changed horribly. Like the *theatrum mundi* set of *Giant,* the illusory world that has yielded only relics for Mona, the five and dime of the present action has suffered the depredations of time, seeming to be still undergoing accelerated change as the camera with care and lingering attention moves over it. The relics consist of the tattered decorations of the reunion, the crumbling set of the five and dime, and in a corner the relic of Sissy's dream, the newspaper announcing another coming, the Ice Capades. As relics, they announce the decay of a cherished world and the disappointment of human wishes; and in the presentation they maintain the power of relics to involve and to move.

The audience, as it is being released into its own world by the appearance of the credits, is yet not freed from the attraction of the past, of the happy reunion dissolving into the past. The camera ensconces the trio in a happy image of their past, and transforms the image of its world, the event of reunion, into a past for the audience. Ever mobile, moving toward the inviting front door and the painfully sunlit exterior world, it pulls back into the dark interior, into the dark attic of its devising—perhaps recognizable even as the eikastic dark of Plato's cave—and proclaims the artist's kinship with Mona, the artist of illusions. In our "intense longing for illusion" and in our recognizing the primordial "need of rapt vision and delightful illusion," we might with Nietzsche come to see that "we ourselves are the very stuff of such illusions" (32–33). This artist shows us, however, not the ultimate "radiant vision of pure delight" but both the possibility of laughter and the "reflection of original pain, the sole ground of being: 'illusion' here is a reflection of eternal contradiction, begetter of all things." In citing Nietzsche here I have reversed his image of movement from originary pain to radiant vision, thinking to echo the artist who brings us back down to the earth, to origins, to the undeniable condition of a present that cannot shake itself free of the past. The artist of the earth affirms the contradictory needs for illusion and reality, the improbable possibility of laughter, and the potential for discovery, transformation, and reunion.

The reunion of *Come Back to the Five and Dime Jimmy Dean, Jimmy Dean* is a manifold of reunions—of the fan club, of the self, of worlds, of past and present, of illusion and reality, of art and artist and audience. But it is not a reunion that establishes a final unity or a metaphysical vision. It is rather a tentative excursion that allows for change, the anticipation in Gadamer's *Bildung,* rather than what Gadamer describes as the Hegelian "completion through the movement of alienation and appropriation in a complete mastery of substance, in the dissolution of all concrete being, reached only in the absolute knowledge of philosophy" (*Truth and Method,* 15). Growth and development—"formation," a word that yields "transformation"—entail the idea that for Gadamer is implicit in the root of *Bildung: Bild,* image or picture. "In Bildung there is Bild [11].... [T]he general characteristic of Bildung [is] keeping oneself open to what is other—to other, more universal points of view" (17).

My exploration of the mirror or photographic/cinematic image has entertained the play of images as being both concrete as appearance and ideal as paragon; both the directly perceived and the represented.

The play as representation is both mirror and its own truth. As the characters confront images and ideas, the audience reflects that engagement in that the play, like the written text, is not only image and interpretation for the audience but also revelation of the play's truth. *Bildung* is not then a matter of traveling a road to a destination but rather a tracing of Heidegger's hermeneutic circle, a process of discovery that leads back to union with self and with others. "To recognize one's own in the alien, to become at home in it, is the basic movement of spirit, whose being consists only in returning to itself from what is other" (*Truth and Method*, 14). This movement might be thought of as Nietzsche's reconciliation of the human to nature, "nature's reconciliation with her prodigal son, man," in the advent of the Dionysian (*Birth of Tragedy*, 23), but it might be seen more acutely as Gadamer's reunion.[23] Through the risk of departure from the familiar and predictable and the journey into the alien or strange, with the consequent depreciation and humbling of the autonomous self, the voyager might discover both the authenticity of the alien other and the possibility of an enriched self.

The outcome for the celebrants of a reunion, the participants brought together in the mirror or in the theater, is a possible transformation of relationship to oneself, to others, and to the world. Since Altman the artist of the mirror expresses this truth as tentative and uncertain, his images being "deceiving to the eye," the resolution is not a liberation into the pure sunlight of Plato's noesis but rather an exposure to the illusion of mobility, of discovery, that disturbs images of gods and safe places. The audience might speculate on and reflect the characters' opportunity to experience recognition and transformation. Like Joanne, the play is a duplicitous appearance that allows us a chance to reconfirm or to modify values in connections made, in the harmony of reunion. The happy resolution of images is caught by the mirror's light out of the dark cave of the past, and the camera's withdrawal into the inner darkness leaves the audience to its own devices, its mobility and reflexivity, its speculation.

5
The Play: Presenting, Recollecting, Projecting

M<small>Y APPROACHING IDEAS AND PLAYS—COMING BACK PERSISTENTLY</small> to the idea of the play, its transformation into a structure involving an audience and its being a createdness, and ending as persistently in speculations on that createdness for an audience entailing the idea of its creator—has not at all times appeared to acknowledge the difficulty in playing between abstraction and the moment's seeing. It is all too easy to talk about residual ideas as if they were timeless, when they are in their actuality caught up, as in a play, in the activities of being presented here and now, of being recollected and adapted, and of being projected toward and for consequences, particularly toward possible audiences in the future. In talking about the ideas and the plays, I have imagined myself performing that idea of activity Heidegger presents as an image of circling; a circling not among ideas only but among and toward plays presenting their own ideas that in effect—as in my talking about Altman's film—require extension: back, toward talk about inherited ideas of human beings and worlds, authors and audiences; and forward, toward the concern in this chapter with temporality. If the idea of temporality identifies all things as in time, and recognizes them as vulnerable to the fluctuations of being in time, it would encourage seeing those things as participating in their moments *and* within their world, would provoke recognition that the idea of the temporal essentially entails the idea of community.

Experiencing the action of the play is inherently the experience of a world that is imaginatively constituted, the play being a mimesis of the building of a world. The constitution of a world is personal, both in the characters' and the audiences' beliefs formed out of their past and their assumptions by which the individual reads the moment; and it is communal, in the agreed-upon premises that shape events into coherence and predictability. For the individual and the group, those understandings might on any occasion encounter what appears as something contradictory, alien, or perverse. As drama, the action arouses in the audience an anticipation that the events will cohere, will lift themselves out of the random, accidental, incidental, or cryptic goings on that fill mundane time, that they will take on and confer meaning.

Significance and importance are attained, not by establishing perfect clarity and closure, but by negotiating between the sense of satisfaction in the completeness of presence and the sense of looking into the mystery. If significance might be satisfactorily achieved in a perfectly transparent mimesis of probability and necessity, felt importance lies in and through the enigmatic, which reaches toward the profound and the anticipation of deeper understanding. The play is comprised of the disparity of temporality: its existence is possible only as immediate experience, the coming together in time of audience and represented event or text, and possible only as a moment in the frame of time and preparedness. The ideas emerging from an action are historical and communal, in that they have been constituted in the world of the play and the worlds of the audience.

The audience apprehends essences that might corroborate its understandings or might affront and confound them. Challenged, it might tenaciously hold to known values as refuting the play's truth; or it might thrust those values on the play and see only its own identity of the moment reflected there.[1] The play and the audience come together, however, in the moment that looks to the past and to the future, and if the play's being seems remote because it is recovered by us from a world not our own, Sophocles's Athens of our distant past or Shakespeare's London somewhat closer to us, its remoteness is felt not merely as a distance in time but as a disengagement of world or community as well. In a play of our own time, Eugene Ionesco's *The Chairs* for instance,[2] the world is remote and unsettling, meaning is not immediately forthcoming, and the audience is given to understand from the outset that its expectations must be flexible, its readiness must be a readiness to become attuned to the mysterious and to be satisfied with what is unresolved.

In *The Chairs* the event is dislocated in space and time: outside there is "water under the windows, stretching as far as the horizon" (113); the "half-light," growing "stronger and stronger as the invisible guests continue to arrive" (132), becomes "powerful light . . . cold, empty," when the emperor arrives (147); and when the play ends the main door stands "wide open onto darkness" (160). If Paris ever existed, and it "must have existed because it collapsed" (116), its time is declared by the Old Man to have been long ago: "It was the city of light, but it has been extinguished, extinguished, for four hundred thousand years." The remoteness of this alien world from ordinary expectations, its surprising energy and intensity, encourages letting it

5: THE PLAY: PRESENTING, RECOLLECTING, PROJECTING

be what it is to be, grounded as it is in the appearances of representation, in the illusion that is the condition of discovery. Its disruption of the expectations of established conventions, forms, and modes of drama calls for a readiness to be engaged in the essence, the Eidos, of the play, which is the audience's engagement in that "transformation into structure" in which the play achieves ideality.

The value sought in Husserl's "bracketing" and Heidegger's "turning" and "letting be" is enabled, it would seem, by the energy, the force, the assertiveness of the enthralling spectacle, which seizes the spectator with the power Longinus attributes to the sublime. Longinus's metaphor of the sublime as, metaphorically, an overwhelming natural force like lightning or tornado that flashes out of the foundation laid by rhetoric implies that power of the immediate, the appearance here in this moment, to capture the imagination of the audience. In this concentration of attention, however, the totality of involvement is not wholly originated, satisfied, and concluded in the immediate impact, ending in the closure of applause that acknowledges the final curtain as an end. If, as Heidegger argues, "The Being-alongside which discovers circumspectively in concern, amounts to letting something be involved—that is, to projecting an involvement understandingly" (*Being and Time*, H 353), then the representation of the work of art *as a work* and the representation of images and ideas *as images and ideas of something* are directed temporally toward the past and the future. The relationships and connections extend beyond the immediate, attracting toward the openness and uncertainty of possible resources that might yet appear as meaningful and the potential continuation of the work in what Heidegger refers to as an "ecstatical unity" (*ekstatischen Einheit*). Establishing a relationship of concern with the world of the work would be an "*awaiting* of what it [that concern] is involved in" and "the *retaining* of that which is thus involved. . . . The awaiting of the 'towards-which' is neither a considering of the 'goal' nor an expectation of the impendent finishing of the work to be produced. It has by no means the character of getting something thematically into one's grasp. Neither does the retaining of that which has an involvement signify holding it fast thematically. . . . Letting something be involved is constituted rather in the unity of a retention which awaits" (353–54). The sense of deferral implicit in Heidegger's talk about the readiness-to-hand of "equipment," about the bearing of concern, about the inextricability of awaiting and retaining, seems to be reiterated by the energy and boldness of the work's gathering to itself its assertion, apparently being revealed in its presence, and its withholding itself from the "impendent finishing," from an audience's "holding it fast thematically," from getting it "thematically into one's grasp." It seems paradoxically on the one hand to require attention and care, to necessitate seeing it as it is, to oblige apprehending its appearance in the moment, and on the other to ask for deferral to its inaccessible depths and absences, to invite feeling its hyperbolic mystification, to admonish answering with trepidation its enticement to interpret.

As an imaginative world, the play is in itself, like the images and ideas it presents, a particular instance of the idea of the play that reaches into the past and the common reservoir of dramatic experience. Ideas of the human being, the world, and the play demonstrate not only the quality of allusiveness but also what is essential to any such reference, direct or oblique: the possibility of duplication and repetition. If what happens to the idea of the home or the hero cannot happen without the ideas of home or hero, then it happens as a reflection of the idea; and the idea in the present image extends the possibilities of further reiteration or transformation of the idea. The presentation is a playing back into the past and forward for the future. The mimesis occurs in the field of the mimetic, its repetition of mimesis in worlds within worlds amplifying the display of repetition. Only with the idea of the play as repeatable, as deriving from the idea of mimesis, is the originality of a new play possible; and only with the play's repeatability as a mimesis is its continuity to be maintained in reproduction. Each new staging appears as if in reference to the possibility of past productions, perhaps directly and consciously alluding to earlier productions. Staging, costumes, and acting style might attempt to recall the elements of the Greek stage, evoking a sense of historical connections, or they might strive for detachment from that past for the sake of contemporary relevance, as a production of Mozart's *Marriage of Figaro* set in a modern high-rise might translate the opera's political consciousness and exaggerate it in modern American idiom, dress, and locale.

The film drama would seem to attain a permanence that arrests the free allusiveness of reproduction, establishing the film itself as text identical in repetition rather than transformational. Yet the presumed invariability of the performance, barring circumstantial differences such as breaking film or audience distractions, manifests the essential temporality of even this fixed form and reveals the primordial relationship in mimesis. The play's mimesis in representing a world, in the fusion of performance and represented world, is the mimesis of an audience's participation in and reiteration of that *bildung*. Both film and audience are constituted in the event as in "the unity of a retention which awaits," and the retaining of previous performances is for the individual generative and temporal, as the reproductions of a play on stage are contextual and anticipational. The film play and the audience share in the awaiting, the anticipation of surprise and astonishment, the proleptical uncovering of significance. If the stage or film play were not presumably constituted as offering the possibility of fresh discovery and insight, if the mimesis were thought to be already perfectly and fully apprehended, it might nevertheless be revisited nostalgically, with the anticipation that it would merely provide a return to the past and no more; but it might become a repetition like the commuter's monotonous daily ride—which, however inattentively experienced, is never reducible to the certainty of unalterable recurrence. The diurnal journey of the commuter might become something like a drama for the playful and imaginative traveler, and such an audience could be charged perhaps with misapplying the aesthetic sense to actual events. Making the dull ride an entertainment, alerting the attention to sudden differences and revelations of purposefulness, and readiness for the adventure of discovery are the qualities of awaiting or anticipation that engage the audience in the play.

The genuine aesthetic attitude entails the childlike submersion of the self in the presence that is potential revelation of something mysterious, possible emergence of design and significance from the play of illusion. The magnetic attraction of the work is to the self yielding to the work and taking the work to self as an unfinished deepening of significance, unfinished because temporal. As repetition, either of the "same" play or of the play as actualizing the idea of play, as repetition of the essential expectation of other plays, the event is not merely a duplication in the present: it is awaited as possibly uncovering what had remained covered up in all previous experiences; it is anticipated as the rediscovery of what has been recognized but not retained; and its appearance in a moment that can only be its own is to an audience that repeats only the idea of audience, not the perfected and fixed identity of any past audience, individual or communal. The play's condition of imaginative encounter, the meeting of the playful imagination with a play of imagination, can be disruptive of the set convictions that retain and maintain the closure of assurance that reality is known, known completely and retained fully. The play is retained in the memory of an uncompleted being who can only anticipate the fusion of the past as mediation and as prelude to the fullness, but not the finality, of occasion. Going to see a familiar play is the anticipation of an event to be revisited, a free occasion for re-viewing the retained memory of the play against the unfinished or deferred grasp of meaning, the "event of withdrawal" that "attracts us by its withdrawal" (Heidegger, *Basic Writings*, 350).

The certainty of full and accurate memory is, like the assured convictions of truth in ideas of identity and world, a presumption ever vulnerable to revision. Essential to remembering is the ineluctable experience of memory as entailing failures of retention and the loss of what has been retained. The individual certain of memories retained as if indubitable presence attains that certainty only in its assertion against the awareness that retention itself is not full and certain, that forgetting is the ground of possibility for remembering. The febrile attempt to remember the forgotten exhibits the perpetual reformation of the constituents of identity and the reassuring structures that have established a world's continuity. In that accounting against erosion, the impulse to convert detritus into souvenirs and relics is a preservation that builds, creates, organizes, and connects. Memories that retain content as souvenir attest to the attraction to what is past, what passes and has passed away, preserving—for instance in the photograph of something or someone as it was—not only the retained image but also its accessibility only as recollection, its moment of being that is preserved only in looking back. The souvenir's images of the ephemeral are reminders of the need to retain and are recovered in nostalgia; they confirm temporality as loss, as the strife between conservation and erosion. Memories transformed into relics look to the past as bearing significance into the present and toward the future. The memory of an enriching event of bestowal, an endorsement of conversion and growth, like the memory of another's influence that has become coexistent in the individual's character, is essentially an enablement and preparation for the future. Mighty destroying events and persons, the holocaust and Hitler, mass murders and depraved killers, produce relics and are signs of destruction that test endurance and prove the possibility of survival, amelioration, and augmentation. Having become, through what is retained as cherished fabrication of the present, a capability yet to increase, the unfolding being looks to the relic as extension of the self, as anticipation, even assurance, that directs attention toward and awaits the future.

The cultural memory retains the past in this doubleness of apprehension, as the nostalgia for the lost, for what has passed away, and as the energizing event or figure through which history gathers character and action into significance, purposefulness, and design. A culture's nostalgia erects statues and celebrates events as memorials to the past, and the need and satisfaction are in placing them at points along the line of history, "at that time," preserving them in tribute to the past. Although the satisfaction involves the recognition of origins and the retaining of memories, the memorializing elevates the images as of another and a different time; and, like the personal photograph, they are accompanied by a sense of unredeemable loss. Profoundly evoking a sense of time's dilapidations, as does the memorial, the relic in addition affirms the endurance and efficacy of what has passed, its maintaining an essence that is and will be not just a memory but an influence and operative vitality. Having contributed to the formation of the present as what is here, what has become, the relic embodies the anticipation that, in its overt signs of tattered fragility, its essence—which is the fusion of the relic's significance with the recipient—will remain in force. The relic energizes through participation, drawing to itself the participant's contribution, capacitating the present, encouraging transformation and the submission of identity to the as yet unformed and undiscovered.

When the play is retained as a memorial to what has been possible, it is established bearing that quality of a past greatness or of a historical artifact that maintains its difference and its locality as antecedent. A culture pays tribute to the souvenir, to past achievement that calls for recognition of the work's importance, and it is installed like a fixed and unyielding equestrian statue or like a photograph against the inescapable deterioration or temporal recession that separates what was from what is. A culture's reception of that memorial of the past asserts its own relationship to the play and the play's world as determining how the play is retained. The multiplicity of attitudes in a culturally diverse world maintain a conflictive spirit of preservation, the play being retained at the sufferance of its interpreters' utilizations of it. Established as canonical, it might answer to the primitivistic demand, satisfying the craving of nostalgia for greatness in the past. To the spirit asserting independence from the past and conviction of attained rectitude, the play's utility is as an object of revision or repudiation, and it represents the past as mistaken or false, established in delusion and partiality. The play as a memorial entails contradiction. It is at one extreme the historically determined object that bestows its meaning as original and singular; and it must be looked up to. At the opposite extreme it is the perennially reinterpreted object vulnerable, like the statue of Lenin, to disparagement or praise; and it is at the disposal of the contemporary.

The play enduring as relic solicits a forfeiture of the sure and confident grasp that has custodial control of the past in the contemporary; it heightens the awareness of inevitable change and loss and extracts from that awareness a sense of urgency, the need for realization and union in the storm of destruction. The play as relic is not differentiated as a tribute to the past or as an artifact weighed in the scale of contemporary convictions but is embraced as a potency bringing with it the familiarity that makes it accessible and the withholding that requires attunement, openness to its strangeness and remoteness.

Theories of the drama that postulate ritual affect, the communal benefit of participation, direct the interest toward the play's potency, toward the occasions that fuse participants and empower them.[3] The achieved harmony neither effects a closure denying the anticipation of further discovery and increase nor maintains a differentiation holding the origin and past of the play out as absent, lost, or concealed, needing to be brought into the present as memorial.

Thinking the idea of the audience as individual rather than community might advert to psychological rather than ritual theory, but need not be founded in a psychology. If the essence of the audience is not to be abstracted in the distinction between individual and community, then the essential experience of the play, the abstraction deferred, is a fusion, the audience participating by giving itself over to the action that unfolds itself as an event of the moment. Holding itself apart from the play, the audience might receive it as a memorial preserving an image from the past and differentiating its world from that of the audience. As a relic actuated in intimacy and mutual dependence, the play is neither audience nor performance—nor text, source, absence—but generative event grounded in anticipation, expectation, a motive to effect transformation in the event that expatiates and speculates. The audience, retaining memories of past experiences of drama, particular plays and ideas of the play, contributes to the action by becoming impartial, freely engaged in letting appear what is to be presented. The impartiality is not a forgetting but a retention of the past experiences that have been generative in the potential experience in this event, as this occasion is a preservation and *bildung* toward what has not yet been attained. As relics, the remembered events are freed from "living convictions" and achieve the status of play. Memory itself becomes the preservation and contribution of vital experience to what might be experienced, rather than a retention of images fixed in their occurrence in the past.

Memory, then, like the relic, attests to the continuity extending beyond the moment and the individual, appearing as a figure of bestowal in that it is creative, anticipational. Like the relic subsuming and transmuting the value of the memorial, it achieves the value of a tribute to the future. As a figure or image, memory itself has been established and retained as an idea of bestowal, in the Greeks' Mnemosyne. Archaic, born from heaven and earth, Uranus and Gaea, Mnemosyne is the mother of the Muses and hence the source of poetry, and as generative force she represents, for Heidegger, a "thinking back" (*Basic Writings*, 352). Rather than conceiving Memory as the content of what is retained, "mental representation," Heidegger characterizes it as an activity, "the gathering of thought upon what everywhere demands to be thought about first of all. Memory is the gathering of recollection, thinking back." The activity of the poet or playwright becomes constructive, reconsideration as well as retention, the making of something memorable from the remembering. Gadamer, who follows Heidegger in interpreting Mnemosyne as a representing and discovering activity, refers to her as "the muse of memory and recollective appropriation."[4] That appropriation is not, however, a conversion of history, detritus, souvenirs, and memorials to the personal free from influence—or the contemporary world free from the past—but an accommodation that is on the one hand a tribute to Mnemosyne herself, who "rules here as the muse of spiritual freedom," and on the other a tribute to influences and continuities that weave the fabric of time and project the past toward the future.

The essence of the play as Mnemonic is the activity appropriating and propagating relics in the recollection of tributes and in the assertion of the tribute anticipating its reception, retention, and transformation into further tribute. The play's activity in gathering and preserving what is to be presented recalls not only the past but also the paying of tribute in the past, and its assertion as commendation becomes an expectation of reiterated commendation. An audience's applause signifies the tribute that is thematic in the play, the play's enfolding the spectator into the structure of relationship made possible by retention and awaiting. The freedom of the play is a lifting of appropriated participants into the continuity that is alluded to even in its being seen as play. In repeating the idea of the play it alludes to the past—to plays, images, and ideas that endure as potential in being available in memory—as it alludes to the future: to outcomes and consequences of the play as play, the applause, its continuance in memory, its contribution to salvaging and making memorable what slips away, its serviceability as affect and relic, its readiness to participate in succeeding acts of tribute.

The play that appears overtly as a tribute makes thematic the "gathering of recollection, thinking back," an emphatic quality recognized in the play called the "memory play." This designation only accedes to the play's abundance in calling attention to its being, like all plays, a gathering and bestowal for Mnemosyne. The play that seems to question the possibility of retention and continuity, the efficacy of the tribute, as does Ionesco's *The Chairs,* is nonetheless a bearer of the idea of tribute, constitutes in itself and calls for tribute. Ionesco's play, presenting that world of suspect memory, the house encompassed by water and darkness and dislocated in time, is an action anticipating the tribute. The "message" the Old Man wants to "deliver" (118) to the world, "radiating upon posterity the light of my mind . . . thus making known to the universe my philosophy" (157), is a certainty of his preserved identity: "the inner life, peace of mind, austerity, my scientific investigations, philosophy" (133). His sometimes awaking "in the midst of absolute silence" that is "a perfect circle," with "nothing lacking" (145) in the perfect circle's having become silence, implies solipsism; and his and the Old Woman's deficiencies and contradictions of identity—his being "general factotum" (114) rather than accomplished as "head president, head king, or even head doctor," her slipping into the role of an "old prostitute" (132), their striving to establish identity as retained images of child and parent, their submission of themselves to the Emperor as "servant, your slave, your dog, arf, arf" (148)—belie the constitution of dramatic character as full representation of human identity and integrity (except, of course, that they are consistent in their inconsistency).

The intensity and excess of the Old Man's desire for homage to be expressed by the Orator seem to be determined by the characters' images of themselves derived from the past, images of both the world and themselves in it. The degenerated present world, the "stagnant water," the "bad smell" and the mosquitoes (113), in which "it is dark already" at "six o'clock in the evening ... wasn't like this before." The Old Man's appeal, "Surely you remember," is an incitement to recall the past, even though the Old Man is "tired" of "examples from history." The story, "*the* story" (115), the Old Woman elicits from him is his story and also hers, and it is about the journey to the garden where "the grass was wet" (116) and "through the garden" to the village, the place "called Paris" reduced, primitivistically, to the innocence of the minimal. The ideas of the remembered place are recaptured in the "monotonous" re-telling of the "same story ... every single evening" (115), and they are, the Old Woman says, regenerative: "every evening" she becomes "new again" (115) when they "amuse" themselves "by making believe" (114). The story is not, however, productive of change and growth; her mind being as if "a clean slate every evening" (115) is not a preparation for and anticipation of discovery but a readiness for the rote of the memorial narrative, which is congratulatory and comforting. Her identity is rooted in fragments of the past, the mere allusion in her name, Semiramis, establishing no vital connection to the founder of dynasties; and the Old Man's referring to her as his "worthy" and "faithful helpmeet" (133, 157), rather than conferring on her the potency of Eve, reveals her function as a fetcher of chairs to be a parody of the helpmeet.

The Old Man's noble aim, to reveal a lasting and constructive truth to the world, is doubly thwarted. Suspended between the idea of embodying a final truth for the future, the "perfected ... real system"

(146), and the atavistic recurrence of the child in him, he is debilitated, unable to deliver the message. In addition, the Orator, the third performable character in the play, is mute; his attempts to convey a message on the blackboard convey in language the fragments of meaning that remain in the images from the past—Paris, the garden, Semiramis, Tristan and Isolde (133); "ANGELFOOD ... ADIEU" (159–60)—that do not contribute to a new harmony, wholeness, or understanding. Debilitated, like the Old Man, the Orator retains and performs an impotent image from the past: "He's a typical painter or poet of the nineteenth century ... histrionic in manner, conceited ... like an automaton" (154–55). An idea of the artist or the poet, he is not endowed by Mnemosyne, neither retaining and enriching the past nor eliciting a corresponding tribute from the audience. "Satisfied" with his performance "and a little solemn," he is "faced with the absence of the hoped for reaction" (160) and withdraws, "gliding like a ghost." The Old Man and Old Woman have sacrificed themselves in order to "die in full glory ... to become a legend" (158), which could have been established, if not a failure, as worthy of tribute; their poet, if not mute and incoherent, could have voiced the tribute; and their audience, attuned and anticipative, which was to have received and applauded, retained and grown from the tribute, is visually represented as a blank.

The stage audience, only imaginatively constituted until the Orator has left the stage empty, attains a momentary aural presence in that emptiness. As an idea of the audience, it responds appropriately to the debilitation, fragmentation, and ineffectuality of "real" character and action in the play. Articulate in "bursts of laughter, murmurs, shh's, ironical coughs" (160), it renounces the Orator and the message, creating out of incoherence a certain consistency, out of shards and detritus an imaginative congruity. In a world of dissolution and inauthenticity, the audience acts appropriately; its alienation is voiced as a recognition of insignificance and meaninglessness, the disruption of continuity and the loss of purpose. Its substantiality is a remonstrance against the insubstantiality of the Orator: "just as the invisible people must be as real as possible, the Orator must appear unreal" (154). As they fill the stage, invisible but imaginatively real, they take their places in a theater that is, indeed, a recollection and a tribute to theatrical design. The chairs are arranged facing the dais, forming "regular rows, each one longer as in a theatre" (139),[5] producing on stage an extension and a duplication of the actual audience, both audiences arranged to witness the performance from the dais, the stage upon the stage.

The stage is, in contradistinction to the Old Man's "perfect circle" of "absolute silence," a perfect half-circle, a design that alludes to the theater of the past. The half-circle of the stage is completed by the half-circle of the audience in the Vitruvian theater, a theater conceived architecturally and rendered effective for both practical and ideal purposes.[6] A mimesis of cosmic design alluding to ideas of another dimension of reality that makes the actual world a *theatrum mundi* and the stage an imitation of that structure, the theater represented a place of union, wholeness, and revelation. Relating one dimension to another, uniting audience and stage, the Vitruvian theater was designed for both visual and auditory effects, the presentation of spectacle and poetry. Ionesco's presentation of the spectacle renders the semicircular walls of the stage, with their ten doors, an arena of frenzied activity; the Old Woman's precisely determined exits and entrances in creating an audience with chairs builds to farcical climax. The Old Man's attempt to express his desire for immortality or at least to outlast the flesh is spoken as a macabre poem about the old couple's inability to be united in death, as they are separated by the invisible audience in life. This poetry of the stage suffers, as do heroic images and ideas from the past, a decline, a reduction, a trivialization. Although it might serve as a tribute to implacable mortality, to the radical isolation that prohibits their sharing the same tomb and the same worms, that assures their rotting "in an aquatic solitude" (158), the nobility of desire for individual transcendence of time in tribute—"We shall not be forgotten"—is trivialized as having a street named after them.

This paltry *theatrum*, its audience being "all that is left from humanity" (157), brings down noble conceptions of the stage into the context of commedia dell'arte. If, however, "with such leftovers one can still make a very good soup,"[7] what is to be made of what is left over need not be only a tribute to earth's destructions, to the brute factuality of existence, to nihilism and despair. In the depreciation of "making" the metaphorical soup, the idea of artist as maker is retained, and the soup to be made is, in this play, made with the precision and skill of the artist who is a craftsman. The remembrance of the past is constitutive in the play as tribute, not only in that retention of the idea of the stage's impact and efficacy, the zany busyness laid incongruously and strangely on the classic design, but also in the idea of remembrance itself and in the idea of anticipating the establishment of relationship between artist and audience.

The *ubi sunt* complaint, more than a lament for an unrecoverable past, persists as a recollection of the formal expression of loss, and any echo of it alludes to François Villon's voice and the voices of others that establish a continuity making the echo both possible and meaningful. If the Old Man's "almost whimpering" to La Belle "Où sont les neiges d'antan?" (132; *Les Chaises,* 150) seems parodic, it establishes in the allusion both the complaint and the memorableness of the poet's voice. Ovid's assurance, in the epilogue to the *Metamorphoses,* that although "the devouring ages can destroy" the "mortal body"[8] his "words shall be / Upon the lips of men" argues that he will have an audience, far in the future, that will pay tribute to his voice. Having ended the *Metamorphoses* with an account of Julius Caesar's apotheosis, his tribute to nobility of character and identity, Ovid anticipates his own contribution to and participation in the preservation of a world. The Old Man's desire for "apotheosis" (*Chairs,* 157) fervently appeals to the Ovidian Orator to make him a Julius Caesar and asks that, like Ovid, the Orator should "neglect none of the details of my private life." Ovid has, of course, made full and appropriate use of the details of Julius Caesar's public life; and both the Old Man's life and his poet, their debasement of noble images, their incongruities and incoherence, effect disarray in the *theatrum mundi* and a garbled echo of poetic tribute for an estranged, disillusioned, or distracted audience.

For the Old Man nothing is left of Paris "except a song . . . a lullaby, an allegory" (116), and nothing is left of the stage except a parody, fragmentary echoes and mocking allusions to ideas of the past. In an imposed consciousness of that detrition, the making of a play and establishing of relationship with an audience, transforming it into a structure of play, are improbable. The "leftover" audience is not a pure and simple representation of the actual audience, however, though its presence in disembodiment is expected to evoke a more substantial reality than do the remnants, the trappings, of the artist in the Orator's embodiment. That expectation involves the artist in imaginative formation, the retention and development of the idea of the audience in both imagined audiences, the one on stage and the one not yet realized. The playwright's repetition and transformation of the Vitruvian stage is both a disfigurement and a tribute; the Old Man's tribute "to the owners of this building, to the architect, to the masons who were kind enough to erect these walls" (156), is an allusion to the theatrical metaphor wherein the architecture of the stage represents the architecture of the house, the castle, the world—Shakespeare's "little O," the fourth-wall convention of realism. The playwright's creation of an imagined audience on stage is a reiteration of the tradition in plays of the past that have incorporated in them audiences (for plays within the plays) that allude to the audiences the plays anticipate, hope for, need fulfillment in.

The refractory audience of *The Chairs,* imagined as integral in disintegration, plays its part in a drama that presumes an imaginative engagement with the anticipated audience. The "laughter, murmurs, shh's, ironical coughs" become audible and fade, lasting "long enough for the audience—the real and visible audience—to leave with this ending firmly impressed on its mind" (160; "l'esprit" [*Les Chaises*, 180]). The "real and visible audience," like other audiences in the past that have glimpsed themselves represented in the play, are both brought into the structure of the play and granted their freedom in the playwright's tribute that requests tribute in return. They are free to see or not see themselves in that stage audience, and the possible apprehensions of themselves are manifold; what they are not free to do is to not be, not have been, an audience. They have been afforded the opportunity to realize the idea of audience in the play's structure of relationships. If they applaud, they pay tribute not only to the play as an individual achievement but also to its preservation and transformation of the idea of the play recovered and reconstituted in the activity of Mnemosyne. The idea of the artist still capable of recalling from the world's flotsam a coherence in the play, wrought with difficulty out of improbability, calls for an idea of the audience that can be brought into momentary unity, that can be touched and can reciprocate.

Questioning the authenticity and efficacy of residual ideas, *The Chairs* evidences the questioning in rich allusion, provocative hints for discerning the song of the long lost garden and city as "lullaby" or "allegory." The reciprocating audience might recognize the play's repetitiveness as satisfying the baby's need for lullaby, as answering its own need for the reassurance and soothing effects of lullaby; or it might set out in pursuit of the intellectual pleasure of garnering comprehensive allegorical meaning; or it might in recognizing its possibility in the stage audience know itself as cast out among the shards and ephemera of a turbulence out of which the Mnemonic imagination creates designs.

In the drama of Anton Chekhov, which directs the questions of character and representation toward a world struggling to maintain its sense of continuity in the angst of dissolution and the scattering of forces, the remembered past is evoked in melancholy; and the characters themselves, unless they are capable of planting themselves firmly in the present and acting by conviction, are incapacitated by an awareness of being dissolved in the general disintegration. In *The Three Sisters*, the sisters' longing for a return to Moscow remains a dream from the past that takes its place among other disabled hopes and illusions. Irina's cry at the end of act 3, "only let's go to Moscow! I implore you,"[9] becomes in act 4 a voicing of despair: "if it's not my fate to live in Moscow, then so be it. . . . You can't do anything about it" (147).

Although Chekhov's plays are rich in allusion, as when in *The Cherry Orchard* Lopakhin refers to Varya as Ophelia,[10] the abundance of the past seems to have slipped away for characters like Lyubov, and what remains are ghosts of the past. While the forces of destruction loom, incomprehensible and relentless, as in the indeterminate power of banks and economics that has the estate in its grip, human figures from the past appear within the orchard. Gaev expresses the sense of mystery and the inability to deal with it: "and the orchard will be sold to pay off debts. Strange, isn't it . . . " (176); and Trofimov says that Lyubov and Gaev "no longer notice that you are living in debt, at the expense of other people" (189–90). The "generations of human beings" staring at them from "every cherry tree in the orchard" are, at the end of act 2, Trofimov's abstracted images of the guilt the living bear for ownership of "land and serfs . . . living souls" (189) in the past. Trofimov's solution to the burden is to gain a "clear idea about our relation to the past . . . to begin living in the present . . . [to] first of all redeem our past and then be done with it forever" (190). Although he professes a certainty that this redemption requires "exceptional labor . . . endless work," he is like the others who, he says, "just philosophize, complain of boredom, or drink vodka"; and like them he hopes for future happiness that is only "felt impressions . . . visions I can't explain."

Trofimov's ghosts from the past are a rhetorical device, serving to depict a "philosophy" that has not become its own praxis; he "just" philosophizes and feels vague intimations of future happiness that might or might not be realized in his returning to the university at the end of the play. For Lyubov the ghost appears near the end of act 1, following a lament in which the pain of the present and the memory of the past are inextricable: "If only the heaviness I feel in my heart, the millstone I carry now, were suddenly taken away forever, if only I could forget my past!" (176). The image of her mother that appears "walking in the orchard" is vivid and personal—Lyubov "laughs jubilantly" and cries, "See, it's Mama."—yet she knows that the figure is an illusion, that "it just seemed to me I saw her," that what looked like a woman is only "a white small tree bending down." Lyubov's ghost is not abstracted to serve a conviction, but even in its acknowledged illusoriness it contributes to the enduring pain and remembered or imagined happiness that intensify the need for future happiness. Memories are recalled or formed and serve in a field of loss in which happiness, if it is to be found, must be created: as a happiness in the past and therefore in the impotent, painful recollection; or as an escape from the pain of the moment.

How that escape provides resolution or concession is dependent on how the characters conceive the problem and their relationship to it. Whether in the individual's power to determine outcomes or in vulnerability to others' actions and to determinative influences beyond those others, resolutions are not likely to bring unmixed satisfaction. Varya's resolute caretaking is no more effectual in addressing the problem than is Lyubov's compulsive giving of herself and money. Lopakhin's "saving" the cherry orchard, an offer made in act 1, answers to practical, economic needs, and will make "your cherry orchard . . . happy, rich, sumptuous" (174), although the house and orchard must be destroyed in order to attract tenants to the summer places that will supplant them. Since he knows that his success has not changed him, that he is "just a peasant through and through" (166), his exhilaration at the end of act 3 is contaminated by the sense that his owning the cherry orchard is "only a dream" (200) and by the regret, for Lyubov, that she would not "listen to me before" (201). Gaev's solution to the threat of loss, presented in act 1 as an alternative to Lopakhin's, is to seek financial aid from the "dear aunt, the countess," who "doesn't care one iota for us" (178); and the insufficient support from her does not save the estate. Facing and solving real problems in a world of contingency and deprivation remains contingent even for those who take things into their own capable hands. For those like Pishchik who trust their salvation to others—to the generosity of others, to chance and the lottery (175), to good health inherited from the "very same horse that Caligula had seated in the senate" (191), to the "extraordinary" good fortune that brings Englishmen to find "some kind of white clay in the ground" and sign a lease for "twenty-four years" (207)—awaiting good luck might turn out as well as practical judgment and hard work. Self-trust and dependency, capable management and submission to powers beyond themselves, seem like contradictory solutions to problems that, for the characters, provide choice and disclose the question of responsibility.

The play is essentially about the questions of remembering and preserving what is derived from the past as the past appears in the present need to act, to solve problems, in the present event. This articulation of past and present intensifies as a sense of urgency in the need to discover sources of energy and sponsorship. Gaev's seeking relief from the aunt and Pishchik's trusting to some protective power of good fortune are like Varya's reliance on "God's will" (176) and her dream of throwing down the keys of responsibility and "walking from one holy place to the next . . . walking and walking" (169–70);

all three express an impulse to trust and seek an enduring and caring benevolence beyond the troubled affairs into which they are cast. Trusting to Varya's god or Gaev's "Dear, honored bookcase," the "receptacle for books" whose "very being has been directed to the shining ideals of cardinal good and justice . . . upholding . . . in generations of our line personal courage and faith" (174), characters might preserve the idea of trust that has been established in religion or in those books the bookcase perpetuates. In remembered and unremembered instances of miraculous intervention, the world has assembled and made possible Pishchik's belief in good fortune. In Gaev's books remain those instances that uphold Gaev's belief in "cardinal good," a foundation of courage and faith. If in actuality the characters seem embedded in and vulnerable to circumstance and their own lack of coherence, blown like Dante's Paolo and Francesca upon the winds, they like Dante's lovers feel the love that cannot transcend isolation in their limbo; and they generate a sense of the appropriateness of allusion to paradigms of love and separation, to literary characters like Ophelia who suffer like themselves. Such instances of conflict are not the conflict of love and strife, attraction and repulsion, but the prevailing need for love, sympathy, and understanding, the need the characters can still express better by touching one another than in words, opposed by a principle of distraction, misdirection, discrepancy, and deferral. Although Lyubov arranges a moment for Varya and Lopakhin to make a commitment to marriage, the agreement does not take place, not because they are unwilling or because of conflict between them, but because of hesitation and digression.

Gaev and Pishchik provoke comparison and contrast to literary or actual characters from the past who are not distracted from problems needing resolution but turn to or await intercession from a higher power. Vergil's story of Aristaeus is told in book 4 of the *Georgics*,[11] a work devoted to giving practical advice on rural life and to championing the advantages and satisfactions of that life, which is attainable if thorough knowledge of husbandry and understanding of origins are united to labor. The story told within the story of Aristaeus, Proteus's narration of the Orpheus legend, is about love and loss, Orpheus's reclaiming Eurydice from the underworld, losing her again, irrevocably, and mourning throughout the rest of his life and in death. Aristaeus, like Orpheus, acts courageously and decisively, but unlike Orpheus carries out his mission successfully. A beekeeper whose bees have been destroyed, Aristaeus seeks advice from his mother, who advises him to go to Proteus to learn the cause of the hardship. The Protean power of changing shape demands of Aristaeus strength and tenacity, and he is successful in learning, from Proteus, that his loss is Orpheus's punishment for his guilt in Eurydice's death and, from his mother Cyrene, how to make sacrifice and receive a new breed of bees. As the *Georgics* establishes a model of how to live in a world that requires knowledge and endurance, strength of commitment and capability, the story of Aristaeus illustrates this pious and successful life attuned to powers and resources both mortal and immortal.

The world and characters of *The Cherry Orchard* invoke these ideas, not as reassurance that perseverance and labor are efficacious in constructing a happy life or that trusting to benevolence is rewarded with miraculous assistance—though these beliefs persist within the play—but as a vague sense of old coherence, productivity, and security lingering in memory but ineffectual in a world of dissolution and estrangement. Firs remembers that courageous action in the past, the freeing of the serfs, made everyone "glad, but what they were glad about, why, they didn't even know themselves" (185); and that action produced the conditions of the present, in which "nowadays" the masters and the peasants "are all mixed up, and you can't tell one from the other" (186). For Firs, the cherry trees were prolific in the past, like Aristaeus's bees, because the trees and husbandry were in consonance: the "dried cherries . . . were soft and juicy, sweet and a good smell to them. . . . They knew a way of doing it at that time" (173); and now "No one remembers it." Reading Lopakhin as like Aristaeus only calls into question his motives and reveals that his actions have had grievous effect on Lyubov and that his success is illusory. Announcing at the end of act 3 that he has bought the estate, he admits that he might be delirious, drunk, insane, or daydreaming, that if "it's only a dream, it's only something that seems to be. . . . This is the fruit of your imagination, concealed in the shadows of uncertainty" (200–01). His anticipation that the abundance of the cherry orchard will be regained grows out of that illusion, since he realizes that "nowadays the summer resident only drinks tea on his balcony" (173). His nebulous wish, hardly a promise, is that "it *might happen* he'll take up farming his own plot of ground, and then your cherry orchard will become happy, rich, sumptuous" (my emphasis; 173–74). Pishchik's awaiting and receiving good fortune to resolve his problems is a quizzical anomaly, the miraculous salvation that is neither a probability in this world nor an assurance that his trust to miraculous intercession is viable. The stability and fulfillment of a past world having withdrawn, characters who are blown together by the winds of contingency are sorrowfully aware that they dwell in loss, and they recall but are unsure of the past as a source of happiness.

There is no reasonable expectation of miracles, heroic endeavor, or human intercession in this world, except as accompanied by or subject to whim. Pishchik's salvation only demonstrates that in a world out of control the improbable is as believable and meaningful a resolution as would be the outcome of keen sight, sure knowledge, and capable action. Lyubov sees through Lopakhin's pose of strength and confidence and berates him, eliciting his confession that he is "as big a lunkhead and idiot" as his father (185), who "didn't understand anything" and "taught me nothing." Lyubov's complaint follows Lopakhin's inability to hear the "music coming from somewhere . . . our celebrated Jewish orchestra" (184) and his irrelevant comment that he has seen a funny play: she says that "probably there wasn't anything funny in it. Going to see plays isn't what you people should do. Try looking at yourselves a little more often and see what gray lives you all lead. How much of what you say is unnecessary" (185). Her apparent solution to a gray life and unnecessary talk is introspection, observing oneself rather than going to see plays for entertainment. Her own introspection and confession, however, which precedes this exchange, has revealed but not resolved her "sins," her profligacy, her punishment for a "stupid and degrading" life (184). She moves with the others in gestures, motions, and travels that bring them toward union and concerted effort, which the play's action reveals to be only dissatisfaction, the failure to realize the self in relationship with others. The questionableness of all their solutions—Trofimov's belief in ideals and the future, Lopakhin's sense of control and self-determination, Varya's dogged performance of duty, Lyubov's generosity and love, Pishchik's trusting to good luck (and Yepikhodov's assurance of bad luck), Gaev's reliance on an unlikely agent of deliverance, Firs's unyielding service still governed by the past—is a reminder that they represent not the solution of problems or the probability of finding in discrepancies a satisfactory resolution, but the condition of irresolution and uncertainty in a world of vacillation and cross-purposes.

That image of a world proves, again, not to be a show of meaningless detrition but a speculation on purposes and powers of individual and community, and it addresses the question of power in representing the possibility and the idea of artist in such a dissolving world. In Chekhov's appraisal, the function of the artist is to represent that condition, and it is indeed the condition in his created world that might or might not be judged by an audience to truly represent an actual world. "It's none of the artist's business to solve narrowly specialized problems" like "the destinies of capital" and "the harmfulness of hard drinking," he wrote to A. S. Suvorin,[12] arguing that the artist "observes, selects, surmises, composes—actions which by themselves presuppose a question at their very beginning"; the artist's only obligation is "*the correct posing of a question,*" not "*the solution of a problem.*" In these observations Chekhov elides a distinction between the problem represented in the imagined world and the artist's problem in presenting it. In Lyubov's admonition to Lopakhin, the play is presumed to be a mere entertainment, a diversion producing laughter, as are Sharlotta's tricks and illusions. It would seem that Chekhov places himself somewhere between the playwright whose responsibility is to resolve perplexities and the one who is pure entertainer. While he does not have answers that would require a "specialist's knowledge," that of the scientist, social scientist, psychologist, theologian, or philosopher, he nevertheless has something to say that goes beyond a moment's diversion. Sharlotta seems to be a speculation on what might become of the artist in a world that trivializes even pleasure and entertainment. Her incessant talking and performing were an annoyance on Anya's journey to Paris; she "kept on talking and doing her silly conjuring tricks the whole way" (168). Anya seems to find little pleasure in an entertainment, and as Lyubov's advice to Lopakhin implies, mother and daughter share this attitude.

If the play is not mere entertainment or diversion but the work of a craftsman for whom "question and intention exist in creative work . . . design . . . previously thought-out intention" (*Letters,* 88), the audience is evidently expected to recognize and respond to what the play is. In the play's design, the audience might discover itself and sense its serious implication with the characters. In enjoying the play, it might recognize that the conjoined ideas of the artist and the play, prima facie an entertainment, is reflected not only in the world designed by an artist for an audience but also in a character whose assumed function is to entertain. Attitudes within the play like Anya and Lyubov's establish a question of aesthetic engagement that remains speculative so long as the play is perceived as a presentation of problems rather than a solution, and observing Sharlotta as an artist only confirms that her enthusiasm and panache are signs of the artist's excessive bestowal of her gifts upon others. Saying that the playwright is being descriptive rather than prescriptive imposes no right response on the audience, no proper lesson to be learned, nor does that observation confine the dramatist to preconceived notions of the artist's social function.

Sharlotta might seem a parody of the artist, but in her gratuitous displays, her showing of things through tricks, she exposes the artist's "problems and purposes" in "design," creating illusions that her audience knows to be illusions and receiving their willingness to be accomplices and their admiration. She reveals as well possible manifestations and transformations of the idea of artist in a world splintered from its past. In her rootlessness she represents a more profound absence of origins and deprivation of the sustenance of tradition than do the characters who are identifiable by their places in societal structure. She does not know how old she is, but thinks of herself as "very young" (180); when she was a child her parents "used to travel from fair to fair and give shows" and she did "all sorts of tricks"; and, although after her parents died she was taken into a German woman's home and became a governess, she still feels absolute isolation. She does not know "where I come from and who I am . . . who were my parents. . . . I feel alone all the time, all alone, I don't have anybody at all and . . . and who I am, what on earth I'm here for, is beyond me" (180–81). This deprivation not only isolates her but also frees her from the responsibility to become one with others (who become, willy-nilly, her audiences) in their worrying over their problems or to give them advice on practical negotiations. As an idea of artist on the verge of community she is doomed to freedom, freedom from serious responsibility to take ethical positions or actions involving her in their affairs; and her audience is, like the audience of Chekhov's play, reciprocally free.

Her freedom from the role of responsible artist, as for instance the social critic of "narrowly specialized problems," makes her relationship with her audience an ethical one grounded in the grace of the artist's bestowal. She refuses to perform in act 1 because "I don't want to" (175), but in act 3 she provides an interlude for the characters anxious about the fate of the cherry orchard, a diversion from their troubles. She performs card tricks and ventriloquism, which Anya has referred to as "silly conjuring tricks" (168); she makes Anya and Varya appear from behind a lap robe (192–93); and she appears in the ballroom (198) performing something apparently like the "*salto-mortale* and all sorts of tricks" (180) she did as a child. As marginal, she cannot in act 4 share the illusion of happiness the others are wresting from their sorrow, Anya's saying that "this is the beginning of a new life" (205), Gaev's having "started to feel cheerful" (206), even Lyubov's "sleeping fine"; she asks, or demands, "please find me another job, won't you? I can't go on like this." Yet she has performed one last ventriloquistic trick, responding to Gaev's saying "Happy Sharlotta, she's singing!" by picking up "a bundle which resembles a baby in swaddling clothes," making it cry, consoling her "fine little boy," then abruptly throwing it down. This performance is far different in spirit from her entertainment in act 3, which has been directed entirely toward an appreciative, applauding audience. The baby seems to be an expression of her own futility: "I feel sorry for you, so sorry!" Perhaps it is intended as an affront to their attempt to face a brave new world after "the whole thing was settled once and for all," to falsify their actual affliction and dismay by forcing an illusion of well-being. The baby boy, in both its essence as a new life, a fresh beginning, and in her expression of sympathy for it, is cast aside in a shocking refutation of illusory hope. It is repudiated as the efficacious and consolatory symbol of beginnings, the newborn child as innocent potential in a new dispensation and therefore a sign of resolution.

Sharlotta's performances, her playing with illusions, do not amount to the poet's judicious advice of the *Georgics,* but they might represent the voice of the artist among her own shards of time and share with the playwright's representation implications concerning the creation of illusions for engaging an audience in such a world. In the entertainment as a gratuitous showing to others, the artist offers amelioration, momentary respite from the rigors of life, in the invitation to share an illusory pleasure. The skill displayed in extraordinary dedication to creating a coherence, a harmony, is an excessive expenditure, a lavishness, opposed to and arising from the necessary eking of daily subsistence from meagerness and penury. In bestowing that gift, Sharlotta speaks to their shared predicament and to the possibility of happiness without deferment or dependency. In representing illusion as illusion she engages her audience in ideas of the human inclination and power to create illusions and invites speculation on both the creation and the acceptance of them. Having created a momentary illusion of the living child in a bundle and brusquely destroying the image, demonstrating it to be a false idea devoid of the power to represent hope for the future, she makes a serious comment in a brief dramatic presentation. Her little work of art reiterates the cruel solicitude others express in real life when they confront another's constructed and preserved image of self with a counterimage. Lyubov's advice to Lopakhin about seeing himself rather than a play is of consequence, eliciting his confession that he is a fool and understands nothing; when she demobilizes Trofimov's pretensions to philosophical understanding, calling him "simply an immaculate prude ... a laughable eccentric boy, some kind of freak" (196), he refuses her definition of him and declares that "All is over between us!" Like the showing in Sharlotta's trick, the artist's representation has the power of influence, in presenting an image provoking thought and inviting an audience to see something and become engaged with it, but it does not have the power to determine the outcome of that presentation any more than Lyubov's showing Lopakhin and Trofimov themselves produces sure results.

With the knowledge that the artist is no longer central to establishing and preserving tradition by providing authority, instruction, and

5: THE PLAY: PRESENTING, RECOLLECTING, PROJECTING 173

resolution, a responsibility he disavows in affirming what his business still might be, Chekhov retains an idea of the artist as marginal. Sharlotta identifies herself as the artist who is peripheral, incidental, as T. S. Eliot's Prufrock identifies himself with such as Polonius rather than with Hamlet: "an attendant lord, one that will do / To swell a progress, start a scene or two, / . . . almost ridiculous— / Almost, at times, the Fool" (8). Sharlotta's disconnectedness at the end of the play is an acknowledgment of her origins, and she remains the wanderer while the others console themselves with the dream or pretense that their travels are toward new purpose or, for Lyubov, at least a fragile durability. The artist as a wanderer is elusive and free of the commitments and responsibilities dictated by tradition as interpreted and imposed in her or his own time, but not free of tradition and the past itself, of the withdrawal that attracts. As the memory provokes in retention itself a concession to loss, the idea of the artist is retained in the repudiation of the traditional image. The play made out of diverse recollections need not reconcile that diversity and contrariety in a resolute determination of how the present articulates with the past, which images and ideas from the past are required and remain viable, and how actions can fortify and assure a future by repudiating or preserving what has been.

The playwright might represent that diversity rather than try to abstract from it a closure of truth directly applicable to the world of this moment: might be concerned with reflecting what appears in the world of the play, squarely as it is seen; with incorporating memories in a design retrieved from felt disintegration; with constructing from enervation an exuberant tribute. The play as tribute given freely by the mobile artist might attest to possibilities remaining in the world—the will to continue in the face of loss; endurance through dedicated labor; achievement through reliance on powers beyond the self; creation and preservation through the transformations of memory—possibilities fulfilled and unified in the artist's presentation of the play to and for the audience. Incorporating images lifted out of an imagined rubble, the design becomes a tribute to objects of virtu that call to be preserved and to preservation itself, to the liberality of the artist making something of ravelment, and to the possibility of continuation through an audience's bestowal of itself. The achieved harmony of the play becomes, like Sharlotta's tricks, the music that is spontaneous, arising without practical justification as a mysterious impulse that provokes and resists resolving interpretation. Like the "sound of a string breaking" at the end of act 2 (188), it will be interpreted; but it will incorporate and it will be the music that is a momentary harmony arising from disharmony and mystery, affecting and passing in a moment.

The exuberant coherence of the work, generated as a strength out of enervation and erosion, achieves the *enargeia* desired in classical rhetoric. The vitality appearing is an inherent embodiment, in the appearance, of the *enargeia* itself as well as the affective image presented, as in rhetoric the *ethos* is the total character and values of the rhetorician as constituted in argument, the quality of the rhetor's persona or being. The play that represents this *enargeia*, which is associated in Heidegger's thought with the idea of *Lichtung*, having to do with both illumination and alleviation (*Basic Writings*, 384n), showing and changing, achieves its concentration and intensity, as Gadamer observes, under "the penetrating gaze of Mnemosyne" (*Relevance*, 46). The accomplishment in the activity of "forming or cooperating in the play of form . . . lies in retaining what threatens to pass away." It "reveals the human experience of finitude in a unique way and gives spiritual significance to the immanent transcendence of play as an excess that flows over into the realm of freely chosen possibilities." The play that intensifies and makes portentous this knowledge of fading light, the pallor of Lyubov's "gray lives" and the "half-light" of the stage in *The Chairs*, becomes Heidegger's lighting and lightening, an accomplishment acknowledging the diminishment that incites a remonstrance in shining.

The artist in Tennessee Williams's *The Glass Menagerie*, the playwright who appears in stage directions and "Production Notes," constructs a world as lighting out of darkness, presented as the contemporary infused with the past; the time is "Now and the Past."[13] This world, which echoes imaginings of hell, is a mass of the "enslaved" whose habitations are linked by fire escapes, an "accidental poetic truth, for all of these huge buildings are always burning with the slow and implacable fires of human desperation" (3). Architecturally, it is "hive-like," an image suggesting not the social order and productivity of bees but the "one interfused mass of automatism" that avoids "fluidity and differentiation." Its "dark, narrow alleys which run into murky canyons of tangled clotheslines, garbage cans and the sinister latticework of neighboring fire-escapes" evoke the image of a prison represented in Giovanni Battista Piranesi's *Carcere*, its fire-escape-like walkways placed indefinitely and uncertainly, not progressing within coherent design and toward clear destinations but standing as fragments in confusion and disjunction within oppressive space. The hell of "warty growths in overcrowded urban centers" in the world of *The Glass Menagerie* is a maze whose fire escapes are the means of access to private worlds, each its own hell, rather than

5: THE PLAY: PRESENTING, RECOLLECTING, PROJECTING   175

routes of escape from it. Trapped in the world of destitution and haunted by dreams of a better past or frustrated by elusive intimations of escape and fulfillment, the inhabitants, like those of *The Cherry Orchard,* bear the present by looking beyond it, by attempting to create an illusion of happiness from the remains of ideas and images, the detritus of the present.

Like characters in *The Cherry Orchard,* Amanda, Laura, Tom, and Jim search the past for remnants of value that might alleviate their sense of futility. They preserve icons as memorial to the accomplishments and beauty retained in the memory, images that promised a better future than this and bear, in being remembered, a sense of broken promises and disappointed hopes. For Laura and Tom, and for Jim himself, Jim was in high school "shooting with such velocity," was so accomplished in basketball, debating, and singing the "male lead in the annual light operas" (61), that his working now at "Continental Shoemakers" (27) is an incomprehensible decline to his current participation in a gray existence. On the other hand, retained images of debility and suffering confirm the plausibility of this life—Laura's present incapacity recalls memories of her "clumping all the way up the aisle" in the high school auditorium (94). The icon of the father "in this larger-than-life-size photograph over the mantel" (5) represents the discrepancy of memories and the forfeiture of the assurance and support signified in the idea of the father. Although he might represent for his son Tom a source of resentment and grievance, Tom presents him as having successfully escaped from this world, as Tom hopes to do, the "telephone man who fell in love with long distances" (5–6) having become the wanderer. Amanda "picked" him instead of one of her promising "beaux" (10–11), who in her fabrication of a past notably died tragically but left their widows consoled by a fortune; and he abandoned her to a life of penury. Contradictory memories reveal not only the fallibility and inaccuracy of memory but also its preserving through flawed efforts the constitution of significance and worth. Jim tries to remember Laura and has a dim sense of recognizing her, but he recalls a name that is not hers, "Blue Roses" (95). The name originated when Jim misunderstood the word Laura used to explain her absence from school, "pleurosis," his conversion of an unfortunate reality into a lovely image that became, for him, her name, and he has preserved it. When he falters in recognizing her, she provides the name he retains but cannot associate with her, and he observes the problematical quality of memory, "Isn't it funny what tricks your memory plays?" (92).

The memory participates in the creation of illusions, which might be seen as a falsification of the past in Amanda's trying to replay her luminous past for Laura, to prepare Laura for "gentleman callers" like those she had "one Sunday afternoon in Blue Mountain" (8); but it entails as well the impulse of the imagination to transform the ordinary or disagreeable into a beauty to be cherished. When the lights go out and Tom has paid his dues to the "Union of Merchant Seamen . . . instead of the light bill" (77), Amanda recalls or creates a story that attests to the value of relics from the world of the "nineteenth century, before Mr. Edison made the Mazda lamp" (86). The "lovely old candelabrum that used to be on the altar at the church of the Heavenly Rest . . . was melted a little out of shape when the church burnt down" (87); the lightning that caused the fire was, as the revivalist Gypsy Jones intimated, God's retribution "because the Episcopalians gave card parties." As a primitive source of light suffused with the dignity of legend, it has the power to recapture the intimacy of candle light, and she anticipates its efficacy in her bestowing it on Jim and Laura for their romantic scene.

Jim's Blue Roses and Amanda's Blue Mountain, both retained as imaginative transformations, are personal memories; the candelabrum attains for Amanda the distinction of a holy relic, preserved in legend and still capable of imparting a magical glow in a time of need. The playwright's story, like Amanda's candelabrum, is imaginative creation derived from images of the past. If the play has, as Tom says, a "social background" that is a "shouting and confusion" of the blind (5), out of that chaos and dismay images of a cultural past are preserved. They seem to mockingly proclaim the destitution of the now, the infernal world, but they are invoked as a resonance in sounds and images that honor the past in radiating in the present. The playwright's attempt to "strengthen the effect of what is merely allusion in the writing" (x) by the use of legends and images on a screen at times seems derisive, as in scene 5 the legend, "Annunciation" (49), reveals in the allusion the profound discrepancy between the angel Gabriel's announcing to Mary that she will bear a savior whose incarnation will transform the world and Tom's announcement that Laura will have a "gentleman caller." The allusion implies Tom's deprecatory attitude toward Amanda's demand that he provide the gentleman caller in order to free himself. The allusion in the play's first legend, however, not only appears as Tom's ironic counterpoint to Amanda's recounting the legend of her gentleman callers but also echoes the passionate lament that is Tom's own. "Ou sont les neiges" (6) echoes Villon as the play's pervading consciousness of a degenerated world and as its impetus to search the past for viable images and to transform them.

The "memory play," according to the "Production Notes," aims at

5: THE PLAY: PRESENTING, RECOLLECTING, PROJECTING 177

realizing through "unconventional techniques . . . a more penetrating and vivid expression of things as they are" (ix); and those things as they are are neither surface realism nor an acceding to the hopelessness and powerlessness of enslaved creatures in a dismal world. The artist's service to Mnemosyne is to affirm that "truth, life, or reality is an organic thing which the poetic imagination can represent or suggest, in essence, only through transformation, through changing into other forms than those which were merely present in appearance." The "single recurring tune . . . like circus music" (xi) and the visual image of "delicately spun glass" are united in invoking ideas of distance, fragility, change, and sorrow; but the resultant nostalgia is not a pathos of utter desolation and remoteness. The images serve "as a thread of *connection* and allusion between the narrator with his separate point in time and space and the subject of his story" (my emphasis).

In suggesting that Tom and Laura are connected through allusion, Williams distinguishes the mnemonic value of allusion, in that the connection achieves a unity through transformation. The image of Laura is not a memorial to the unredeemable past but achieves a relical power to influence and therefore to unite her with Tom and to inspire his tribute. She is lighted in the play so as to make her "distinct from the others" (xii); the light should have "a peculiar pristine clarity such as light used in early religious portraits of female saints or madonnas. A certain correspondence to light in religious paintings, such as El Greco's, where the figures are radiant in atmosphere that is relatively dusky," translates her out of the dusk of her world and transforms her into an image of the holy. Like a saint fixed in the final tableau with Amanda, whose "silliness" is converted into "dignity and tragic beauty" (123), Laura remains an image from the past that, because images pursue him, Tom cannot escape: "I am more faithful than I intended to be" (124). The wanderer has not escaped the world of detritus, where "cities swept about me like dead leaves (123)"; his world is still "nowadays . . . lit by lightning" (124); he is isolated among strangers in cities. The images that haunt him, the music and the glass, retain the power of relics to evoke Laura, and his memory can express "truth, life, or reality . . . only through transformation."

Tom's transformation of a world he is powerless to change is a lighting of the memorable, a preservation in theatrical light for the sake of retaining or bestowing significance and coherence. Laura becomes, like Petrarch's Laura, the inspiration from the past that calls to the poet and gives voice to his remonstrance against the "dead leaves," the meaninglessness and incoherence of his world. The continuity affirmed in his tribute is that maintenance beyond the personal achieved by the artist's transformation into structure, which unites author and audience in the play. Images recalled and connections made through allusion reveal Laura through those lighted images, and lifting her out of the darkness unites her with the playwright who remembers and transforms her. Presenting his images, he unites his play with an audience, realizing for the audience the impulse he shares with them, the need to preserve what is always passing away in a world of change and depreciation. His exaggeration amounts to sentimentality, he confesses (5), but his achievement will be measured in the setting up of a world that becomes a lighted place for the audience. The "social background" he establishes is a world of political revolution, "dissolving economy," and violence; and the people in it, that mass that avoids "differentiation," are entrapped in the battles of history that sweep around and over them, powerless to influence circumstances or control events in their world. Lacking vision—"their eyes had failed them, or they had failed their eyes"—they cannot see significance or dignity in their own lives. The *theatrum mundi* Tom presents, the little world of Amanda, Laura, and Tom, is given to the audience as "truth in the pleasant disguise of illusion" (4), and as a product of memory it is constituted to show that in the world of disillusionment and dismay there remains, in the little worlds of all the characters, an instinct to convert the dismal into beauty, to make an ideal world through the imagination that recalls a past radiance. The stage discloses Tom's imagined world through "the transparent fourth wall of the building and the transparent gauze portieres of the dining-room arch," Tom having entered and delivered his first speech to the audience from downstage, standing on the audience's side of the scrim. The first scene, with Laura and Amanda seated at the dining room table, is thrice removed from the audience, seen as at a distance through the double walls that become transparent by means of interior lighting.

Like the other characters, Amanda has the artist's instinct to make beauty out of her bleak world. Her governance of that world is demonstrated in her beginning the play's action by calling Tom to join them for dinner, and her "silliness" is grounded in the discrepancy of that governance. She must eke out their lives in the real world, an endeavor that requires fortitude and persistence, coercion of her children and making herself, for Tom, an "ugly—babbling old—*witch*" (28); but she preserves illusions of a past that yield hope for the future. Practical measures, sending Laura to "Rubicam's Business College" (22) to prepare for a "business career" (19), are mingled with the failed image of herself as belle making a successful marriage, an image she imposes on Laura in the pursuit of the gentleman caller. Her histrionic instinct— "a bit of acting" (14)—dominates in the confrontation with Laura, who has practiced "Deception" (18) in "amusing" herself rather than going to school. Inspired by the prospect of a beau for Laura, the "image of the gentleman caller" Tom identifies as Amanda's "obsession" like an "archetype of the universal unconscious" (22), she becomes director of a play generated from and infused with her memories: she transforms the apartment into a stage for courtship and costumes herself and Laura for their performance. The transformation of Laura, which is "a momentary radiance, not actual, not lasting" (63), is effected with a new dress "colored and designed by memory" (62), and Amanda's dress is "resurrected from that old trunk" (65). Amanda's exuberance, her excess, is the spontaneous impulse to create an ideal from the ordinary, with a purpose to influence an audience, the "emissary from a world of reality" (5).

Although this artist's endeavors are misdirected in the attempt to directly influence the actions of an audience, obscuring the differentiation between the stage and the real world, Amanda shares with Tom the need to transform and elevate through the hyperbolic presentation. Her failure reveals the ideas of contingency and vitiation borne in the actuality from which the artist wrests her ideas and against which the work of art strives. The disappointment in her ineffectuality is not for lack of an appreciative audience, but the circumstance, for Amanda, of Jim's existence beyond the play, his surviving ambition and his engagement to be married. Jim brings with him the capacity to dream, to magnify the actual, that is there as potential in all those desperate lives and is presumed to be there in Tom and Williams's potential audiences for their play. Jim plays his role for Amanda with gusto, courting Laura, urging her to share the "limelight" of the candelabrum (89), and bestowing on her those same ideas generated by Tom: trying to persuade her that her "being different" is not inferiority but uniqueness, he argues that others are "not such wonderful people.... They walk all over the earth. You just stay here. They're common as—weeds," but she is "*Blue Roses*" (111). He in effect elevates her into the fixed tableau Tom, the wanderer, creates; and like an idea fixed in images in the memory, she accompanies the one who departs from her—as the unicorn Jim will "treasure" as a "souvenir" (120) and as the "familiar bit of music" or "piece of transparent glass" that haunts Tom (124).

Laura, like Tom, seeks refuge, not merely from Amanda but from the painful corrosion of circumstance—for her, secretarial school; for him, the shoe factory—which keeps them enslaved like the others who make up that undifferentiated mass. The refuges they seek are little worlds providing respite from the world of the blind, places they go to see, to have presented to them illusions of control and magic, images retained for their diversion. Laura's deception of Amanda required spending days walking in the park and going into "places to get warmed up" (18), the "art museum," the "bird-houses at the Zoo," the movies, and "the Jewel-box, that big glass house where they raise the tropical flowers." As a spectator, she saw art preserved and birds and flowers protected in enclosed worlds that took her into their warmth. As an artist, she creates her own little world of light and warmth, the world of the glass menagerie that needs care and appreciation, and her audience of the moment, Jim, eagerly plays his role for her as he does for Amanda. His insufficiency is, as with Amanda, not an unwillingness to play a role but—as Williams observes of the possible real audience in the "Production Notes," "a lack of attention in the audience" (x)—his being distracted with his own real life. Laura only with difficulty calls his attention to the glass collection and presents the unicorn to him, which he fails to identify, as her "favorite one" (105). After he has enticed her to dance and accidentally breaks the unicorn, he still calls it a "little glass horse with the horn" (109) and guesses, not remembering, "that it was your favorite piece of glass" (110). Laura's own fragility, represented by Tom in the image of glass, generates a miniature world that enfolds her and becomes a private place lacking a competent audience.

Tom's excursions to the "Paradise Dance Hall" (46) and to the movies are not Laura's retreat into privacy, her becoming the lone spectator of the artist's own little world, but reveal his urge to be involved, to engage in "adventure" (47). He knows that the dance hall, with its "large glass sphere that . . . would turn slowly about and filter the dusk with delicate rainbow colors" (46), provides only an illusion of fulfillment and union with others. The "hot swing music and liquor, dance halls, bars, and movies, and sex that hung in the gloom like a chandelier and flooded the world with brief, deceptive rainbows" (47) were, in the narrator's interpretation, fleeting moments, "compensation for lives that passed like mine," that were not capable of enduring against the world's strife: "All the world was waiting for bombardments." At the movies, however, Tom is not merely a spectator of the "very long program" on the screen (31). In the stage show he becomes an assistant to "Malvolio the Magician," whose wonderful "tricks" include transformations of water into whiskey and fish into birds; and whose "wonderfullest trick of all" is escaping from a nailed coffin (32). That Tom points up the relevance of this trick to himself—"there is a trick that would come in handy for me"—reveals his kinship with other artists who perform tricks for an audience. Having an audience is essential to the trickster and the playwright, an audience that is ready for engagement and adventure,

5: THE PLAY: PRESENTING, RECOLLECTING, PROJECTING 181

that anticipates and delivers itself over to the event. His audience, like Sharlotta's, makes itself a willing device in the artist's design.

Tom's engagement with the audience in his play presumes its willingness to respond to his expectations, his presentation of himself establishing an intimacy that asks the audience to trust him while he tells them that he deals in illusions and sleight-of-hand. Confessing, "Yes, I have tricks in my pocket, I have things up my sleeve" (4), he distinguishes himself from the magician, who "gives you illusion that has the appearance of truth. I give you truth in the pleasant disguise of illusion." Distinguishing himself from Plato's magician, he appeals to the audience to let itself be taken into the "disguise of illusion," into the transformation into structure, to allow him the freedom the author of the stage directions allows him: "The narrator . . . takes whatever license with dramatic convention as is convenient to his purposes." The truth he presents is the truth of an idea that can be created out of his memory of the actual; and the transformation of an actual Laura, who has withdrawn into the past and continues to haunt him in images that appear in the present, is the elevation of the image in a play that is tribute.

Transcending the personal, the play becomes a tribute not only to the idea that might be preserved as image in an art museum or a glass menagerie but also to the artist's imperative to preserve and to confer significance in the work of art that transforms an audience into the structure of the play. This artist's requirement is an audience that can give itself to the work of art and let the work give itself as art, that can become a participant in the transformation into a structure achieving ideality. The play's excess in its presentation, the gratuitous performance for another, does not in its giving constrain but is an opening up, a liberation of the audience to the play of ideas made possible in showing, including the idea of the play as entertainment for an audience that might begin in curiosity and end in care. Heidegger distinguishes the way "Care" becomes "concern" and "circumspection" from the way "curiosity . . . concerns itself with seeing, not in order to understand what is seen (that is, to come into a Being towards it) but *just* in order to see. It seeks novelty only in order to leap from it anew to another novelty . . . just in order to have known" (*Being and Time,* H 172). Tom's anticipation is that his audience will become a genuine player, transcending curiosity, in the structure of relationship that will unite it with the artist, as he uses his tricks to sustain the image of Laura and endow her with the power of a relic. The audience, taken into his representation, has bestowed upon it the moment of illumination that is a unitive sympathy, even a sentimentality, arising out of the darkness.

To attempt to play the role of participant, to assume the identity of the audience as idea, in Jean Genet's *The Maids* is to question the possibilities and the manner of engagement, to be involved in aesthetic theory, to live the question of the audience vitally. To experience this play is to be confronted by the strange, which threatens and casts the audience into the confusion and degeneration that are the miasma from which the play arises. Testing the limits of expectation and satisfaction based in retained ideas of the artist and the play, the play also tests the audience's capacity to yield itself, to place at risk its own assurances garnered as an understanding of its world and reflected in its expectation that it will grasp and acquire an understanding of the play's world. The theatricality of this *theatrum mundi* demands adjustment and accommodation to what does not provide the clarification of an emerging cohesive world; it exposes the audience to the sheer energy of creative will deprived of the artist who, like Tom and Sharlotta, while performing sleight-of-hand engages an audience agreeably and to ostensibly benign purpose. The represented transformations in *The Maids* arise from the intensity of will to rise, to transcend debasement, and at the same time to descend in pejoration of, in dragging down and shattering, exalted, protected, and venerated images. As if deprived of perspective, a base for distinguishing what is actual from the unreal, the audience is exposed to an exaggerated display of illusions that dissolve into other illusions. As artists, Claire and Solange generate performances that are repetitions of the past, struggle through ritual toward release from the past, and create the drama that is willed to achieve finality and resolution. The play is the realization of character that exalts and destroys itself, negates value in the affirmation of virtue, and negates sanity in the certainty of convictions as it seizes the audience in that dark design of creation and demolition.

Claire and Solange are passionately absorbed in performing an action that spins out of both personal and communal pasts and, being known, provides a pattern wherein identity can be assumed and conflict regulated by the commitment to work out the design. The audience is cast apart from the maids' intimacy, radically alienated. Its discovery of the unknown is based, however, not in utter chaos, absurdity, or insanity, but in an elemental plot recognizable as bearing familiar ideas of character and action. Aristotelean probability is discernible in the maids' passion to destroy objects of hatred. Caught up in their furtive game, Claire playing Madame and Solange playing Claire, the maids are interrupted by the alarm clock that is used to announce the limit of their freedom and the necessity of preparing for Madame's return. In their own identities they continue to reveal both

5: THE PLAY: PRESENTING, RECOLLECTING, PROJECTING   183

their conflict with each other, love alternating with domination and submission, and their conflict with Madame, Claire's "anonymous letter" having been an instrument in Monsieur's being taken to jail.[14] After the telephone call from Monsieur declaring that "the judge let him out on bail" (58), they are terrified and, recalling how Solange failed to kill Madame (59), plan to kill her by putting "ten pills" of phenobarbital in her tea (66). Madame's return repeats the themes of love and domination, the maids' hostility disguised as meekness and their hatred as love; and her departure, after she is told about the telephone call, leaves them free to resume the "ceremony" (55): Solange (as Claire) killing Claire (as Madame) in the kitchen and Claire reappearing to drink the poisoned tea. This understanding of the play's action comes, not from a simple unfolding of action and revelation of character, but as appearances bearing the idea of illusion, which compels an audience's heightened involvement and affronts its self-possessed identity and anchored values.

From the beginning, the maids' assumption of roles, their mobility in moving in and out of identities, places the audience's understanding at risk. As the play begins, Claire's calling Solange "Claire" (37) as well as "Solange" (38) thrusts the audience into a forest of ambiguity, and the discrepancy in Claire's playing Madame is revealed when she as maid intrudes in the rite. Her passionate retention of her own identity does not yield entirely to the role, and her castigation of "Claire" for bringing "those odors from some foul attic" (40) unites her with Solange in that place "where the lackeys visit us at night." When she breaks the illusion with the plea "Let's skip the business of your prayers and kneeling" and lapses into talk of the "half-naked milkman" (41), Solange recalls her to the performance: "Madame is forgetting herself, Madame—." In creating and playing the role, Claire is not "forgetting herself" as Claire, and the exposure of dark design in the ritual performance is revelation that they are painfully aware of the past out of which their world and being are constituted. If Claire speaks "of the smell of garrets, it is for memory's sake" (40). The garret is both a prison and a private and secure room, a place to go "if you must whimper" (42). As if a "little altar to the Holy Virgin" (40), it is a place to dream and to preserve the cherished past, but it does not provide a base of reality and a truth of the self apart from this world of illusion. Its flowers are paper, unlike these real ones on stage whose profusion is oppressive. In one psychological maneuver, the maids' degradation and confusion induce a compulsive repudiation of what they actually are and, in a contradictory gesture, an ardent preservation and empowerment of that identity in its attempt to transcend itself, to rise above their debased condition. Their febrile struggle for transformation carries with it the bewilderment that instigates and confounds their efforts, and the audience is delivered into that perplexity.

The resolution they seek becomes the play's utmost irresolution. When the fact that Solange has in actuality killed Claire with the gloves is revealed to be an illusion, apparently but not certainly an element of the ritual, Solange's extended speech of exultation, "addressing characters who are imaginary, though present" (91), reverts from resolution to ritual repetition. Perhaps a variation and improvisation, it nevertheless remains embedded, in the structure of the rite, as preparation for the ultimate sacrifice. Since the progression toward that finality proclaims mistrust and delusion, the assurance with which Claire takes command, her having "decided to take the lead" (96), does not free the action in a transcendence of futile recurrence. Her self-immolation cannot be trusted as authentic and actual, although an audience's ambivalent desire for resolution, mimetic of the maids' passion to end their play, might authorize its exulting with Solange in the play's final speech. If Claire's death is actual, there is probable and believable cause for the sense of release from bondage, from both the debased condition and the compulsive repetition of the rite, in Solange's declaration that they will now be "beautiful, joyous, drunk, and free!" (100; "Nous serons belles, libres et joyeuses" [*Les Bonnes*, 92]). Solange's failure to kill Madame, whether believed as fact or accepted as an element of their imaginative design, establishes uncertainty and indecisiveness as the base of resolution, calling into question Claire's determination of a conclusion. Thinking of the play's action according to expectations of probability, the Aristotelean granting of the audience's demand for revelation of an understandable pattern, might raise the objection that Claire is seen drinking the tea and thereby achieves closure; but the doubt is cast ahead of the act and there is no assurance that Claire has poisoned the tea. The repeated collapsing of the actual into the illusion and revelation of the real erupting from the unreal obscures the ground of determinativeness and mingles the dimensions of game and reality. Solange's final speech, echoing the ecstatic oration that follows her illusory killing of Claire as Madame, is a clarion call into the void, a pure cry of triumph against degradation and deprivation; but it is a rejoicing that might celebrate the gaining of freedom from the ritual action or might remain embedded in it.

The accomplishment of these artists, the maids whose identities are interdependent and interchangeable, whose roles represent an antipathy of domination and subservience seeking tranquility in the memory of love, is not indubitably transcendence of that strife and anguish.

They effect a nullification of the orientation toward values that would finally distinguish the real from the illusory and malevolence from benevolence. Yet their creation of possibility out of mistrust and alienation, as expression of hope, allows an audience's involvement, and the impugning of living convictions calls into question the audience's fortified security in endowed beliefs and values. The assault on conventional virtue places the audience in the subservient role, casting it into a mimesis of the maid as Madame being dominated and abused by the inferior, the outcast, the criminal. The call for the audience's taking part, merging, and identifying with character echoes, however, that remembrance of love—"Do you remember? Under the tree, just the two of us? Our feet in the sun?" (64)—which is retained in the recurrence of violent rite. The uncertainty arising from the illusion requires a questioning, a turning toward what is to be discovered, an allowing of certainties to be put into the abeyance of the game. There remains the doubleness of possibility for the audience—to play the role of victim or be caught up in and merged in love with what is hateful and horrifying. Its disquiet might reflect the horror of Claire, who is exhilarated by thoughts of the Maenads (who mutilate indiscriminately the weak as well as those blessed or cursed by the gods) slaughtering Madame, carrying "her off to the woods" (65), cutting "her to bits by the light of the moon." Claire expresses her abomination of the act in which she is imaginatively engaged: "Murder is a thing that's . . . unspeakable!" This consciousness of the self enfolded in Apollonian dictates and at the same time alienated, freed, or cast out from them affords no resolution through evaluation and choice, judgment and discrimination. The giving of self to the enthusiasm of the game puts into abeyance any final determination of the worth of the game and as well any assurance of its outcome and consequences.

If the maids alienate and are alienated from the audience, their creation is an arrogation of power distilled in the exorbitance of the creation itself. Ambivalent toward an audience, needing one but fearful of being seen, they know security only in the abject solitude of the garret, where Solange says she "didn't have to put on a show. . . . no mirrors, no balcony" (50). From Madame's balcony Claire could, according to Solange, greet "the populace which has turned out to parade beneath her windows" (51); yet she fears that the light in the room makes of it a stage, wondering whether they can be seen by "the people opposite" (48). Solange's contempt for Claire's performances, her "playing queen, playing at Marie Antoinette, strolling about the apartment at night" (50), seems to be directed toward the cowardice of the performer's playing in the dark: "you thought you were invisible on your balcony" (51). Even the ultimate audience, God, is to be both sought and guarded against: "We know that it's for Him that the last act is to be performed, but we mustn't forewarn Him. We'll play it to the hilt" (84). When, however, Solange plays her prolonged scene after killing Madame/Claire, she turns from the "characters" on stage "who are imaginary, though present" (91), and "steps out on the balcony. Facing the night, with her back to the [actual] audience" (93), she creates with rhetorical *enargeia* the scene of triumph, a scene in which the heroine and the audience are united in the consummation of action. She calls to them, "Out on your balconies to see her making her way among the shadowy penitents!" (94). Having turned her back on the real audience for her performance on the balcony toward the darkness, a performance trammeled in illusion, she addresses the real audience in her final speech. "Facing the audience" (99), she represents a challenge to that audience, presents a dare to yield to her eloquence, to believe, to become one with her, to share her ignominy and her exaltation. As she called the imagined audience "out on your balconies" to participate in the imagined rite, she presents to this audience the *enargeia* that witnesses transformation into beauty and freedom and at the same time affronts that audience with the idea that it has, like the maids themselves, its garrets and balconies, its darkness and little light, its secrecy and need for love.

For the audience as for the maids, then, the possibility of love can arise from discord and deprecation, from cruelty and contempt, through the improbability of transformation, through the tenuous *bildung* of beauty and freedom out of detritus, the scattered remains of an aesthetic. In a world in which the aesthetic has been demeaned, all but obliterated, for the sake of waging the wars of domination and subjugation, protecting and promulgating the theories that establish virtue on the one side and error on the other, *The Maids* appears to represent that world's potential for animosity and destructiveness. The reasonable analysis and disengaged observation of such phenomena, taken up in the spirit of science, might make of the maids a study in teratology, a pursuit of their strangeness as an oddity to be understood psychologically or sociologically; they might be classified among other creatures in the category of monsters. Such analysis might satisfy the curiosity that seeks to know the strangeness of the something other. An archaeological approach might, however, recognize that they not only reveal the potential for monstrosity in their time but also carry the weight of the past from which monsters, human cruelty, destructiveness, and duplicity are borne in legend, myth, and history. It might recognize too that their longing for an innocence and their feverish attempts to recover love, to reunite fragmented beings suffering the anguish of estrangement, is a faint light remaining and must be accounted for in any archaeology.

If the aesthetic remains as a faint light, it remains a possibility the maids exploit in their call for and to an audience. The possibility of aesthetic engagement with the maids would have to be educed from an audience, whether the undifferentiated mass or the presumptuously discriminating, by coercing the alienated, entrapping the self-possessed, seducing the virtuous. Solange's appeal to Claire—"Don't laugh—ah! above all, don't laugh at my grandiloquence" (46; "Ne riez pas. Ah! surtout ne riez pas de ma grandiloquence" [*Les Bonnes*, 26])—calls the audience's attention, not merely to her virtue or vice, her strangeness or her monstrosity, but to her hyperbolic eloquence. An audience that can surrender to her speeches at the end of the play and to the play's eloquence remains capable of enacting the aesthetic. The total mediation of the play might put into abeyance the audience's strengths, including its "aesthetic differentiation" (Gadamer, *Truth and Method*, 85–87), its expertise; and the maids' exorbitant dramatization of fierce creation that is an "extraordinary combination of luxury and filth" (76) takes the chance that "Everyone's listening, but no one will hear" (90). The audience is free to repudiate them, their creation, the play; to remain secure and captivated in the toils of the actual. If it loses and finds itself in their web of illusion, if it is delivered into a genuine relationship of care, it might come to appreciate the experience itself as it echoes and at the same time dismantles the idea of sublimity.

The improbability of the sublime's appearing in the maids' world, in which archaic ideas of the sublime are passé, becomes a possibility in an idea inherent in the sublime itself, an idea of the sublime that the maids manifest. The sublime, stripped of the metaphysical and relocated in the subjective—notably in the empiricism that provides a psychology for Joseph Addison's and Edmund Burke's discussions of the sublime and in Immanuel Kant's aesthetic—retains the idea of violence, the sublime's assault on the subject. Kant's distinction of the sublime from the beautiful opposes the playfulness of the beautiful to the sublime's earnestness "in the presentation or faculty of presentation . . . the imagination";[15] and the simple pleasure of beauty's attractiveness is opposed to the complicated attraction and repulsion of the sublime, which is not pleasure but "negative pleasure" (300). It "seems to be no sport, but a dead earnest affair of the imagination" (299). As opposed to the satisfaction to be had in experiencing the beautiful object, which conveys a sense of purposiveness that can become useful in our regarding nature not "as mere mechanism" but "enlarged to the concept of nature as art" (301), the sublime seems to "contravene the ends of our power of judgment, to be an outrage on the imagination, yet it is judged all the more sublime on that account" (300). Sublimity of the imagination does not lend credence to understanding actuality by "anything leading to particular objective principles" (301)—by Aristotelean probability—but rather, the sublime being subjective, there is generated in the experience of it only "a feeling in our own selves of appropriateness quite independent of nature." If the violence of the imagination, the violation of lucid purpose, in the maids' representation does not lead to "particular objective principles and corresponding forms" by which their actions can be understood and their natures judged, they retain the qualities of the sublime that elude conformability to a world that can be apprehended as designed and purposeful. Their representation "excites ideas of the sublime" as a power Kant attributes to nature "in its chaos, or in its wildest and most irregular disorder and desolation, provided it gives signs of magnitude and power," in that their intensity, their excitement of a sense of disaster and destruction, and their imaginative aggrandizement elevate the action beyond the scope of the beautiful.

The ideas of qualities of the sublime that remain are not, however, an intact theory of the sublime, locating it in the subject, but have become in a world of detritus scattered, deflected from a sense of center and continuity. The heightened violence is "all the more sublime" because it does not answer to reasonableness and probability in this world. The maids' compulsion to realize this purposive use of the imagination can be expressed only in language and ideas brought down from exalted ideas of the past—nobility has to be rediscovered in what is possible, essences must be found in the actual. A name and operative meaning for nobility might be sought by Wallace Stevens in words like "peculiar" and "eccentric";[16] Ideas might become "notions" for T. S. Eliot; and the sublime might be called by the "lesser" name, "beauty." When Solange uses the word "beauty" it evokes a sense of the sublime that appears in a play embarrassed by great ideas of the past. When she declares that "The great thing is to end in beauty" (88), she affirms that purposiveness of the violent imagination and anticipates that distillation of the sublime in the exalted *enargeia* of her final speeches.

As an antiquated idea, the sublime can be affirmed in a degenerate world only by the force of an imagination that scavenges from the wreck of noble ideas and authorizes its own activity as a violent seizure and transformation of the world's violence. In Kant's bringing the sublime down from metaphysical heights to relocate it in the subject, this diminishment covers up the archaic question of its essential purpose as established in Longinus's treatise, which is to link and to transcend the privacy of the subject's dark garret. The ideas of power and violence remained, in such instances as Wordsworth's spots of time, under the influence of the Longinian sublime. Longinus's rhetorical sublime was a "single blow" out of rhetoric's persuasion, casting a spell, exerting "invincible power and force," tearing "everything up like a whirlwind."[17] This location of the event of the sublime in the relationship of the work and the audience, the work's getting "the better of every hearer," attributes to the work itself, in which the *ethos* of the author remains, that determinative power to capture and enslave the audience, whose power to control and choose whether or not it will be persuaded is overcome.

Paradoxically, this idea of the enslavement of the audience addresses an essence, an instinct, that involves the human being, who is "no humble or lowly creature" (35.2), in ideas of transcending, connecting with what is beyond the self, understanding meaning and purpose, and thereby achieving freedom. The audience genuinely engaged in a work is enslaved by it and thereby gains freedom. Being "spectators" brought "into life and into the universe as into a great festival," we, because of an "irresistible desire for anything which is great and, in relation to ourselves, supernatural . . . travel beyond the boundaries of our surroundings" and seek to know "what we were born for" (35.2–3). Returning to the paradox in his *peroratio*, Longinus wonders whether the slavish mentality is not overcome, as "one of the philosophers" has proposed (44.1), by the freedom of a democratic state, since in bondage "the inability to speak freely and the consciousness of being a prisoner at once assert themselves, battered into him as they have been by the blows of habit" (44.4). Longinus's answer is that pettiness and ignobility are not to be understood by finding "fault with the present situation" (44.6) but by recognizing the true sources of bondage that appear to be expressions of freedom: the love of wealth and pleasure, which generate "greed, pride, and luxury," which "breed in turn those inexorable tyrants of the soul, insolence, lawlessness, and shamelessness" (44.7). True bondage is not imposed from without but generated from within; enslavement by the sublime is a lifting up and freeing to the discovery of relationship and purpose through the capacity to love what is greater than the self. The bondage of the self to what preserves and augments the self is broken by the assault from the alien sublime and the reciprocal submission of the subject, even if in unwilling astonishment, to that assault.

The paradoxical linking of the ideas of enslavement and freedom in the sublime, its power to overwhelm and its aim to liberate and exalt, frees the imagination to "travel beyond . . . boundaries." It is not in *The Maids* an accomplishment of Longinus's vision sub specie aeternitatis. It is, however, an expression of the desire to recover lost dignity and innocence, a desire that seems like a vague recollection of the Longinian sublime. The hope that the play's audience—assaulted, deluded, disoriented, vulnerable to eloquence—can be caught up in that tattered dream is an anticipation that it can spontaneously, for the moment, free itself from the fetters of its world, its alienated and tawdry state, as represented in the play's brutality and victimization. Through the capacity to reciprocate, to love and admire what appears struggling, improbably and outrageously, even arrogantly and viciously, out of the mire toward an image of beatitude preserved and proclaimed by the obstinacy of creatures of the mire, the audience might lose and discover itself. It is not only assaulted by the representation of human bestiality and depravity but also liberated to share the illusion that even in bondage and isolation, in the garret and the cave, the impulse to rise from that disgrace persists.

In the affirmation that spites detrition, in the leap that defies Horatian equanimity, the audience represented by the maids in their imagination might achieve a momentary and problematical transcendence in the imaginative passing "beyond the boundaries." To Claire/Madame's question, "Are you offering me the dreary exile of your imagination?" (43), the audience might respond that, yes, we share the exile and the imagination that renounces it. Forfeiting the sanity and security of the Horatian poet, the maids represent the "mad poet" who is "on a rampage, / Stampeding unlearned and learned alike, in his rage / To recite."[18] Leaping like Empedocles "into Aetna . . . to his fiery fate," they wish "to be thought an immortal god," and their vision contains the Horatian warning against giving oneself to the spell of sublime eloquence. "Sensible people avoid" the mad poet like Genet and his maids because, "once he's caught you, he'll . . . read you and read you and read you and read you to death." The grandiloquence of Solange reveals what remains as a potential idea of the sublime, the transformation through eloquence, poetry, and aesthetic fusion that is itself, especially in our time, suspect and perhaps merely an illusion. The feverous imagination of this artist would confound living convictions in an embrace that casts into abeyance the comforting illusions of a reality built out of calamity; it would offer an improbable sublime moment in creating a singular challenge to unite in strange beauty.

The artist's representing the gesture that is an image caught from the transitory, that moment arising in extremity, tests the possibility of realizing momentary transcendence. Yet the gesture is made possible as an image drawn from the past and as an intimation of the mystery, the ineffable, that cannot be brought "thematically into one's grasp." The work as tribute to and preservation of what is past, even if in

5: THE PLAY: PRESENTING, RECOLLECTING, PROJECTING

shards, and to the anticipation of an audience's reception and retention of it is not fulfilled and completed in applause but, like the relic, is carried forward into the future. It is retained as influence and as memory, both in mediating possible experiences of drama and attracting to itself, calling audiences back to the remembered play that, in the recollection, is anticipatory. To the extent that it has not been fixed and held fast thematically, that it was in the presentational and unitive act representing not only the presence in a moment but also the attenuation of moments, it offers an opportunity to recover the moment as not yet fully grasped. When the work has established that relationship of care that transcends curiosity, it does not release nor is it released; but in that *bildung* is generated a freedom to see again and to see more, to experience again and afresh.

The power and eloquence of mortal artists like Tom Wingfield and Solange, the angel of earth, bestow in the sentimentality, histrionics, or perversity of their performances a range of affect from trivialization to profundity. Their plays become, for an audience, an acknowledgment that the illusion of the present bears in what it makes as its reality the images and ideas of the past that can be worn down, trivialized, transformed, put to bizarre use, retained as ideals. As their plays might become preservation and honor to plays and makers of the past and in turn merit tribute from their audiences, they reiterate the possibilities in reaching toward others and hoping for responsiveness. Ideas of authors and of worlds, both the worlds they derive from and the worlds they make, remain available and diverse icons retained in and viable for the historical community. Retained as well is the idea of retention itself, as plays make speculative their allusiveness to inherited worlds and makers of worlds.

In plays' echoing from the past, they invite speculation and the discovery or making of connections. An audience might recognize and feel in the febrile authorship of Bergman's *Fanny and Alexander,* in the ways makers of plays think about and realize the *theatrum mundi* metaphor, a revitalization of the frenetic and dour artist of Ibsen's *The Master Builder.* The imposing or oppressive power felt in the image of the artist as god can be, as these plays demonstrate, debilitating or rejuvenating, as can be god-like influences from the dimension beyond, the realm of god, or from mysterious dimensions that impinge on the present world. As this contemporary film might be felt to be a commentary on, as allusion to, ideas about the artist of rebellion against the artist of omnipotence in the earlier play, two contemporary dramas, again a film and a play, might be considered as comparable ways to reach back into the past to speculate on the Adamic image as it relates to the idea of the artist. Bernard Pomerance's *The Elephant*

Man and Harold Pinter's *The French Lieutenant's Woman* provoke thought of the earth-bound and earth-generated artist manqué as maker of work and world. The Adamic figures must, in their assumptions about their life's missions, obligations, and endowments, contend with the enigmas that seem to come from and remain beyond them, especially as realized in the mysteries of the female and the artist. All of these plays have in common a sense of mystery that, reflected in the audience, can be resolved neither by getting into one's grasp the ultimate truth of worlds beyond or withdrawn into the past nor by fully identifying with, understanding the powers and psyche of, the artist.

Rebellion and Reconciliation: Ibsen's *The Master Builder* and Bergman's *Fanny and Alexander*

Entertaining ideas of the artist generates not only the image of the creator of peopled worlds who fills the role of the artist as maker but also of that figure undergoing the vicissitudes of being in the world, playing out the *bildung* of self in a world of strife and discord as well as harmony. According to the RCA Victor trademark—the terrier listening to "His Master's Voice"—the god speaks through the machine. The absent artist who speaks *ex machina* is a creator, the author of this wonderful experience that takes us beyond our ordinary, and in speaking he/she is manifest as a presence that seems to come from another dimension of reality, a truer or more real dimension, perhaps. The imperatives of one divine maker, the God of testament, are embedded in His message to the world, making their claim or demand. Coming directly, for instance to Job as a voice from the whirlwind ("I will demand of thee" [Job 40.7]), or through an intermediary, as when the angel tells Joseph in a dream that he should "fear not to take unto thee Mary thy wife" (Matt. 1.20), this message from another world demonstrates the authority and control of the agent as maker of His lesser world. In the lesser dimension, as the earthly artist creates a world, imitating the act of divine creation, her or his making of a world might range from pious mimesis to iconoclasm. If the voice of God might seem to descend from the heavens, the human artist in Ibsen's *The Master Builder,* Halvard Solness, might respond by standing atop the steeple at Lysanger to announce his rebellion; if it might be heard through the voice of an agent, as when in Bergman's *Fanny and Alexander* Edvard counsels Alexander in the ways of Truth, the nascent artist Alexander might defy that fervent spokesman for God's Truth with obstinate though silent refusal.

In Ibsen's *The Wild Duck*, the "claim" or "demand" that Gregers Werle brings to the Ekdal family when he comes "down from the heights"[19] is a claim of the "Ideal." Gregers's rectitude and his austerity, like Edvard's in Bergman's film, reflect or "stand in for"[20] the quality of seriousness or sincerity of that other dimension from which his moral imperatives are promulgated. His certainty of knowledge reflects the authority and the truth of the mind of the creator (who like god in Plato's *Republic* is One, unchanging, and true). The question of the truth is, of course, essential to the maker of representations, and the artist's need to know and to act on the truth—Solness' and Alexander's—is instinctive, expressed as a will to disobey, to question and ultimately to deny the authority of heavenly or Platonic Ideals and to seek on the earth whatever truths they can find or make. The aging Solness has chosen to make homes for human beings to live in together (and is now, initiating a new phase, constructing for himself a home with a tower); and the child Alexander has populated little worlds, little theaters, with creatures of his imagination for the entertainment of the other children. Given a "local habitation and a name," these artists' ideas answer to no stentorian call from a bright world above.

If the received Ideals and Truths are fixed, eternally unchangeable, they are determined and set in another dimension, beyond the earth. That other world, acceded to in the traditions of Platonic philosophy and Christian theology as a "superior" world, is felt to be as genuine and imposing as merely human values and accomplishments are uncertain, tentative, fluctuating, and ephemeral. The Ideal, projected metaphorically above and beyond, in its essential absence has to be sent down by a voice or a sign. If the essence of Ideal truth lies in its changelessness and univocity, the artist who relinquishes access to absolute truth turns earthward in search of serviceable truths, seeking among beings of this world for what is good.

The disfranchised artist, however, need not and perhaps cannot retreat into the self, finding in pseudo-romantic privacy, in some still point of origin, a source of inspiration and truth. In both plays, the artist is dependent on other influences than a god-centered One. If ideas are relocated in things of the earth, essences are to be discovered in experiences, and the artist's temporality entails a dialectic of discovery and a concomitant mobility. Being mortal artists, Solness and Alexander engage in processes of discovery and realization, and their *Bildung* is enacted in the *theatrum mundi* that reflects as well as challenges the transcendent dimension.[21] Their progress and development, and the consequences of their actions, are as different as their ages, the old architect and the unformed boy, but both are cast out into a strangeness that is new involvement and discovery. Trusting in their relatedness to others in this process, risking involvement, is the essential condition for their making their ways in and attempting reconciliation with the world.

Although not deprived of connectedness, these artists in their need for self-realization reveal in the idea of artist that idea of isolation and privacy. Solness's sense of alienation is not merely the result of personal disillusionment or a sense of guilt. Having conceived of himself as standing apart from the world, he has assumed a stance of heroism. Poised high above the world, on top of the tower he had built for God, he inaugurated his calling of service to human beings by repudiating God's will and declaring his freedom: "I said to Him: Hear me, Thou Almighty! From this day on, I'll be a free creator—free in my own realm, as you are in yours" (854). Not only was his moment of courage endangered by the human beings below, "one of those little devils in white . . . screaming up at me" (805), but also his career has come to naught: "Nothing, nothing—it all comes to nothing" because "human beings don't know how to use these homes of theirs" (855). Solness' and his wife Aline's own home is like other homes, a place of alienation, error, and loss rather than a place where people "could live safe and happy, feeling what a sweet thing it is to be alive in this world" (825). The alienation is a heroic pose against lack of appreciation—from God above, from mortals below.

That felt isolation is for Solness an estrangement from his past as well as from god and other people of the moment, although he feels in and for himself, contradictorily, an inheritance, a special endowment. His elevated solitude in that memorable moment ten years ago is that of a flawed character, signifying his attachment to the past, his idea of himself generated out of epic or tragic images of the hero. Entangled in the mundane, with a jealous wife whose passivity is menacing, with unpromising but threatening adversaries whose presence is enervating, he is no builder of castles for the Norse gods, no participant in the epic struggle between the gods and the giants. But he harbors secret thoughts of his exceptional nature. Although his source of power and influence is hidden, mysterious, even dangerous, he is certain that something comes to him, as for Socrates Ion's power comes through the mysterious rings.

Solness's potential derives, like Ion's, from the dimension of thought, not only in idealized conceptions of his role and calling but also in the secret working out of his thoughts or wishes: he is one of those "chosen people who have a gift and power and capacity to *wish*

5: THE PLAY: PRESENTING, RECOLLECTING, PROJECTING   195

something, *desire* something, *will* something—so insistently and so—so inevitably" (830). The house burned, not because he knew about and did not correct a condition that could cause a fire, but because he wished it (830); Kaja heard his unspoken wish and answered him by offering herself as his assistant (797); Hilda came with her own demand but possibly in response to his secret desire, his "call" (833). Although he is not unsympathetic toward others, as for instance in recognizing that Aline "had a talent for building too" (826), his identity is built on a sense of otherness, a dispensation, which makes his relationships with others matters of secrets, liaisons, and hidden negotiations rather than reciprocity in shared endeavors and mutual dependence in social relationships. Solness's metaphysical terror exhibits Promethean isolation, the solitary hero attracting to himself and encountering the gods' power; he experiences not the impenetrable darkness beyond human community, the void of unknowing that enforces human participation in the scene of mortality, but the force of will concentrated either against him or—to echo a thought rich in implication throughout Ibsen's plays—for his sake. If Hilda comes for his sake, as emissary from the unseen world, then she only confirms his being set apart, chosen, whether for good or ill, and his heroic suffering is sanctioned by his uniqueness.

Alexander moves, on the other hand, in a deferential world, the child allowed to wander romantically solitary, like Edward Young's poet: "In the fairyland of fancy, genius may wander wild; there it has a creative power, and may reign arbitrarily over its own empire of chimeras."[22] In their apparent isolation, whether thrust upon them or sought, both Solness and Alexander retain and show signs of the romantic need for purposeful withdrawal from others. The film opens with Alexander directing his own private play, his creation of a little world being a mimesis of the artist in the larger world, which is a world of the theater making little worlds for its own and others' entertainment. His being let alone and left free to create is not, however, abandonment. When he moves back toward the family, calling their names, his isolation confirms the abiding presence of others. The mystery of the private self, far from invalidating the possibility of communion, establishes the necessity of accepting uncertainty, irresolution, and disclosure to others. The fallible generosity that characterizes his world is human fallibility and the human understanding that the individual's freedom is a condition of the world's benevolence. This world's magnanimity is grounded in an assurance of others' letting one be, and this consolation seems to reflect the encompassing dimension. The god of tradition is celebrated in a Christmas pageant that confirms blessedness and the permission to realize individual and collective undertakings, but this limited approbation does not resolve ultimate questions and purposes, nor does it put to rout the encompassing darkness.

The stage on which the artist must realize, must build, the self receives definitions from the past and must define itself in its time as a lighting within that darkness. According to Oscar in his speech early in the play, which with Gustav's at the end frames the play's action, outside the theater is an alienation, a "harsh world"[23] that drives the artists of the theater back into their world. If Oscar sees the little world as a world of "orderliness, routine, conscientiousness, and love," Gustav, reiterating the necessity of kindness and affection in our trying "to take pleasure in *the little world*" (208), recognizes too that among us and beyond there is imperfection, mere human vulnerability and tenuousness, selfishness and error. On our part we must have our "subterfuges," and the actors represent us in providing "our supernatural shudders" (207). In the little world of make believe we have represented to us those characters and events, mortal and metaphysical, that make us shudder. We cannot hope to control or grasp with our understanding the sublime, which bestows on us the recognition that our finite world is all we have to be happy in. These two eloquent, derivative speeches, Oscar's in the beginning and Gustav's at the end, constitute a message from, in, and about this world that is contradicted by the eloquence of Edvard's assertion that truth and reality are generated elsewhere.

This world of the theater is, of course, the one into which Alexander is born and to which he returns after separation and initiation, after his forced encounter with the alien world of Edvard. Edvard's stark white world of absolute conviction is enabling for Alexander, constituting a ground for *bildung,* for return to his world and himself, and his imprisonment is instrumental in that growth and development. Edvard is one of those mysteries, embedded in this world, that produce shudders. Rather than discovering evil set apart as coming from the outside, recognizing the unfathomable duplicity of Edvard affirms the evil within, the existence of interpenetrating realities, Oscar's "harsh world outside" that appears among us when Gustav's actors give us our "supernatural shudders," as Oscar was, while playing the Ghost in *Hamlet,* himself dying. The inside and the outside, the human and the alien, are not to be isolated from one another, their boundaries known and their difference established; like the theater and the world, they impinge and reflect, and the alien might appear in the mirror of ourselves.

The supernatural appears with the force of the sublime in the world of Isak, into which Alexander is thrust after the escape from Edvard.

5: THE PLAY: PRESENTING, RECOLLECTING, PROJECTING   197

Alexander has been thrown from the rich clutter of the theatrical milieu into the harsh gravity of Edvard's house, and his journey back home entails experiencing an illuminating reality. If Edvard's regimentation and scrupulous authoritarianism certify his method as the way of Truth, his ostensible forthrightness and rectitude belie darker purposes and deeds, both in his past and in the present. Isak saves the children by a trick (a ruse comparable to the device practiced by the Venetian fishermen when they spirited the body of St. Mark away from Alexandria and brought it to Venice for righteous ends, even though those ends had to be legitimized by fictions). The trick distinguishes him as an artist of the marvelous, and his home confirms this role. His nephew Aron, appropriately named for a high priest, presides over a puppet theater. With his puppets, he declares, he is God. His puppet theater like Alexander's little theater, for instance the drama of Arabella and her mother's ghost, can cause shudders, calling up figures and intimations from a mysterious world beyond. The profuse, luxuriant, theatrical trappings of Isak's house are the setting for Alexander's losing his way and encountering the strange, the eerie. Oscar's ghost appears, assuring Alexander that death does not separate them, that he cannot leave Alexander—as he has assured Emilie before his death; and Alexander's fusion of identity with Ismael, writing Alexander and reading Ismael, opens up for Alexander implausible connections between actions in Isak and Edvard's worlds, mysterious knowledge of unseen events.

In these two plays the dimensions of this world and another are essential structuring. The world apart from the human, where both Solness and the Ekdahls' god presumably dwells, does not give itself in clear and definitive terms. Although, projecting attributes of their own world into the beyond, the inhabitants of Alexander's world feel a beneficence from beyond and Solness's community feels the stern authority of God, as does Edvard's, the spiritual or ideal dimension is not discerned by means of pure revelation but discovered in the challenges to understanding that come with intrusions from the unknown. In both plays, the mystery makes itself known in the immediate dimension, not only revealing by surprise but also revealing the incompleteness of revelation.

This perplexing connectedness and problematical relationship between worlds, between the imagined present and other worlds of a play, between individuals and little worlds within those worlds, between the worlds of the plays that refer across time, are essential representations of the structure of relatedness between play and audience. The transformation into structure of idea raises questions in the duplicative worlds of the plays and in the unresolved worlds of the audience: themes of knowledge and identity, discovery and concealment, the dialectic of withdrawal-defense-isolation-separation and approach-discovery-fusion-union, rebellion and reconciliation. The characters in these plays are mimetically engaged in the requisite activity that engages us: standing open to surprise, Heidegger's "astonishment" that is the beginning and the accompaniment of philosophy and of plays' ideality. Solness and Edvard embody a principle of control, the need for maintenance of order for the sake of self; their domains are theirs by possession and domination. While our moment of commiseration for Edvard comes to us only when in his suffering he cries out that he is "horribly awake" (196), our concern for Solness follows his prolonged development and reflects his consternation that his will, his decisions, and his calculations do not effect his goals. Alexander, on the other hand, seeks experience and suffers things to come to him; and, even when he tries to flee them, as when he avoids his dying father, they come to him nevertheless. He explores the mysterious, the attractive horror; lacking the adult commitment to a vested accomplishment, Solness and Edvard's defensiveness for the worlds they have built, he is ready to be astonished.

In the play's domain being ceded to the audience, the audience might reflect, ambivalently, the impulses of either Solness or Alexander, or both of them. To make the play one's own might mean gaining dominion, forcing it toward complete disclosure and measuring it by one's own understanding and values, leaving no mystery, no unresolved and perhaps irresolvable questions. This is the satisfaction Aristotle addresses in his insistence on probability or necessity, with the implication that the play gratifies, reassures, confirms order and meaningfulness in its revelation of intelligibility. But if Heidegger is justified in attributing his thoughts about astonishment to Plato and Aristotle, Aristotle's rather neglectful observation that wonder is essential to tragedy reveals something more problematical than the resolution that comes with full and final understanding. A mode of readiness for astonishment is anticipatory; it is a standing open to further astonishment and a letting of the refractory unknown remain unknown. The ultimate astonishment would be the end of astonishment, the closure of knowledge in that absolute intelligibility. The story of Alexander exemplifies what will in the future remain this openness to discovery in that it is a story about beginnings, preparation, *bildung;* and it maintains, even requires, respect for the mystery of forces beyond this world's understanding. Alexander has only begun his discovery, but what he has seen is taken in by him, informs his maturation, and dwells with him. The past endures in relical power capable of reasserting itself, as the ghost of his father assures

Alexander of his enduring benign presence and influence and as the apparition of Edvard (in the film, not in the published script) reminds Alexander that his rancorous influence will endure, admonishing him that "You can't escape me."

If readiness to be astonished implies the anticipation of further revelation and the readiness to receive the alien and assimilate the strange, then other dimensions might not be merely constituted by or projected from ourselves, generated and therefore governed by us; in the astonishment of their appearing, becoming present to us, they bestow themselves: in their appearing and as they are. Otherness and the alien are not, however, comprised only of the powers, wills, or presences appearing to Solness and Alexander from another dimension. These artists' own pasts and the others who people their own world are no less mysterious or problematical than are visitations from unseen, felt dimensions beyond. If, as I have suggested, Edvard reveals an obscure will to power sanctioned by his bequeathed authority and if Solness's need for control is fortified by his secret image of himself drawn from heroic images from the past, then the past remains operative in the drama of their lives. They maintain the past and utilize it to their own purposes. Solness's ineffectual repudiation of the past is signified in the fact that he does not read anymore, though he "used to try, in the old days" (820). Like Hilda, he "can't connect with" books. Solness's compulsion to free himself, as Hilda advises him, to be "all alone" in his "right to build" (821), produces his "solitude and silence—endlessly . . . brooding on that same idea." His competitiveness directs itself both toward the eternal god, the supreme authority, and toward all men who might like himself aspire to authority, men of his world like Brovik and Brovik's son Ragnar being read by Solness as having dark, hidden purposes against him.

Alexander's receptivity to others—to his father and uncle Gustav, the nominal rulers of the theater world; to Isak and Aron, figures of power in their world—denotes his freedom, a freedom not of cutting himself loose from others but of assimilation and complaisance. To be free is not to retreat in "solitude and silence—endlessly," to brood with Solness, in Schiller's terms, on the "twofold seriousness of duty and of destiny" (80). Alexander has the freedom to wander, to hide, to create and through creation interpret reality—interpretation ranging from the "lie" that his mother sold him to a traveling circus to the "truth" about Edvard's children—and this freedom can manifest that "lack of earnestness" that Schiller associates with play: "Man only plays when he is in the fullest sense of the word a human being, and he is only fully a human being when he plays." In reaching into the past for an understanding of Edvard's nature, whether truth or fiction,

Alexander is refusing the segregation that Edvard enforces on life and art. When Edvard counsels Alexander in the way of truth, in the necessity of distinguishing between the lie and the truth (90), play and imagination become the exclusive rights of those who are not serious; imagination is "held in trust for us" by the others, the artists (92). Edvard presumes to know them and to categorize and isolate them, while Alexander is vulnerable to the play of the world, the uncertainty and not knowing that keep him receptive to "historical" figures, to ghosts of the dead and gone that will continue to appear in the future, and receptive as well to the living.

These ranging modes of being in the world, from the congeniality and complaisance of involvement to the alienation and isolation of self, are ways of embodying ideas of love and strife, domination and submission, grasping and letting be. Solness actualizes a contradiction in elevating himself above, divorcing himself from others and his past while suffering dependence on them and submission to them, feeling a loss of freedom; it is as if he reveals his essence, his ground of being, to be strife; his vital need, his unrealized being, to be love and harmony. Alexander's conflict is with an abstracting force, with Edvard as a representation of the principle of division, categorization, and separation; but this intrusion into his world wages war against what is fundamental for him, the principle of love and harmony. A humorous moment illustrating the way conflict appears in Alexander's world of concord is Alma's slapping Maj, a gesture not without provocation and one that could be expected to generate further conflict in the love triangle; but it is a momentary action without protracted effect or interest. With Alma's knowledge and apparently her approval or at least her compliance, the relationship between Maj and Gustav is sustained, producing one of the baby girls in the last scene.

The principle of domination, as I have characterized it, produces the conflict between lord and servant, master and slave, and generates the need for freedom. It has been treated in this discussion as evidently an ancestral male stereotype, since I have scarcely mentioned the plays' women until I pointed to Maj. I have, however, consciously avoided the question of the stereotypical female in order to observe opposed tendencies without identifying them as male and female. Domination, power, rule, constraint, separation, and estrangement on the one hand and on the other—not freedom, isolation, and heroic solitariness or reversal of the power roles—but self-determination in community, fulfillment in union and reconciliation, identity generated out of communal experience, growth through participation and harmony, these are opposed characteristics that have been, since the world was created out of Chaos and Love was born, in one way and another opposed as male and female, in the Olympian gods Ares and Aphrodite, in Empedocles's love and strife. It would seem, however, that as Heracleitean paradox the male and female are not only undeniable opposites but also interdependent. Bergman's play being named for Fanny *and* Alexander suggests that she is as important as he; that the title of Ibsen's play is an epithet for the male protagonist implies his detachment and isolation in the need for mastery.

The possible human relationships have been structured as idea including, in addition to that between god the father/artist and the human being, the involvements of male and female. The reunion of Hilda with Solness is crucial, instigating the play's action, while the unobtrusive presence of Fanny accompanying Alexander is unremarkable except that it must be noticed as at least raising a question; it is a presence to be regarded. If there is something enigmatic about Fanny's quiet attendance, the enigma of Hilda proclaims itself, for both audience and characters in the play, as requiring discernment, care, and circumspection. If we at first take the challenge posed by these two characters as having to do with the questions of enablement and suppression, the ideas and roles of male and female, we might be led to encounter, with the male artists, the extremity of interpretation and the limits of understanding; these two female characters are enigmatic, for the audience as well as for Alexander and Solness. The idea of the female takes us, in both plays, to the limits of knowing, definition, and the comforting sense of power that comes of interpreting. Alexander's encounter with Ismael takes him to the edge of reason and, for us and from our familiarity with Aristotelean theory, to the limits of dramatic probability; and it is the culmination of his adventures before his homecoming. Ismael's identity is a mysterious fusion of male and female; his allusive name, interpreted by him as meaning "he will be a wild man" (198), is appropriate to his being Alexander's alter ego, but his voice, persona, and sensuality in caressing Alexander are feminine. He speaks Alexander's thoughts and wishes, "saying your mental pictures aloud" (200); but, going beyond the mystery of knowing Alexander's subjective experience, he speaks Alexander's wishes that are, like Solness's, being realized in the objective reality. "I merge into you," he declares, and Alexander now "clearly sees the burning figure" (Edvard) that Ismael has just described. As idea, this fusion might be a consummation that is mimetic of the doubling of the hero in myth or the marriage of male and female, perhaps the Jungean reunion of anima and animus or the liberation of Nietzsche's dionysian spirit. Ismael's declaring himself to be Alexander's "guardian angel," however, bestows a particularity on their relationship that is not felt in entertaining the broad ideas of the male doppelgänger or the union of male and female.

As Ismael is provocative and quizzical in generating and obfuscating the idea of the female, his identification of himself as Alexander's "guardian angel," linking the ideas of the female and the guardian angel, further provokes speculation on ways these ideas and others might be related. The male guardian angel might appear at times of crisis or care, as in Milton's *Paradise Lost* Raphael comes to Adam and Eve, first warning them of Satan's threat and then relating the past events that are background to their immediate predicament. Embodying the idea of guardian angel, such a being appears from another dimension executing his role as protector, guide, and instructor; offering for the recipient security, direction, and understanding. In the Christmas play that opens *Fanny and Alexander,* Emilie plays a female angel who warns Joseph and Mary of Herod's threat and assures them that "all ends well this holy day" (24). The guardian angel embodied as woman might like Ismael cause supernatural shudders or might like Emilie play the role as bland, matter-of-fact reassurance of harmony between worlds. The guardian angel might like Emilie's descend from that superior dimension or might like Ismael appear within the world or from a world within it.

Neither a darkly glowing energy like Ismael nor a bright messenger like her mother's angel, Fanny is no authorized guardian angel from this or another dimension; she seems, nevertheless, to be an angel of earth, sustaining and supporting Alexander, offering him guidance and protection. She is protective and supportive of Alexander; for instance, in the scene in which Amanda challenges Alexander's understanding of Isak's lesson that the human being "bears chasms, heavens, and eternities within him" (122). Fanny responds to Amanda, "If you're so afraid of what can't be seen you'd better get yourself another brother and sister" (123). Like the angel, she has assumed the responsibility to take a message from her dying father to Alexander, responding when Oscar asks that she "Tell Alexander there's nothing to be afraid of": "I'll tell him" (75). As an angel with him, on and of earth, Fanny might well provide another assistance to Alexander beyond maintaining protection, defending him, and conveying advice. She shares with him the first vision of Oscar's ghost (82).

That sharing includes, as in her identification with his thoughts against Amanda's, an imaginative participation. Alexander's story of Edvard's wife and two daughters, their being imprisoned and starved "for five days and nights" (121) and their fatal attempt to escape, is a product of the imagination and has been anticipated by Fanny. When Emilie, Amanda, and Alexander revealed that they knew the story of the drowning, Fanny extrapolated a haunting by the "two pale little girls" who will come to "entice Fanny to a deep part of the river" (110). Fanny, then, unobtrusively serves as angel to Alexander, but with a distinctive quality. Like Wallace Stevens's "angel of reality . . . the necessary angel of earth" ("Angel Surrounded by Paysans," *Palm*, 354), she helps to attune the poet or artist to earth's "liquid lingerings," its "tragic drone," and her influence is "of the mind," the imagination. Thinking of Fanny in this light is not meant to lift her out of her ordinary status, abstracting her as merely an idea, as representing the idea of the angel, to the extent that she is no longer apprehended as sister, as unobtrusive but persistent child-accomplice. After all, in the epilogue she plays the role of mortal observer in Alexander's play about the "dying man," when "Death has taken shape in the nursery" (210). She plays a supporting role to the dying hero while the mature women, her mother and grandmother, are prepared at the end of the play to assume roles in "a new play by August Strindberg . . . that abominable misogynist" (216).

Her relationship to Alexander suggests, however, the idea of a figure far less spectacular than that of the imposing angel. The artist receives a presence that influences and inspires, activating and empowering the imagination. Milton's "Heav'nly Muse . . . didst inspire" Moses,[24] the invocation in Book III asks the "Celestial Light" to "shine inward . . . / . . . that I may see and tell / Of things invisible to mortal sight" (3.51–55). The spiritual guide of the poet or artist is the muse, who has a double identity. She might be thought of as an abstract generative force behind and absent from the work of art, the personal genius guiding the creator; but she might appear as well embodied, a figure in the work: in Milton's voice calling his muse, his invocation to an ambiguous but identifiable source, or in Dante's Beatrice, Petrarch's Laura. Fanny's complicity with Alexander is a quiet, profound influence, not a spectacular appearance but an enduring presence, support, and inspiration. When Alexander tells Justine, "his audience" (120), his story of a visitation by apparitions, Fanny attests to the veracity of his story by declaring, "I've seen them too." She abets Alexander in his telling of "things invisible to mortal sight." If the idea of her sharing attributes with the muse is to be entertained, she should be recognized too as an "angel of earth": inconspicuous, grounded, mortal. Contemplated as muse, she instantiates the ideas of administering to and inspiring the artist, and her presence and influence are generative in this artist's creating his work.

Hilda's relationship with Solness is less clearly as guardian angel or muse, though she can be seen as bearing the signs of either. While Fanny's unassuming presence maintains a constant and beneficent influence on Alexander, encouraging his imaginative excursions and enriching his *bildung,* Hilda's appearing to Solness, suddenly and dramatically after exactly ten years, startles and surprises him. Like Gregers Werle in *The Wild Duck* and like an angel from another dimension, she comes down from the heights—Solness knew her ten years ago when he "built a tower on the old church . . . up at Lysanger" (801); Dr. Herdal met her "last summer . . . at one of the mountain lodges" (800); and Mrs. Solness met her "up *there* . . . at that health resort" (801). Her descent would designate her an angel of the ideal, and she comes with an assurance that seems to authorize her demand for a kingdom. Her authority, however, is not endorsed by known and trusted divine or ideal purpose illuminated through her mediation. Nor is she an angel of earth like Fanny, a merely human being administering to Solness's human needs, which include the need for involvement, participation, reciprocality. Answering his call (833)—if indeed he has called her by means of his extraordinary powers—she would seem to be a muse, invoked and inspiring. However obscure and possibly duplicitous her motives and origin might be (Is she angel or muse, troll or devil?), her transaction with Solness, like the muse's, has to do with things of the mind, of imagination. The castle he will build for her must be "very high up—and free" (847), and even though Solness finally stipulates that it must be "one with solid foundations" (848), it will represent the freedom of the imagination to create "castles in the air." The freedom would be expressed in another message to god: "Hear me, Almighty God—you must judge me after your own wisdom. But from now on, I'll build only what's most beautiful in all this world" (856).

Hilda's inspiration of Solness can be read, however, only from the context of the master builder's confusion and dismay. Without the solace of god or community, he lives in dark isolation, and she appears as a personal muse, feeding his desires by the force of will—whether his as a demanding call or hers as undecipherable purpose. She represents for Solness not only the liberation and power of the imagination but also the incarnation of anguish and doubt. Cut off from a creditable and reassuring past, he lives amidst a presence of distrust and suspicion. Declaring an improbable past to be true—his climbing the tower and afterwards kissing her (a child) "many times" (807)—she elicits from him a ready belief and trust. "Isn't it strange," he says, "that all these years I've been going around tormented by . . . a search for something—some old experience I thought I'd forgotten" (811). If Solness does not remember the heroic image from which he derives his identity, he cannot remember the vital experience that seems to be a clue to his being, the shadowy "old experience" that Hilda provides as a truth or perhaps a figment. If a muse, she is indeed the daughter of Mnemosyne. As daughter of Mnemosyne, she would ask to be read as bringing to light the inexorableness of the past, out of which come not only the voices of the gods but also the formative images and ideas that must be encountered in the contemporary.

The muse is a medium, a spiritual connection with "things invisible to mortal sight," making possible and animating the artist's construction and interpretation of a world. Meaningful apprehension of continuity—connectedness of self and other, relationship of this world to the past—is the value of the muse's service to the artist's imagination: not free, random play or escape into sequestered fantasy but reconstruction and reintegration. The invisible might be filled by imaginative projections of another world or imaginative constitution of design in this one, but imaginative activity is not productive of absolute, definitive truth or reality. (Alexander's truth about Edvard's daughters is contradicted when the girls appear to declare his story a lie [144].) There must be, then, in the play of the imagination, a certain irresolution and openness to what is yet to come as an ongoing mediation of past, present, and future. Whether or not Hilda's attendance on Solness is enabling, she instigates his repetition of that act of the past, climbing to the top of the tower, which proves to be the fatal act of the tragic hero. She might be interpreted as offering Solness the salvation of self-determination, the apprehension and resolution of vision, the marriage of minds and identities in his union with her. She might, on the other hand, be seen as merely revisiting on him his stasis, his immobility, his being locked in, bounded by the archaic image of himself as tragic hero; in nourishing his dramatic image of himself alone confronting God, she then confirms an impotent image from the no longer vital and sustaining past, the past that is a souvenir. Paradoxically, his movement toward heights returns him to his debasement, as his freeing himself from the past dooms him to live by its images and re-perform his own past.

My suggestion of opposed readings of Hilda, sympathetic and antipathetic, her being possibly the genuine muse or, as she and Solness observe, possibly the troll of the spirit, is meant to defer these and other possible resolutions of meaning. Neither is simply true and a negation of the other; both are imaginative interpretations that, each in itself, aim to gather images into coherent and meaningful design. The satisfaction and sense of power that come with a definitive reading are grounded in the expectation of experiencing probability and necessity, the dramatic imperative that empowers us, like Solness's god, to judge the play "after [our] own wisdom." Less comfortably, we might with both Solness and Alexander be aware, even painfully, of the discrepancies and counter-truths that appear in the impingement of worlds or beings. Our activity in our relationship to the play is mimetic of the relationships of interpreters in the plays. Desiring resolution and certainty, we might recognize with the characters, or through their failure to recognize, that after all we stand open to wonder and are vulnerable to astonishment that arises from mystery. The anticipation of resolution that stands out before us is more primordial, brought forward into every new experience of the play, than the revelation of probability and necessity. Both Fanny and Hilda have in their enigmatic presence brought forward the idea of mystery: Fanny in her bland participation and Hilda in her provocative disclosures. Neither is in fact a muse, but both allow a possible understanding in terms of the idea of the muse, daughter of Mnemosyne. They raise for the audience the ideas of "things invisible to mortal sight" and direct us to understand them in their individual identities, in their relationships with others, in their possible revelation of self through likeness to troll, angel, muse, Jungean archetype, Nietzschean "Dionysiac wisdom" (*Birth of Tragedy,* 132). But while taking a part on the side of the artist and fostering the imagination, they remain for the audience veiled or obliquely seen, reminders of the limits of knowing and the incompleteness of truth.

Solness or Alexander as the artist, then, as creator of the self in the building of worlds for others' sake, must look forward and backward. The builder must have recipients of his worlds imbued with his truth, must have projected audiences for his creations, as a reason for creating and bestowing. He needs, just as essentially, his agents connecting him with his past, approving and abetting his enterprises, attributing significance and worth to the products of his energies, encouraging his imaginative projections of the past for the present and the future. In creating their little worlds—homes, castles, stages, stories, magic-lantern shows—both artists require not only the intimate attendant spirit but also freedom to discover and to create, freedom from a domineering god. Each needs others in building an idea of himself, as artist, creating his works, being the artist as defined by the past and as potential, not only within tradition but also in rebellion against it. Like Solness, Alexander has a quarrel with God, who as represented in his ambassador Edvard is Apollonian. It is uncertain whether Alexander's "isolated words ... bastard ... shit ... piss—prick" during the funeral procession (80) are directed toward God or Edvard, but after Aron has played God to frighten Alexander, Alexander applies the same language to God: "If there *is* a God, then he's a shit and piss God" (195). Alexander has been experiencing, in the house of Isak, the lessons necessary to his reunion with the theater world. His father's ghost has taught him that he must not be cynical about people, that "You must be gentle with people. . . . By and by you will understand" (184). Aron now teaches him that "Everything is alive. Everything is God or God's thought" (194).

The complex idea and manifestation of the artist working to build within and for his world an imaginative reality that speaks for him and bears his relationship to the work and the world cannot be appreciated as independent of the idea of the world the artist inhabits. The mortal creators' sense of freedom and power or subjugation and debility derives from a sense of relatedness to forces and influences beyond the self—gods, angels, muses, fellow beings in their worlds, audiences in or, like gods and angels, beyond their worlds. Solness's confrontation with God and his rebellion are not unrelated to his involvement with Hilda and the other participants in his world, and that rebellion against god is not relieved to the end of his life; he reiterates in his last scene with Hilda the determination to build as he pleases "what's most beautiful," without God's permission or approval (856). His vision is shared only with Hilda, and his intention to climb the tower is withheld from Ragnar, Mrs. Solness, and Dr. Herdal.

Alexander's responsiveness to others, on the other hand, entails definition and building of a world that allows a reciprocal granting of freedom. The lessons Alexander learns from Aron and his father are about both his world and himself as human being and artist; his father the actor and Aron the puppet master, artists themselves, teach him about God and people; and both show him in their own qualities, in their living the role of artist, what they are as human being in a kind of world. Aron demonstrates as well, by example, that the artist does not have to challenge and repudiate others, including God, in order to affirm individual autonomy in creating. Having proposed Isak's belief that God is vitally immanent in all things of the earth and having then heard Alexander's rebuttal that God's essence is excremental, Aron "politely" finds Alexander's "theory . . . very interesting" and declares, "I for my part am an atheist" (195). He represents one possible role of the artist, identifying his art as sorcery that operates on the Aristotelean principles of intelligibility and believability. He "prefers to show what is understandable," evidently aiming like Coleridge to bring the supernatural down to the level of what must be probable to be understood; and "it is up to the spectators to provide what is not." If the spectators provide what is not understandable, then they are involved in Aristotle's question of the play's action being circumscribed by the irrational, and they contribute their own metaphysical interpretations, bringing to the performance their own capacity to experience Gustav's "supernatural shudders." Aron has no need to discount anyone's transcendental constructs, which are the presumptions brought to his performances and the source of the audience's experience of the wonderful, the mysterious, the "what is not" understandable.

Gustav considers this interpretation of the artist in his final speech, in that human beings "must live in the little, the little world" (207). They "love what [they] can understand," and for them "people must be intelligible." Ordinary human beings all, the Ekdahls "must be able to grasp the world and reality." If, then, they require understandability in ordinary experience, they need the stage as well, to "give us our supernatural shudders." While Gustav and Aron both imply, in the need for understanding, a sense of the probable in what is possible, their structures of relationship between the probable and the wonderful are like mirror images: Aron conceives of the stage as presenting what is intelligible, and the audience, in its "real" dimension, providing "what is not"; Gustav imagines real people needing an understandable world and going to the theater to experience the mysterious and the wonderful. The apparent contradiction in these two views lies in the distinctions and oppositions felt in conceptions of the world, in the felt relationships between actuality and art, life and the stage. One is presumed to be grounded in predictability, understanding, the boundaries of the mundane; the other seems free to explore, not only in imitations of the ordinary but also in flights of fancy toward the boundless. If, however, we consider the audiences, Aron's who "provide what is not" understandable and Gustav's who are "given . . . supernatural shudders by the actors," we observe the essential problem in both interpretations, the prime concern and beginning of Husserl's philosophy. Who generates the supernatural, the audience or the actors? Who determines what is real, the subject bringing along its presuppositions, its ideas and ideals, or the objectivity out there on the stage that must be received, recorded, and understood?

If we agree to Husserl's pragmatic bargain not to require resolution of the question, not to have finally to agree with either Gustav the actor/manager or Aron the puppet master, but to settle for the experience of the play as intentional experience of the essence that might appear, then the stage and the world will not be reducible to abstract duality and isolated as two opposed dimensions, one real and the other unreal, one determining and the other determined. Participating in a relationship of intentionality, the stage and the world become in this view generative of the illusion that appears as truth or fiction and generative as well of the idea of opposition in the distinction between truth and fiction; and the enterprise is a collaboration. Aron's reluctance to impose a single truth on either dimension or on other subjectivities in the world is revealed in the way he prefaces his statement about the roles of artist and audience: "A *sorcerer like me prefers* to show what is understandable" (195; my emphasis). The language he uses in citing Uncle Isak's metaphysics would allow either dimension its reality: "we are surrounded by realities, one outside the other" (194). And this openness toward questions of truth and reality amidst life's illusions is a quality of the world Alexander is absorbing as essential to his *bildung*.

Aron's meditation on inner and outer dimensions, on "realities, one outside the other," and on the need to understand their relationships, is anticipated by Oscar's opening speech, which Gustav echoes in his closing speech. Gustav will refer to the real world outside the theater as "the little, the little world," and Oscar declares his love for "this little world inside the thick walls of this playhouse" (26). Oscar's little world is the little world of the stage encompassed by the reality outside it; Gustav's little world is the outside world that is a *theatrum mundi*; outside that world is yet another world, the encompassment questioned in these plays; and so forth. To the extent that Oscar's little world of the stage reflects the big world, it serves to aid our understanding: "Outside is the big world, and sometimes the little world succeeds for a moment in reflecting the big world, so that we understand it better." These "realities, one outside the other," are problematically involved in the question of mimesis, and their structure in duplicated in yet other dimensional relationships. If the individual human being expediently and instinctively, as interpreter in a world, unreflectively agrees with Descartes's considered resolution that "Cogito ergo sum," then the ground of relationship is with another "outside" reality. If the represented world of the stage helps us to understand the larger world outside, then the larger world outside, as *theatrum mundi*, helps us to understand the encompassing reality. I have referred to the metaphysical dimension ruled by Solness and Edvard's God as being a realm above and beyond this world; and either of that dimension or appearing from yet another are the ghosts, spirits, and supernatural forces that influence or appear in this one. The palpable, ghostly figures like Oscar and Edvard who appear in the real world are no less real and embraced than are those of flesh and blood. The mystery beyond becomes better understood when it is manifest in the present.

To be manifest is to become palpable, as when appearing to Helena Oscar lets her hold his hand (128); and what is manifest is illuminated, brought to light. Heidegger plays with this metaphor of lighting, not only as the clearing in the forest, *Lichtung*, which becomes "light, free and open" (*Basic Writings*, 384), but also as "that which gleams and radiates" (385). Implicitly, if the stage or little representation of a world is a clearing, then it is a place to which the audience comes and in which it sees as reflected light something of itself; and that seeing is recognition, understanding directed back toward itself. If, however, what appears gleams or shines, then it like Gustav's actors is a giving agent, provocateur, freeing the audience to discover the strange and unknown, to become aware of more than the little world of the present and the self. In little worlds within the play and in the little world of the play, illumination can appropriate that quality of gleaming, as in Oscar's story about the chair and in Aron's story about the mummy.

In Oscar's fanciful anecdote for the children, his audience (41), and in the lesson Aron teaches Alexander about the mummy (194), the object produces its own light and makes connections not only with an indeterminate dimension beyond the ordinary but also with the mystery of the past, from which its power seems to arise. The extraordinary chair, "the most precious chair in the world," raises the question of its luminosity, "why it shine[s] in the dark." Made in China "three thousand years ago by the emperor's jeweler for ... the most beautiful woman in the world" (43), it has come into the children's possession and must be cherished: "Touch it gently, sit carefully, talk to it." In capturing the children's imaginations, Oscar has endowed the chair in his fiction with the power to shine, and the shining reveals both its history and its worth. It has reassured the children not by reflecting the truth of their world directly but by putting them in relationship with a strange and wonderful shining object that they should cherish because of what it is in the present and was in the past, what remains with the force of a relic. When Oscar withdraws, the chair shines, and his return in the role of villain demonstrates that Fanny has learned the lesson. His trying to destroy the chair makes her angry: "Don't do that to the chair!" Like the stage, the chair radiates and takes the spectator to itself, and like Longinus's power of the sublime as whirlwind or lightning it enthralls and energizes the audience with its own *enargeia*.[25]

Even if the mummy's shining is an artist's trick, Aron's presenting it, a real object, needs no flight of the imagination to allow its shining, only Aron's darkening the room. The mummy's luminosity raises those questions of origins and audiences' engagements with the mysterious that Oscar has demonstrated in his story of the chair. The understanding cannot grasp the reason for the mummy's luster: "Dozens of learned men have been here and ... can't explain why she shines" (194). Yet if a mummy "dead for more than four thousand years" still breathes and shines, it reveals in its shining that "there is much that is strange and cannot be explained." Fanny's reaction to Oscar and the chair, her loss of the distinction between the real and the unreal, truth and fiction, self and performance, produces a full engagement from which the audiences Aron refers to withhold themselves. Demanding what can be understood and believed as probable, audiences as "learned men" repudiate the alien. "Anything unintelligible makes people angry. It's much better to blame the apparatus and the mirrors and the projections." Such audiences contribute their own alienation and withdraw into the shelter of their reality, where life is real and they are in a place where they can maintain their Apollonian dream of order and control. The sorcerer "brought up as a magician" (195) in his parents' "conjurer's theater" (194) might appear self-contradictory in choosing "to show what is understandable," but Aron's argument seems to be based in the idea of the artist as Aristotle sees him. The playwright must allow the audience its expectation that he will show them what is probable or necessary. Hence they can approve the work as imitating the truth as they know it. They are then being dared to venture forth toward the "strange" that "cannot be explained" and to discover their capacity to "provide what is not" by, like Fanny, giving themselves to the mysterious while letting it be what it is, by being open to astonishment.

Like other ideas in *Fanny and Alexander,* this lofty seriousness about dramatic theory is displayed in a rhythm of the serious being deflated by the trivial, the comic, the affably human. Being of serious intention in quoting Gustav, I have truncated his statement about "supernatural shudders," which ends with another need we have for actors, "our mundane amusements" (207). Aron's dissertation on the mummy ends with a digression on the "fiasco" of a real ghost appearing during a performance and disrupting the illusion. Oscar's performance with the chair concludes with Emilie's coming to ask, "Are you all out of your senses?" (44). These artists know that their truths are infected in their origin, which is the depreciated state of "mundane amusements." The serious is, like the metaphysical, not relegated to a higher dimension apart, with only an authorized agent bringing messages down from it. Unlike Edvard's truth, which must be understood, accepted, and emulated as radiating from a spiritual dimension through a priest of truth, truth is engendered through actors' interpretations, ghosts dwell on earth, and the serious exists in play. The people who inhabit the *theatrum mundi* and play on the stage can be fallible, comic, perverse, mistaken, trivial, deluded, or mean, as Oscar and Gustav assume in their orations. Oscar describes himself as "comically solemn" (26), and Gustav declares that his "wisdom is simple" (206). They know that solemnity and wisdom reside among them, that these values are not reserved to the province of philosopher kings or vested priests; and they know that as human attributes those values are adulterated in their immanence. The human aptitudes for love and enmity, participation and selfishness, kindness and effrontery, wisdom and simplicity, solemn rite and comedy, are capacious, all potentially in play in the extensions of self toward others who cannot be fully known and controlled any more than ghosts and supernatural phenomena can be understood and contained within the boundaries of understanding.

In *Fanny and Alexander* and *The Master Builder* critical questions are located at the site of worlds' impingements: of experiencing self and other, of present and past, of a world and other worlds, of a mimetic stage and a real world, of a constituted world and an imagined or suspect other dimension. The overtly suspect dimension, from which ghosts appear and causality remains mysterious, is thematic in these plays, and it is dealt with in our world with language that specifies phenomena we can understand as real or unreal. Alexander experiences the phenomenon we call clairvoyance, seeing events occurring evidently at the moment but not in his presence, with Ismael serving as his guiding spirit or angel.[26] It would seem that Alexander is engaged in psychokinesis as well, since Ismael summons Alexander's "evil thoughts" (199) and declares voodoo dolls to be "a rather clumsy method when you think of the swift and straight ways that evil thoughts can go." Declaring, "You have in mind a man's death. . . . I know your wish," he assists Alexander in the performance: "All you have to do is not to hesitate at the last moment" (200). It is after Ismael's description of Edvard that Alexander now "clearly sees the burning figure as it staggers and howls."

Solness thinks of himself as an "agent" ("a person who apparently initiates telepathic communication" [Knight, 545]) in influencing others to do his bidding, and he thinks that his wish for the fire has been a "call" to the "helpers and servers" (*Master Builder*, 830), whether trolls or devils, good ones or bad ones (832). Solness seems also to have executed a "call" in a different sense,[27] in that his concentration on the image of the "crack in the chimney" was a means to "force my way to success" (829). His call was efficacious, he supposes—even though the real cause of the fire was "in a clothes closet, in quite another part of the house" (830)—because he recruited the help of spiritual forces. Solness and Alexander are engaged with mysterious forces in activities that go beyond the improbability of seeing what cannot be understood as seeing: through indecipherable agents they participate, or seem to, in a power of causation that is perhaps even less explainable than is their extrasensory perception.

5: THE PLAY: PRESENTING, RECOLLECTING, PROJECTING   213

Alike in accepting the existence of something beyond their understanding to which connections are made, or which makes connection with them, Solness and Alexander differ in the ways they profit from this engagement. Alexander, as I have suggested, incorporates the alien to himself, returning to the little world of the Ekdahls and continuing his artistic enterprise, making a play for entertaining himself and others. The play rehearsal Emilie watches near the end of *Fanny and Alexander* is an "awful spectacle" (210), and Amanda seems to be an awesome personification of death, Fanny greeting her as "all-powerful king, emperor of all the worlds" (109). The "mysterious activity" of the play is profoundly serious to the participants, a lighting of the darkness of death; yet it is nothing more than a fanciful idea played out in their imaginations for pleasurable effect, for "supernatural shudders." Their playmaking reflects their world's diversions and anxieties.

Solness's reception of immeasurable influence is a taking to himself, in his privacy and alienation, the power he can gain to satisfy his own needs, and his goal is utterly serious, a matter of life or death. In his pursuit of freedom Solness cannot escape the determination of life as categorical, as his being either guilty or innocent (827), free or determined; his ties with the past severed, he being unable to read, he is inexorably, as he says, "chained to the dead" (845). In his pursuit of happiness he cannot resolve the schism of felicity and responsibility, and he declares that he "can't go on living without joy in life" (845). The artist's pleasure in creation, ostensibly the song of joy in moments of fulfillment, is heard only by Hilda. When in the final action Solness climbs the tower, Hilda hears "the singing—a tremendous music" (859), but Ragnar thinks "it must be the wind in the treetops." When Hilda tells Solness that he sang on the tower at Lysanger—"It sounded like harps in the air" (805)—Solness declares, "I've never sung a note in my life." The song Hilda hears is not, however, a song of joyous creation but a battle song. What she heard at Lysanger was Solness's declaration to God that he would henceforth be "a free creator" (854), and when she hears the "tremendous music" Ragnar does not hear, Hilda sees Solness "struggling with" someone (859). Solness's creating began in an "honest and warm and fervent" desire to please God (853), and since his piety dictated that building churches was "the noblest thing I could do with my life ... He should have been pleased." God made him "complete master in my own realm," taking his and Aline's children from them, isolating him from others, so that as master of creating in this world he would "enhance His glory" as creator in the other (854). As imitator of God, Solness reflects His austerity; as builder of houses for human beings, after his first rebellion, he carries himself aloof from the mortals who do not know how to be happy in those homes; the second rebellion, building "only what's most beautiful in all this world" (856), will be a further solipsistic retreat, not only from God but also from other human beings.

If he will build, for himself and Hilda alone, castles in the air, his commitment to his art and his sober, even dour idea of it contain no joy. His idea of the disembodied beautiful is as stringent as the representations of pure ideals Plato would have the artist imitate. Solness's discrepancies, the gulf between the actual and the ideal, duty and happiness, bondage and freedom, truth and falsehood, utility and diversion, earnestness and play, produce not a genial acceptance of the unknown and uncontrollable as an opening toward wonder but an emphatic closure upon choice and self-determination. To choose the way of the ideal, to aspire, to climb upward again, is to denounce the actual, the mundane, the earthly; the discrepancy in his end is the difference between Hilda's staring "fixedly upward" (859) after his fall, her "dazed triumph" (860), and the perceptions of the others: he has been "smashed to bits. . . . His whole head's been crushed" (859). Instead of reconciliation, Solness has sought heroic isolation; and from the townspeople's view he has achieved a naturalistic fall to earth.

In Solness and Alexander's encounters with the dimension beyond the *theatrum mundi,* the profound mystery, both artists rebel against the god of logos, the source of the absolute, order, and intelligibility. Embedded in crass actuality, Solness is met by an ostensibly liberating spirit whose encouragement to idealism confirms his heroic, perhaps defunct image, souvenir, of himself as tragic hero. He embraces this obscure force, not knowing whether she is angel or troll, muse or devil, and his failure echoes the defeat of the tragic hero without the affirmation of its meaning. Having abandoned—or been abandoned by—the past, lacking a sense of continuity, he announces and reiterates his freedom while continuing to dwell under the dark influence of the past. In Solness's world of usurpation and the sincerity of a jealous God, the artist's seeing like God in watching others, his needing the power of God to make the world in an image of the self, reveals a self who demands mastery while being at the same time dependent on God, others, and the past.

Solness's god out there, beyond, prevails, and the rebellious artist has not in the end grown or changed; the god with whom Alexander is reconciled is Aron's god, immanent in the actual and in the possibilities of imaginative creation. Alexander, afloat in his world's promiscuous mingling of nationalities, religions, beliefs, and passions, rejects the oppression of a monomaniacal truth and lets others' truths come to him. He is carried by others' actions into a dark, mysterious world and returned miraculously, or by stage trick, to the world of the theater. Not knowing quite what to make of the various dimensions of truth and not seriously concerned to settle all matters of truth, he makes a play in the nursery about a dark, profound truth while his mother and grandmother prepare to make another in the "little world." Reconciled to the play of life, he is let be free to create his little drama as a provocation to discover and feel the force of the strange and mysterious. He absorbs and confirms the alien, the threatening, and the possibilities of fulfillment in human works as well as in gods and dimensions beyond; he reflects his world's muddled, sometimes brilliant and accomplished, sometimes bumbling and laughable making; he confirms abundance and amiable love in a world of discrepancy, degression, and withdrawal.

If the artist as maker assumes like god the power to make a world, that created world engages an audience in a structure of relationships between worlds—heaven and earth, the world of the play and the world of the audience, these worlds in relationship to doublings of worlds in the play world—and presents to the audience the ideas of mimesis and identity, truth and reality, influence and power, freedom and knowledge. That mimetic audience, then, reflecting on the play's resolutions, is imaginatively engaged in the idea of reconciliation, both in the way the play's conflict is resolved as a representation or transformation of Aristotelean form and in the way the worlds of audience and play are brought together. The outcomes of the plays are not only the finality of Solness's crushed skull or the rejoicing in a new dispensation for Alexander and the Ekdahls, but also the potential discovery of yet new meanings and values in the events. The idea of reconciliation is realized in the possibility of our fusion of horizons with others, other worlds, plays, and in our ability to conceive of affirmation as well as denial, Heracleitean "measure" as well as strife, reconciliation as well as alienation, marriage as well as divorce.

ADAM AND THE ARTIST: POMERANCE'S *THE ELEPHANT MAN* AND PINTER'S *THE FRENCH LIEUTENANT'S WOMAN*

When God put Adam "into the garden of Eden to dress it and to keep it" (Gen. 2.15), He also brought the animals "unto Adam to see what he would call them: and whatsoever Adam called every living creature, that *was* the name thereof" (2.19). Naming and dominion, having power over and responsibility for the garden and giving names to the creatures of the world, together imply that such sovereignty requires as well clear sight; open-eyed, clear perception is necessary to knowing and empowerment. If Adam does not see what transpires in the garden with the serpent, after being cast out of the garden he nevertheless suffers, united still with Eve, an awakening to sight of a new reality: "the eyes of them both were opened, and they knew that they *were* naked" (3.7). In discovering, maintaining, or recovering relationship to a world, sight and language are essential, whether in the play of recognition and defining relationship or in the play of creating relationship through imagination and metaphor. That constituting involvement with others in a world is the essential condition of being human, whether others and the world are presumed to be unproblematical, directly and fully known—as when the object is substantively and adequately represented by the word—or worlds and others are experienced as inherently involved in the doubleness and the principle of similarity in metaphorical uses of language.

Bernard Pomerance's stage play *The Elephant Man* and Harold Pinter's film play *The French Lieutenant's Woman*, doubling the plot of John Fowles's novel, invoke the figures of Adam and Eve, raising the questions of the adequacy of perception and language; and they negotiate between conceptually opposed but mimetically reflective worlds: here and there beyond, past and present. Both plays dramatize the profound need to hold dominion in the known world, to make things right and bring them together in unity, coherence, and the intellectual grasp of things as they are. They dramatize as well the mysterious opening of that world into another, the intrusion of the alien into the diurnal, the terrible challenge of the unknown that threatens annihilation and offers the possibility of growth and transformation.

In the worlds of these plays, the Adamic figures—Treves in *The Elephant Man* and Charles/Mike in *The French Lieutenant's Woman*—share with Adam both stature in a world and qualities of mind that are manifest as needs to observe, to interpret, and to control. Treves and Charles appear, paradoxically, disclosing the vulnerability of Adam's innocence and armed with the self-assurance provided by the scientist's knowledge. The scientist is comfortable in his accomplishments, in his command, which is achieved in the rigorous discipline of studying that Baconian book of nature. Like Adam, he is a lord in his world, responsible to maintain order and to rule his domain beneficently. Charles, a disciple of Darwin, has dedicated himself to promoting scientific understanding; Treves, doing the good work of a man of medicine, devotes himself to serving society and specifically to improving the lot of Merrick. Their self-image entails an assumption

5: THE PLAY: PRESENTING, RECOLLECTING, PROJECTING   217

of power over objective realities in their real world, and they involve themselves in interpreting it, their interpretation beginning in the scientist's sharpened powers of observation.

Like Adam the namer, they bestow order on their worlds through the power of language. Treves knows human nature as scientific determination, can describe the signs of Merrick's disease as "papillomatous extrusions . . . osseous deformities,"[28] has written "books on Scrofula and Applied Surgical Anatomy" (1); and he is interpreted by Gomm as being identified by as well as endowed with this technical language. Lecturing on Merrick, he has access to the restricting and conclusive metaphors of naturalism—cauliflower, radish, fungus, tuberous roots—which serve to define Merrick's nature. Having a comfortable grasp on social reality as well, he lectures Merrick on the meaning of the word "home" (25–27). Charles, too, knows scientifically the names of fossils—for instance, the echinoderm named Micraster Coranguinium (29)—and he feels the pressure of social determination when Mrs. Poulteney refers to the "gross disorders on the streets" (34). When he seeks to understand the enigma of Sarah Woodruff, also known as "Tragedy" (13) and "whore" (23), he goes to Doctor Grogan for a lecture on the three classifications of melancholia: natural, occasional, and obscure (40).

If, however, Treves and Charles, like Adam, trust to the establishment of security achievable in a known world, accept their responsibility to maintain and improve it, and rely on the language that helps to clarify, define, and classify it, they are troubled by discrepancies. Sarah endangering herself on the sea wall entices Charles in rebuffing him, and the name "Tragedy" encourages his curiosity. Treves is ready with a glib response when in the opening scene Gomm advises him that his rewards for "industry, accomplishment, and skill" will be an "excellent consolation prize" (1–2). Taken aback, he declares that he does not know what Gomm means by the word "consolation," recapitulates his accomplishments, asks himself, "Consolation for what?", and declares that he has "excessive blessings. Or so it seems to me." Both Charles and Treves will encounter, specifically in Sarah and Merrick, the recesses of another human being that reflect the concealment beyond, becoming representative, mimetic, of the mystery encompassing the dominion of Adam.

Sarah and Merrick, objects of the scientists' intense, perhaps excessive though benevolent curiosity, not only represent a different—the artist's—way of seeing things but also appear for Charles and Treves as enigma, as the appearance of something in their comfortable worlds that calls into question, that challenges their assurances of a completed and autonomous self and their understanding, their comfortable grasp, of reality. Sarah and Merrick are in fact artists, both creating imaginative representations that transcend the ordinary, reaching beyond the order of the world that encloses and confines them. Merrick's motive for building the model of St. Phillip's is indicative of his propensity to dream, to indulge illusions; he began building only when he saw that St. Phillip's "really was . . . an imitation of grace flying up and up from the mud" (38); and he must surely make an imaginative connection, seeing that image as mimetic of the artist, reflecting himself, whose beastly head is full of dreams. Sarah creates paintings that in the beginning represent her tormented, dark soul—hardly the reassuring or undisturbing mimesis of realistic portraiture—and in the end see the world brightly; the transformation in her painting represents an idea of the artist being realized and revealed in the work, her *bildung*.

As artists, Merrick and Sarah adopt a sometimes wry playful attitude toward language, and the play of language becomes a means of projecting beyond the constraints of the word conceived as simple correspondence; language becomes in itself a play of creativity, a freedom to speculate about transcendence and mystery. Sarah startles Charles by appropriating the language of the world and its power of domination when she labels herself "Whore" (45). She knows the creative power of language to transform mere fact reiterated as pure word, even though creation through language might not correspond to simple truth. Her creation of an image of herself, for Charles, in a story of her past is an attempt to tell a truth like the truth of her self-portraits, and it is revised in another version of truth when Charles asks her why she lied, and in a third version when he finds her at Windermere. The truth of her contradictory stories is a developing truth, a transformation in the verbal that reflects a transformation of her self.

Merrick's first words in the play are ambiguous, either a mishearing or a playful transformation: the man's presentation of the Pinheads as "Queens of the Congo" is echoed by Merrick as "Cosmos? Cosmos?" (8). He reveals in this scene a trait that belies his condition, a playfulness with language that shows wit, honesty, sympathy, and a certain sophistication. When the Pinheads seem to know only one word, "Allo!", he says, "Little vocabulary problem, eh? Poor things" (9). The playfulness of a minimally human creature like Merrick reveals something in him like the mystery of the degraded Sarah, a potential to create of the self something more than the world can define in a word. The artist plays with language and actuality and makes a play of them, or makes of them a play that escapes into the realm of illusion, the naive Adamite's untruth.

The Adamic figure names, knows, and holds dominion, making of his fallen world a practical truth and making himself at home in it. His dedication is not totally, however, to the unmediated harvesting and shepherding in that world. While he labors in his commitment to build and improve the social conditions of its homes and palaces in consonance with its hospitals and courts, he recalls or feels the need to remember that other world, the lost dream, the enclosed garden that is as undeniably designed and structured as the edifices he can build. Treves and Charles are not fully realized in and constrained by their self-definition and indifferent to the call from the unknown, the forgotten other world and the strange beings different from themselves and in some strange way free of their self-imposed coercion. Therein lies the mystery of these Adams. In both plays, the Aristotelean imperative of probability or necessity in action and character falters before the question of inciting motivation. Why do Treves and Charles pursue Merrick and Sarah? Answers might be that they follow the instinct of the scientist, curiosity and the desire to resolve uncertainties; they follow their social instinct to help others by ameliorating the world's suffering for individuals as well as for humanity in general; or their need for diversion and amusement takes a morbid turn when they become interested in the grotesque, the outcast. Perhaps the contradictoriness of these answers is in itself an answer; to resolve them might be to accept them all and dwell in contradiction or to settle on one, excluding other viable possibilities, none of which is determined by the action. If the action allows the possibilities, it establishes them in a ground of uncertainty, and the mystery is there as intimation that beyond Adamic dominion lies the unknown, another world, whether forgotten and calling to be uncovered or an obscure desire, like the third category of melancholia, the obscure, that remains unsatisfied by the works, accomplishments, and consolations of this world and, according to Grogan, remains for the scientist Hartmann of unknown cause: "he doesn't know what the devil it is that caused it" (40).

The artist knows, holds dominion over, and creates—through metaphorical relationships to this world—a very different sort of world, with sometimes strange or alien values that challenge comfortable relationships, disturb order and design, and thwart expectations. As a work of art presented to an audience, it stirs in them the admiration of the wonderful, the awe of the mystery, that does not answer to practical needs and aims in governing affairs in this world but embodies the idea of excess and calls for the audience's capacity to reflect its exorbitance. The illusoriness of that world, its echoing the vague, unsatisfied dream of adventure and discovery, perhaps even the foundation of a new order, disrupts the Adamic complacency felt in the factuality of the one real world with the anticipation or the imagination of something beyond. Adam's waking with Eve into a new reality, their knowing they are nakedly ashamed, is an irrevocable movement from one dimension into another, a movement that converts the old reality into a dream, a memory, a lost simplicity and beauty. Merrick's power to dream, realized in his model of St. Phillip's, is the artist's creation of an ideal reality that affronts the mundane with the intensity of its aspiration and its improbability, and the created world mediates between the past and the future. When he tells Mrs. Kendal that he does it "with just one hand, they all say," she says, "You are an artist, John Merrick, an artist" (38).

The artist leads us—not without and perhaps in spite of the knowledge, certainties, and powers by which we maintain and hope to control our actual world—into a second, an imagined world. The artist's power over us and this imaginative world is only, as we experience it in *The Elephant Man,* "The Weight of Dreams." Since the model, an ideal image, does not "dominate the play visually" (v) as Pomerance originally intended it, it does not compel and constrain a sense of two worlds in abutment and tension. In Edward Albee's *Tiny Alice,* the "huge doll's-house model of the building of which the present room is a part"[29] is a center and a duplication of action, and it is unmistakably a microcosmic and hyperbolic manifestation of the idea of a *theatrum mundi*. Pomerance thinks, however, that "the building of the church model constitutes some kind of central metaphor, and the groping toward conditions where it can be built and the building of it are the action of the play" (*Elephant Man,* v); and Merrick makes it clear that the artist's making such a model is allusive, not only to the past, historical images of an art that points toward heaven but also to reiterated theories of art and the artist in general. His echoing Plato in saying that he makes his "imitation of an imitation" elicits Treves's somewhat revisionist interpretation of Plato: "Plato believed this was all a world of illusion and that artists made illusions of illusions of heaven" (38). Merrick's church as an idea and representation of a truth and reality points toward a world beyond that legitimizes the strain and excess of the ambition to transcend a debilitated condition.

The other world that plays against the actual world of *The French Lieutenant's Woman* is, like that image of St. Phillip's, a central and compelling metaphor, easily becoming, in speculating on or talking about the film, the action itself—the story of Charles and Sarah that is being filmed and stars two rather elusive actors named Mike and Anna. The world of the sideshow and court in *The Elephant Man,*

5: THE PLAY: PRESENTING, RECOLLECTING, PROJECTING 221

with the hospital a mediating structure between crass, depraved, or self-serving human beings and the unconstrained possibilities of what they might be, is precisely the actual world of London from 1884 to 1890. The actual world of *The French Lieutenant's Woman* is the present, 1979, during the filming of the script,[30] and the action of the novel being translated to film begins in 1867. The consciousness of that past creates the other world, as does the narrator of Fowles's novel, with a sense of difference. Mike and Anna demonstrate that difference for the audience as their customs, habits, attitudes, language, and values are recognized as alien to the social structures, inherited beliefs, and preserved conventions of that Victorian world, which is only beginning to wake up to the transformation threatening the stability of empire. That world the actors are creating evokes in them a sense of nostalgia for or curiosity about its quaint attitudes and strange convictions; Anna enriches her understanding of Sarah by studying the statistics of London's prostitution establishment in 1857 (18). The Victorian world's attraction, the actors' fascination with it, reveals their living in the late twentieth-century world as not only a freedom from old conventions but also a vulnerability to the fluidity of change and the casual choices that might be made without the constraints of heavenly, institutional, or communal guardianship. When a telephone call wakes Mike and Anna, in the first scene that develops their identifies apart from the roles they play, their nudity, their language ("Christ, look at the time" [9]), and their apparently casual sexual relationship define them as antithetical to the roles they play. Mike, however, reveals his identification with Charles. Charles's protracted and agonizing decision to flaunt convention, to break his engagement to Ernestina and marry the French Lieutenant's Woman, is translated by Mike into the modern idiom. Although he is married to Sonia and Anna has a lover, David, he like Charles is improbably eager in his serious pursuit of the mysterious woman, willing to take unreasonable risks. When Anna complains that his answering the telephone means "they'll know you're in my room, they'll all know" (9), he responds, "I want them to know."

Both Mike and Anna are revealed not only, for the audience, as commentaries on the characters they play but also as discovering or interpreting themselves through identifying with those characters. Their casual demeanor toward their own lives belies the seriousness and intensity of the characters they play, but they recognize the difference and playfully assume the Victorian identity for themselves and for their world. Anna's feigned anxiety—"They'll fire me for immorality. . . . They'll think I'm a whore"—is a reading of Anna and the film company through the spectacles of Sarah and her world. Mike's reckless pursuit of Anna, echoing Charles's fascination with Sarah, seems, if somewhat parodic, to be a genuine desire for the profound commitments and the fervent sincerity possible in a lost world. In a world where all truth is elusive and the individual's freedom is realized in an atmosphere of dissolution and evasion, the unreclaimable world is not forgotten; but neither is it a source of consolation and reassurance, except as it remains an attractive idea or can be transformed into dramatic illusion. Since knowing that it is, like the present world, fallen allows no primitivistic retreat into the illusion of an ideal state, characters like Anna and Mike can play themselves off, self-consciously, against what seems alien and eccentric, while they feel the tug of a mysterious force from the past. If Mike and Anna's attitude toward the world of the past seems condescending or supercilious, they betray in their apparent insincerity the embarrassment of loss and the longing for lost values embodied in the characters they play.

The dissatisfaction of the Adamic heroes Charles, Mike, and Treves leads to their consternation about the fact that, desirous of something that eludes them, they lack, in Gomm's word, the "consolation" against restlessness and their strange aspiration to go beyond their accomplishments. Yet all three have attained the consolation of an ideal world contained within and ostensibly incidental to the arena in which their labors are productive. The ideal place is on the one hand a representation of the reward for mastering earthly conditions through labor and gaining self-esteem through succeeding in the world; it is on the other hand an emblem of a world apart. Their involvement in affairs of the world preserves the idea of a garden as a still center to which the man of the world can return as to a primordial condition.

The idea of that protected and protective place in *The French Lieutenant's Woman* appears in the sense of its being lost; in the fragile architecture of home with garden, the building of it as a haven apart from the world's negotiations; and in the febrile, even vague anticipation that in the future there might be a better, happier place, a *locus amoenus*. In the novel, Charles's misadventure is resolved by Fowles in the freedom of a modern ambivalence toward the past, the audience of fractured sensibility that is given an option to see Charles finally abandoned, lost, unreconciled, or reunited with Sarah. The offered choices of an ending for the novel allow, of course, that in the irresolution and indeterminacy of the reader's time, in the flux of uncertainty and the hesitation before the closure of a story's ending, the supercilious temper might prevail. The choice need not be taken seriously, as a choice that must be made, if the audience shares with the author both that attraction to the seductive past and the ache of the present's sense of distance from a quaint innocence. Pinter's play divides the choices, delegating to Charles the reconciliation and to Mike the abandonment; but the complication of identities in the actor Mike, whose liberation from the fiction he has played is incomplete, mirrors the confusion. Abandoned at Windermere by Anna, he calls out, standing in for Charles, "Sarah!" (104). Charles has regained the idyllic place, reunited in a garden world with Sarah, who has transposed the elements of her name, Woodruff, creating a new identity as Mrs. Roughwood. Mrs. Roughwood's residence at Windermere is identified as "the new house" (98), and Charles first sees it in "a glimpse of white walls through dense shrubbery" with "the sound of playing children." The interior is "white, full of light" (99), with sounds of a piano and laughter. The powerful image of sylvan retirement, where Sarah is free to be the artist, "free to do my own work" (100), propels the imagination beyond the brief confrontation of Charles and Sarah, beyond any doubts about the veracity of her third account of herself, and the reunion of lovers is complete in an edenic place.

The attainable refuge, the garden in which Charles would find fulfillment through marriage to Ernestina, is forfeited by the scientist who has caught a glimpse of something beyond his understanding. As Adamic man, Charles has sought fossils, the origins of life, in "the vast wilderness of the Undercliff" (20), and the sublime setting becomes the site of Sarah's forbidden solitude and his tracking of the mysterious woman (or, according to Grogan, the locale in her scheme to entrap him [51]). If the dark mysteries of nature are tamed in the enclosed garden, then it is appropriate that, endangering his pledge to Grogan and himself—"I shall honour my vows to Miss Freeman" (52)—in order to deepen his involvement with Sarah, Charles departs for London leaving Ernestina in the garden. Caught in his fabric of secret motives and temporizing, he assures her that "the true charm of the world resides in this garden" (59). Charles's identity has been determined by his role as scientist and lover, proper gentleman and complaisant conductor of business. With Mr. Freeman's offer to be his "guide" if he should, as son-in-law, be "disposed to explore the world of commerce" (11), the comfort and security of that garden should give him no cause to desire anything more. As a haven within the structure of the world's occupations, it could be a little world within and oblivious to strife and labor, achievement and disappointment. In abandoning the consolations of that world, Charles has pursued at risk a mystery, the illusion that becomes transformed into a consummate love in an ideal place, safe as immaculate idea from the actuality of commerce.

Mike, like Charles, abandons the actual woman in the actual garden for the sake of his fascination with and desire to grasp the illusion. Mike's pursuit of Anna is contaminated from the beginning—not by the naiveté that is essential, like Merrick's, to pursuing the dream; nor by the possibility that the dream he pursues is an illusion, is deceiving—but by his confusion. Anna's identification with Sarah, which is ostensible and perhaps to some extent feigned, enables that confusion. In scene 73, cut from the film, she and Mike toy with the idea of their relationship and playfully confuse themselves with Charles and Sarah in scene 72, when Sarah says, "I prefer to walk alone" (24). When Mike echoes the line, Anna responds, "Me? Not me. Her" (25); and when he asks if she meant to be provocative she says, "Well, it worked. Didn't it?" On the beach, Mike questions her about looking sad, and she seems, in looking "towards the Undercliff" (42), to be either lost in or acutely conscious of playing Sarah's melancholy. Mike's confusion is pointed up in David's questions to first Anna and then to him about the choice of an ending for the film. Anna responds to the question with certainty: "I've decided. . . . I want to play it exactly as it's written" (83–84). She could mean that she wants to film both endings of "it," the novel; or that she wants the ending that has already been written for the film; or, reflexively, that she wants Sarah to perform one ending of the novel and Anna the other. Mike's response to David's question is that "We're going for the first ending [of the novel]—I mean the second ending" (95), and he diverts David's question "Which one is that?" with another question: "Hasn't Anna told you?" His confused cry to Anna in the end—"Sarah!"—comes from the barren set of the white house that, as empty film set, now mocks the reunion of Sarah and Charles. Mike has run "up the stairs on which he first saw 'Mrs. Roughwood'" (104), finding the trace of Sarah, her "long red wig," and going into "the white room" where "moonlight falls"; and his call is toward her departing "white car."

Mike has pursued his ideal love to the ideal place, and it is empty. Caught up with profound seriousness in the illusion, he fails to see that he has converted his actual garden into a plaything. At the lunch he has arranged in order to see Anna, what others refer to as Mike's "lovely house" and "lovely garden," his "great garden" (94–95), are the haven he enjoys neglectfully. Sonia tells Anna that she, not Mike, "looks after it," that he is "pretty lazy"; and when Anna says that she envies Sonia "for being able to create such a lovely garden" (96), Sonia responds, "I wouldn't bother to envy me, if I were you." Mike's confusion is not merely a disorientation induced by Anna's spurning him but a failure to distinguish between the necessities of Adam—

who takes his responsibilities to his garden seriously, practices the skills of his profession, and strives to realize them in and for the world—and the artist's need for dreams. Mike's confusion of the roles of actor/artist and man of responsibilities in the world is debilitating. There is a certain ruthlessness in the artists Sarah and Merrick, a determination to transform the artist her/himself through the creation of art, perhaps a purpose true of the enigmatic Anna as well. Treves and Mike, drawn toward the dream of transcendence, lose their established footing on the solid ground while Charles is saved by the sincerity of his commitment to what seems to be, in the end, the sincerity of the woman and artist Sarah.

Treves's consternation follows, like Mike and Charles's, on the disclosure of obscure meanings that call them toward something beyond their understanding. Gomm, who represents compromise with actuality and adaptation to things as they are, perplexes Treves with the word "Consolation." The mentor who gives sound advice about the world and negotiating one's way in it knows the enfeeblement of himself in that world, and he knows the necessity of establishing a home in it. In the first scene, when he predicts that Treves will come to know what he means about accomplishment as a "consolation prize" (2), he asks if Treves has "bought a house" (1), and Treves replies, "On Wimpole Street." To be at home in the world is to accept it and its consolations, and Treves's refusal to consider them consolations confirms that he has not accepted that unregenerate world for what it is and for what it allows in the construct of a *locus amoenus* within it.

As his dismay grows, represented in the dream of Merrick's becoming the lecturer on Treves, the mirrored identities place Treves under the evaluative gaze of the sub- or supra-human. From this dream-Merrick's point of view, which is a view held within Treves's dream ego, Treves's "terrifyingly normal head ... allowed him to lie down normally, and therefore to dream in the exclusive personal manner, without the weight of others' dreams accumulating to break his neck" (61). His normality paradoxically makes him one with his community in their having "exclusive personal" subjectivity and their lacking genuine participation and care. Treves's normality isolates him in his own "personal" exclusiveness and confuses him, in that the privacy of his assumption that he sees the world's problems clearly and is capable of alleviating them maintains in him "a disabling spiritual duality" (62). The identity he assumes has "projected a normal vision of benevolent enlightenment" that is a "self-mesmerized state" (61); his Apollonian vision is an illusion. Satisfied "at being at the hub of the best of existent worlds," he is "incapable of self-critical speech, thus of the ability to change." Treves's accountability to his world is authorized by the illusion that his essential relationship to his world is benevolence based in understanding, rather than exclusiveness, and by the concomitant illusion that the world participates in his essential benevolence. His establishment, security, and authority are not, however, invulnerable to the stirrings of conscience; long before the dream, Merrick has disturbed his complacent assumptions about propriety and conformity with questions that made Merrick already a Socratic mentor. The discussion about nakedness, following Mrs. Kendal's demonstration of nakedness to Merrick, reveals in Treves a depth of feeling that he cannot express to Merrick. Only after Merrick has gone out does Treves answer his questioning why Mrs. Kendal will not come back: "because I don't want her here to see you die" (58).

Treves's dissatisfaction that he does not hold Adamic sway over his world grows from the experience with Merrick, which Treves has expected to be a further disciplined and responsible step toward the fulfillment of his own identity. Even though he can name and thereby see conditions and beings in that world, there is something in and beyond himself that he cannot grasp, a consciousness exacerbated by the discovery that Merrick bestows a truth of human being that is not satisfied by normalcy, by Treves's having established for himself an ethical communal function and a home with a garden. As language fails him, in the scene entitled "They Cannot Make Out What He Is Saying" (63), he expresses his despair to the Bishop as a new conviction, "I am sure we were not born for mere consolation" (65). He does not speak the premise of that certainty, which is the uncertainty about what he was born for. His complaint is that, as Adam, he has believed in himself and his power to bring mystery into the confines of his guardianship, to transform the strange, the less than human Merrick into ordinary Adam. Intuiting his own metaphorical relationship to Adam, he declares that he is "an awfully good gardener" (66). The Bishop, he says, would "like my garden too. My dog, my wife, my daughter, pruned, cropped, pollarded and somewhat stupefied." The garden has been for Treves that tranquil center, located within the bustle and superintendence of life, that obligatory attempt to actualize the memory of the ideal place. As Treves's power to control language deteriorates, he tries to reveal what has been wrong in his and the Bishop's caring for Merrick, their shepherding having been to "take such good care of anything, anything you, we, are convinced . . . is not very dangerously human." Merrick, Treves has learned, is not the animal-like human being who might be brought with Treves's care to a minimally adequate human condition; he is "very dangerously human." Merrick has revealed his nature in his aspiration, his contradiction of debasement and humiliation, and the revelation becomes a threat to establishment and order. His power to dream of beneficence beyond the human exposes Treves's human accomplishment as blind constraint and forced conformity to the words and convictions of a little world. If Merrick dies into the darkness, he is attended by the "Queens of the Cosmos" (67), not into oblivion but into "Beautiful darkness' empire" (68), the darkness of the unknown and of possibility, "light's true flower."

Treves, Charles, and Mike build within the confines of a dimension that affords them a home, and they preserve the idea of the perfect place, the remembered garden, within that constructed dominion. Troubled by what comes to them through Merrick, Sarah, and Anna as mysterious, they recognize its appearance, its intrusion into their regulated lives, as from a darkness beyond their lighted world. Yet it appears not as a power of darkness breeding only debilitating confusion and consternation but as an illumination of their own confusion, an exposure of their error in presuming mastery and self-determination. The real world, a little world of light and order where life's business is transacted by a capable Adam, contains a perfect little world as primitivistic ideal; and its security is breached by intimations of meaning beyond these characters' intellectual grasp, intimations that are an incitement to venture into the alien darkness. To name that unknown as mystery or darkness is to metaphorically place it outside the known and the light, and to say that it is beyond them generates that idea of a substantial world out there. That it is an undefined and uncontained otherness, however, does not provide the substance that would make it another actual world for which this world is a *theatrum mundi*. To name that unknown a fiction, on the other hand, would be to bring it yet again within the dictates of the known.

If it is materialized by the imagination, as Merrick projects a god of light in a heaven, or as the Pins devise "Beautiful darkness' empire" that is "light's true flower," then the aspiring imagination is giving human habitation and name to the unknown; that aspiration to see it, to let it be visible, is not an Adamic naming but an expression through metaphorical relationships. Merrick's model and Sarah's drawings are the artist's attempt to express what is ineffable except through the artist's representation. Sarah's images of the "old woman on her death bed" in the beginning (9) and of children in the end (100) are an artist's renderings of something that needs to be brought to light, evoked not only as expressions of Sarah's psychology but also as having to do with the idea and meaning of herself as a woman. She is in the beginning conceived and expressed by herself as the abandoned woman, destitute, alone, dependent, dying; and in the end she has gained her freedom as a woman and an artist in a light, sylvan home with children, in a garden world beyond the architecture of man's city.

The artist's need to explore the undetermined, to address the mystery with images and metaphors that are only possible expressions of it, liberates the artist in that venture from the predetermined roles and practical enterprises that mark the agent of Apollonian order; and the liberating need is, from the point of view of the practical and reasonable Adamic man, itself an element of the mystery. When the Adam catches a glimpse of and aspires to the mystery that attracts, that draws him beyond reason toward the enigma, his self-doubt and bewilderment reveal his betrayal, not only of his acquired stature and duty but also of the protected dream, the memory of a lost world that has been reconstructed as at the heart of reality. The impulse to create or memorialize that insubstantial dream as a habitable place is excessive; it is a manifestation of the dissatisfaction that makes him vulnerable to the woman's and the artist's inaccessibility, the mysterious otherness that seems to offer a vision of what he cannot see and say, the mysterious otherness of the artist who attempts to reveal the ineffable.

Brought into the confines of the garden, the woman has become for Mike, Charles, and Treves the safe and consoling helpmeet—Sonia, Ernestina, Treves's wife—who abets his endeavors and reassures him of their significance; she is, as a necessity in that little theater, typecast. Ernestina is for Charles that benign spirit, receiving his gift of the echinoderm with fitting surprise and appreciation (28) and lamenting that she is "horrid" for taking the part of Mrs. Poulteney, that "horrid old woman," against Charles (36). Treves, confessing his stupefaction, has recognized that his imperative to prune, crop, and pollard his garden has resolved the dream into a dog, a wife, and a daughter who are "somewhat stupefied." Mike, divested in his world of the restraining structures that demand care and accountability, has nevertheless established his garden world—"Mike's house" (94–96)—at the center, relegating the custody to Sonia. Although Sonia appears to be a stable and trusting helpmeet, she reveals in her elusiveness the irresolution and unpredictability of others in her world, their inaccessibility, which is the mystery appearing at the heart of the world. Her enigmatic response to Anna's envy that she is "able to create such a lovely garden" redirects the question of mystery toward the securely pruned, cropped, and pollarded garden.

For the Adamic man, the artist and the woman represent the aspiration to extend the vision, to discern light out of the darkness, both in the work of art and in the being of the artist. Merrick incorporates

5: THE PLAY: PRESENTING, RECOLLECTING, PROJECTING   229

the idea of the woman, of course, as well as the idea of the artist. His contradictory nature incarnates the "sickening stench" of "fungous skin growths" (6), the signs of most degraded "indecency" and "disgrace" of human being, along with singular beauty. The right hand, rather than displaying the strength and rectitude of an overseer, is like the fin of a sea creature; the left arm, the sinister, is "a delicately shaped limb covered with a fine skin and provided with a beautiful hand which any woman might have envied." If the "useless" right hand cannot build edifices like the hospital that is his home, the feminine left hand creates the "imitation of grace flying up and up from the mud" (38).

Although reflected in and reflecting his work, this artist Merrick is not defined and restricted by the Platonic conception of the artist's mimesis as a mirroring of the actual. Constrained by the world's finitude and complaisant toward its demand for a literal and true representation of itself, that mimetic artist whose power resides in Plato's mirror falls always under the world's judgmental gaze; he is, like Adam and others in the world, responsible, accomplished, established within its structure. Pleasing the world, he gives them back an image of themselves. As Merrick is interpreted by his audience to be that Platonic artist, he becomes a mirror to them, the admirers who approve him because he reflects what they approve in themselves. For the Bishop he is "religious and devout" (39); for Gomm, "practical"; for the Duchess, "discreet" (40); for Treves, "curious, compassionate, concerned about the world." Mrs. Kendal's finding him, like herself, "gentle, almost feminine . . . honest within limits . . . rather odd . . . hurt . . . helpless not to show the struggling" is to see herself mirrored in him, but the mirror reveals in her idea of herself those qualities for which the mirror is inadequate. The partial honesty, the strangeness or eccentricity, the alienated hurt and helplessness are not traits of the stereotypical accomplished actress or the woman of the world, the Duchess whose essence is discretion, but ideas of Mrs. Kendal as woman. The mirror's deficiency rests in its limited power, the ability to reflect only presence, surfaces that are already there in the design and structures of the world.

Mrs. Kendal's idea is of the woman not entirely revealed, not fully represented in the role, enigmatic because ever creating herself. Her appreciation of Merrick is not, finally, for his surface reflection of her surface but for his probing mind, the play of imagination that seems adequate to pursue the mystery, as he demonstrates in speculating about Romeo and Juliet. Romeo's holding a mirror up to Juliet in order to see the sign of life, breath, does not yield a living woman for him; he sees "nothing" (33). The nothing, as nothing, dismays; and the mirror revealing the nothing, in its failure to reveal the possibility of life, reunion, and love, is not a truth but an illusion: "Looking in a mirror and seeing nothing. That is not love. It was all an illusion." The lost woman, Juliet, is not brought back into the world and enshrined in the perfection of a lighted place; the mirror that cannot see her cannot find her. The Adamic man wielding the mirror can reveal, as a mimetic artist, only what is already there, safely ensconced; as a practical architect of edifices in the world he can only confine and fix the fragile memory of the garden within the structure of that world. The artist whose imagination probes the darkness for the invisible and for the possibility of reunion with it—whether degraded human being with god, abandoned man with woman, fractional being with self, or depreciated world with the faintly remembered dream—pursues not deluding chimeras but potentiality.

The faint recollection of a dream, unremembered as a virtual past and anticipated only as answering a vague deficiency, a need for something more than the attained, might be domesticated in the framework of reality as an illusion of bliss, a secure retreat, a mimesis of utmost satisfaction in the world; or it might become the haunted pursuit of a strange fulfillment discoverable only in the jeopardy of encounter with Merrick, Sarah, and Anna. Hazarding their contentment, Treves, Charles, and Mike move through confident and casual exploration, perhaps most essentially born of curiosity, toward the "dangerously human"; and they confront the mystery with their demands to understand and to be understood. Representing but one resolution, the happy ending, Charles attains his goal by submission to Sarah, accepting her verbal account of herself as true or as unquestionable and, more importantly, yielding to her freedom as an artist. Mike is bereft, his own uprootedness, ostensible freedom, and negligence blinding him to the possibility of Anna's sincerity as an artist. As their blasé world fragments and scatters relationships and identities, individuals constantly eluding others, Anna, whose premise is concealment, is even less accessible to an audience's understanding than is Mike. She seems, however, to be intent on her performance as the artist creating Sarah. Selecting material for Sarah's dress in the scene at Windermere, she says, "Yes, I think I'm going to like her in this" (88), revealing, as opposed to Mike's losing himself in Charles, a professional concern and a consciousness of the image she wants to create. In the earlier scene when she and Mike play at their relationship's reflecting that of the characters, he diverts the interest in Sarah and Charles to Anna and himself. Whereas he "enjoyed" the scene they have just filmed and wonders whether she finds him "sympathetic" (25), amending the question with "I don't mean me. I mean him," her concern is for the performance: "I never know ... Whether it's any good." The difference between Anna and Mike as artists seems to be the distinction Aristotle makes between the capable poet who "can easily change character" (an accomplished Anna) and the mad or frenzied poet who is possessed or loses his proper self (an Adamic Mike).

The artist intent on making the obscure palpable concentrates the vision and incarnates it as the work of art, caring that the realized expression engages and stimulates an audience. Merrick's announcement when he places the "last piece on St. Phillip's" is the terse, echoic statement "It is done" (66), and he leaves it to speak for him and for itself. The tangible sign wrought by the artist is intended to capture the imagination of that audience, to shake the foundations of its fortified reality, to express the dream that can be lighted out of the darkness, to entice it toward the sinister and the "dangerously human." As the artist embodies those virtues, she/he is realized and remains an idea of the artist in the character created by the actress, the image drawn by the pictorial artist, the model constructed by the debilitated architectural artist.

The work of this artist remains for the world, that audience caught up like Adam in its own contrived world dedicated to and built on its convictions, an enticement to wonder. The work of art not only entices an audience to engagement in its appearing but also reveals its withdrawal as it appears. The residual wonder is not contained, is not resolved by the professional literary or social critic's Adamic power.[31] The audience as critic, and like Adam holding sway in the real world's business and trying to encircle it with his or her own understanding, must cede presumption of full understanding in order to enter the mysterious territory into which the poet directs us.

The Adamic man's capacity for wonder, tamed in the construction of the domestic imitation of the garden, is nevertheless an impulse capable of responding to, inherently in need of, the disquieting appearance that calls for an audience. If the work of art calls for and generates a sense of wonder, aspiration, admiration, or love, both in its being and in its expectation of the audience, then it is not susceptible to the constraints of total intelligibility but addresses the need for growth and transformation. The audience's vulnerability to signs of abundance and excess, gratuitous bestowal without practical demand, is the detection of a nobility or sublimity that becomes, in the audience's approbation and appreciation, reflected tribute. Applause transcends the moment in that it as response calls for more, affirms the anticipation of revelation, echoes the aspiration in creating, and participates in the memorializing of the tribute that pays respect to potentiality in discovery and transformation. The work of art, whether creation of character in role, building a model as tribute to architectural tributes, or making a play that is a world constructed in honor of and for a world, embodies the artist's tribute to the past for the future, which is improbable mediation and reconciliation in contextual strife, alienation, and perplexity.

6
Call and Recall: The Play of Imagination

TURNING BACK ONCE MORE TO THINK OF WALLACE STEVENS'S "PLAIN sense of things" recalls the question of how a world, all that seems substantial and enduring, is constructed in imaginative activity into a reality that, in spite of all our certainties, holds our future uncertainly in trust. While eliciting the faith necessary to live in it, it reveals in momentary glimpses its illusoriness that calls forth doubts about permanence, certainty, and repeatability; identity and community; causality, purpose, and consequences; truth and goodness. In such moments, the comfortable habitation grown uncanny, a structure of interpretation recognizes the one and the other dimension, the familiar and the strange, the familiar grown strange, as at a theater. Appearing in these moments is the idea of illusion, not an illusion that merely and simply opposes itself to the firm base of reality but illusion as the appearance of something that is not in the first place real or unreal but indeterminate, as playing against or even mocking the "natural standpoint." In its appearance *as* play, the play affronts the casual and complacent acceptance that things are as they seem to be. The familiar loses its firmness, its dependability; and in being felt as insubstantial becomes less an assurance that it does not participate in and derive from the play of illusion. As involving illusion, it stimulates an activity that plays with the questions of reality and truth, an activity that is interpretation approaching the mysterious, the uncanny, which is the offer of a chance to discover.

In this spirit of play, the drama presents an illusion that, satisfying the expectations of dramatic illusion, challenges interpretation and calls for recognition of its truth. To see the play as primordial illusoriness is to refrain, to resist engagement, and to remain apart. To see it as an appearing and to play with it is to contribute, to give to the play the self's separate identity in a yielding to the possibility of discovery and becoming. Thus engrossed in the activity, the player becomes one with the play, its world, its characters, in mimetic action and identity. Neither lost in delusion nor invincible against the play of illusions, the audience becomes, once in and of the illusion, less a determinate judging self and more a possible self as other. Open to the play of illusion, the audience is capable of imaginatively making and remaking a sense of reality, performing in the action that is both life, the making of a world, and drama, the mimesis of a world.

Presenting itself as a mimesis of a world made possible by illusion, the play raises the questions of relationship and connection between worlds and identities. Its call is to an audience made ready to participate by being accustomed to dramatic tradition: to drama that has endured from the past, having created worlds for other worlds, and to drama that appears for the first time in the present, whether to endure or not. The audience of plays, film, and television is indubitably involved in the representation, both interpreting and contributing to the making of a world. If, however, it takes the play and its own relationship to the play lightly, it might withdraw from the experience unaware of the play's call and its transformative power as well as the audience's own mimetic activity. Uncaring, it might return to its own reality as if the play had been merely sleight-of-hand and entertainment. Freed of care, it might, as Heidegger describes Dasein's curiosity, be concerned to grasp all things, far and wide, just in order to demonstrate the facility of that grasp. Ostensibly caring, it might play the critic, knowing and proficient, judging and analyzing, maintaining an "aesthetic" differentiation: "Versatile curiosity and restlessly 'knowing it all' masquerade as a universal understanding of Dasein" (*Being and Time,* H 178). The play might, however, become a voice of the "call" that Heidegger considers a call of conscience (H 269–80), originating not in another discreteness, another individual or a metaphysical source, but in Dasein, in the human being and its world. If the world of the play calls, as conscience and consciousness, the play bears, in its mimesis and its anticipation of an audience's mimetic involvement, an imaginative ethical truth and an insistence. The audience's quasi-ethical relationship to the play, its involvement being as if a seriousness, is the granting of a possible seriousness to and in the nonserious, the allowing of the authenticity of the other that attracts the personal to itself. The extravagant mimesis in the doubling of worlds within the play, presenting the idea of the audience in the play, calls to that audience in its capacity as stand-in and illuminates the idea of the audience's mimetic and metaphorical relationship to the play.

The intensification of metaphorical relationship in this doubling is compelling, an importunate call toward the questions of reality and truth, an attraction to deeper play. A mimetic showing that, as Gadamer says, "enables us to see more than so-called reality" (*Relevance,*

129) elicits and makes evident the game being played, the displacement of bland and complacent acceptance of "so-called reality" as the only satisfaction of the authentic. With Gadamer's premise that "The 'as if' modification of poetic invention . . . clearly make[s] possible a form of participation that is beyond the reach of contingent reality," the appearance of the *theatrum mundi* metaphor in the play not only entices an audience toward the pleasure of that unfolding but also captures it in the transformation into a structure of ideality. Even in the creation that "reduces participants to the level of exploited consumers" and in which the "mere onlooker" maintains the "safe distance" that "regards the encounter with the work of art as nothing but enchantment in the sense of liberation from the pressures of reality through the enjoyment of a spurious freedom" (129–30), the appearance of worlds within worlds and identities hiding/revealing identities provokes a heightened awareness and becomes an illumination, a call for involved thinking about relationships. The rising consciousness of the idea of a *theatrum mundi* calls for the audience to become an idea of an audience, to become speculative.

In the representation in which an actual world or character is confronted by an illusory one and in which the illusion demands the question of its reality, as in ghostly manifestations, the appearance presents the activity of withdrawal; the secure locus of the real is being withdrawn as the illusory attracts, pulls thought toward its elusiveness, its withdrawal. In Heidegger's *Was heisst Denken* (translatable as "what is called thinking?" and as "what calls for thinking?" as Heidegger turns around the question [*Basic Writings*, 359–61]), the event of the withdrawal "touches" the human being "in the surely mysterious way of escaping him by its withdrawal" (350). The withdrawal is, in Heidegger's thought and in a play's representation of ideas, an event in a moment, a temporality. Heidegger's account of our holding to what holds us in our essential being recognizes memory as our means of holding and giving "thought precisely because it remains what must be thought about" (345); but since "what is to be thought about turns away from man, has turned away long ago" (348), that "event of withdrawal could be what is most present in all our present, and so infinitely exceed the actuality of everything actual" (350). The play's presenting the withdrawal of the illusory from the actual is essence of the play's being; in the doubling of the *theatrum mundi* metaphor the play sharply calls attention to the question of mimesis and the need for discovery: not a divorcement from, a denial or falsification of, the actual, but the opening of play with it. In the imaginative play, the freedom gained is not a release from the actual but a liberation toward discovery and transformation of what must always be returned to as the actual.

That inconclusive discovery and rediscovery, the journey out toward the mystery and back to constituted actuality, mutatis mutandis, is made possible by the unconstrained play of imagination. The imagination does not directly and immediately effect desired ends in the actual; it is not "creative" of a supplanting actuality. Its freedom is to range between the known and the unknown, the perceptible and the lethean in it, to entertain ideas of what is possible. Images of the strange, the fantastic, and the improbable; images retained and transformed by the memory; and images that seem to explain the state of things as they are, even the "plain sense of it, without reflections," are set in play as a freedom from the contingent, with the aim to make sense of the sensory. Yet this activity articulated with represented images in the play is not the free play of a private imagination but a listening to the call of that representation and those images that are there and have been there, that are reiterated and novel. If the call is *zu den sachen selbst,* to what is essential in appearances, the imagination creating a sense of the whole in the illusion of a reality necessitates submitting to the representation, giving and caring, letting it appear. Husserl's admonition to look and look again in attempting to discover an essence, an activity made possible by putting into abeyance the saltatory impulse that protects the subject from genuine participation, still reminds us that the freedom to discover is achieved in the abasement that is an advantage. Knowing not to presume and rely on—impose—great knowledge is the humbled condition made possible in a world descended and declined from the heroic, god-driven past.

An essence remaining in the world's memory is the anticipation that it is possible not to be alone, that in the possibility of sharing even the ideas of deprivation and solipsism, sharing occurs. In the withdrawal of others and what has been, there remains an idea of transcending the self in a momentary touch, an event essential to the play's mimesis that calls for the audience's mimesis of an action. There remains a cogency in eccentricity that in its strangeness calls for rapt attention, listening and seeing ecstatically, an excess that is mimetic of the play's exuberance. Giving thoughtfulness to what might appear as an essence need not be an intrusion of the individual desire to impose order through control, through getting into one's grasp and exposing secret meanings that resolve meaning. Letting appear, in an imaginative and speculative entertainment of ideas, is being involved, not only in the presence that speaks of this moment but also in the withdrawn and withdrawing. Ideas that remain as echoes of the past, affirmed or transformed, repudiated or grown strange, might provide

6: CALL AND RECALL: THE PLAY OF IMAGINATION 237

illumination without effecting resolution. Retaining and cherishing the work, caring to see it again and letting it work in the memory, is in itself a freely imaginative mimesis of the work's retention and preservation through re-creation; and the desire to share ideas about it becomes a tribute to its sharing and to the possibility of touching another as the play touches, in the attempt to think in the "event of withdrawal" that "could be what is most present in all our present." The play and its world speak in that withdrawal, a voice that expresses the cramped space of the little world of the present and the limited knowledge of even the moment as it recedes; and it speaks of the *enargeia* that in still attempting to call out to another is not yet silenced by the mysterious withdrawal and the mystery of continuation.

The play's appearance and withdrawal instigate the audience's mimesis of that *enargeia*. To keep on going, to keep on talking—about the play's élan that is attenuated in the condition of being in mystery, about the mystery, and the encounter with it—the interpreter might try to express a love for the play that has touched her or him, might want to retain the play and keep going back to it as tribute that unites with others who participate in it. In such desire is repeated, as retention, the play's representation of that desire to retain its relics. Taking this desired task entirely seriously, trying to see the profound truth of the play and talk about its gravity, gives the interpreter an importance, an authority, a professional edge that is indeed desirable. To play the role of the rhapsode, however, to be driven like Ion, in Socrates's pursuit of truth, from the presumption of knowledge and certainty toward the comic, accedes to the lightness of being that the imaginative work—metaphorical, mimetic, allusive, and illusory—confesses itself and its world to be. The diminishment—of world, human being, artist, and audience—leaves the critic in an embarrassment, and her or his imperative to secure the self against attrition turns the critical and professional authority away from the withdrawal toward legitimate and respected activities. Such activity is the preservation of theory itself, which is historically, philosophically, psychologically, or sociologically valuable; and even the fragile, dubious product of the avowed minor artist's activity retains its value as souvenir in the professional architecture of the theoretical.

If, however, the world is uncertain, formative or erosive, rich in hope and hollow in dismay, a truth of it that remains and is told is that desire persists and laughter is possible. Whether gay and joyous, ironic and wry, or sardonic and brutal; whether angelic, Dionysian, or satanic, laughter arises out of the recession toward mystery and in the play is a lightening elicited from and by the somber. As the artist might be an entertainer, playing tricks for an audience, practicing a confidence game in creating illusions, the play might become a game designed to reveal to and receive laughter from the audience. The play might present a truth of reality as the joke of the world imitated in the joke of the play. The interpreter who gets the joke, the participant in seeing and interpreting a way of being in the world, reflects the idea of play in an arena of lamentation, becoming indeed like Ion and his poet "a light and winged and holy thing." Attempting to talk about the play that jokes involves the interpreter in the embarrassment of appearing to explain a joke, but if the discussion retains a quality of Ion's unabashed enthusiasm, the pedantic and solemn might be brought down to reflect and mediate the spirit of the work. Not to be embarrassed by a play, even a frivolity, of language, metaphor, and imagination is not to abandon the search for thoughtfulness, care, and circumspection in circling toward the drama; it is to admit that the play of imagination and language manifests the withdrawal into the alien, reveals the dissolution and detrition of a world that withdraws as it is being made.

If the play rises up with panache to offer and play with questions, it might begin with the premise that the world is imagined to be, in knowing or idle talk about its detrition and Lethean oblivion, a fallenness peopled by the deaf and the blind. If the spectator is deprived of sight, as in Samuel Beckett's radio play *All That Fall,* then the joke is about both the participants in the language game, who cannot see the action, and on language itself: the play questions the commonplace that knowledge is a kind of seeing, plays with "serious" thought that cannot free itself of the play of metaphorical thought. The metaphor of eyesight, appearances, and illumination was instinctive for Husserl as it had been for Plato, and it can be argued that the philosophical tradition echoing the metaphor calls for thinking about knowledge as hearing.[1] As a radio play, Beckett's play is rich in sound effects—animals, "sheep, bird, cow, cock, severally, then together";[2] the train, bells, whistles; Christy's cart, Mr. Tyler's bicycle, Mr. Slocum's car; "dragging feet"; wind and rain; the woman's "same old record" (55), "Death and the Maiden." Human voices—sighs, sobs, breathing, panting, humming, laughter—and language—the urgent and unrestrained talk, the assertion of identity to and for others, devising conversation and society out of silence—evoke a world of animation and busyness, curiosity and desire; a world of inconsequential activity of the moment that betrays the knowledge of degeneration and loss, expressed as sorrow, lamentation, and nostalgia.

Like the joke, the play distills a sense of awareness that the ordinary perception of things, the complacency of living convictions, is awry when knowledge and its consequent certainties are presumed to be grounded in seeing. As Dan tries to convey to Maddy his sense that "nothing happened" when the train stopped, she seems to make the usual mistake of the sighted: "Did you not spring up and poke your head out of the window?" (49). Calling her attention to his debility, he asks, "What good would that have done me?" and she clarifies, amends, or hides her assumption: "Why to call out to be told what was amiss." She has had to make a similar adjustment with Mr. Slocum; to her questioning "what Dan will say when he sees" her torn frock Mr. Slocum responds, "Has he then recovered his sight?" (14): she had meant to ask, she says, what Dan will "say when he feels the hole." Deprived of sight, the alienated human being like Dan makes his or her way in the world and builds a world from limitation, and hearing both provides his evidence for concluding that "nothing happened" and reveals his dependency on others who might tell him "what was amiss." The radio-playwright's telling what is amiss grants to the audience the privilege of sharing Dan's blindness and provokes reconsideration of the prosaic assumption that to know is to see. "'Let me see,' said the blind carpenter as he picked up his hammer and saw." What can Dan do to protect himself against the suspicious interpreter who presumes to see into the mystery of things, Maddy or the audience, but reiterate his claim that "nothing happened"?

The nothing that happens in *All That Fall* is allusive, echoing and mocking the something that happened in the story of Oedipus. The tragic events, characters, and thought of Sophocles's play are put into abeyance, shattered, raised as a question among other questions, pertinent or impertinent, inconsequential or calling for resolution; and Sophocles's metaphor of knowledge, Oedipus's seeing, is mocked and solemnized in Dan. Dan is not accessible for the ulterior uses that would be made of blind Oedipus at Colonus, both the persuasions of Creon and Polyneices to let his life and death fulfill their needs and the blessing his blessedness confers on Theseus and Athens. Dan's refusal of himself—his privacy—and of answers to questions is not Oedipus's withdrawal into mystery, the hero's enigmatic translation and the secrecy that conceals his grave and ensures his continued influence as a relic. Dan's dying has been long, unaccompanied by miraculous signs; he has been "given up" by the doctors on the day Maddy proposed marriage to him (43). His blindness is not a climactic and heroic gesture proving self-knowledge and acceptance but "a great fillip" attached to the other circumstances that constitute the process of his dying.

As an interpreter, however, Dan has in common with Oedipus the king, and with audiences and interpreters who can see themselves in him, a curiosity and a desire to settle questions, to provide answers that reassure and resolve; Oedipus's certainty about his parentage, which blinds him to the truth, is reflected in Dan's accomplishment of knowledge, his erroneous certainty about Grimm's Law (50), his knowledge of the derivation of the word "buff" from "buffalo" (55). Dan's mathematical mind, adding and subtracting, calculating costs, recalls Sophocles's metaphor and diminishes Oedipus's grappling with his dilemma as a problem in choice and computation: either Laius was killed by one man or by several, and singular is not plural. Descending the steps to the station, Dan declares that he has "been up and down ... five thousand times and still I do not know how many there are" (38). When Maddy pleads that he not ask her to count, he objects: "Not count! One of the few satisfactions in life?" (39). The pleasure of counting is not countermanded by its ineffectuality. Alone in his compartment on the train, Dan defines his problem as a choice between the cost of "business" and the cost of staying home (45–46). His "mind began to work" on the expenses of travel: "Add to this— or subtract from it—rent, stationery, various subscriptions ... and a thousand unspecifiable sundries, and it is clear that by lying at home in bed ... with a change of pyjamas once a fortnight, you would add very considerably to your income. ... One has these moments of lucidity." One does not, if he is Dan, arrive at a climactic recognition that transforms his life and preserves it as a paradigm of character, of strength and integrity; if he vociferously maintains his secrecy, that action is not toward an ultimate clarity that gives the shape of context to the mysterious.

Although Dan shares qualities of mind with Oedipus, Maddy too shows the persistence of Oedipus, asking importunate questions about whether hinnies can "procreate," about Freudian implications in her own "preoccupation with horses' buttocks" (51). She is like Oedipus and Dan in that her acquired knowledge is a reassurance of self, proof of identity, uniqueness. She seems to be proud that people find something "bizarre about my way of speaking" (3), and she accedes to Dan's observation that "one would think you were struggling with a dead language" (48). Her delight in knowledge of the esoteric goes beyond the intellectual contrast between their dying language—as Dan says, "like our own poor dear Gaelic"—and the language of the lamb, which "has not changed, since Arcady" (49); and her knowledge is riddled with uncertainty and error. Maddy claims to have learned certain truths from a voice of authority, "the Regius Professor" (54): the sparrows "weren't sparrows at all," and it was not an "ass's colt" but a hinny that Christ "rode into Jerusalem or wherever it was." Her guesses can be not only indifferent—"wherever it was"—but also imprecise; neither "Lead, Kindly Light," nor "Rock of Ages" was sung on the Lusitania, nor on Maddy's second guess, "Or was it the Titanic?" (26). Her demonstration of knowledge is flawed by a continual loss of memory: she quotes, "Sigh out a something something tale of things" (5). In her pride of intellect she is the Oedipal interpreter, the would-be solver of riddles like the Sphinx's, though her questions and answers are of little consequence beyond the self compared to the tragic and restorative ends of Oedipus's pursuit; and her persistent questioning is, like her language, exaggerated, intense, histrionic. When Dan reiterates "I know nothing" (41), she insists: "But you must know! You were on it! Was it at the terminus? Did you leave on time? Or was it on the line? (*Pause.*) Did something happen on the line? (*Pause.*) Dan! (*Brokenly.*) Why won't you tell me?"

Retaining and cherishing the idea of Oedipus, attracted to his appealing representation of attributes that can be imaginatively shared and affective and can affirm our communal integrity, an audience might become painfully subject to and affronted by the world represented in *All That Fall*. Curious like Maddy it retains the desire to see itself in Oedipus and is gratified in the illusion that appears in metaphorical seeing. Desiring continuity and significance, it is confronted with fragmentation and detrition, not only the world's affronts to order and regularity such as a train's being late but also the individual's proclivity to distraction and irrelevancy. What remains of the idea of Oedipus is to be found only in shards. To be "at home" in this world is, as Maddy complains, a "lingering dissolution" (7). To try to make sense of it is to be defied by distraction, interruption, diversion, discrepancy, irrelevancy, uncertainty, and ignorance. Persistent, like Maddy—now Jocasta, now Oedipus—an audience comes to represent the discrepancy of the accommodated ego in that "lingering dissolution." Cast out of yet responsive to that Oedipal world of probability and necessity that rewards the quester with the clarification of destiny, the interpreter finds the self caught by Dan's allusion to Dante's interpreters, the damned magicians and prognosticators who presumed to see into the mystery, into the beyond. To seek a source of guilt in Dan, for instance the locus of Oedipal hamartia, or to conclude that as in our time Oedipus serves to explain Freudian psychology, is to seek resolution of the intractable in Dan and, as he stands in for us, in ourselves. To expose the truth of Dan, to understand the play and bring it into the coherence of cause and effect, motive, and resolution, is to go, as Dan says, "like Dante's damned, with their faces arsy-versy" (42–43). Yet in Dan and in the play itself the enigma appears, an enticement to the gratification of resolution and certainty, to grasping the play firmly and holding it fast.

The question posed to Oedipus by the Sphinx presents an image of a being that goes on four feet in the morning, two at noon, and three at night; and Oedipus's identification of the image as a human being confirms not only the power of that same being's intellect to solve riddles and to recognize itself in the enigma but also the gratification of its intellect in the power gained through the demonstration. Whereas detective and mystery fiction demonstrates such solving in the hero's or heroine's action and in the implicit challenge to the audience to outguess Holmes or Miss Marple, the mysteries for Oedipus the interpreter, both the Sphinx's riddle and the identity of the murderer, would have been familiar to Sophocles's audience and probably would not have constituted a vital suspense in the experience of the play by any later audiences. The ingenuity of Sophocles's audience might well have directed itself toward ideas that arose from the action, questions of guilt and innocence, fate and freedom, love and hatred, pride, arrogance, cruelty, or honesty. Oedipus's resolution of the question, however, and his actions following that discovery, complete an action that is a pursuit of knowledge and constitution of a design. Oedipus's formalized encounters with others is a centripetal motion toward the questions that must be answered, a motion that sweeps in from the periphery, finally, the messenger who comes to bring good news and the shepherd whose clear memory of a moment in the past makes it no longer possible for Oedipus to hold separate the identity he protects and the one he has cursed. As the questions about the killing of Laius and the prophecies have to be brought together, accomplishing a unity, the separate identities have to be merged for revelation and completion of the design.

The design of *All That Fall* extends, not toward the explicable that affirms human purpose and worth within the alien and indecipherable, but toward the heart of the mystery that is the condition of being human. Dan, the creature who "thumps the ground with his stick and pants incessantly" (34), who goes on three feet at night, contemplates reducing his meager existence from the daily journey on "these cursed steps" and "this hellish road" (39) to the immobility of home, where he would sit "on the remnants of my bottom counting the hours—till the next meal." The journey Maddy makes to retrieve Dan is a circle out to the station, up the steps, into the community, and down again with Dan for an uneventful return in a trip eventful only as a "surprise" celebration of Dan's birthday. This motion is unlike Oedipus's journey, which is intended as an escape from home that, as with the questions and the identities, discovers the one in the other, the presumed familiar in the alien, home at the furthermost point in the journey from home. In the riddle of the Sphinx Oedipus recognized

6: CALL AND RECALL: THE PLAY OF IMAGINATION   243

the human in the enigma, and in the question of the identity of the man at the crossroads he discovers his father and himself, himself as son and husband and father—and murderer; the encounter yields his parents and his children. In the flight from parents and home he discovers that he has found true home and parentage, his parents and himself as parent, and the outcome of marriage.

For Dan and Maddy, home is reduced to that essential union, the marriage that is fragile in its carnality and barren, the one child having died who would now be, according to Maddy, "in her forties . . . I don't know, fifty . . . getting ready for the change" (10). Home is not the arena of action, as it is for Orestes and Oedipus, but a place of seclusion and *otium,* a place where, with the blinds drawn, Maddy can read to Dan about Effie and the Major, where the woman "all alone in that great empty house" can play "all day the same old record . . . Death and the Maiden" (55). The security that Dan and Maddy have achieved is the familiarity of a marriage isolating them from others, the predictability and inconsequentiality of days with little variation and little promise. Maddy's going to the station to commemorate Dan's birthday only reveals his forgetting it, but she confirms their shared dependency in her reassurance that Dan can "just cling to me and all will be well" (39). They find in the refuge of one another the comfort that mitigates the disease of their lives, their distress that remains unalleviated either by knowledge and accomplishments or by messages from God's representative, the preacher. The text tomorrow will not be Hardy's "'How to be Happy though Married'"—Hardy has died (56)—but "'The Lord upholdeth all that fall and raiseth up all those that be bowed down,'" a promise that causes them to "join in wild laughter." Their outburst treats the consolation as a joke that, whether a cosmic or a cultural subterfuge, provides for them a shared recognition and a consolidation of identities against the illusion. Experiencing the pain and "lingering dissolution" of their lives at home and abroad, they are one in endurance and lamentation, and in their laughter they are united against a religion that mocks them, children who jeer and "pelt us with mud" (42), and the world in general, those at the station who are for Maddy "such horrid nasty people" (36).

Neither the journey—a pattern of rising and falling, getting up and getting down with or without help—nor the marriage—which persists against the world in the comforts of home where, Maddy promises, "We shall hang up all our things in the hot-cupboard and get into our dressing-gowns" (55)—achieves importance beyond mere subsistence. Their defiance is not the eminent defiance of Oedipus against forces that keep an eye on him and hold him accountable for his actions, but an ineffectual remonstrance against their dependence and unimportance. Maddy affirms her identity against the world by insisting that she is not invisible: "Am I then invisible, Miss Fitt? Is this cretonne so becoming to me that I merge into the masonry?" (22); "Do not imagine, because I am silent, that I am not present, and alive, to all that is going on" (29). Dan declares his violence as a "wish to kill a child" (42), an unfocused and mysterious urge, and Dan does not reveal an attempt to understand either the urge or what restrains him.

In the depreciation that calls into question the certainties upon which an identity is constructed, the deficiency in self-knowledge and knowledge of the other vacates the center of self and of home. Dan's abrogation of the Oedipal search for full comprehension is a withdrawal from himself and of himself from his wife. Maddy's importunate demand for an answer to "what happened" leads to the mystery that appears from the answer to a question; and as opposed to the action of the detective story or *Oedipus Rex,* that opening and linking of questions is the end rather than the beginning of the action. The mystery that is Dan eludes Maddy as she plays the detective, holding firmly, like Miss Marple in her apparent distraction, to the question; and Jerry's running to return the "something" Dan dropped at the station (57) provides her an opportunity to ask it again. Delaying his return to the station, she asks "what the hitch was . . . what kept the train so late" (58); and Jerry replies that "It was a little child fell out of the carriage. On to the line . . . Under the wheels" (58–59). Since the play ends after this statement with the sounds of Maddy and Dan going toward home in the "Tempest of wind and rain," Jerry's explanation seems to satisfy Maddy's curiosity and, for the audience, to fulfill or to quiet the demands for dramatic structure.

Maddy's urgent questioning is casually, even perfunctorily, silenced by an answer that explains the train's delay but offers no assurance that what seems to be an accident has anything to do with Maddy or Dan except by coincidence. If Dan's reaction to Jerry provokes in the audience a suspicion that he is attempting to avoid suspicion, the audience might go arsy-versy interpreting, sifting evidence that in a well made play might yield certainty and resolution; and Dan could be either exonerated or taken away, handcuffed, known to be the murderer. To pursue the question, even if to conclude that the pursuit is inconclusive, is to follow a conventional dramatic directive to see or make connections and coherence. Considering the elusive identity and unseen actions of Dan reveals that the desire to receive an answer, to arrive at a conclusion, is a presupposition of dramatic form that expects and is expected to provide a satisfaction. This play teases the audience, provokes pursuing the mystery as represented in Dan, who withdraws from the revelation.

6: CALL AND RECALL: THE PLAY OF IMAGINATION 245

The object that Jerry delivers seems, as a thing to be seen and recognized, acknowledged and explained, a formidable sign pointing the finger at Dan. A questionable thing, it has no ascertainable connection to the question about the train's delay. The palpable object, an image that calls for recognition, is like the image described by the Sphinx a challenge to interpretation, and like the Sphinx's riddle this object calls for the question of identity: who is this being that presumes to know itself and to hold sway by intellectual grasp of the other? The other question out of Maddy's mind for the moment, she persists in asking what the object is and describing it visually: "It looks like a kind of ball. And yet it is not a ball" (57). Since it belongs to Dan, or since he is at least willing to claim ownership, it exaggerates the mystery of identity; refusing to explain or specify, he only answers, twice, "It is a thing I carry about with me!" An object that generates the idea of a ball seems to create a link between itself and the child killed (or not killed) by Dan (or not by Dan)—a ball is a child's toy—and to instigate interpretive connections that will resolve the question of Dan. Yet it is not a ball. Whatever it might be, it is not an actual ball familiarly known and recognized as something a child would play with; it therefore does not establish a connection to the other question; but it does assert in its appearance to Maddy—which Dan confirms by touch before he acknowledges that it is his—that, one with him in marriage and suffering, she does not even know that he carries about with him a "something" that cannot be identified by seeing what it looks like.

To receive Maddy's testimony of how she perceives the object, that "it looks like a kind of ball ... yet it is not a ball," is to remain deprived of visual perception and dependent on language as sound, to rely as Dan would have relied on others had he poked his "head out of the window ... to be told what was amiss." Like Dan, the audience cannot verify Maddy's speculation by sight; unlike Dan, it cannot confirm what the object is by touch. The imagination might concretize the visual image—as something bright and stonelike, as something dark, amorphous, and pliable—and generate connections between it, Dan, and the child; but the imaginative activity would not bring the play into a form that accomplishes a full and satisfactory revelation of identity and confirms the efficacy of the traditional mimesis. The play might, like the mysterious object, look like something that it is not—the form that was shaped in the past according to prescribed recognitions and reversals answering the demand for completion and intelligibility. It might seem the more disturbing because it ends with the heightened questioning that amounts to the fancifulness of conundrum.

The riddle "What is it that is black and white and re(a)d all over?" locates the pun in the question, and the answer "Newspaper" might as well be "book" or "text." The play becomes an expression of both the playfulness of the joke that asks such questions and the profound enticement of the will to deduce and count, to infer and bring things around to rightness in a fastidious circularity. To provoke and betray that desire, to lead toward and end with a question that ought to be a beginning, is to leave the audience open and vulnerable to the "lingering dissolution" that is the lives of the characters and the *detrimentum* of the world that finds itself in them; it is to represent itself as the play that is not a play insofar as it cannot be what the play has been, the *spectacle* grounded in the metaphor of recognition as *seeing*. If in its play with dramatic form it evokes and abjures the past, lovingly recalls and mocks what it cannot be of what has been, then it can be what it is, a dwelling in the mystery that continues to tell the story that Dan is goaded to tell, his "composition" (49) explaining that he does not know what happened, that "I have never known anything to happen."

Dan's attenuated story about nothing happening points to the play about nothing happening, as Maddy's question about the mysterious object points to the question the play raises about itself as object of experience. His story about nothing happening and her question about the thing seen, reflective of the play itself, make of it a joke that plays against ordinary perceptions and expectations. Taking it as reflecting something of the world's knowledge that the shining edifice of the past has fallen into disrepair, the audience recognizes the febrile, persistent talking as not just a presumption of knowledge but an affirmation of continuance. As in Edwin Arlington Robinson's villanelle "The House on the Hill," the talk is negation that affirms talking itself. The decayed house attracts and raises the question, "Why is it then we stray / Around the sunken sill?"[3] Poetry is powerless to influence the fate, to revoke the loss, of those who "are all gone away," whose stories, like the story of Dan and Maddy, call out to be told, "And our poor fancy-play / For them is wasted skill." Yet in the conclusion that "They are all gone away, / There is nothing more to say," the poem affirms that there is something more to say, since there is something being said; there is an audience engaged and listening. Ursula K. Le Guin speaks, for the writer of fiction and drama, the audience, and the critic, of this urge to memorialize that produces the tribute and the relic; and inherent in this desire is possibility of future participation. In her essay entitled "It Was a Dark and Stormy Night; or, Why Are We Huddling About the Campfire?" she affirms the need by letting others speak, by practicing what she calls the novelist's "habit of ventriloquy":[4] "'Even in this place one can survive, and therefore one must want to survive, to tell the story, to bear witness' (Primo Levi, from Auschwitz)." The storyteller makes a tale her own and bestows it on the listener. "Insofar as I have remembered it, it is mine; and now, if you like it, it's yours. In the tale, in the telling, we are all one blood. Take the tale in your teeth, then, and bite till the blood runs, hoping it's not poison; and we will all come to the end together, and even to the beginning: living, as we do, in the middle" (30).

The play, like narrative, continues talking, retaining the past and telling a story, to an audience that comes to listen and to see, to—like the rat of Stevens's imagination, the "silence of a rat come out to see"—participate in and maintain the experience. For the critic as for the creator of a narrative or a drama, going to "a symposium on narrative and" getting "eaten in the forest by a metabear" (Le Guin, 22) does not resolve us into full intelligibility and away from the necessity of the imagination. The liberation from the actual mimetic moment that the imagination realizes in the play calls for acceptance of the fact that, although we share in fallenness in our world and in the world of the play, our knowledge is held together by the imagination, which is not incapacitated; nor is it preempted by the abstraction that follows it as authoritative and professionally accomplished interpretation. Becoming and not becoming Dan and Maddy, interpreters break the silence of listening by trying to talk about imaginative experience, to hope that "we will all come to the end together, and even to the beginning: living, as we do, in the middle."

If the engagement with the play is that mysterious transcendence of the self in "identification with," the yielding of the actual self of the moment to the play of possibility in being one with another, then talking about the play is an attempt to retain and preserve. Although the understanding must be satisfied in the construction of the probable, in the assurance that the seen and heard can be experienced as evidential, the value in the collaboration to maintain the play is not to preserve its historical or archaeological meaning, its worth as a souvenir. The imaginative delight and the desire to experience and reexperience the play through communality are realized in the interpretation's accepting its arsy-versy dependency, like Dan and Maddy's, on the imagination's keeping it up in the telling and retelling. Connecting and letting go, releasing the self and the play from the strictures of getting it "thematically into one's grasp" and "holding it fast," is a way of acknowledging the tenuous accomplishment of union in the withdrawal, the unfathomable mystery beyond the horizon. Knowledge of the play, which involves the clarification that what is not known is not known, prevails only so far as the audience yields to the play, gives itself to the play in the activity of taking it to the self and attempting to preserve it through memory and through finding the language of tribute.

Notes

Chapter 1. Speculation: Seeing and Imagining

1. Leon Golden, trans., *Aristotle's Poetics* (Englewood Cliffs: Prentice-Hall, 1968), 11. I cite the *Poetics* as well, for comparative purposes, from other translations: Gerald F. Else, *Aristotle's Poetics* (n.p.: Ann Arbor-University of Michigan Press, 1970); and S. H. Butcher, *Aristotle's Theory of Poetry and Fine Art: with a Critical Text and Translation of* The Poetics, 4th ed. (New York: Dover, 1951).

2. Deprived of the source, neither having access to an original text nor capable of reading classical Greek, I cite Douglas Young's translation after making comparisons with others (*The Oresteia*, trans. Douglas Young [Norman: University of Oklahoma Press, 1974]). Subsequent references to *The Oresteia* are from this edition.

3. Siegfried Wenzel, "Chaucer's Pardoner and His Relics," *Studies in the Age of Chaucer* (Knoxville, Tenn.: New Chaucer Society, 1989), 37.

4. Wallace Stevens's little poem with the ironically playful title "Lebensweisheitspielerei" (*The Palm at the End of the Mind* [New York: Knopf, 1971], 383–84) invokes a past golden world as a consciousness, a memory, in this diminished state, this "dwindled sphere." Subsequent quotations from Stevens's poems are from this edition.

5. For Maurice Merleau-Ponty, phenomenological perception is not "pure," but made possible by the "setting in which all disclosure" is "a realm of truth, a *world*" (*Phenomenology of Perception*, [Atlantic Highlands, N.J.: Humanities Press; London: Routledge, 1962], 17). Merleau-Ponty describes a "moment" of seeing the "funnel or masts" of a ship as "indissolubly fused with" the ship, *as* ship, when from his angle of vision they become distinct as beyond the trees from which they emerge. Martin Heidegger's "interpretation . . . grounded existentially in understanding" (*Being and Time* [New York: Harper, 1962], H 148) is "the working-out of possibilities projected in understanding," and such "circumspection . . . has the structure of *something as something*. . . . In dealing with what is environmentally ready-to-hand by interpreting it circumspectively, we 'see' it *as* a table, a door, a carriage, or a bridge" (H 149). (I cite *Being and Time* as Macquarrie and Robinson refer to the later German editions in their index.)

6. Wallace Stevens, "The Plain Sense of Things," *Palm*, 382–83. Edward S. Casey's phenomenological description of the imagination—in which he stresses the primacy of the imagination as activity, as event, in the title—establishes a clear and precise description of the faculty that can be called "imagination" (*Imagining: A Phenomenological Study* [Bloomington: Midland-Indiana University Press, 1979]). In this attempt to describe accurately, he must counter on the one hand the excessive claims of a residual romanticism and on the other the commonplace pejoration of imagination as mere illusion, the "honorific connotation" of the word "imaginative" and the "dishonorific connotation" of the word "imaginary" (Casey xv–xvi). What is found to be essential to imagination, in his clarification of it, is its intentionality. The "act phase" (40–48) and the "object phase" (49–58) are interdependent; "the

fundamental correlativity of act and object phases is what establishes imagining as ineluctably intentional" (57).

7. There are convincing and instructive arguments concerning these themes; for instance, Bruce Wilshire's *Role Playing and Identity* (Bloomington: Indiana University Press, 1991). Wilshire is concerned about the usefulness of the theater in a time of need; more serious than I, he pursues the idea of being human, the ontological problem of identity. Subsequent quotes from Wilshire are from this edition.

8. In our time the theorists, critics, and historians of drama often express a sense of the uneasy articulation of their theme, drama, which requires imaginative engagement, and their responsibilities as analysts, theorists, or historians. Richard Hornby, for instance, writes an able and influential scholarly book about drama and "metadrama," which "can be defined as drama about drama" (*Drama, Metadrama, and Perception* [Lewisburg: Bucknell University Press, 1986], 31). He bases his enterprise in the discipline of structuralist and semiotic thought, which is encouraged when things fall comfortably into categorical structures—as when "overt metadrama" can be identified in its five "possible varieties" (32). Yet in this "metadramatic experience" the audience feels "unease, a dislocation of perception . . . [and] This 'seeing double' is the true . . . subject of this book." Another capable critic, Lionel Abel, is fascinated not only with the "metaplay" but also with his own scholarly/critical acumen and, in steering toward the sharp contrast between tragedy and "metatheatre" (*Metatheatre: A New View of Dramatic Form* [New York: Dramabook-Hill & Wang, 1963], 113), predicts early on that he will "answer all the old questions—once and for all" (41). Stretching the limits of the scholar's persona, Thomas R. Whitaker, critical of the way "dramatic criticism of the usual kind . . . posits a critic who is a fixed identity and a play that is external to the critic and to everyone else" (*Fields of Play in Modern Drama* [Princeton: Princeton University Press, 1977], 7), allows, in the liberal play of imagination, his own text to move ever further into the "Fields of Play" that the text is about. The "I" becomes "we" and progressively a multiplicity of possible assumed identities insisting not only that the play is "the form of our shared acting and witnessing, a distinctive field of playing that we compose within the intersubjective field of play that makes it possible" (6), but also that "language itself is a participatory act" (8). Even a capable historian of recent American drama, C. W. E. Bigsby, acknowledges and values this insight that the drama of a world imaginatively "inventing itself" is expressed by the stage, which reveals "the extent to which the imagined can become the actual, the self be reborn in a myriad of guises, a singular thought become a communal truth" (*Modern American Drama, 1945–1990* [Cambridge: Cambridge University Press, 1992], 341). Questions of illusion, identity, and worlds addressed to the activity of invention remind us, in that invention is process rather than end, that questions remain or reappear in answers. Implicit and pervasive in what I have said and cited—"seeing double," "fields of play," a world "inventing itself"—is my point of departure, the immediacy of drama's presentation.

Chapter 2. Mimesis: The Play

1. These words echo from Wallace Stevens's "Things of August" (*Palm*, 355–61), a poem concerned with that time of year when "the sense of the archaic touched us at once / In a movement of the outlines of similarity" (359). That sense evokes the images of the past—"the wanderer, / The father, the ancestor, the bearded peer, / The total of human shadows" (360)—as both "an old and disused ambit of the soul" (355) and "A new text of the world" (360). Being "touched" by the "archaic," engag-

ing in an "old and disused ambit," going around and back over the ancient shadows, makes the audience both a shadow moving among the "outlines of similarity" and, like those shadows, a presence "bright as glass" in the moment of experience.

2. Gadamer argues that in the play "the thing represented is there (Das Dargestellte ist da)" (*Truth and Method* [New York: Crossroad, 1991], 113). Children, playing at "dressing up . . . are not trying to hide themselves, pretending to be something else in order to be discovered and recognized behind it; but, on the contrary, they intend a representation of such a kind that only what is represented exists." Subsequent references to this work are from this edition.

3. Edmund Husserl launches his investigation of the way toward a "pure phenomenology" by characterizing our involvement in and perception of a world of objects and values: "Our first outlook upon life is that of natural human beings, imaging, judging, feeling, willing, '*from the natural standpoint*'" (*Ideas* [New York: Collier-Macmillan, 1962], 91). Subsequent references to this work are from this edition.

4. The dethronement of "logocentrism" is a mission in much contemporary theory, a seminal essay representing this conviction being William V. Spanos's "Breaking the Circle: Hermeneutics as Dis-closure" (*boundary 2* 5 [1977]: 421–57).

5. In his consideration of our finding aesthetic pleasure in the "Disagreeable" or "Terrible," Addison says that "When we look on such hideous Objects, we are not a little pleased to think we are in no Danger of them. . . . The more frightful Appearance they make, the greater is the Pleasure we receive from the Sense of our own Safety" (*The Spectator* [Norman: University of Oklahoma Press, 1974], no. 418, 566–68). Subsequent references to Addison's *Spectator Papers* are from this edition.

6. Heidegger's turning is a pervasive maneuver in his thinking, a turning back to look at the way he has come. For instance, the reversal of the title "from 'Being and Time' to 'Time and Being'" is representative of the turning that is "not a change of standpoint from *Being and Time,* but in it the thinking that was sought first arrives at the location of that dimension out of which *Being and Time* is experienced, that is to say, experienced from the fundamental experience of the oblivion of Being" (Martin Heidegger, "Letter on Humanism," *Basic Writings* [New York: Harper, 1977], 208). Subsequent references to *Basic Writings* are taken from this, the first, edition.

7. Gary Larson, *PreHistory of the Far Side* (Kansas City: Andrews and McMeel, 1989), 262.

8. The "transformation into structure" (*Truth and Method,* 110–21) is a fusion of all participants in the event, a temporal structure comprised of all who are found and lost in the event, including the spectator.

9. Clifford Geertz, "Deep Play: Notes on the Balinese Cockfight," *Myth, Symbol, and Culture* (New York: Norton, 1971), 15.

10. Jackson I. Cope, *The Theater and the Dream* (Baltimore: Johns Hopkins University Press, 1973), 23.

11. Golden, *Aristotle's Poetics,* 30 (chap. 17, l. 17–19). In Butcher's translation of these lines, this poet, in contrast to Socrates's mad or inspired Ion, has "a happy gift of nature . . . [and] can take the mold of any character" (17.63).

12. Such notions of the reader/audience might range from the psychology of Norman Holland, as seen for instance in his early *Poems in Persons* (New York: Norton, 1973), to Wolfgang Iser's developing in *The Implied Reader* (Baltimore: Johns Hopkins University Press, 1974), under the influence of Roman Ingarden's phenomenology, ideas of the reading process. Inclinations to subjectivize the idea of audience make it more manageable, make analysis of it more accessible and comprehensive, and escape the problems that arise with the uncertainties about the subject in Heidegger's herme-

neutic and in discussions of plays that confuse (or identify) represented and imagined stage audience with a natural audience.

13. Samuel Taylor Coleridge, *Biographia Literaria* (London: Oxford University Press, 1954), 2:11. Subsequent quotations of Coleridge are from this edition of the *Biographia Literaria*.

14. Harold Pinter, "The Black and White," *Complete Works: Two* (New York: Evergreen-Grove, 1990), 242. Except where indicated, subsequent quotations of Pinter's plays are from *Complete Works*.

15. Maggie Verver's having to make connections, to interpret relations and to be related, is anticipated in the connections Charlotte "might have been" making when the antiquario suggests how the bowl might be broken by "dashing it with violence—say upon a marble floor" (Henry James, *The Golden Bowl* [Harmondsworth: Penguin, 1966], 106). For Charlotte "they were a connexion, marble floors; a connexion with many things: with her old Rome, and with *his*; with the palaces of his past, and a little, of hers; with the possibilities of his future." The challenge is central in *A Passage to India*, and the epigraph to *Howard's End* is "Only connect. . . ."

16. George Lakoff and Mark Johnson trace the up-down metaphor in ordinary use (*Metaphors We Live By* [Chicago: University of Chicago Press, 1980], 14–21), suggesting that the up-down structure can involve the question of knowledge, the unknown being up in the air, the known being grasped: "It's easier to grasp something and look at it carefully if it's on the ground in a fixed location than if it's floating through the air" (20). The women's game of inversion—one correcting the other's statement of direction—is a comic expression of conflict involving knowledge and power. Knowing whether something is up or down is in itself a reassurance of knowledge, and correcting another's perception is an assertion of superior knowledge.

17. O. B. Hardison stresses the cognitive value of Aristotle's mimesis and concludes that "A tragedy should be made totally intelligible; the pleasure derived from it is learning; and the pleasure of learning ultimately absorbs the pity and fear aroused by the action" ("Epilogue: On Aristotelian Imitation," Golden, *Aristotle's Poetics*, 295).

18. I here cite the Butcher translation (9.39). Golden reads, "For there is more of the marvelous in them if they occur this way than if they occurred spontaneously and by chance" (18).

19. I have argued in my article "Dimensions of Mimesis" that *No Man's Land* reflects Sophocles's *Philoctetes*, making oblique reference to the epic past, to both characters and their world.

20. E. H. Gombrich, *Art and Illusion* (Princeton: Princeton University Press, 1969), 219.

21. I receive and extrapolate ideas about "ambulatory" and "saltatory" from William James's thinking of the opposed qualities of mind in philosophy: the inclination to amble toward experience in no particular direction and with no predetermined end that seems rather irresponsible and unaccomplished compared to the more vigorous thinker's leaping upon and definitively circumscribing ideas (*Pragmatism and The Meaning of Truth* [Cambridge: Harvard University Press, 1978], 245–50). Pursuing this metaphor of ambulation would lead to observing the mobility of Heidegger's thinker as he/she enters or makes clearings in the forest of interpretation.

22. E. D. Hirsch's argument for a clear and conclusive distinction between meaning and significance is grounded in this need for a controlled intelligibility.

23. The ferment of critical activity in the last half century has been surveyed by Vincent B. Leitch, who records one critical objection to Norman Holland's psychoanalytical theory: "his own readings were solipsistic and merely confessional" (*American Literary Criticism from the Thirties to the Eighties* [New York: Columbia

University Press, 1988], 223). This objection might be raised against the subjectivist theory of David Bleich as well.

24. Lucina Gabbard, *The Dream Structure of Pinter's Plays* (Rutherford: Fairleigh Dickinson University Press, 1976), however, displays psychoanalytical design in Pinter's plays, an interpretation that refers the work of art directly to Freudian schemata.

25. Ingarden, provoked by attacks on his philosophical consistency in *The Literary Work of Art*, attempted in *The Cognition of The Literary Work of Art* to strengthen his case for the cognitive value of the aesthetic experience.

26. Friedrich Schiller, *On the Aesthetic Education of Man* (New York: Ungar, 1965), 74.

27. Hans-Georg Gadamer, *Philosophical Hermeneutics* (Berkeley: University of California Press, 1977), 15.

28. Derrida is interpreted by Foucault, in Spivak's reading, with careless attention and "virulence," but Foucault's criticism, as quoted by Spivak, is revealing: "A pedagogy that tells the pupil that there is nothing outside of the text . . . gives to the voice of the teacher that unlimited sovereignty which permits them [the students] to read the text indefinitely" (*Of Grammatology*, translation and introduction by Gayatri Chakravorty Spivak [Baltimore: Johns Hopkins University Press, 1974], lxi-lxii).

29. In reader response theory, attempts to answer the question "What reader?" often aim to name and fix readers as, for instance, "characterized" and "implied" opposed to "real" readers (W. Daniel Wilson, "Readers in Texts," 858). Such ontological distinctions need not be invoked so long as the reader remains ideal (rather than Ideal)—remains, that is, ideas of an audience reflexively engaged.

30. Derrida's deferral of presence is not my point. The presence-absence dialectic settles an issue against the probability of presence, but the question remains moot so long as author or audience remains a speculative value rather than being conceived of as ontologically definite. It would be expedient to agree with Wallace Stevens in talking about "fictions," provided that "fictions" are agreed to be neither true nor false but tentative and amendable conceptualizations, versions of truth. If we must argue against the certainty of those who "have been a little insane about the truth" ("The Noble Rider and the Sound of Words," *Necessary Angel* [New York: Vintage-Random House, 1951], 33), we might assume for rhetorical effect that "Poetry is the supreme fiction, madame" ("A High-Toned Old Christian Woman," *Palm*, 77-78). Subsequent references to the essays in *The Necessary Angel* are from this edition.

31. In this context, Husserl's bracketing becomes not a means to attain philosophical assurance but a psychological activity, a felt uncertainty.

32. These words again echo from Stevens's poem "Lebensweisheitspielerei" (*Palm*, 383-84). It is in this diminished world and "indigence" of human beings that there might be "a few words spoken." Then surprisingly, improbably, "Each person completely touches us / With what he is and as he is."

CHAPTER 3. IDEAS: AUDIENCE AND AUTHOR

1. Robert Frost, "The Oven Bird," *Poetry and Prose* (New York: Holt, 1972), 54.

2. The audience conceived as imaginative possibility in the event resists abstraction, classification, and closure as a structure determined prior to the event, even the tripartite structure Sidney Homan proposes: the actual audience offstage, the "playwright's use of onstage audiences" (*The Audience as Actor and Character* [Lewisburg: Bucknell University Press, 1989], preface, n.p.), and the conceptual, self-

conscious, or "philosophical" audience. The "actual" audience remains hypothetical and moot, and the audience as idea, philosophical or self-conscious, might be actualized in, for instance, ideas of community as well as of subjectivity. Homan's three audiences lose their discrete identities, finally, in his characterization of drama: "The play is, properly, an imaginative collaboration among all those present, a union of seeming opposites acknowledging that what unites reality and the theater is the principle that identity is an ongoing process between perceiver and the perceived, that *reality* itself is not an exclusive term" (163). Herbert Blau's audience is no less authentic for its elusiveness; it "is not so much a mere congregation of people as a body of thought and desire. It does not exist before the play but is *initiated* or *precipitated* by it; it is not an entity to begin with but a consciousness constructed" (*The Audience* [Baltimore: Johns Hopkins University Press, 1990], 25).

3. John Keats, *Letters*, vol. 1 (Cambridge: Harvard University Press, 1958), 193–94. Subsequent quotations of Keats's letters are from this edition.

4. I am thinking of Ernest Jones's study of Hamlet (*Hamlet and Oedipus* [Garden City: Anchor-Doubleday, 1954]), which still stands as a classic example in the anachronistic Freudian analysis of characters in literature.

5. As with other translations of plays, I compare English texts with the original-language text when I am capable, and I compare translations when I cannot. The problem of translation calls into play the question of origin—the idea of a pure and accessible source—and leaves the question open even when we think we have before us *the* authentic version of the play. Even in comparing translations, an imaginative (re)construction of a text that is neither absent nor present but in the process of appearing is essential to the experience. While referring to the Edward Storer translation of the "original version" of *Six Characters in Search of an Author* in *Naked Masks* (New York: Dutton, 1952), I cite the Anthony Caputi translation in *Eight Modern Plays* (New York: Norton, 1966) because the translation seems more true to the original; for instance, the title of the play being produced by the company, *Il giuoco delle parti* (*Naked Masks*, 212), is bland in Storer's translation ("Mixing It Up") and in Caputi's translation ("The Game of Parts") seems not merely more "authentic" but verbally provocative of ideas in and about the play.

6. David Mamet, *House of Games* (New York: Evergreen-Grove, 1987), 34.

7. Although I quote from *The Standard Edition* of Melville's *Works* (New York: Russell, 1963), I derive Melville's attribution of the review to the "Virginian" from *The Norton Anthology of American Literature*, edited by Nina Baym et al. (New York: Norton, 1989), 2131n.

8. Nathaniel Hawthorne, *Works: Centenary Edition*: vol. 8 (Columbus: Ohio State University Press, 1972), 90. Subsequent quotations from Hawthorne's writings are drawn from the *Centenary Edition*, *The American Notebooks* in vol. 8, *Mosses from an Old Manse* in vol. 10 (1974), and *The Scarlet Letter* in vol. 1 (1962).

9. Butcher 9:37. The argument—for an audience's being conditioned to believe that what has actually happened is possible and believable in the dramatized events—is clear in Golden's translation (17) and in Else's (33).

10. Eugene O'Neill, *Long Day's Journey into Night* (New Haven: Yale University Press, 1956), 12.

11. My entertainment of ideas about *The Dumb Waiter*'s structures of relationships entails this essential and problematical relationship among author, work, and audience as I see it reflected in the manifold of relationships between other subjects and objects in his plays. In addressing the problem of understanding Pinter's plays, Richard Schechner acknowledges their "conceptual incompleteness" while arguing that "structurally each play is complete" ("Puzzling Pinter," *Tulane Drama Review*

11.2 [1966]: 177). Naming Pinter the "'disinterested' artist," he finds the plays "paradigmatically theatrical," the play being, "finally, an illusion" (184). Thomas Van Laan directs attention to the audience ("The Dumb Waiter: Pinter's Play with the Audience," *Modern Drama* 24 [1981]: 494–502), whose "filling in"—what I would call the audience's need for clarity and finality—is the source of the problem. The characters reflect this impulse, as in Ben and Gus's filling in about the old man and the lorry and about the killing of the cat (Van Laan, 495–96). Pinter wants us to "question ourselves" as "uneasy collaborators" (499), to "review our assumptions about reality" (500). He is "playing with us and playing us in order to make sure that our responses get called into play and into *the* play" (501). Both critics seem to be leading toward thought of the *theatrum mundi* topos in that the solid actuality, the assumption of clear and final knowledge about the author's and the audience's world, is called into question.

12. Martin Heidegger, *What Is Philosophy?* (New York: Twayne, 1958), 81. Subsequent references to this work are from this edition.

13. Husserl argues that the empiricist's "requirement of a return to the 'facts themselves'" is restrictive: "he takes for granted without further question that experience is the only act through which facts themselves are given. But *facts (Sachen) are not* necessarily *facts of nature,* the fact world in the ordinary sense" (*Ideas,* 74–75).

14. The bracketing becomes, in effect, a freedom of the imagination: "This attempt to doubt everything should serve us *only as a device of method,* helping us to stress certain points which by its means, as though secluded in its essence, must be brought clearly to light. . . . The attempt to doubt everything has its place in the realm of our *perfect freedom*" (*Ideas,* 97).

15. Frederic V. Grunfeld, *Rodin: A Biography* (New York: Henry Holt, 1987), 250.

16. John Keats, *Poems* (Cambridge: Harvard University Press, 1978), 373. Subsequent quotations of Keats's poems are from this edition.

17. Katharine Worth suggests that *The Room* evokes the "metaphysical questions about human identity" in "the medieval miracle and morality plays, with their besieged souls and deathly visitations" ("Pinter's Scenic Imagery," *The Pinter Review* 1 [1987]: 32). She connects the vertical structure of the house, with an upstairs and a basement, to Freudian or Christian allegorical structure—a connection I consider worthy of further speculation.

18. *Sacrifice of Isaac. Chief Pre-Shakespearean Dramas* (Cambridge: Riverside-Houghton, 1924), ll. 60–62). Subsequent references to this play are from this edition. I cite *The Dumb Waiter* from Pinter's *Complete Works: One.*

19. Quoted in Robert B. Burlin, *The Old English Advent* (New Haven: Yale University Press, 1968), 8.

Chapter 4. Ideas: Human Being and World

1. T. S. Eliot, *The Wasteland and Other Poems* (New York: Harvest-Harcourt, 1962), 13. Subsequent reference to Eliot's poetry are from this edition.

2. Ben Jonson, *Timber or Discoveries* (Westport, Conn.: Greenwood Press, 1976), 71.

3. Tennessee Williams, *A Streetcar Named Desire* (New York: Signet-New American, 1947), 37. Subsequent references to this play are from this edition.

4. According to Aristotle, the poet "must necessarily imitate things one of three possible ways: (1) the way they were / or are, (2) the way they are said or thought to be, or (3) the way they ought to be" (Else 25:67).

5. Vergil, *The Aeneid* (New York: Rinehart, 1953), 157. Subsequent quotations of this work are from this edition.

6. Luigi Pirandello, *Naked Masks* (New York: Dutton, 1952), 139. Subsequent references to this play are from this edition.

7. I was led to this connection with Klee's angel of earth by hearing a paper by Mark Luprecht ("Paul Klee and the Angels of Modern Times," *Eighteenth Annual Conference on Literature and Film,* Tallahassee, Florida, 28–30 January 1993). Robert Alter observes the influence of Klee's *Angelus Novus* on the thinking of Walter Benjamin and Gershom Scholem and relates the image to Franz Kafka's thought (*Necessary Angels* [Cambridge, Mass.: Harvard University Press, 1991], 113–20).

8. The play is "Robert Whitman's theatre work *Light Touch*" (ix).

9. Henrik Ibsen, *The Complete Major Prose Plays* (New York: Farrar, 1978), 239. Except as noted, further references to Ibsen's plays are from this edition.

10. Einar Haugen, *Ibsen's Drama* (Minneapolis: University of Minnesota Press, 1979), 10.

11. The presence of the metaphor in Young's text is in agreement with the usual translation: when Electra asks whether Orestes is "setting a snare for" her, he responds, "If so, the trap I make entraps myself" (ll. 220–21).

12. Aristotle represents Electra's recognition of Orestes as a process of "reasoning" that is based in seeing similarity: "'Somebody like me has come; nobody is like me but Orestes: therefore he has come'" (Else, 17:46).

13. The imaginative dimensions of the *theatrum mundi* metaphor are open and invite extrapolation. Following the logic of metaphor's analogical structure, the union of the one world with the other in likeness and difference establishes the extension of the comparison of either world with yet another. If we think of two worlds in a relationship as being either lighted or in darkness, as opposed in seeing-knowledge and blindness-ignorance, their relationship can be imagined as an unlimited play of possible repetitions, and this fairly elemental structure of thought is the unifying activity of imagination, of mimesis, and of what we call "identifying with" another: "I am like, or feel like, that other; that other is like, or feels, as I feel." The dimensionalizing mode of this metaphorical activity is perhaps too elemental to need this graphic representation:

Extrapolated inner world	Inner world	World	Outer world	Extrapolated outer world
	Dark>	<Light		
		Dark>	<Light	
Dark>	<Light		Dark>	<Light

14. The Houses of Athens, Argos, and Thebes were connected, if distantly, in their genealogy. Argos and Athens shared bloodlines that could be traced back to Pelops.

15. Gadamer's interest in the mirror as speculation (*Truth and Method,* 465–66) is not unrelated to his idea of drama as play transformed into "Gebilde," structure (110); he characterizes relationships between the picture (painting or photograph), the copy, and the mirror (134–41). The copy fulfills its function merely in *referring* to the painting, but the mirror and the painting *represent* what is to be revealed. "What is in the mirror is the *image* of what is represented and is inseparable from its presence" (139; my emphasis). The painting or picture presents *not an image but a world* from which it, as representation, cannot be isolated. Like the play, the picture constitutes its representation of its world, for which the picture realizes "an *increase in being*" (140).

16. In making this connection of the photograph and the film with the mirror, I recall E. H. Gombrich's observation about works of art: "Works of art are not mirrors, but they share with mirrors that elusive magic of transformation which is so hard to put into words" (*Art and Illusion*, 6). Gombrich's concern with the literal mirror focuses on its power of illusion regarding size, its small image being seen as life-size (6, 279, 300). I have only recently, since ideas in this paper were fully developed, seen the translation of Lucien Dällenbach's *The Mirror in the Text*. The ideas explored by Dällenbach are provocative and confirm what he would consider to be my "intuitions." The methodical critic, whose approach is through a "structural typology" ([Chicago: University of Chicago Press, 1989], 42), argues well for what might seem freely imaginative in my discussion. I think I am not in bad company with C. E. Magny, however, whom he considers "cavalier," imprecise, "unable to control her metaphors," "infecting" the term "abyme" with "metaphysical meaning," and producing a "critical hotch-potch" (21-24). My idea of Magny is of the critic who does not presume to be a pure analytical subjectivity standing apart from and observing the text as object.

17. Robert Self, objecting to an "auteur theory" that predetermines an ideal conception of the artist as endowed like a "divine . . . maker" ("Robert Altman and the Theory of Authorship," *Cinema Journal* 25 [1985], 3), would free the artist Altman from a restricted single identity, biographical or ideal. For Self, as for me, the idea of the artist involves the "articulation of contradictions in the film text," heterogeneity, a "plurality of authorial voices"; the "name of the author" involves "the names of other artists" (4-6). Helene Keyssar, taking a suggestion from Tzvetan Todorov, suggests that Altman's role as director can be characterized as collaborative: "we would follow the name Altman with a slash and the name(s) of others with whom the particular text at hand was created" (*Robert Altman's America* [New York: Oxford University Press, 1991], 11-12).

18. Ed Graczyk, *Come Back to the 5 & Dime, Jimmy Dean, Jimmy Dean* (New York: Samuel French, 1976), 55. Subsequent references to Graczyk's play are from this edition. I cite Altman's film from the Viacom videotape, 1982.

19. It is possible to extend this comparison, but I do not intend to argue that Graczyk (or Altman), Williams, and Ibsen constitute a sequence of influence, rather that the comparison is speculative. To extend and leave open this comparison, however, I would observe that there is in all three plays an intruder who attempts to influence and in some degree succeeds: Gregers Werle; Jim, the gentleman caller; and Joanne.

20. Gadamer, *Truth and Method*, 269-77. Instead of deploring the inevitability of our involvement in the hermeneutic circle and our established understandings, our ways of seeing, Gadamer urges us to overcome the fears of prejudice and of misunderstanding. The excursion into the alien and unknown can open us up to what is to be disclosed, and we can return enriched (*Philosophical Hermeneutics*, 15); "The important thing is to be aware of one's own bias, so that the text can present itself in all its otherness and thus assert its own truth against one's own fore-meanings" (*Truth and Method*, 269). Encountering the *theatrum mundi* as expressed in the play within a play seems to me a prime instance of this opportunity to stand open to what appears, since our assumptions about probability and believability in our own world might be required to adapt to the rules of the play's world and again, along with the understandings of the personages in that world, to the rules of the play within their play.

21. Friedrich Nietzsche, The Birth of Tragedy *and* the Genealogy of Morals (New York: Anchor-Doubleday, 1956), 26. Subsequent references to Nietzsche's thought are from this edition.

22. Nietzsche's representation of god as transcendent Subject is, like Sir Philip Sidney's, drawn from a long-honored metaphor. Sidney's poet vies with nature and rises above her; whereas "Her world is brazen, the poets only deliver a golden" (*Selected Prose and Poetry* [New York: Rinehart-Holt, 1969], 108). In this power to create an idealized world the poet imitates God, the "heavenly Maker of that maker" (109). Sidney's apologetic stance, his admission that this might "be deemed too saucy a comparison," seems to anticipate a conclusion that the poet's power to create a "golden" world is a disparagement of God the artist, considering what has become of God's golden world. The fall, of course, the cause of man's "infected will," is also the origin of nature's brazen state. It seems that our image of the artist, while it retains godly attributes, precludes trust in the cosmic image. Subsequent references to Sidney's ideas are from this edition.

23. In his analysis of *Truth and Method,* Joel Weinsheimer observes that the story of the prodigal son is the "primal story of Bildung ... and it is no accident that a Bildungsroman such as *Great Expectations* should make explicit use of that biblical paradigm" (*Gadamer's Hermeneutics* [New Haven: Yale University Press, 1985], 70). Bildung, as Weinsheimer characterizes it, "always has this structure of alienation and return, excursion and reunion," homecoming and reunion being appropriate terms for an event that is a beginning, an anticipation.

Chapter 5. The Play: Presenting, Recollecting, Projecting

1. Jean-Paul Sartre considers this expectation in contrasting the bourgeois and epic theaters:

> The bourgeois theater is therefore subjective, not because it shows what is going on inside the head of the character ... but because the bourgeoisie wants a representation of itself which is subjective. That is to say, it wants produced in the theatre an image of man according to its own ideology and not man *seeking through* this sort of world of individuals who see one another, of groups which form judgments about one another, because then, the bourgeoisie would be contested. ("Beyond Bourgeois Theater," *Theatre in the Twentieth Century* [New York: Evergreen-Grove, 1963], 133; my emphasis)

2. I quote the English translation of *The Chairs* from Ionesco's *Four Plays* (New York: Grove, 1958). The French text quoted is from *Les Chaises, Le Théâtre d'Eugène Ionesco,* vol. 1 (Paris: Gallimard, 1954), 129–80.

3. Ritual theories might derive from reading Aristotle's "catharsis" as of communal affect; Francis Fergusson's conception of the tragic pattern as a working out of purpose, passion, and perception considers the audience's sharing of this event: "Purgation ... seems to be connected with the ritual origin of tragedy, and with the 'ritual expectancy' which the audience must still to some degree have had in Aristotle's time" (*The Idea of a Theater* [New York: Anchor-Doubleday, 1953], 245).

4. Hans-Georg Gadamer, *The Relevance of the Beautiful and Other Essays* (Cambridge: Cambridge University Press, 1986), 10.

5. "les chaises, tournées vers l'estrade, dossiers à la salle, forment des rangées régulières, toujours augmentées, comme pour une salle de spectacle" (*Les Chaises,* 158).

6. Frances Yates pursues the "'Idea' of the Globe Theater" as it presented "the most important aspects of the ancient theatre," the Vitruvian form. This theater was

"designed to give fullest support to the voices and the gestures of the players as they enacted the drama of the life of man within the Theatre of the World" (*Theatre of the World* [Chicago: University of Chicago Press, 1969], 188–89).

7. "qui êtes les restes de l'humanité, mais avec de tels restes on peut encore faire de la bonne soupe" (*Les Chaises*, 176).

8. Ovid, *Metamorphoses* (Oxford: Oxford University Press, 1986), book 15, 379. Subsequent references to Ovid's poem are from this edition.

9. Anton Chekhov, *Plays* (New York: Norton, 1977), 144. Subsequent quotations of Chekhov's plays are from this edition.

10. Bristow's introduction, xvii. Not to mistranslate Ophelia, as does Lopahin, is to admit the loss in translation (Bristow, xxiii) and to recognize that translation, as interpretation, is an act striving for coherence in the awareness that loss is inevitable. "Chekhov has interlaced his language with threads of folk song, folklore, poems, and literary allusions that stitch point to patterns of meaning that are easily understood or felt only by audiences familiar with the Russian language and environment" (xvii).

11. Vergil, *Works: The Aeneid, Eclogues, Georgics* (New York: Modern Library-Random House, 1950), 346–52.

12. Anton Chekhov, *Letters* (New York: Viking, 1973), 88. Subsequent references to Chekhov's letters are to this edition.

13. Tennessee Williams, *The Glass Menagerie* (New York: New Directions, 1966), viii. Subsequent references to this play are from this edition.

14. Jean Genet, *The Maids and Deathwatch* (New York: Grove, 1962), 49. Subsequent quotations of the English translation of the play are from this edition. I quote the French text from *Les Bonnes* (n.p.: Marc Barbezat, 1963).

15. Immanuel Kant, "The Analytic of the Sublime," *Critique of Judgment, The Philosophy of Kant* (New York: Modern Library-Random House, 1949), 299. Subsequent references to Kant's philosophy are from this edition.

16. As Stevens surveys the "great pond" in the "absence of the imagination" only to affirm the imagination, he pursues the idea of nobility that can finally be seen and expressed as "peculiarity" ("The Noble Rider and the Sound of Words," *Necessary Angel*, 33); and he affirms the remnants or transmutation of the imagination and nobility in the images of the fragmented, distorted, and temporalized circling that becomes "eccentric" in, for instance, "Notes Toward a Supreme Fiction." Birds, angels, and poets enjoy the "mere repetitions" of their own songs, "the going round / And round and round, the merely going round" (*Palm*, 231–32); and "we enjoy like men, the way a leaf / Above the table spins its constant spin / . . . its spinning its eccentric measure."

17. Longinus, *On Sublimity* (Oxford: Clarendon, 1965), 1.4.2. Subsequent references to Longinus are from this edition.

18. Horace, "The Art of Poetry," *Satires and Epistles* (Chicago: University of Chicago Press, 1959), 290–91. Subsequent references to "The Art of Poetry" are from this edition.

19. In Dounia B. Christiani's translation, the expression might be "claim of the ideal" (*The Wild Duck* [New York: Norton, 1968], 44) or "demands of the ideal" (48). Fjelde translates the expression "Summons to the Ideal" (*Plays*, 448). Einar Haugen characterizes Gregers as a man who "has come out of the wilderness, down from the heights," with a "messianic complex" (83). Haugen observes a "code" in Ibsen's works that opposes the "calling" toward the heights to the "imperative of love," which is a pull toward the depths (93). Subsequent references to *The Wild Duck* are from the Christiani translation, and I cite *The Master Builder* from Fjelde's *Plays*.

20. Bruce Wilshire considers some plays to be "paradigmatically theatrical" because "they reflect in their manifest content the structure of any theatrical event. That is, in them actors stand in for characters who stand in for other characters. The audience member stands in through the actor's standing in" (23).

21. *Bildung* for Gadamer transcends the subjective in that the individual incorporates the "alien" encountered in experience and, although effecting a "return to oneself ... finding oneself again" (*Truth and Method*, 14), does not obtain "complete mastery ... in the absolute knowledge of philosophy" (15). The achievement of *bildung* is reintegration, not only of self but also with others: "The universal viewpoints to which the cultivated man (gebildet) keeps himself open are not a fixed applicable yardstick, but are present to him only as the viewpoints of possible others" (17).

22. Martin William Steinke, *Edward Young's "Conjectures on Original Composition"* (New York: Stechert, 1917; n.p.: Folcroft, 1978), 52.

23. Ingmar Bergman, *Fanny and Alexander* (New York: Pantheon, 1982), 26. Subsequent references to this play are quoted from this text.

24. John Milton, *Complete Poems and Major Prose* (Indianapolis: Odyssey, 1957), 1.6–7. Subsequent references to Milton's works are from this edition.

25. Heidegger observes that *Enargeia* "has the same root as *argentum* (silver).... In the Greek language, one is not speaking about the action of seeing, about *vidēre*, but about that which gleams and radiates" (*Basic Writings*, 385).

26. Guides are "benevolent spirit entities, often close relatives, allegedly assigned to mortals as a protective influence over the latter during earthly existence; guiding spirits or 'angels'" (David C. Knight, ed., *The ESP Reader* [New York: Grosset, 1969], 547). Subsequent references to this work are from this edition.

27. The call is "the ESP symbol selected by the subject in trying to identify a target" (Knight, 546).

28. Bernard Pomerance, *The Elephant Man* (New York: Evergreen-Grove, 1979), 30. Subsequent references to the play are from this edition.

29. Edward Albee, *Tiny Alice* (New York: Pocket-Simon, 1966), 22.

30. Harold Pinter, *The French Lieutenant's Woman* (Boston: Little, 1981), 8. Subsequent references to the filmscript are from this edition. When I refer to the film I am citing from viewing the videotape *The French Lieutenant's Woman*, screenplay by Pinter and directed by Karel Reisz (MGM/UA, 1981).

31. The capable and thoughtful interpretations of such critics as William E. Holladay and Stephen Watt might be instructive concerning the hypothetical (presumably actual) audience of the play (and Lynch's film) seen as melodrama and "freak show" (William E. Holladay and Stephen Watt, "Viewing the Elephant Man," PMLA 104 [1989], 880); and the critic fulfills her/himself as the paradoxically proficient and bemused scientist, the not-yet-challenged Charles or Treves. In Bruce Wilshire's reading, instead of the audience's participating "in the pornography [that] exceeds the Victorians'" (Holladay and Watt, 880), the relationship between Merrick and Mrs. Kendal confirms "his possession of those universal traits essential to his being fully *human*" (Wilshire, 10); and Wilshire speaks for himself and for the audience as having been genuinely engaged in the transformative experience of the play: "we come home to ourselves as we believe we are: beings of inexhaustible particularity as well as indefinitely extendable horizons of human concern and identification."

Chapter 6. Call and Recall: The Play of Imagination

1. For Don Ihde, *Listening and Voice* (Athens: Ohio University Press, 1976), a phenomenology of sound might effect suspension of the urge to detemporalize—the

instinct to make permanent—that is encouraged by the inherited static visual image. Deprived of the visual metaphor for the moment, the perceiver might become more sensitive to the abstracting impulse that accepts and applies the inherited force of the visual metaphor without question.

2. Samuel Beckett, *All that Fall* (New York: Evergreen-Grove, 1957), 1. Subsequent references to this play are from this edition.

3. Edwin Arlington Robinson, *Selected Poems* (New York: Collier-Macmillan, 1965), 9. Subsequent references to Robinson's poem are from this edition.

4. Ursula K. Le Guin, *Dancing at the Edge of the World* (New York: Perennial-Harper, 1989), 27. Subsequent references to Le Guin are from this edition.

Works Cited

Abel, Lionel. *Metatheatre: A New View of Dramatic Form.* New York: Dramabook-Hill and Wang, 1963.

Addison, Joseph. *The Spectator.* Edited by Donald F. Bond. Vol 3. Oxford: Clarendon, 1965.

Aeschylus. *The Oresteia.* Translated by Douglas Young. Norman: University of Oklahoma Press, 1974.

Albee, Edward. *Tiny Alice.* New York: Pocket-Simon, 1966.

Alter, Robert. *Necessary Angels: Tradition and Modernity in Kafka, Benjamin, and Scholem.* Cambridge, Mass.: Harvard University Press, 1991.

Altman, Robert, dir. *Come Back to the Five and Dime Jimmy Dean, Jimmy Dean.* With Sandy Dennis, Karen Black, and Cher. Viacom, 1982.

Aristotle. *Poetics.* Translated by Gerald F. Else. n.p.: Ann Arbor: University of Michigan Press, 1970.

———. *Poetics.* Translated by Leon Golden. Commentary O. B. Hardison, Jr. Englewood Cliffs, N.J.: Prentice-Hall, 1968.

Baym, Nina, et al., eds. *The Norton Anthology of American Literature.* 3rd ed. 2 vols. New York: Norton, 1989. Vol. 1.

Beckett, Samuel. *All that Fall.* New York: Evergreen-Grove, 1957.

Bergman, Ingmar. *Fanny and Alexander.* Translated by Alan Blair. New York: Pantheon, 1982.

Bigsby, C. W. E. *Modern American Drama, 1945–1990.* Cambridge: Cambridge University Press, 1992.

Blau, Herbert. *The Audience.* Baltimore: Johns Hopkins University Press, 1990.

Burlin, Robert B. *The Old English Advent: A Typological Commentary.* New Haven: Yale University Press, 1968.

Butcher, S. H. *Aristotle's Theory of Poetry and Fine Art: with a Critical Text and Translation of* The Poetics. 4th ed. New York: Dover, 1951.

Casey, Edward S. *Imagining: A Phenomenological Study.* Bloomington: Midland-Indiana University Press, 1979.

Chekhov, Anton. *Letters.* Edited by Avrahm Yarmolinsky. New York: Viking, 1973.

———. *Plays.* Translated by Eugene K. Bristow. Norton Critical Edition. New York: Norton, 1977.

Coleridge, Samuel Taylor. *Biographia Literaria.* Edited by J. Shawcross. 2 vols. London: Oxford University Press, 1954.

Cope, Jackson I. *The Theater and the Dream: From Metaphor to Form in Renaissance Drama.* Baltimore: Johns Hopkins University Press, 1973.

Dällenbach, Lucien. *The Mirror in the Text.* Chicago: University of Chicago Press, 1989.

Derrida, Jacques. *Of Grammatology*. Translated by and Introduced by Gayatri Chakravorty Spivak. Baltimore: Johns Hopkins University Press, 1974.

Eliot, T. S. *The Waste Land and Other Poems*. New York: Harvest-Harcourt, 1962.

Fergusson, Francis. *The Idea of a Theater*. New York: Anchor-Doubleday, 1953.

Fish, Stanley. "Interpreting the *Variorum*." *Is There a Text in This Class?: The Authority of Interpretive Communities*. Cambridge: Harvard University Press, 1980. 147-73.

Frost, Robert. *Poetry and Prose*. Edited by Edward Connery Lathem and Lawrance Thompson. New York: Holt, 1972.

Gabbard, Lucina P. *The Dream Structure of Pinter's Plays: A Psychoanalytic Approach*. Rutherford: Fairleigh Dickinson University Press, 1976.

Gadamer, Hans-Georg. *Truth and Method*. Translated by Joel Weinsheimer and Donald G. Marshall. New York: Crossroad, 1991.

———. *The Relevance of the Beautiful and Other Essays*. Translated by Nicholas Walker, edited by Robert Bernasconi. Cambridge: Cambridge University Press, 1986.

———. *Philosophical Hermeneutics*. Translated by David E. Linge. Berkeley: University of California Press, 1977.

Geertz, Clifford. "Deep Play: Notes on the Balinese Cockfight." *Myth, Symbol, and Culture*. Edited by Clifford Geertz. New York: Norton, 1971, 1-37.

Genet, Jean. The Maids and Deathwatch: *Two Plays*. Translated by Bernard Frechtman. New York: Grove, 1962.

———. *Les Bonnes et comment jouer les Bonnes*. N. p.: Marc Barbezat, 1963.

Gombrich, E. H. *Art and Illusion: A Study in the Psychology of Pictorial Representation*. 1960. Bollingen Series 35. Princeton: Princeton University Press, 1969.

Graczyk, Ed. *Come Back to the 5 & Dime, Jimmy Dean, Jimmy Dean*. New York: Samuel French, 1976.

Grunfeld, Frederic V. *Rodin: A Biography*. New York: Henry Holt, 1987.

Hardison, O. B., Jr. "A Commentary on Aristotle's *Poetics*." Golden, 53-296.

Haugen, Einar. *Ibsen's Drama: Author to Audience*. Minneapolis: University of Minnesota Press, 1979.

Hawthorne, Nathaniel. *Mosses from an Old Manse*. Vol. 10 of *Centenary Edition*. 1974.

———. *The American Notebooks*. Vol. 8 of *Centenary Edition*. 1972.

———. *The Centenary Edition of the Works*. Edited by William Charvat et al. 11 vols. Columbus: Ohio State University Press, 1962-.

———. *The Scarlet Letter*. Vol. 1 of *Centenary Edition*. 1962.

Heidegger, Martin. *Basic Writings: From* Being and Time *(1927) to* The Task of Thinking *(1964)*. Edited by David Farrell Krell. New York: Harper, 1977.

———. *Being and Time*. Translated by John Macquarrie and Edward Robinson. New York: Harper, 1962.

———. *What Is Philosophy?* Translated by William Kluback and Jean T. Wilde. New York: Twayne, 1958.

Hirsch, E. D. "Three Dimensions of Hermeneutics." *New Literary History* 3 (1972): 245-61.

Hocks, Richard A. *Henry James and Pragmatistic Thought*. Chapel Hill: University of North Carolina Press, 1974.

Holladay, William E., and Stephen Watt. "Viewing the Elephant Man." *PMLA* 104 (1989): 868–81.

Holland, Norman N. *Poems in Persons: An Introduction to the Psychoanalysis of Literature*. New York: Norton, 1973.

Homan, Sidney. *The Audience as Actor and Character: The Modern Theater of Beckett, Brecht, Genet, Ionesco, Pinter, Stoppard, and Williams*. Lewisburg: Bucknell University Press, 1989.

Horace. *The Satires and Epistles*. Translated by Smith Palmer Bovie. Chicago: University of Chicago Press, 1959.

Hornby, Richard. *Drama, Metadrama, and Perception*. Lewisburg: Bucknell University Press, 1986.

Husserl, Edmund. *Ideas: General Introduction to Pure Phenomenology*. Translated by W. R. Boyce Gibson. New York: Collier-Macmillan, 1962.

Ibsen, Henrik. *The Complete Major Prose Plays*. Translated by Rolf Fjelde. New York: Farrar, 1978.

———. *The Wild Duck*. Translated by Dounia B. Christiani. Norton Critical Edition. New York: Norton, 1968.

Ihde, Don. *Listening and Voice: a Phenomenology of Sound*. Athens: Ohio University Press, 1976.

Ingarden, Roman. *The Literary Work of Art: An Investigation on the Borderlines of Ontology, Logic, and Theory of Literature*. Translated by George G. Grabowicz. Evanston: Northwestern University Press, 1973.

———. *The Cognition of the Literary Work of Art*. Translated by Ruth Ann Crowley and Kenneth R. Olson. Evanston: Northwestern University Press, 1973.

Ionesco, Eugène. *Four Plays*. Translated by Donald M. Allen. New York: Grove, 1958.

———. *Les Chaises*. *Le Théâtre d'Eugène Ionesco*. Vol. 1. Preface by Jacques Lemarchand, 129–80. Paris: Gallimard, 1954.

Iser, Wolfgang. *The Implied Reader: Patterns of Communication in Prose Fiction from Bunyan to Beckett*. Baltimore: Johns Hopkins University Press, 1974.

James, Henry. *The Golden Bowl*. Harmondsworth: Penguin, 1966.

James, William. Pragmatism and The Meaning of Truth. Cambridge: Harvard University Press, 1978.

Jones, Ernest. *Hamlet and Oedipus*. Garden City: Anchor-Doubleday, 1954.

Jonson, Ben. *Timber or Discoveries*. Edited by Ralph S. Walker. Westport, Conn.: Greenwood, 1976.

Kant, Immanuel. *The Philosophy of Kant: Immanuel Kant's Moral and Political Writings*. Edited by Carl J. Friedrich. New York: Modern Library-Random House, 1949.

Keats, John. *Poems*. Edited by Jack Stillinger. Cambridge: Harvard University Press, 1978.

———. *Letters*. Edited by Hyder Edward Rollins. Vol. 1. Cambridge: Harvard University Press, 1958.

Keyssar, Helene. *Robert Altman's America*. New York: Oxford University Press, 1991.

Knight, David C., ed. *The ESP Reader*. New York: Grosset, 1969.

Lakoff, George, and Mark Johnson. *Metaphors We Live By*. Chicago: University of Chicago Press, 1980.

Larson, Gary. *The PreHistory of The Far Side: A Tenth Anniversary Exhibit*. Kansas City: Andrews and McMeel, 1989.

Le Guin, Ursula K. *Dancing at the Edge of the World: Thoughts on Words, Women, Places*. New York: Perennial-Harper, 1989.

Leitch, Vincent B. *American Literary Criticism from the Thirties to the Eighties*. New York: Columbia University Press, 1988.

Longinus. *On Sublimity*. Translated by D. A. Russell. Oxford: Clarendon, 1965.

Luprecht, Mark. "Paul Klee and the Angels of Modern Times." *Eighteenth Annual Conference on Literature and Film*. Tallahassee, Florida, 28–30 January 1993.

Mamet, David. *House of Games*. New York: Evergreen-Grove, 1987.

Melville, Herman. *Billy Budd and Other Prose Pieces*. Edited by Raymond W. Weaver. Vol. 13 of *The Works of Herman Melville: Standard Edition*. 16 vols. New York: Russell, 1963.

Merleau-Ponty, Maurice. *Phenomenology of Perception*. Translated by Colin Smith. Atlantic Highlands, N.J.: Humanities Press; London: Routledge, 1962.

Milton, John. *Complete Poems and Major Prose*. Edited by Merritt Y. Hughes. Indianapolis: Odyssey, 1957.

Nietzsche, Friedrich. *The Birth of Tragedy and The Genealogy of Morals*. Translated by Francis Golffing. New York: Anchor-Doubleday, 1956.

O'Neill, Eugene. *Long Day's Journey into Night*. New Haven: Yale University Press, 1956.

Ovid. *Metamorphoses*. Translatd by A. D. Melville. Oxford: Oxford University Press, 1986.

Pearce, Howard. "Dimensions of Mimesis: Sophocles' *Philoctetes* and Pinter's *No Man's Land*." *All the World: Drama Past and Present, Volume II*. Edited by Karelisa V. Hartigan, 65–74. Washington: University Press of America, 1982.

———. "A Phenomenological Approach to the *Theatrum Mundi* Metaphor." *PMLA* 95 (1980): 42–57.

Pinter, Harold. "The Black and White." *Complete Works: Two*, 240–43.

———. *Complete Works: Two*. New York: Evergreen-Grove, 1990.

———. *Complete Works: Four*. New York: Evergreen-Grove, 1990.

———. *The Dumb Waiter*. *Complete Works: One*, 127–65.

———. *Complete Works: One*. New York: Evergreen-Grove, 1990.

———. *The French Lieutenant's Woman: A Screenplay*. Boston: Little, 1981.

Pinter, Harold, screenwriter. *The French Lieutenant's Woman*. Directed by Karel Reisz. MGM/UA, 1981.

Pirandello, Luigi. *Six Characters in Search of an Author*. *Eight Modern Plays*. Edited by Anthony Caputi. New York: Norton, 1966.

———. *Naked Masks: Five Plays*. Edited by Eric Bentley. New York: Dutton, 1952.

Plato. *Great Dialogues*. Translated by W. H. D. Rouse. New York: Mentor-NAL, 1984.

Pomerance, Bernard. *The Elephant Man*. New York: Evergreen-Grove, 1979.

Robinson, Edwin Arlington. *Selected Poems*. Edited by Morton Dauwen Zabel. New York: Collier-Macmillan, 1965.

Sacrifice of Isaac. *Chief Pre-Shakespearean Dramas*. Edited by Joseph Quincy Adams, 117–24. Cambridge: Riverside-Houghton, 1924.

Sartre, Jean-Paul. "Beyond Bourgeois Theatre." Translated by Rima Drell Reck. In *Theatre in the Twentieth Century*, edited by Robert W. Corrigan, 131–40. New York: Evergreen-Grove, 1963.

Schechner, Richard. "Puzzling Pinter." *Tulane Drama Review* 11.2 (1966): 176–84.

Schiller, Friedrich. *On the Aesthetic Education of Man in a Series of Letters*. Translated by Reginald Snell. New York: Ungar, 1965.

Self, Robert. "Robert Altman and the Theory of Authorship." *Cinema Journal* 25.1 (1985): 3–11.

Sidney, Sir Philip. *Selected Prose and Poetry*. New York: Rinehart-Holt, 1969.

Spanos, William V. "Breaking the Circle: Hermeneutics as Dis-closure." *boundary 2* 5 (1977): 421–57.

Spivak, Gayatri Chakravorti. Preface. In Derrida, *Of Grammatology*, ix-lxxxvii.

Steinke, Martin William. *Edward Young's "Conjectures on Original Composition" in England and Germany*. New York: Stechert, 1917. n.p.: Folcroft, 1978.

Stevens, Wallace. *The Palm at the End of the Mind: Selected Poems and a Play*. Edited by Holly Stevens. New York: Knopf, 1971.

———. "Imagination as Value." In *The Necessary Angel: Essays on Reality and the Imagination*. New York: Vintage-Random House, 1951.

———. "The Noble Rider and the Sound of Words." In *The Necessary Angel: Essays on Reality and the Imagination*. New York: Vintage-Random House, 1951.

Van Laan, Thomas F. "*The Dumb Waiter*: Pinter's Play with the Audience." *Modern Drama* 24 (1981): 494–502.

Vergil. *The Aeneid*. Translated by Kevin Guinaugh. New York: Rinehart, 1953.

———. *Works: The Aeneid, Eclogues, Georgics*. Translated by J. W. Mackail. New York: Modern Library-Random House, 1950.

Weinsheimer, Joel C. *Gadamer's Hermeneutics: A Reading of* Truth and Method. New Haven: Yale University Press, 1985.

Wenzel, Siegfried. "Chaucer's Pardoner and His Relics." *Studies in the Age of Chaucer*. Vol 11. Edited by Thomas J. Heffernan. Knoxville: New Chaucer Society, University of Tennessee, 1989.

Whitaker, Thomas R. *Fields of Play in Modern Drama*. Princeton: Princeton University Press, 1977.

Williams, Tennessee. *The Glass Menagerie*. New York: New Directions, 1966.

———. *A Streetcar Named Desire*. New York: Signet-New American, 1947.

Wilshire, Bruce. *Role Playing and Identity: The Limits of Theatre as Metaphor*. Bloomington: Indiana University Press, 1991.

Wilson, W. Daniel. "Readers in Texts." *PMLA* 96 (1981): 848–63.

Worth, Katharine. "Pinter's Scenic Imagery." *The Pinter Review* 1 (1987): 31–39.

Yates, Frances A. *The Art of Memory*. Chicago: University of Chicago Press, 1966.

———. *Theatre of the World*. Chicago: University of Chicago Press, 1969.

Index

Abel, Lionel: *Metatheatre: A New View of Dramatic Form*, 23, 250 n. 8
Addison, Joseph, 31, 187, 251 n. 5
Aeschylus: *Agamemnon*, 19, 20; *Choephoroe*, 92, 125–32; *Eumenides*, 125; *Oresteia*, 125
Agamemnon, 19, 20
Albee, Edward: *Tiny Alice*, 220
allusion, 136, 160; to Ophelia, 165
Altdorfer, Albrecht, 53
Alter, Robert, 116; *Necessary Angels*, 116, 256 n. 7
Altman, Robert, 132, 134, 257 n. 19; *Come Back to the Five and Dime Jimmy Dean, Jimmy Dean*, 132–50
Apollonian, 121, 122, 143, 148, 185, 211, 228
Aristaeus, 167
Aristotle, 13, 14, 16, 23, 29, 31–33, 38, 41, 48, 50, 53, 58, 62, 77, 85, 106, 127, 198, 215, 231, 249 n. 1, 255 n. 4, 256 n. 12; catharsis, 59, 158; design, 62; the marvelous, 51; mimesis, 23, 33, 48, 49, 133; the poet, 231; *Poetics*, 23, 32; probability or necessity, 198; wonder, 48, 50, 53, 62
Artaud, Antonin, 40

Bacon, Francis, 216
Beckett, Samuel, 66, 238; *All That Fall*, 238–48; *Endgame*, 67
Benjamin, Walter, 116
Bergman, Ingmar, 191, 192; *Fanny and Alexander*, 192–215
Bigsby, C. W. E., 23; *Modern American Drama, 1945–1990*, 23, 250 n. 8
bildung, 154, 186, 191–193, 196, 198, 204
Blau, Herbert, 68; *The Audience*, 68, 254 n. 2
Bleich, David, 55, 253 n. 23

Brecht, Berthold, 48; verfremdungseffekt, 48
Bristow, Eugene K., 259 n. 10
Burke, Edmund, 187; the sublime, 187
Burlin, Robert B., 97; *Old English Advent*, 97
Butcher, S. H., 14, 50; *Aristotle's Theory of Poetry and Fine Art*, 14

Caputi, Anthony, 72; Translator, *Six Characters in Search of an Author*, 254 n. 5
Casey, Edward S., 22; *Imagining: A Phenomenological Study*, 22, 249 n. 6
Chaucer, 21
Chekhov, Anton, 35, 106, 164, 170; *The Cherry Orchard*, 106, 165–74; *Letters*, 170; *The Seagull*, 35; *The Three Sisters*, 164
Christiani, Dounia B., 193, 259 n. 19
Coleridge, Samuel Taylor, 44, 45, 70, 207; *Biographia Literaria*, 44, 45
Cope, Jackson I., 40; *The Theater and the Dream*, 40
critical theory: feminist, 54; Marxist, 54; psychoanalytical, 54; reader–response, 54, 55; subjectivist, 54

Dällenbach, Lucien, 133, 257 n. 16; *The Mirror in the Text*, 133
Dante Alighieri, 203, 241; Beatrice, 203
Darwin, Charles, 216
Derrida, Jacques, 59, 60, 238 n. 28; deconstruction, 59; deferral, 60, 253 n. 30
Descartes, René, 209
Dionysian, 122, 143, 148, 237
Dumb Waiter, The, 82

Eidos, 104
El Greco, 177
Eliot, T. S.: "Preludes," 103, 188

Else, Gerald F., 14; *Aristotle's Poetics,* 14
Empedocles, 201
enargeia, 174, 186, 237
Endgame, 67
Euripides, 142, 143; *The Bacchae,* 142

Fergusson, Francis, 158; Purgation, 158, 258 n. 3
Ficino, Marsilio, 40
Fish, Stanley, 59; interpretive communities, 59
Fjelde, Rolf, 193
Forster, E. M., 48, 252 n. 15; *Howard's End,* 48; *Passage to India,* 48
Foucault, Michel, 59, 253 n. 28
Fowles, John, 52, 216, 222; *The French Lieutenant's Woman,* 52
Freud, Sigmund, 71, 241
Frost, Robert, 63; "The Oven Bird," 63, 64
Frye, Northrop, 40

Gabbard, Lucina, 55; *The Dream Structure of Pinter's Plays,* 55, 253 n. 24
Gadamer, Hans-Georg, 25, 29, 30, 33, 35, 36, 38, 41, 44, 45, 58, 66, 67, 71, 132, 139, 144, 158, 174, 187, 234; bildung, 132, 149, 150, 154, 186, 191, 193, 196, 198, 204, 260 n. 21; game, 134; Gebilde, 132, 256 n. 15; mirror, 133, 136; mirror as speculation, 132; Mnemosyne, 159, 174; *Philosophical Hermeneutics,* 58, 257 n. 20; "reflection," 134; *Relevance of the Beautiful,* 234; "speculation," 133; speculum, 132, 140; "total mediation," 134; transformation into structure, 38, 134, 153, 197, 251 n. 8; *Truth and Method,* 30, 35, 251 n. 2, 257 n. 20, 260 n. 21
Gasset, José Ortega y, 40
Geertz, Clifford, 39; "Deep Play: Notes on the Balinese Cockfight," 39
Genet, Jean, 182; *The Maids,* 182–91
Golden, Leon, 14, 41, 49; *Aristotle's Poetics,* 14, 49
Gombrich, E. H., 53, 54, 57, 61, 98, 133, 139; *Art and Illusion,* 54, 57, 139; the Egyptian, 57, 61; mirror, 133, 257 n. 16; speculum, 140
Graczyk, Ed, 135, 137, 257 n. 19
Grunfeld, Frederic V., 88

Hamlet, 15, 196
Hardison, O. B., 49, 252 n. 17
Haugen, Einar, 123, 193, 259 n. 19; *Ibsen's Drama,* 123
Hawthorne, Nathaniel, 74–78; "The Custom-House," 77; "The Minister's Black Veil," 76; "My Kinsman, Major Molineux," 76; "Rappaccini's Daughter," 77; *The Scarlet Letter,* 77
Heidegger, Martin, 22, 24, 25, 30, 33, 38, 45, 48, 52, 57, 59, 65, 85, 88, 90, 118, 151, 153, 155, 158, 181, 198, 209, 210, 234, 235; alethia, 65; astonishment, 85, 86, 88, 198; *Being and Time,* 34, 48, 57, 249 n. 5; call, 234; Care, 181; curiosity, 181; Dasein, 34, 49, 60, 100, 234; enargeia, 174, 210, 237, 260 n. 25; "idle talk," 100; letting be, 153; lichtung, 65, 209; Mnemosyne, 158; "The Origin of the Work of Art," 86; "reciprocative rejoinder," 90; turning (Kehre), 33, 153, 251 n. 6; *What Is Philosophy?,* 85; withdrawal, 235
Heracleitus, 201, 215
Hirsch, E. D., 54, 252 n. 22
Holladay, William E., 231, 260 n. 31
Holland, Norman, 44, 55, 251 n. 12, 252 n. 23
Holmes, Sherlock, 242
Homan, Sidney, 68; *The Audience as Actor and Character,* 68, 253–54 n. 2
Homer, 62; Odysseus, 48; *The Odyssey,* 51
Horace, 190
Hornby, Richard, 23; *Drama, Metadrama, and Perception,* 23, 250 n. 8
Horne, Lena, 42
House of Games, 74
Husserl, Edmund, 24, 25, 29, 30, 32, 33, 35, 45, 48, 55, 61, 68, 70, 86, 101, 104, 139, 153, 158, 208, 236, 238; bracketing, 61, 87, 104, 153, 253 n. 31, 255 n. 14; Eidos, 68, 70; epoch, 61; *Ideas,* 68; intentionality, 55; "living convictions," 105; "the natural standpoint," 29, 251 n. 3; zu den sachen selbst, 86, 255 n. 13
Ibsen, Henrik, 78, 120, 137, 191–93; *An Enemy of the People,* 78; gengangere, 123; *Ghosts,* 120–25, 129; *The Master*

Builder, 191, 192–215; The Wild Duck, 137, 193, 204

Ihde, Don, 238; Listening and Voice, 238, 260–61 n. 1
imagination, 18, 61, 104
Ingarden, Roman, 55, 253 n. 25; The Cognition of the Literary Work of Art, 55; intentionality, 55; The Literary Work of Art, 55
Ionesco, Eugene, 152, 159; The Chairs, 152, 159–64
Iser, Wolfgang, 44; The Implied Reader, 44, 251 n. 12

James, Henry, 48, 147; The Golden Bowl, 48, 252 n. 15; "The Jolly Corner," 147
James, William, 54, 252 n. 21; Pragmatism and The Meaning of Truth, 54
JFK, 29
Job, 46
Johnson, Mark, 49; Metaphors We Live By, 49, 252 n. 16
Jones, Ernest, 71; Hamlet and Oedipus, 71, 254 n. 4
Jonson, Ben, 105
Journey, 55; Odyssean, 55
Jung, Carl Gustav, 142, 201, 206; anima, 201; animus, 201

Kafka, Franz, 116
Kant, Immanuel, 187, 188; the sublime, 187
Keats, John, 69, 83, 89; Letters, 69; Negative Capability, 69; "Ode on a Grecian Urn," 89
Keyssar, Helene, 135, 257 n. 17
Klee, Paul, 116; angel, 116; "Hero with Wing," 116
Knight, David C., 212; "Guides," 212, 260 nn. 26 and 27

La cage aux folles, 43
Lakoff, George, 49; Metaphors We Live By, 49, 252 n. 16
Larson, Gary, 37; The Far Side, 37, 38
Lear, King, 46
Le Guin, Ursula K., 246; "It Was a Dark and Stormy Night," 246
Leitch, Vincent B., 55; American Literary Criticism from the Thirties to the Eighties, 55

locus amoenus, 222, 225
Long Day's Journey into Night, 78, 79
Longinus, 153, 188, 189, 210; the sublime, 189, 210
ludere, 89
Luprecht, Mark, 116

Maenads, 185
Magny, C. E., 133
Mamet, David, 74; House of Games, 74
Marlowe, Christopher, 15
Marple, Miss, 242
Melville, Herman, 74–76; "Hawthorne and His Mosses," 74
memory play, 176
Merleau-Ponty, Maurice, 22; Phenomenology of Perception, 22, 249 n. 5
Metamorphoses, 163
Metaphors We Live By, 49
Milton, John, 202, 203; Paradise Lost, 202
mimesis, 48, 49, 54, 87, 236
Mirandola, Pico della, 40
mnemosyne, 158, 159, 164, 205
Mozart, Amadeus, 154; The Marriage of Figaro, 154
mystery, 50

New Criticism, 54
Nietzsche, Friedrich, 143, 144, 150, 201, 206; Apollonian, 206, 258 n. 22; The Birth of Tragedy, 143, 206; Dionysian, 201, 206

Odysseus, 48, 51
Oedipus, 241
Oedipus Rex, 32–33
Ophelia, 165
Orpheus, 73, 167
Ovid, 163; Metamorphoses, 163
O'Neill, Eugene, 78, 82, 108; Long Day's Journey into Night, 78–82

Petrarch, 177; Laura, 177, 203
phenomenology, 48, 55
Picasso, Pablo, 73
Pinter, Harold, 45, 46, 82, 87, 192, 216; "The Black and White," 45, 46–62; The Dumb Waiter, 53, 82–102; The French Lieutenant's Woman, 87, 192, 216–31; No Man's Land, 52

Pirandello, Luigi, 72, 110, 134; *Henry IV*, 110–15, 134; "Il giuoco delle parti," 72; *Six Characters in Search of an Author*, 70, 72
Piranesi, Giovanni Battista, 174; *Carcere*, 174
Plato, 14, 32, 36, 58, 72, 76, 85, 139, 181, 193, 198, 214, 220, 229, 238; the artist, 229; Eidos, 103, 153; "Ion," 237, 238; the magician, 181; mimesis, 133; the mirror, 76, 133, 135, 229; *The Republic*, 193
Pomerance, Bernard, 191, 216; *The Elephant Man*, 191, 216–31
Proteus, 167

reader response theory, 59, 253 n. 29
Revenger's Tragedy, The, 67
Robinson, Edwin Arlington, 246; "The House on the Hill," 246
Rodin, Auguste, 88, 101; "The Hand of God," 101

Sacrifice of Isaac, The, 82, 89–102
Sartre, Jean-Paul, 152; "Beyond Bourgeois Theater," 152, 258 n. 1
Schechner, Richard, 84, 254–55 n. 11
Schiller, Friedrich von, 56, 59, 62, 199; "On the Aesthetic Education of Man," 56
Schindler's List, 29
Scholem, Gershom, 116
Self, Robert, 135, 257 n. 17
Shakespeare, William, 163, 165; *Hamlet*, 15, 42, 196; Juliet, 229; "little O," 163; Ophelia, 165; Romeo, 229
Shaw, George Bernard, 78
Sidney, Sir Philip, 144, 258 n. 20
Six Characters in Search of an Author, 70, 72
Socrates, 73
Sophocles, 15, 52, 239, 242; *Oedipus*, 239–44; *Oedipus at Colonus*, 239; *Oedipus Rex*, 32–33, 239–44; Orestes, 243; Philoctetes, 52
Spanos, William, 31, 251 n. 4
spectacle, 246
Spivak, Gayatri Chakravorty, 59, 253 n. 28
Stevens, Wallace, 21, 22, 28, 52, 60, 62, 66, 116, 188, 203, 233, 247; angel, 116; "Angel Surrounded by Paysans," 116–17, 203; "A High-Toned Old Christian Woman," 60, 253 n. 30; "Lebensweisheitspielerei," 21, 62, 249 n. 4, 253 n. 32; *The Necessary Angel*, 52, 60; "The Noble Rider and the Sound of Words," 60, 188, 253 n. 30, 259 n. 16; "Notes Toward a Supreme Fiction," 116, 188, 259 n. 16; "Of Modern Poetry," 64; "The Plain Sense of Things," 22; "Things of August," 28, 250–51 n. 1
Storer, Edward, 72
Stormy Weather, 42
Strindberg, August, 89; *A Dream Play*, 89
sublime, the, 187
sublimity: versus Aristotelean probability, 188
Suvorin, A. S., 169

Theatrum mundi, 40–43, 52, 58, 64, 66, 71, 80, 84, 87, 90, 104, 108, 116, 128, 134, 139, 144, 146, 148, 162–63, 178, 182, 191, 193, 209, 211, 214, 220, 227, 235, 256 n. 13
Todorov, Tzvetan, 135

Ubi sunt, 162

Van Laan, Thomas, 84, 255 n. 11
Vergil, 108, 167; *Aeneid*, 108; Aristaeus, 167; *Georgics*, 167, 172
Victor/Victoria, 43
Villon, François, 162, 176
Vitruvian theater, 162, 163
Vitruvius, 162

Watt, Stephen, 231, 260 n. 31
Weinsheimer, Joel, 150; Bildungsroman, 150, 258 n. 8
Wenzel, Siegfried, 21
Whitaker, Thomas R., 23; *Fields of Play in Modern Drama*, 23, 250 n. 8
Whitman, Robert: "Light Touch," 119
Williams, Tennessee, 106, 136, 137, 174; *The Glass Menagerie*, 136, 174–81; *A Streetcar Named Desire*, 106–9
Wilshire, Bruce, 23, 193, 231, 260 n. 20; *Role Playing and Identity*, 23, 250 n. 7
Wilson, Daniel, 59; "Readers in Texts," 59, 253 n. 29
Wordsworth, William, 70, 83, 189; "ego-

tistical sublime," 83; "spots of time," 189
Worth, Katharine, 90, 255n. 17

Yates, Frances, 162; Vitruvian form, 162, 258–59n. 6

Young, Douglas, 19, 127; Translator, *Oresteia*, 19, 127
Young, Edward, 195

Zola, Emile, 78